# TH
# BOOK OF HEBREWS

the Smart Guide to the Bible™ series

BE SMART · BE INSPIRED ·™

Robert C. Girard

Larry Richards, General Editor

THOMAS NELSON
*Since 1798*

NASHVILLE   DALLAS   MEXICO CITY   RIO DE JANEIRO   BEIJING

*The Book of Hebrews*
The Smart Guide to the Bible™ series
Copyright © 2008 by GRQ, Inc.

Published in Nashville, Tennessee, by Thomas Nelson. Thomas Nelson is a trademark of Thomas Nelson, Inc.

Thomas Nelson, Inc. titles may be purchased in bulk for educational, business, fundraising, or sales promotional use. For information, please e-mail SpecialMarkets@ThomasNelson.com.

Scripture quotations are taken from the New King James Version® (NKJV), copyright © 1982 by Thomas Nelson, Inc. Used by permission. All rights reserved.

To the best of its ability, GRQ, Inc., has strived to find the source of all material. If there has been an oversight, please contact us, and we will make any correction deemed necessary in future printings. We also declare that to the best of our knowledge all material (quoted or not) contained herein is accurate, and we shall not be held liable for the same.

General Editor: Larry Richards
Managing Editor: Michael Christopher
Scripture Editor: Deborah Wiseman
Assistant Editor: Amy Clark
Design: Diane Whisner

ISBN 10: 1-4185-1008-4
ISBN 13: 978-1-4185-1008-4

Printed in the United States of America
08 09 10 11 RRD 9 8 7 6 5 4 3 2 1

# Introduction

Welcome to *The Smart Guide to the Bible*™—*Hebrews*. This is another in a series of books that make the Bible fun and easy to understand. This is not a traditional Bible study or commentary. It is an entirely new kind of commentary that I hope will change your outlook on the Bible forever.

## To Gain Your Confidence

*The Smart Guide to the Bible*™—*Hebrews* is designed to make the Bible user-friendly. I have tried to write with a light touch and good humor while using a sound educational approach. I've put out the welcome mat and invited you to participate in an exciting adventure of enlightenment and joy as you discover what the Bible is about.

The best source of information for understanding the Bible is the real thing—the Bible itself. That's why this book often uses other Bible references to shed light on Bible statements. Oddly enough, that's also what the author of Hebrews does! Every chapter of the book of Hebrews is loaded with quotations from the Old Testament, which the author clearly believes to be an oracle, a message directly from God, inspired by God Himself. The Hebrews writer knew: The Bible is its own best commentary.

## What Is the Bible?

In the front pages of most Bibles you will find a table of contents listing the 66 books contained in the Bible, with page numbers. The list will be in two sections—an "Old" Testament list of 39 books and a "New" Testament list of 27 books. Different authors and poets, of Hebrew heritage, wrote the Old Testament between BC 1400 and 400. The New Testament was written (also by Jewish authors) in the 60 years between AD 40 and 100. Centuries later, scholars divided the books of the Bible into numbered chapters and verses to make it easier for us to locate its stories and teachings. Thus "John 3:16" identifies the third chapter of the book written by John, and the sixteenth verse of that chapter.

## Old Testament/New Testament—What's the Difference?

The Old Testament reports events that happened before the birth of Jesus Christ, mostly centering on the nation of Israel. The New Testament tells about the birth, life, teachings, death, and resurrection of the historical person, Jesus, and about the movement begun by the people who believed He was the Son of God. The New Testament book of Hebrews shows us vital links between the two testaments.

## Sprechen Sie Deutsch? ¿Habla Usted Español?

Most of the Old Testament was originally written in Hebrew, the official language of the Jews, the nation of Israel. The New Testament was written in Greek. Greek, like English today, had become the universal language, spoken and understood all over the world. Alexander the Great (356 to 323 BC), who preceded the Romans in conquest of the Middle East, spread a dialect called *koine* (koy-nay) or "common" Greek. As the Greek empire spread, Alexander instituted the use of koine Greek from Europe to Asia. New Testament authors wrote in common Greek so their books and letters could be read and understood by people all over the Roman Empire.

Most Jews spoke and wrote Greek. Some sections of the New Testament seem to indicate that Jesus was fluent in three languages—Greek, Hebrew, and Aramaic (the language used by homeland Jews. By Jesus's time the Old Testament had also been translated into Greek and copied onto papyrus scrolls. New Testament writers most likely also used papyrus.

## Which Translation of the Bible Should You Read?

Today, English-speaking people have a wide range of good Bible translations from which to choose. I used several different translations in the preparation of this commentary. In addition, I often looked at verses in the original language of the New Testament (Greek). However, for this series we chose to use the New King James Version (NKJV) of the Bible as the default version, meaning that most of our quotations will come from that. It faithfully expresses the words of the original Bible writers in clear and contemporary English.

## A Word About Words

There are several interchangeable terms: Scripture, Scriptures, the Word, Word of God, God's Word, etc. All these mean the same thing and come under the broad heading, "the Bible." I may use each of these terms at various times.

The word "Lord" in Old Testament Hebrew refers to Yahweh, the Old Testament's most special name of God. In the New Testament, "Lord" is a term of respect, like "sir." Sometimes it's a reference to God, or a title for Jesus.

# You've Got Mail!

The New Testament book of Hebrews is a letter. First century letters (including all the New Testament letters except Hebrews and 1 John) typically began with a salutation identifying the writer and the person or persons to whom the letter was addressed.

Hebrews is different. It includes no salutation. You have to dig for clues in the letter itself to figure out who wrote it, and who it was written for. Hebrews ends, however, like a typical letter, with personal notes, good wishes, and a farewell.

On the other hand, in the first-century world the term "letter" or "epistle" referred to a wide variety of written communications. Thus Hebrews is more like a sermon or a lecture that became a letter. It's about as long as a typical sermon—taking less than an hour to read aloud. Many scholars today think that the Hebrews Letter was first delivered as a sermon, or teaching, in one of the house churches in which Christians met, then was sent from house church to house church in cities across the empire.

Picture a scribe in the audience taking notes on the preacher's message. After the meeting the note-taker turns his notes into a letter and sends it to other people.

# How to Use the Smart Guide to the Bible—Hebrews

Here's how I suggest you approach the book of Hebrews. Sit down with this book and your Bible. Then, before you begin your verse-by-verse study, read the entire book of Hebrews all the way through, in one sitting. It takes about half an hour. Then:

- Start this book at chapter 1.
- As you work through each chapter, read the Scriptures that it references, from your Bible.
- Answer the Study Questions and review with the Chapter Wrap-Up.

In addition, the sidebars are loaded with definitions and other helpful bits of fascinating information, as explained below.

# Why Study Hebrews?

The book of Hebrews will help you see how Old and New Testaments are linked—how they are two parts of the same astonishing story. Like no other New Testament book, Hebrews helps us understand the Old Testament. Even more important, Hebrews helps Christians today comprehend the exciting reality that they are inseparably linked with a living Savior who cares, listens, speaks, and is there to help in every situation of their daily lives!

# Is Hebrews Hard to Understand?

Recently, I heard a TV preacher tell his audience: "Hebrews is the most difficult book in the New Testament."

I don't necessarily agree but I think I understand the problem. Hebrews is loaded with unfamiliar ideas and terminology relating to the Jewish priesthood and the Old Testament sacrificial system, which are unfamiliar to most twenty-first-century readers. Not to worry! This commentary will help you understand many of those unfamiliar terms and ideas. They'll come alive with significance for your life.

Hebrews is a phenomenal book, loaded with information and insights found nowhere else. Hebrews will help you better understand Jesus's life, death, and resurrection, and it will uncover the rock-solid foundation on which Christian faith is established.

Jesus said that His Holy Spirit will guide us in discovery of "all truth" (John 16:13 NKJV). It helps to read and study the Bible with an open heart, expecting God to light up your life in surprising ways.

Where do you turn when you are under terrible pressure and your faith is taking a beating? The theme of Hebrews, repeated in various ways throughout the book, is a slogan to help you keep your head in the midst of challenge and change.

The slogan and "open sesame" to spiritual power for the tough stuff of life is:

"Looking unto Jesus" (Hebrews 12:2 NKJV)

Hebrews is relevant today because exploring it helps you understand the importance of Jesus in your life, from situation to situation, right here and now!

## Hebrews Cheer: "Jesus Is the Greatest!"

| | |
|---|---|
| Jesus is the greatest message from God | Hebrews 1:1–3 |
| Jesus is greater than the angels | Hebrews 1:1:4–2:5 |
| Jesus is the greatest human being | Hebrews 2:5–18 |
| Jesus is greater than Moses | Hebrews 3:1–6 |
| Jesus offers the greatest rest | Hebrews 4:1–11 |
| Jesus is the greatest priest | Hebrews 4:14–8:6 |
| Jesus is the greatest mediator of the greatest covenant | Hebrews 8:7–13 |
| Jesus is the greatest sacrifice | Hebrews 9:1–10:18 |
| Jesus is the greatest objective of faith | Hebrews 11:1–12:3 |

# The Search for the Anonymous Author

Clues to the identity of the author of Hebrews are hidden in the writings and deductions of early church historians, apologists and other people throughout history who have studied the Bible intensely. Over the years, scholarly "detectives" have sifted through the Letter to Hebrews over and over, dusting for fingerprints.

## Three Solid Clues—"Fingerprints"

Many brilliant assumptions have been advanced. Still the illusive author remains anonymous. For 2,000 years Bible sleuths have searched among the traces, looking for proof that would crack the mystery:

*Fingerprint A*—The anonymous author was an expert in Judaism, familiar with the temple, priesthood, sacrificial system, and Jewish history.

*Fingerprint B*—The Hebrews' scribe was from Paul's inner circle. Hebrews 13:23 indicates that the author and Timothy, Paul's bosom buddy, knew each other and were planning a trip together. He was someone who hung out with Paul. And, the ideas in Hebrews are distinctively Pauline.

*Fingerprint C*—The creator of Hebrews wrote from the perspective of a Jew living much of his life outside the Promised Land.

### The Letter to the Hebrews . . . Whodunit?

**Clues unearthed by researchers have led one or more students of Scripture to believe one of the following is the most logical suspect to credit for the authorship of Hebrews.**

| | |
|---|---|
| **Paul** | Born "Saul of Tarsus," a free Roman city, 300 miles north of Jerusalem (Acts 21:39). Under Roman law, citizens of free cities enjoyed rights and protections not accorded other Roman citizens (Acts 21:37–22:3; and 22:25–29). As a Christian, Saul's name was changed to Paul (Greek: Paulos (Acts 13:9). He was fluent in Greek, Hebrew, and Aramaic (Acts 22:2). As an apostle, Paul wrote 13 New Testament letters under his byline. Early Christian leaders and teachers were divided about his authorship of Hebrews. Producers of the AD 1611 King James Version of the Bible were so convinced Paul was the author they renamed the letter "The EPISTLE OF PAUL to the Hebrews." Linguistic experts, however, compare the writing in Hebrews with Paul's other letters and insist the writing is not his. It's highly polished Greek unlike anything Paul wrote, and uses 169 words he never used elsewhere. Later creative academics floated the idea that Paul wrote Hebrews in Hebrew and Luke (who wrote better Greek than Paul) translated it into Greek. |
| **Barnabas** | Barnabas was a Levite (Acts 4:36). Thus Barnabas was an expert in Jewish religion, trained for leadership in Judaism. Barnabas was part of Paul's inner circle. He was Paul's first friend in Jerusalem after Paul's conversion (Acts 9:26–27). Barnabas and Paul pastored the Antioch church together (Acts 11:25–26). They were the first team commissioned to take the Gospel to the Gentiles. The author himself describes Hebrews as a "word of exhortation" (Hebrews 13:22 NKJV). It's the kind of letter Barnabas with his unique giftedness would write. His name, "Barnabas," means "Son of Exhortation" or "Son of Encouragement" (Acts 4:36 NKJV). Barnabas was born and raised on the Island of Cyprus, outside the Israeli homeland. He was a Greek-speaking Jew, able to write from both Grecian and Jewish perspectives (Acts 4:36). |
| **Luke** | Luke was Paul's coworker and was known as the "beloved physician" (Colossians 4:14 NKJV). The Greek in Hebrews is closer to Luke's style than Paul's. |
| **Apollos** | Apollos was a silver-tongued, Greek-Hebrew-speaking Jewish expatriate from Alexandria, Egypt and Christian preacher-apologist (Acts 18:24–28; 1 Corinthians 1:3). He had a considerable following in the Corinthian church (Acts 18:24–28; 1 Corinthians 11–13; 3:1–13). Martin Luther believed Apollos authored Hebrews. |

## The Letter to the Hebrews . . . Whodunit? (cont'd)

| | |
|---|---|
| **Priscilla** | Priscilla and her husband Aquila were Paul's comrades at Corinth, Ephesus, and Rome (Acts 18:5; 19:22; Romans 16:3–5; 1 Corinthians 16:10, 19). Some early historical evidence suggests Priscilla was a member of a highborn Roman family; who first converted to Judaism. Then to Christ. If she wrote Hebrews it might explain the author's choice of anonymity. Could it be that antifeminist attitudes in Judaism and society in general clung to the early church, making it difficult for a woman's writings to be considered authentic? How tempting is that prospect—Priscilla, possibly the secret author of Hebrews! Problem: a shortage of evidence. |
| **Philip** | Philip was one of the first team of seven men chosen to carry on and oversee the church's ministry to the hungry (Acts 6:1–5). Philip was an evangelist, an itinerant Gospel preacher (Acts 8:5–40). Whenever Paul was in town he stayed at Philip's house (Acts 21:8). |
| **Clement** | Clement is an "early church father," influential late in the second century, in formation of the fledgling Christian movement. He was the first early Christian writer to quote Hebrews in his own writings. |
| **Mary** | Even Jesus's mother garners a few scholarly votes. Who would know Jesus better than Mary (Acts 1:12–14)? |
| **Silas** | Silas was Paul's partner for the Second Missionary Journey (Acts 15:40; 22–40). |
| **Timothy** | Timothy was called Paul's "true son" (1 Timothy 1:2 NKJV). His authorship of Hebrews is doubtful. Consider Hebrews 13:23. |
| **Epaphras** | Epaphras was a hard-working companion in Paul's ministry. Paul notes his servanthood and fervency in prayer (Colossians 1:7; 4:12). |

# Is That Your Final Answer?

If I must commit myself, the *correct* answer as to the authorship of Hebrews is, most likely, Barnabas. The arguments for his authorship are better than for any of the others. Paul is ruled out because of language issues.

Whoever the person who authored Hebrews, it is clear that he or she was a brilliant student of the Old Testament who knew Jesus well. He understood the meaning of Christ's sacrificial death, and celebrated His never-ending work on behalf of believers. Also, everything this nameless person wrote is consistent with the rest of the New Testament. No writer does a better job of tying Old and New Testaments together and showing how the person and work of Jesus explains secrets hidden in the treasure troves of ancient Judaism. None does a better job of demonstrating how Jesus changes the way people and God can connect and live as friends. No one presents the divine sonship and humanness of Jesus with more clarity and enthusiasm.

## About the Author

Bob Girard spent many years in the pastorate, during which he wrote several influential books and had a popular radio ministry, *Letters to the Church at Phoenix.* For many years Bob wrote adult Sunday school lessons for Scripture Press. He is the author of other books in the Smart Guide to the Bible™ series, including *The Life of Christ* and *Acts.* Bob is now retired and lives in a house he built in Rimrock, Arizona.

## About the General Editor

Dr. Larry Richards is a native of Michigan who now lives in Raleigh, North Carolina. He was converted to Christianity while in the Navy in the 1950s. Larry has taught and written Sunday school curriculum for every age-group, from nursery through adult. He has published more than two hundred books that have been translated into twenty-six languages. His wife, Sue, is also an author. They both enjoy teaching Bible studies as well as fishing and playing golf.

# Understanding the Bible Is Easy with These Tools

To understand God's Word you need easy-to-use study tools right where you need them—at your fingertips. The Smart Guide to the Bible™ series puts valuable resources adjacent to the text to save you both time and effort.

Every page features handy sidebars filled with icons and helpful information: cross references for additional insights, definitions of key words and concepts, brief commentaries from experts on the topic, points to ponder, evidence of God at work, the big picture of how passages fit into the context of the entire Bible, practical tips for applying biblical truths to every area of your life, and plenty of maps, charts, and illustrations. A wrap-up of each passage, combined with study questions, concludes each chapter.

These helpful tools show you what to watch for. Look them over to become familiar with them, and then turn to Chapter 1 with complete confidence: You are about to increase your knowledge of God's Word!

# Study Helps

The thought-bubble icon alerts you to commentary you might find particularly thought-provoking, challenging, or encouraging. You'll want to take a moment to reflect on it and consider the implications for your life.

Don't miss this point! The exclamation-point icon draws your attention to a key point in the text and emphasizes important biblical truths and facts.

**death on the cross**
Colossians 1:21–22

Many see Boaz as a type of Jesus Christ. To win back what we human beings lost through sin and spiritual death, Jesus had to become human (i.e., he had to become a true kinsman), and he had to be willing to pay the penalty for our sins. With his <u>death on the cross</u>, Jesus paid the penalty and won freedom and eternal life for us.

The additional Bible verses add scriptural support for the passage you just read and help you better understand the <u>underlined text</u>. (Think of it as an instant reference resource!)

How does what you just read apply to your life? The heart icon indicates that you're about to find out! These practical tips speak to your mind, heart, body, and soul, and offer clear guidelines for living a righteous and joy-filled life, establishing priorities, maintaining healthy relationships, persevering through challenges, and more.

This icon reveals how God is truly all-knowing and all-powerful. The hourglass icon points to a specific example of the prediction of an event or the fulfillment of a prediction. See how some of what God has said would come to pass already has!

What are some of the great things God has done? The traffic-sign icon shows you how God has used miracles, special acts, promises, and covenants throughout history to draw people to him.

Does the story or event you just read about appear elsewhere in the Gospels? The cross icon points you to those instances where the same story appears in other Gospel locations—further proof of the accuracy and truth of Jesus' life, death, and resurrection.

Since God created marriage, there's no better person to turn to for advice. The double-ring icon points out biblical insights and tips for strengthening your marriage.

The Bible is filled with wisdom about raising a godly family and enjoying your spiritual family in Christ. The family icon gives you ideas for building up your home and helping your family grow close and strong.

**Isle of Patmos**
a small island in the
Mediterranean Sea

something significant had occurred, he wrote down the substance of what he saw. This is the practice John followed when he recorded Revelation on the **Isle of Patmos.**

What does that word really mean, especially as it relates to this passage? Important, misunderstood, or infrequently used words are set in **bold type** in your text so you can immediately glance at the margin for definitions. This valuable feature lets you better understand the meaning of the entire passage without having to stop to check other references.

## the big picture

**Joshua**
Led by Joshua, the Israelites crossed the Jordan River and invaded Canaan (see Illustration #8). In a series of military campaigns the Israelites defeated several coalition armies raised by the inhabitants of Canaan. With organized resistance put down, Joshua divided the land among the twelve Israelite

How does what you read fit in with the greater biblical story? The highlighted big picture summarizes the passage under discussion.

## what others say

**David Breese**
Nothing is clearer in the Word of God than the fact that God wants us to understand himself and his working in the lives of men.[5]

It can be helpful to know what others say on the topic, and the highlighted quotation introduces another voice in the discussion. This resource enables you to read other opinions and perspectives.

Maps, charts, and illustrations pictorially represent ancient artifacts and show where and how stories and events took place. They enable you to better understand important empires, learn your way around villages and temples, see where major battles occurred, and follow the journeys of God's people. You'll find these graphics let you do more than study God's Word—they let you *experience* it.

Introduction

# Chapters at a Glance

## Part Four: Hebrews 11–13  A Long Walk Outside the Camp

# Part One
# HEBREWS 1-4
# THE RADIANCE OF GOD

# Hebrews 1:1-3
# This Surprising God

**Chapter Highlights:**
- To Jerusalem with Love
- The God Who Talks to People
- Discovering God
- The Silent Years

## Let's Get Started

Life for Jews living in Jerusalem during the AD 60s was no easy cruise. It ended in a disaster of "biblical proportions." <u>Zealots</u> sought to rid the nation of anyone suspected of sympathy for Rome. Also referred to as "dagger men," they left a trail of blood and terror in the streets of Israel's towns and cities.

## Christian Beginnings

Within the ancient **Holy City** were several thousand Jews who believed that Jesus of Nazareth was the promised Messiah. However, because they had chosen to align their lives and destinies with the crucified Jesus, <u>opposition</u> from religious and political authorities always confronted them. Many had been <u>imprisoned</u> for their faith. Some had paid with <u>their lives</u>. Still they <u>hung together</u> and watched out for each other through difficult times.

Jerusalem's Christian community was as thoroughly Jewish and committed to Judaism as any segment of the population. They embraced the faith and teachings of Jesus but also maintained their allegiance to the national religion.

*First century AD.* Christian Jews were imprisoned, tortured, and killed for confessing faith in Jesus. Are Christian <u>martyrs</u> a thing of the past? Most certainly not!

*Twentieth Century.* (1) More Christians were tortured for their faith during the 20th Century than in all the previous 19 centuries combined. (2) About 100 million Christians were martyred for their faith during the 20th century—more than the number of people who died in all the wars of that same 100 years! (3) And it's not over yet—an estimated 200 million Christians are presently facing persecution around the world.

**Zealots**
Luke 6:15;
Acts 1:13

**opposition**
John 15:18–16:4;
Acts 4:1–28;
5:17–40; 6:9–14;
etc.

**imprisoned**
Acts 4:3; 5:18; 8:3;
12:3–4; 22:4–5

**their lives**
Acts 22:4; 26:10

**hung together**
Acts 2:41–47;
4:32–35;
Hebrews 10:33–34

**martyrs**
Acts 7:56–60;
12:1–3;
Hebrews 11:33–40

**Zealots**
adherents of a political party committed to driving Roman occupation forces into the sea

**Holy City**
Jerusalem

**go to**

**threatened**
John 9:22

**Way**
Acts 9:1–2; 22:4

**heresy**
sect or party promoting false belief or teaching

**Way**
early name for the community of Jesus followers

# None Here!

Sometime during the "stressful 60s," Jewish temple authorities did what they had <u>threatened</u> since Jesus first appeared on the scene. They officially branded Christianity a **heresy** and banned Christians from the temple.

Christian Jews found themselves on the outside looking in— denied access to the shrine around which their highest aspirations revolved. To them, Jesus and Moses were not only compatible, but many followers of the **Way** felt that Mosaic Law, Old Testament–style worship, and Jewish lifestyle were the best part of being Christians!

Even so, for more than 30 years they had danced a precarious-but-happy shuffle between Christianity and Judaism, hoping they would never have to choose between the two. Suddenly, the temple gates slammed shut in front of them! The smell of the burning morning and evening sacrifices filled their nostrils and made their hearts rejoice, but they could no longer participate.

Families were split. Friends shunned friends. And the pressure to forsake the Way of Christ and return to the security of the ancient traditions became nearly irresistible. Some saw their newfound faith crumble. Many were tempted to jump ship! Some did.

**what others say**

### H. T. Andrews

Under the stranglehold of persecution, the strain upon the loyalty of members of the Christian Church became well-nigh intolerable, and it is not surprising that large numbers of men and women were tempted to renounce the faith.[1]

*Late first century AD.* Christian Jews were disinherited by family and shunned by friends and relatives because of their decision to follow Jesus.

*Today.* If a Jewish son or daughter converts to Christianity, many Jewish families will disinherit him or her. Often the convert is declared deceased, burial services are held, and family and friends break off all contact with the offender.

The calamity of **excommunication** was a tragic accessory to the misery about to overwhelm Christian Jews, but also the whole Jewish nation. In AD 70, Roman legions under Emperor Titus would sweep into Jerusalem and leave its once-glorious temple an inglorious heap of smoldering wreckage, its streets and surrounding countryside strewn with the bodies of one and a half million Jewish dead.

What then would happen to worship and traditions? How, without the temple and the paraphernalia of their historic religion, could a Jew—even a *Christian* Jew—serve God? If ever a group needed a "word from the Lord"—to deal with both their current situation and the one they would soon be facing—it was this group!

## To Jerusalem with Love

Into this bleak and confusing milieu came a letter from a Jewish Christian in Rome, Italy (Hebrews 13:24). It became known among Christians by a line an early reader scrawled at the top of the first page: "To the Hebrews." It was a life raft thrown to a drowning people.

"To the Hebrews" has one message:

*Hang on! Don't jump ship! Stop gazing backward, yearning for what you no longer need. The temple, sacrifices and priesthood, represent obsolete religion—all are shadows that gave only a dim vision and knowledge of God. In Jesus you have the best God has to offer. The ultimate disaster would be to give up God's best for something obsolete and spiritually ineffective. Fix your yearnings and hopes on Jesus and hang in there.*

**severe persecution**
Hebrews
10:32–12:4; 13:13

**excommunication**
be barred from participation in religious community life

what others say

**Larry Richards**

The letter called Hebrews was written specifically to converted Jews. They often felt a deep affection for the way of life they had known from birth, and sometimes wondered if they had been right in committing themselves to Christ.[2]

## When Did the Author Write Hebrews?

Two clues suggest a likely time frame. First, Hebrews was written to an unpopular people about to face <u>severe persecution</u>. This sug-

**go to**

**offered sacrifices**
Hebrews 5:1–6;
8:1–6; 9:1–10:18

**house church**
Acts 5:42; 12:12;
18:7; 20:8; 28:30;
Romans 16:5

**Judea and Samaria**
Acts 1:8

**persecution**
harassment based
on religion

**house church**
small Christian con-
gregations that met
in believers' homes;
no special church
buildings were built
until after AD 250 in
Rome

gests a date prior to Emperor Nero's **persecution** of Christians in AD 64 or 65.

Second, when Hebrews was written the traditional institutions of Jewish worship were still functioning. The writer speaks of them in the present tense. The temple was standing and priests offered sacrifices and carried on with their priestly duties. This suggests a date before AD 70, the year Emperor Titus's Roman legions sacked Jerusalem and burned the temple to the ground, ending the kind of worship Hebrews describes. These clues point to a composition date between AD 60 and 69.

**what others say**

**Merrill C. Tenney**

The epistle seems to fit best into the situation of the late six-ties (AD), when the church at Rome was fearing persecution and when the fall of the Jewish commonwealth was immi-nent."[3]

## Mystery Destination—"To the Hebrews"

The original letter was untitled. But as handwritten copies were made and circulated person-to-person among the early Christians, somebody added a title to identify it: *To the Hebrews.*

But to *which* Hebrews? Jewish neighborhoods existed in cities all over the Roman world. In Egypt the Jewish community numbered more than a million. The original letter may have been dispatched to Christian Jews meeting as **house churches**, in Alexandria, Jerusalem, or some other city under the Roman umbrella.

It was written from the perspective of the harassed Christian minority in Jerusalem and small groups of beleagured believers scat-tered about Judea and Samaria. But while primarily targeting harassed Hebrew believers, the message of the book of Hebrews is relevant to Christians of any ethnic background or nationality, *any-where at any time.*

**what others say**

**Zane C. Hodges**

In the final analysis the exact destination of the epistle is of as little importance as the identity of its author. Regardless of who wrote it, or where it was first sent, the Christian church

**Israel**
Genesis 32:28

**great-grandfather**
Genesis 10:21;
11:16

**promises**
Genesis 12:1–3, 7

**moved to Egypt**
Genesis 46

**infanticide**
Exodus 1:15–16

**escaping**
Exodus 5–15

Abraham, father of the Jewish nation, is the first person the Bible identified as a "Hebrew" (Genesis 14:13 NKJV). As his children multiplied and developed into the **Israelite** nation, the "Hebrews" moniker stuck like fly paper to the whole clan (Exodus 1:15–19).

The original word from which "Hebrew" evolves is *Eber*, meaning "Outsider." It was the name of Abraham's great-great-great-great-grandfather on his father's side.

In Egyptian and Babylonian records, the word "Hebrew" occurs as a less than complimentary term for immigrants and day laborers. When **Potiphar**'s wife falsely accused Joseph of trying to rape her, she pointed her finger at him and screamed, "See, he has brought in to us a Hebrew to mock us" (Genesis 39:14 NKJV). She was using it as a term of racial contempt, like saying, "This rotten foreigner!"

How did the clan of Abraham get tagged with the name "Hebrews," which, depending on where you are, inspires either intense pride or contempt? For much of its history, Israel has been a nation of wanderers. In 2000 BC (give or take a century or two), when Abraham was still living among the **pagans** in ancient Chaldea, God turned his life upside down (or right side up, depending on your perspective) with this instruction:

**GENESIS 12:1** *Get out of your country, from your family and from your father's house, to a land that I will show you. (NKJV)*

Saying "Yes" to God, Abraham became a nomad, living on promises. God promised him the **Land of Canaan**, where he lived for the rest of his life. But in his lifetime he never gained title to this promised land. For a while his descendants lived there as **squatters**. But when the Middle East was gripped by famine the family (then numbering 70) folded their tents and moved to Egypt, where they established temporary residence in a part of Egypt called Goshen.

"Temporary" turned out to be 400 years, much of that time as slaves. During those centuries of hard labor Abraham's descendants had babies and, in spite of **Pharaoh**'s monstrous program of **infanticide**, grew into a nation of hundreds of thousands (some estimate three million). After escaping slavery through God's intervention, God confirmed

**Israelite**
descendant of "Jacob" whose name means "heel catcher," which God changed to Israel, "Prince of God"

**Potiphar**
Captain of Egyptian Palace Guard

**pagans**
unbelievers, worshipers of false gods

**Land of Canaan**
east of the Mediterranean, from seacoast to Jordan River Valley

**squatters**
settlers on property with the intent of claiming the land

**Pharaoh**
title of the ruler of Egypt

**infanticide**
killing babies

**go to**

**refused to believe**
Numbers 13–14;
Hebrews 3–4

**military and spiritual generalship**
The book of Joshua

**Joshua**
Numbers 13:8;
14:6–10

**Caleb**
Numbers 13:6, 30

**Ten Commandments**
Exodus 20

**Promised Land**
Canaan, the home-
land God guaran-
teed to Abraham's
descendants

**Mosaic Law**
Moral, religious,
governmental
principles God
gave Moses—
Exodus, Leviticus,
Numbers,
Deuteronomy

**ethnic Jew**
racially Jewish, born
to Jewish parents

**minority**
an estimated one
third of first-century
Jews believed in
Jesus

**pariahs**
outcasts, despised,
rejected by others

that it was time for them to inherit the **Promised Land** for keeps, free and clear, then and there. But they were scared, <u>refused to believe</u> God's offer was anything but pie in the sky, and turned down the deal.

God was not pleased.

For the next 40 years the Hebrews wandered outside the land—gazing across the Jordan River to the hills of home, never able to get there—always on the road to Lord-only-knows-where. A generation of homeless outsiders. Wanderers. Foreigners. Pilgrims. Aliens. Strangers. In other words . . . *Hebrews!*

When, under the <u>military and spiritual generalship</u> of <u>Joshua</u> and <u>Caleb</u>, the Hebrew people finally claimed the Promised Land as their homeland and moved in, their alien status did not end. Trying to live by God's high moral principles, spelled out in the <u>Ten Commandments</u> and **Mosaic Law**, continued to set Israelites apart from their pagan neighbors. Nonetheless, they settled down to become farmers, merchants, and citizens. For the next 1,500 years, in their better moments they marched to a different drumbeat, their lives and society ordered by God's principles in stark contrast to the wickedness of the surrounding nations. Their commitment to God and His commitment to them guaranteed that even as settlers in the land, at heart they would always be . . . *Hebrews!*

## What's a Nice Jewish Book Like This Doing in the New Testament?

If Judaism (the religion of the Jews) and Christianity are two separate and different religions, then why is there a book among the important documents of the followers of Jesus titled, "To the *Hebrews*"?

If being born an **ethnic Jew** made you an outsider in this world, becoming a Jewish *Christian* through faith in Jesus intensified the alienation! The people for whom the letter to Hebrews was written were as surely branches of Abraham's family tree as any Jews. The epithet "Outsiders!" was never more appropriate than when applied to the **minority** of first-century Jews who embraced Jesus as Messiah. Not only were they misfits in the world at large because of their nationality and unique culture, they were **pariahs** among their fellow Jews because they were linked to the officially censured, crucified Jesus. Their own countrymen called them _traitors_!

## Abraham's Alien Offspring

Now fasten your seat belts. This who's-a-Hebrew business gets even more mind-bending! The New Testament insists that _non-Jews_ (Gentiles) who believe and follow Jesus are _spiritual_ children of Abraham as surely as ethnic Jews. And, as it is for all of Abraham's children, part of the Abrahamic legacy for non-Jewish Christians is that they never quite fit into their world. In secular society, people who give allegiance to Jesus are always "foreign" or "strange" when compared to the people and cultures that surround them. In a real sense . . . "Hebrews"!

In other words, Judaism and Christianity are not two separate religions. Both are rooted in the amazing process by which God reveals Himself to people and bridges the gap between a holy God and sinful man. Through the sacrificial death of His own Son, God made it possible for people to live together with Him, in peace.

The Old Testament records prophecies, proclaimed hundreds of years before their fulfillment, telling Israel that God would send a Jewish-born **Messiah**, a "Son," who would benefit people all over the world. Jesus's birth, life, death, and resurrection fulfilled what the prophets predicted.

## The God Who Talks to People

HEBREWS 1:1 _God, who at various times and in various ways spoke in time past to the fathers . . ._ (NKJV)

To counter the indecision of many Jewish Christians, the writer of Hebrews plunges immediately into the basic beliefs that set Christianity apart from other religions. He begins with one upon which both Jews and Christians agree.

"God . . . spoke."

If anything is woven into the fabric of the Judeo-Christian psyche, it is the importance of the Word of God—spoken, written, read, and obeyed.

The **Torah**, read and interpreted in synagogues, is a library of 39 books recording the words God spoke to Israel. Jesus's followers

**traitors**
Acts 6:11–14

**spiritual children**
Romans 2:25–29;
3:29–30; 4:7–25;
11:11–24

**prophecies**
Genesis 12:3; 2
Samuel 7:12–13;
Isaiah 7:14–25;
Micah 5:2

**Son**
Isaiah 7:14; 9:6–7;
Matthew 2:18–25

**all over the world**
Genesis 12:3;
Acts chapters 10–28

**Messiah**
King sent by God

**the Word**
John 1:1

**Paradise**
Genesis 2:8–17; 3:8

**Torah**
specifically, the first
five books of the
Bible, although the
same term is also
sometimes applied
to the entire Old
Testament even
though the correct
word for that is
*tanakh*

give the **Torah** even greater significance, because they see and hear Jesus Himself speaking through its ancient pages.

## What If God Had Kept Quiet?

The headline "God . . . spoke" is fundamental. If God had kept silent, humanity would now be hopelessly lost, groping in the dark. Christians, because they accept the Bible's teaching, stake everything on their belief that God is a kind and loving Creator who cares for people, is involved in their lives, and maintains relationships with them through His spoken word.

If the Bible and the anonymous *Hebrews* author are telling the truth—and Christians are willing to bet the farm that they *are*—it is no surprise when the Almighty buttonholes someone and talks turkey.

## Discovering God

God makes Himself known and shows Himself to people through two types of revelation:

1. *General Revelation:* Everybody knows something about God. Even you! You were born with an inner sense, an inner consciousness of God's existence and a hunger to know Him. You learn about Him by observing the natural world. If you pay attention to earth and sky, plants, animals, and birds, you discover evidence for the existence of a powerful God of order who provides for and protects His creatures. Looking inside yourself you see

more proof. Creator-built into every human being is a moral alarm that sounds when you mess up. It's your <u>conscience</u>.

It's also part of <u>God's image</u> in human beings. Conscience reveals that God is a moral being committed to righteousness and justice. Not that we ever fully figure God out from general revelation—observing Nature and ourselves. The ancient Bible character, Job, puts it in perspective:

> JOB 26:14 *Indeed these are the mere edges of His ways, and how small a whisper we hear of Him! But the thunder of His power who can understand? (NKJV)*

Job was right. You and I need a lot more information if we are ever going to really know God, and how to please Him.

2. *Special Revelation:* This includes actions God takes to disclose secrets about Himself and His will that could not be discovered without His personal show-and-tell. Special revelation includes God's spoken word (neon signs in our minds!) and the written record in the Bible of His past acts and words. The idea that God Almighty communicates with earthlings runs through the Bible from Genesis to Revelation. References to God's voice, God's speaking, and God's Word appear on almost every page.

God speaks. He wants us to know what's on His mind. People with open minds and hearts can hear His voice and understand. It is possible for ordinary people just like us to listen and understand what God is saying.

**go to**

**conscience**
Romans 2:14–16

**God's image**
Genesis 1:26–27;
5:1;
James 3:9

*Something to ponder*

what others say

**Ravi Zacharias**

If mankind were only mind or intellect, evidence from the physical world would be all that mattered. But there is a depth to our being; a spiritual essence that goes deeper than our intellect. That essence hungers for intimacy. The spiritual, not the physical, is the essence of our being, and only communion with the living God satisfies.[7]

Listening to God's voice is a big deal in the Letter to the Hebrews. Frequently the author reports something God says (see Hebrews 1:5–13; 3:7–11; 4:3; 5:5–6; 6:13; 7:17, 21; 8:8–12; 10:16–17; etc.).

**go to**

**audibly**
Matthew 3:17;
Luke 9:34–36;
John 12:28–29;
Acts 9:3–7

**through His Word**
Psalm 1:1–2;
119:11, 105;
Hebrews 4:12–13;
2 Timothy 3:16–17

**vision**
revelation, insight
from God received
while in a dreamlike
state

**angel**
spirit personage in
service of God

**Yiddish**
hybrid Jewish-
German language
spoken by Jews of
Eastern European
heritage

The letter's entire message may be distilled into the urgent advice near the end: "See to it that you do not refuse him who speaks" (Hebrews 12:25).

> **what others say**
>
> **William L. Lane**
> The central theme of Hebrews is the importance of listening to the voice of God.[8]

## How Does God Speak?

The Bible records hundreds of incidents in which "God . . . spoke in time past to the fathers" (Hebrews 1:1 NKJV). It does not always tell precisely *how* the voice of God was experienced. But here are a few Old Testament examples.

### How God Speaks

| | |
|---|---|
| **Visions** | God spoke to Abram (later Abraham) in a **vision** (Genesis 15:1). |
| **Audible Voice** | God "called" to Hagar audibly "out of heaven" (Genesis 21:17–19) |
| **Angels** | An **angel** spoke God's message to Abraham (Genesis 22:11, 15). |
| **Dreams** | God spoke to Jacob in a dream (Genesis 28:12–13). |
| **Observable Events** | God grabbed Moses's attention with a burning bush, then spoke directly (Exodus 3:2ff). |
| **Moses** | God spoke to the nation of Israel through Moses (Deuteronomy 5:4–6). |
| **Prophets** | God spoke to David through the prophet Nathan (2 Samuel 12:7). |
| **Whispers** | God spoke to Elijah in a "still small voice" (1 Kings 19:11–13). |
| **Scripture** | God speaks through His Word to young people who want to live holy lives (Psalm 119:9–16). |
| **Thoughts** | God speaks a "word behind you" (thought, impression, insight) (Isaiah 30:21) |
| **Implantation** | God speaks by implanting His principles "in their minds, and . . . on their hearts" (Jeremiah 31:33–34) . |

## God's Voice in the "Breaks"

A bit of **Yiddish** wisdom says, with a twinge of fatalism: *Azoy vert dos kichel tzekrochen!* Or, "That's how the cookie crumbles!" God often communicates through "the breaks"—the circumstances over which you have little or no control.

The Bible tells how God speaks to people through volcanic eruptions (Exodus19:18–19); crop failure, recession, or sickness (Deuteronomy 28:15–68); wind, earthquake, and fire (1 Kings 19:12); floods (Isaiah 8:6–8); mental illness (Daniel 4:28–37); and getting gulped by a giant fish (Jonah 1:17—"*a great fish*").

A good question to ask at such times is, "What are You trying to say, Lord?" Then listen.

Hang on to God's promise that "all things work together for good to those who love God" (Romans 8:28 NKJV).

## The Unfolding Exposé of God

> HEBREWS 1:1 *God, who at various times and in various ways spoke in time past to the fathers by the prophets . . .  (NKJV)*

God does not disclose all His secrets at once. "God could not reveal more than men could understand."[8] His special revelation of Himself is **progressive**. It unfolds gradually in two stages.

## Special Revelation Stage 1: The Prophets

HEBREWS 1:1 *the prophets(NKJV)*

The Greek word *prophets* indicates "<u>one who speaks for God</u>." The prophets of Hebrews 1:1 represent the Old Testament. They are a roster of God's spokesmen and spokeswomen, including parents, preachers, priests, kings, judges, wise men, playwrights, artists, poets and singers, whose experiences and messages fill the Old Testament from Genesis (by Moses, author of the first five books) to Malachi (author of the final OT book).

**speaks for God**
Numbers 11:29

**secret agents**
Amos 3:7

When the prophet-preachers of Hebrews 1:1 opened their mouths, God spoke, using the prophet's mind, personality, experience and language.

HEBREWS 1:1 *at various times (NKJV)*

In every generation God has His mouthpieces, into whose hearts and minds He puts His word for the people of that day. The prophets are God's <u>secret agents</u>, handling His mysteries. Time after time, when Israel was in trouble, one or more of these spokespersons

**progressive**
developing from incomplete to complete, from promise to fulfillment

**go to**

**mimed**
Ezekiel 4, 5

**called down fire**
1 Kings 18:30–39

**signs and wonders**
Exodus 7–11;
2 Kings 6:1–7

**died**
2 Chronicles
24:20–21;
Matthew 23:37

**face of Jesus Christ**
2 Corinthians 4:6

**early Christian hymn**
Luke 1:40–55;
68–79;
Colossians 1:15–20;
Philippians 2:6–11;
1 Timothy 3:16

**in the Old Testament**
Isaiah 2:2;
Hosea 3:5;
Micah 4:1

**mimed**
pantomimed,
silently dramatized

**fulfilled**
accomplished,
brought about,
realized

would discern the times, hear God's voice, and risk his or her neck to deliver the truth to those for whom God intended it.

**HEBREWS 1:1** *and in various ways* (NKJV)

These prophets gave speeches, wrote plays, books, songs, answered questions, and quipped pithy quips. As they wrote what God said, it often flowed in Hebrew poetry. They dreamed dreams and saw visions. They <u>mimed</u> in the streets. They <u>called down fire</u> from heaven. They performed <u>signs and wonders</u>. And sometimes they <u>died</u> for telling the truth. Even so, together they produced the Old Testament.

The Old Testament is rich and powerful as a representation of God. But it isn't His finished portrait. The most vivid brushstrokes are left to the New Testament, in which God unveils Himself visibly in the <u>face of Jesus Christ</u>.

what others say

**William Barclay**

The revelation of the prophets had a variegated grandeur that made it a tremendous thing. It was never out-of-date. It was adapted to the need of every age. But, at the same time, that revelation was fragmentary, and had to be presented in such a way that the limitations of the time would understand.[9]

## Special Revelation Stage 2: The Son

**HEBREWS 1:2a** *[God] has in these last days spoken to us by His Son . . .* (NKJV)

With these words the author introduces his big idea—the huge truth that lifts the Christian Gospel above the world's great religions—God *"has in these last days spoken to us by His Son."*

Hebrews 1:2–3 was probably adapted from the lyrics of an <u>early Christian hymn</u> sung by first-century believers to celebrate Jesus as God's One and Only Son, *the* one through whom God speaks His ultimate message of-self-revelation.

*"The last days"* is a phrase used <u>in the Old Testament</u> to point to the AD period in history when the predictions of the prophets would be **fulfilled**. That period of history began with the birth of Christ. It includes the times of the original readers of Hebrews and our

twenty-first century too. It's the era for which Jews (and the whole world) had waited. In these last days (*our* days) the Bible's prophetic predictions are exploding into reality like 4th of July fireworks!

God *"has in these last days spoken to us."* Christians insist that God did not stop talking when the last scroll of the Old Testament became part of the Hebrew Scriptures. Sharp conflict between Hebrew Christians and their Judaic brothers and sisters developed at this point. Traditional Jews believed the Old Testament and Law of Moses contained the complete revelation of God and His will. To the Jewish mind, no further light was needed. Christianity was irrelevant and unnecessary.

*"By His Son."* The author of Hebrews, giving the Christian response, says, in effect, "Hold the phone! God has *more* to say." And He says it through *His Son*. Without the Son, the picture of God is woefully incomplete.

## The Silent Years

Between Malachi (397 BC, the last OT prophet) and Matthew (the first book in the NT) came a 400-year dry spell during which no prophet's voice was heard in Israel. Then, after 400 years God broke the silence. The next word out of His mouth was His greatest and clearest. God's extreme, ultimate Word is not something different from, or foreign to, Old Testament revelation; it is a continuation of the ancient story. In fact, it us the climax of the old, old story!

## The Image of Life

An ancient philosopher defined speech as "the image of life."[10] The image of God's life—God's full expression of Himself—is His Son. The heartbeat of Christian faith is that Jesus (Hebrews does not identify Him by name until chapter 2) is, in a special way matched by no other person, God's living, breathing, touchable, ultimate, extreme *"Word."*

go to

**last days**
Acts 2:17; 3:24

**image of God's life**
Colossians 1:15

**one and only**
John 1:14, 18; 3:16

**Son of God**
John 1:32–34, 49; 20:31;
1 John 5:5, 12, 20

**touchable**
1 John 1:1–3

**Word**
John 1:1–18;
1 Peter 1:22–25;
1 John 1:1

**BC**
Before Christ

key point

**Michael Card**

To say that Jesus is the Word is another way of saying he is God speaking to us. While we struggle with our many "clumsy words," God needs only one Word to perfectly communicate the depth and mystery, the passion and the overwhelming grace of who he is. By that Word, Light became a living being. Manna became man. Wisdom became a person. In Him, Life came to life; all that God is came to us in that One Final Word we call Jesus.[11]

# God, the One and Only

The New Testament, including Hebrews, clearly and candidly declares Jesus is *the* unique "one and only" Son of God Almighty, who existed with God, as God, before anything in the physical universe existed (see John 1:1–14, 18; 3:16). In calling Jesus "Son of God," the New Testament affirms that He is God. This is the big idea of the Christian faith and the book of Hebrews.

Consider these unusual historical events, recorded in the New Testament:

- An angel tells the virgin, Mary, she will bear a man-child who will be known as the "Son of the Highest [God]" (Luke 1:31–32, 35 NKJV).

- At Jesus's **baptism** and **transfiguration**, God speaks audibly, affirming that Jesus is His Son (Matthew 3:17; 17:5).

- Satan attacks Jesus's divine sonship and loses the fight (Matthew 4:3–6).

- Terrified **demons** recognize Jesus as God's Son when He confronts them (Matthew 8:29; Mark 1:23–25; 3:11–12).

- Jesus claims to be the Son of God (Matthew 11:27; 26:63–64; 27:43; Luke 22:70; John 11:4; 14:9).

- Jesus teaches that the **eternal destiny** of men and women turns on their response to Him *as God's Son*, sent by God to rescue them from sin's ruin (John 3:16–18).

- Jesus claims the Son (Himself) and the Father (God) always speak and act as One, and one day at His command the dead will rise (John 5:19–27).

- Jesus's **resurrection** is the clearest declaration and most convincing proof that Jesus is the Son of God (Romans 1:4).

## The Mighty Difference

**no salvation**
Acts 4:12

**resurrection**
rising from the dead

It's quite politically correct today to place Christianity on the same shelf with Islam, Buddhism, Hinduism, New Age, and other religious movements, and to suggest that they are all basically the same. "Take your pick—we all serve the same God," said a naive young woman interviewed on TV recently. As she said it I thought I heard a great rumbling sound as all the members of the early church rolled over in their graves!

*On the contrary*, Hebrews insists that Christianity is not just another of the world's "great religions." The difference—the thing that makes Christianity superior to mere religion of any kind—is the New Testament's insistence that authentic Christianity is *not* a religion but a living relationship, a vital connection with God through Jesus Christ. And its further insistence that the reason Jesus is so absolutely essential to real relationship with God is that He is not merely a prophet or religious teacher; He is not just another guru among a crowd of competing gurus.

The difference is that Jesus is proclaimed, not merely by Christians, but by God Himself, to be the *Son of God*!

True Christianity is not just *about* Jesus. True Christianity is Jesus, the Son of God. He is everything to His followers. Everything in the faith of the New Testament revolves about and centers in Him. There is no salvation without Him. Apart from Him there is no hope of knowing God.

The writer of Hebrews intends to show precisely what it means to say that Jesus is the Son of God. Commitment—or at least openness—to that great idea is essential to understanding this book. Nobody says it quite like C. S. Lewis, in this favorite quote:

what others say

### C. S. Lewis

A man who was merely a man and said the sort of things Jesus said wouldn't be a great moral teacher. He would either be a lunatic—on the level with a man who says he's a poached

**go to**

**the way**
John 14:6

**door**
John 10:7–9

express
explicit, the exact
one

self-disclosure
intentional
revelation of
one's own nature

egg—or else he would be the devil of hell. You must make your choice. Either this man was, and is, the Son of God: or else a madman or something worse. You can shut him up for a demon; spit at him or kill him as a demon; or you can fall at his feet and call him Lord and God. But don't let us come up with any patronizing nonsense about his being a great moral teacher. He hasn't left that alternative open to us. He didn't intend to.[12]

## Truly the Son of God

HEBREWS 1:2b–3 *[His Son,] whom He has appointed heir of all things, through whom also He made the worlds; who being the brightness of His glory and the **express** image of His person, and upholding all things by the word of His power, when He had by Himself purged our sins, sat down at the right hand of the Majesty on high . . . (NKJV)*

The Son of God, Jesus, is God's Last Word. There is nothing more He needs to say to the people of planet Earth beyond what He says in the person of His Son, Jesus. If you are ever to really "know God," it is critical that you come to know His Son. The Son is <u>the way</u> and <u>door</u> to God.

**what others say**

**John R.W. Stott**

Christianity is Christ. The person and work of Christ are the rock upon which the Christian religion is built . . . Take Christ from Christianity and you disembowel it; there is practically nothing left. Christ is the center of Christianity; all else is circumference.[13]

## Seven Amazing Facts About the Son

The first chapter of Hebrews states seven facts about the Son of God, which show why God's revelation through Him is superior to all other forms of divine **self-disclosure**. Remember, as you read this, "the Son" is Jesus of Nazareth, also known as *Christ*.

1. *The Son (Jesus Christ) is "heir of all things" (Hebrews 1:2 NKJV).* As God's heir, everything that belongs to God belongs to Jesus (John 17:10). In twenty-first-century society an "heir" is one who

gains possession of something at the death of another. In first-century culture an "heir" was one who held lawful title regardless of how possession was gained. The Father promised to present to the Son "the <u>nations</u>" and "the <u>ends of the earth</u>" for His inheritance (Psalm 2:8 NKJV). Eventually everything and <u>everyone</u> in the world will be brought together under the rulership of Jesus, God's Son and heir (Ephesians 1:9–10).

2. *The Son is the One "through whom also [God] made the worlds" (Hebrews 1:2 NKJV).* Existing <u>with God</u> from the beginning, the Son is credited with being the agent who, under God's direction and authority, <u>created everything</u>. It's interesting to note that the original Greek word translated as "the worlds" literally means "the times" or "the whole time-bound universe." The times, both "time past" (Hebrews 1:1 NKJV) and "these last days" (Hebrews 1:2 NKJV) are the Son's creations. He supervises everything that happens, to keep it all flowing in harmony with God's purposes and on schedule with God's will.

3. *The Son is "the brightness of [God's] glory" (Hebrews 1:3 NKJV).* "Glory" is appearance, reputation, and honor. "Glory" refers to God's character and nature—who and what God is. "Brightness" means splendor, brilliance, or radiance—rays of light shining from a light source. "God is light," wrote the apostle John (1 John 1:5 NKJV). The Amplified Bible translates this phrase in Hebrews 1:3 to say the Son is "the out-raying or radiance of the divine." In other words, Jesus's personality shines with the magnificent character of God. In the Old Testament, "glory" is often used to indicate <u>God's presence</u>. When we see Jesus, God is present. You can take that to the bank!

4. *The Son is "the express image of [God's] person" (Hebrews 1:3 NKJV).* Originally, the Greek term for "exact representation" was used for the image stamped on a coin or the imprint of an official seal or signet ring in a blob of wax on a document. Exposure to Jesus is exposure to the character and nature of God. This is why **four books** in the New Testament document Jesus's lifestyle, priorities, emotions, reactions, words, and accomplishments. God wants us to see and understand Him. When we look at Jesus we are to be aware that we are looking into the face of *God*!

**nations**
Psalm 47;
Matthew 28:19–20;
Romans 15:8–21;
Revelation 5:9–10

**ends of the earth**
Isaiah 45:22;
Acts 1:8; 13:47;
Romans 10:17–18

**everyone**
Philippians 2:9–11

**with God**
John 1:1–2

**created everything**
John 1:3;
1 Corinthians 1:6;
Colossians 1:16

**God's presence**
Exodus 40:34–35;
2 Chronicles 5:14;
Psalm 85:9

**four books**
Matthew, Mark,
Luke, John

What a brilliant communication strategy! In bold action to communicate in language humans speak and understand, to make Himself known, God dispatched His Son from the heavenly dimension to the streets of planet Earth. The Son volunteered to take on <u>human nature</u>. He lived 33 years as "one of us," delivering God's message in human languages (of which He spoke at least three). Since before time began, the Son was God's expression in the universe. He was and is God with us. He talks our language.

In the opening paragraph of his book on the Life of Christ, John writes in breathless, awe, "And the Word [Jesus Christ] became flesh and dwelt among us, and we beheld His glory, the glory as of the only begotten of the Father, full of grace and truth. No one has seen God at any time. The only begotten Son, who is in the bosom of the Father, He has declared Him" (John 1:14, 18 NKJV).

> **what others say**
>
> **Michael Card**
>
> It is one thing to claim that God looks down upon us, from a safe distance, and speaks to us (via long distance, we hope). But to say that he is right here is to put him and us in a totally new situation. He is no longer the calm and benevolent observer in the sky, the kindly old caricature with the beard. His image becomes that of Jesus, who wept and laughed, who fasted and feasted, and who, above all, was fully present to those he loved. He was there with them. He is here with us.[14]

5. *The Son is currently "upholding all things by the word of His power" (Hebrews 1:3 NKJV).* The original Greek word for *"upholding"* means "carrying along." The Son, who worked with His Father to bring the universe into existence, shares a continuing vital role in the natural world, overseeing its processes and keeping it functioning according to God's will and purposes.

**human nature**
Philippians 2:6–8

Another scripture states the same idea a bit differently: "in [Christ] all things hold together" (Colossians 1:17 NIV). Scientists tell of a mysterious force that keeps the atoms from spontaneously splitting as a result of the natural aversion of positively and negatively charged particles toward each other within the atomic structure. Sometimes this force is called "cosmic glue." Paul, in his letter to the Colossians, identifies Jesus as the Cosmic Glue that keeps the world from disintegrating.

Jesus, as told in the Gospel of Mark, once stopped a life-threatening storm on the Sea of Galilee by simply saying to the wind and waves, "Peace, be still!" His awestruck disciples were left shaking in their boots. "Who can this be?" they gasped with chills running up and down their spines. "Even the wind and the sea obey Him!" (Mark 4:35–41 NKJV).

Think of it! The controversial Galilean teacher with dusty feet and empty pockets is the Almighty Architect-Administrator of time, space, and matter, in the <u>disguise of a slave</u>!

With a few breathless phrases the author of Hebrews has lifted his readers' imaginations to a crescendo of wonder at the astonishing position and power of Jesus—Son and Heir of God, Co-Creator, Splendor of God's Splendor, exact Representation and Perfect Image of God's nature and character, whose Word is so powerful it keeps the universe ticking! It's understandable if we are sometimes caught up in a positively *cosmic* kind of worship.

**go to**

disguise of a slave
Philippians 2:7

barrier
Isaiah 59:2

annul
render void,
invalidate, cancel

---

what others say

**Lawrence O. Richards**

Only Christ's active support enables the universe and all processes in it to continue operation.[15]

---

Worship is a natural response when we consider the wonders of Christ.

6. *The Son "by Himself purged our sins" (Hebrews 1:3 NKJV).* With the next stroke of his pen, the author of Hebrews brings us down to earth and we experience a different kind of astonishment, leading once we "get" it to a more personal kind of worship, centering on the Son's power to **annul** the effects of humanity's sins. The author lifts the curtain of secrecy just a little and we catch an inkling of Hebrews' greatest theme—*Jesus as our High Priest.*

However, unless something is done to cleanse away the contamination of sin in us, it stands as an impenetrable <u>barrier</u> to communication and fellowship with God, who is absolutely holy and pure. Later in Hebrews we will learn that cleansing can only come, and fellowship with God can only be restored, through payment of the spiritual debt our sins have created. It's a debt human beings cannot pay for themselves.

apply it

**go to**

**His own person**
1 Peter 2:24;
Romans 5:6–11

**nail scars**
Luke 24:39–40;
John 20:20, 27

**descent**
Philippians 2:6–7

**ascension**
Acts 1:9–11;
Ephesians 4:10

**work completed**
Genesis 2:2–3;
John 17:4; 19:30;
Hebrews 10:18

**rest**
Hebrews 3:11,
18–19; 4:1–11

**right hand**
1 Kings 2:19;
Psalm 110;
Luke 22:69

**ascension**
Jesus's return to His
Father in heaven

**exaltation**
to be raised in rank
and power

The subtleties of the original language indicate that purification of sins was something the Son of God provided in His own person. He offered *Himself* as a sacrifice to pay our sin debt. The nail scars in His hands and feet show just how personal it was!

This is the first reference in the book of Hebrews to Jesus's ministry as High Priest—a huge theme in the book. Chapters 9 and 10 will spell out in detail how purification of sins took place, as Jesus became both High Priest and Sacrifice for us.

**what others say**

**Ravi Zacharias**

Sin is not the violation of an abstract law. It is an action against a person—the person of God.[16]

**F. F. Bruce**

The wisdom which created the worlds and maintains them in their due order may well beget in us a sense of wondering awe, but the grace which has provided a remedy for the defilement of sin by a life freely offered up to God on our behalf calls forth a sense of personal indebtedness, which the contemplation of divine activity on the cosmic scale could never evoke.[17]

7. *The Son "sat down at the right hand of the Majesty on high" (Hebrews 1:3 NKJV).* Jesus, the Son of God, did what no other person ever did! When His assignment was finished—that is, when He'd completed the job of paying for our *our sins*—Jesus returned to the place of honor and authority He had occupied before His descent to earth as baby and servant-savior. That Jesus did return to His place as Co-Ruler of the universe was a fundamental belief of the early Christians. It introduces a major theme of Hebrews: What Jesus's **ascension** means for His friends.

He "sat down." Sitting signifies work completed and rest.

"The right hand" represents the place of highest honor and supreme authority. "The Majesty on high" is God, King of the universe.

No literal location is intended. God, who is Spirit, has no physical right hand or material throne where Jesus sits beside Him. It's a word picture to describe Jesus's **exaltation** to supremacy in the universe.

## Chapter Wrap-Up

- For Christian Jews the AD 60s brought persecution from religious authorities. In AD 70 Jerusalem and the temple were destroyed, with more than a million Jews killed by the Romans. The Letter to the Hebrews arrived in time to help prepare Christians for these events.

- God speaks to people. He has spoken throughout history. In the past He spoke through the Old Testament prophets. More recently He has spoken through His Son (Hebrews 1:1–2).

- God's revealing of Himself is progressive. The Old Testament is not a complete revelation of God. The New Testament—especially the life and deeds of Jesus—completes the biblical portrait of God. (Hebrews 1:2)

- The Hebrews writer identifies seven things about the Son that show why He is qualified to represent and reveal God to people. (Hebrews 1:2–3)

## Study Questions

1. What are two factors that lead some scholars to conclude Hebrews was written between AD 60 and 69?

2. Before Jesus came, how did God speak to Israel's "forefathers"? Name three other ways or means God used to speak to people.

3. Through whom does God speak most clearly in "these last days"?

4. List five of the seven "amazing facts" that explain why the Son's revelation of God is superior to the revelation of God through the prophets.

5. Of the seven qualities of the Son, in Hebrews 1:2–3, which do you most appreciate? Why?

6. How have you experienced God speaking to you? What was your response?

# Hebrews 1:4–14
# Jesus Christ Is "All That"

**Chapter Highlights:**
- Superior to the Angels
- Hymn to the Greatness of the Son
- As God Is My Witness
- The Conqueror

## Let's Get Started

The major theme that immediately grabs the open-minded reader of Hebrews is that Jesus Christ is the most complete **revelation** of God's character and game plan for human beings. Compared with everything else God has done and is doing, Jesus is at the very top of the class. No one is so great, so effective, or so committed to follow God's Master Plan.

## Superior to the Angels

The popularity of the CBS TV series *Touched by an Angel* and other "angelic" entertainments reflects the general populace's fascination with these here-again-gone-again spirit creatures. Even people who don't believe the Bible believe in angels; for example, before she became a Christian believer, a friend of mine used to describe her daily conversations with a "family angel" who lived in her house, gave advice, and watched out for her family.

On the other hand, the Bible takes a dim view of cavorting with **"familiar spirits."** Angels are spirit beings. There are good angels and bad angels. Good or bad, the Bible insists angels are real.

Angels flit hither and thither from Genesis to Revelation. In the Letter to the Hebrews they are found lurking around each turn of a page—from chapter 1 to chapter 13—sometimes shadowy; sometimes awe-inspiring, audacious; usually on some sort of secret mission for the Almighty.

**go to**

**revelation**
Deuteronomy 29:29;
Amos 3:7;
John 14:21;
1 Peter 1:12;
Romans 1:17–18;
Galatians 1:12;
Ephesians 3:3–4;
Colossians 2:5–16

**familiar spirit**
Leviticus 19:31;
20:6, 27;
Deuteronomy 18:10–12;
Isaiah 8:19–22

**revelation**
disclosure, God's process of making known His character, truth and power

**familiar spirits**
spirit or demon who serves and guides an individual; spirit of a dead person (ghost)

---

**what others say**

**Martin Luther**

An angel is a spiritual creature without a body created by God for the service of christendom and the church.[1]

**go to**

**great moments**
Genesis 3:24; 19:1;
28:12;
2 Kings 6:17;
Isaiah 6:1–7

**God's army**
Joshua 5:13–15;
Luke 2:13–14

HEBREWS 1:4a *[the Son] having become so much better than the angels . . . (NKJV)*

The author of Hebrews is on a single-minded mission—to demonstrate that Jesus, as God's supreme revelation of Himself, is the greatest thing that ever came down God's pike, to help bring people into a loving relationship with their Creator. When the writer selects a word to compare Jesus with everything and everyone else, his word of choice is *kreittoon*, a Greek word meaning "better," "superior," "more excellent, valuable and profitable." Of the nineteen times this word occurs in the New Testament, thirteen are in Hebrews.

In Hebrews 1:4, the writer compares Jesus with all the angels God has ever created and declares that no one and nothing is better than Jesus! He's the top! He's more excellent and wonderful than anything else God ever gave mankind. Jesus is even better than the most glorious angel superstars.

Why would the exhorter who wrote Hebrews take so much space to do this Son-angel comparison? The answer lies in the first-century Jewish mind—what Jews believed about angels.

## Angels in the Middle

First-century Jews were even more obsessed with angels than people are today. Jewish Christians were influenced by the beliefs of their countrymen. Angels jazzed up <u>great moments</u> in Bible history.

Both Old and New Testament words for "angel" mean "messenger." Angels are God's couriers bringing His word and carrying out His will in the universe. The ancient Jews considered angels <u>God's army</u>—*"the heavenly host."* Secret angel names were used by Jews who engaged in forbidden occult practices.

According to William Barclay, an expert in Jewish theology and history, the ancient Jews believed angels were created by God on either the second day of creation (the day Genesis 1:3 says *light* was created) or the fifth day (the day God created *flying creatures*, Genesis 1:20). Angels are not material but, according to ancient Jewish belief, are made of an "ethereal fiery substance like blazing light."[3]

Perhaps the biggest reason for the angel obsession of first-century Jews was belief that God was far, far distant from mere **earthlings**. In Jewish thinking, the difference and separation between God and humans was so great as to make it impossible to know or get in touch with God. First-century Jews were convinced ordinary men and women could not talk directly to such a **transcendent** being. A mediator with access to God's presence was necessary. Angels seemed to fill the role.

The early Jews believed God gave the Ten Commandments and the Law to Moses through angels.[4] Contrary to early Judaic teaching, one of the most powerful messages of Hebrews is that no mediator is now needed between people and God, other than God's Son, who "purged our sins" and now occupies the place of power and authority next to God—"at the right hand of the Majesty on high" (Hebrews 1:3 NKJV). When it comes to standing before God on behalf of people, angels simply cannot cut it! Never could! Don't need to! People can go directly—even *boldly*—into God's presence (Hebrews 4:16), anytime!

Angels did not make this possible. *Only God's Son* could do that. That's why this is the first reason the writer of Hebrews insists the Son is "better than the angels" (Hebrews 1:4 NKJV).

**earthlings**
anyone who lives on planet earth

**transcendent**
above and beyond the universe and human experience

---

what others say

**William Barclay**

In Christianity there is no need for anyone else in between. Because of Jesus and what Jesus did we have direct access to God. As Tennyson had it: "Speak to Him thou for He hears, and Spirit with spirit can meet—Closer is He than breathing, and nearer than hands and feet."

The writer to the Hebrews lays down the great truth that we must always remember—that we need no human personage nor supernatural being to bring us into the presence of God. Jesus Christ broke every barrier down and opened for us the direct way to God.[5]

---

# Watch for Flapping Wings

You cannot read the New Testament without bumping into angels. They became visible and served at strategic points in Jesus's life:

- *At Jesus's birth.* To introduce Him as Messiah to His Jewish contemporaries, God dispatched the angel Gabriel to Mary and Joseph (Matthew 1:20; Luke 1:16) with news about the Christ child's approaching birth. An army of shouting angels appeared and gave the good news to shepherds near Bethlehem (Luke 2:9–14).

- *At Jesus's temptation.* After His temptation by the devil in the desert, angels ministered to Him (Matthew 4:11). Again, after His intense prayer and renewed surrender to God's will in the Garden of Gethsemane, an angel strengthened Him (Luke 22:43).

- *At Jesus's resurrection.* Angels announced His resurrection from the dead (Matthew 28:2–4; Mark 16:5–7; Luke 24:4; John 20:11–13).

- At *Jesus's **ascension**.* Angels materialized to promise His friends that Jesus would return (Acts 1:10–11).

The subject of angels is not a major theme in the Bible. Scripture concentrates instead on the incomparable glory of **Yahweh** (God) and on the wonder of His provision of **redemption** for fallen mankind."[6] Even so, you can learn a lot about angels by studying certain passages.

*key point*

# The Scoop on Teraphs, Seraphs, Cherubs, and Other Spirits

- Angels are mentioned 300 times in the Bible.

- Angels are spirits (Hebrews 1:14). They do not have material bodies but some can assume bodily form (Luke 24:39; Genesis 18:1–19:1).

- Angels are not glorified dead people. God specifically created angels to be angels (Psalm 148:2–5; Colossians 1:16).

- Some angels have wings and can fly (Isaiah 6:1–6; Ezekiel 10; Exodus 25:18; Revelation 4:8).

- Angels are accountable to God and will face judgment for their choices (Job 2:6–7; 2:1–2; 1 Corinthians 6:3).

- Angels sometimes are given superhuman power and knowledge, but their power and knowledge are limited (Job 1:12; Luke 22:31–32; James 4:7; Matthew 24:36).

- Angels are **sexless**, though the male pronoun "he" is used to refer to them. They do not marry or reproduce (Mark 12:25).

- Angels do not die (Luke 20:36).

- There are billions of angels—too many to count (Daniel 7:10; Hebrews 12:22; Revelation 5:11).

- Angels help and serve God's people (Hebrews 1:14).

- Angels care for children (Matthew 18:10).

- "Guardian angels" protect and rescue believers (Psalm 91:11–12; Daniel 3:28; Acts 5:19).

- Angels inform and encourage (Luke 2:9–14; Matthew 28:5–7; Acts 27:23–25).

- Angels communicate God's messages to individuals (Matthew 1:20–23; 2:13, 19; Luke 1:11–20, 26–38; Acts 8:26).

- Angels worship God and Jesus Christ (Psalm 148:1–2; Hebrews 1:6; Revelation 4:6–11; 5:11–14).

- Angels exist to do the will of God and to serve His purposes (Psalm 103:20–21).

- All angels were originally created good, but one-third rebelled against God, were expelled from heaven, and became fallen angels (Revelation 12:7–9; Matthew 25:41; 2 Peter 2:4; Jude 6).

**go to**

**superhuman power and knowledge**
Psalm 103:20;
2 Peter 2:11;
2 Samuel 14:20

**sexless**
neither male nor female

something to ponder

**what others say**

**Billy Graham**

Ought not Christians, grasping the eternal dimension of life, become conscious of the sinless angelic powers who are for real, and who associate with God Himself and administer His works on our behalf? After all, references to the holy angels in the Bible far outnumber references to Satan and his subordinate demons.[7]

**beneficence**
doing good, performing acts of kindness or mercy

**Gnostics**
philosophical/religious movement promising salvation through special knowledge; opposed by early Christians

**synagogue**
Jewish "church," meeting place for study and worship

what others say

### John Calvin

Angels are the dispensers and administrators of the divine **beneficence** toward us. They regard our safety, undertake our defense, direct our ways, and exercise a constant solicitude that no evil befall us.[8]

### Earl Radmacher

Don't become preoccupied with the agents God uses to accomplish his work. Keep your prayers simple. Leave it to God to move his troops where He wants them, to answer your prayers.[9]

## Jesus Is No Angel!

Some early Jewish detractors of the Christian movement taught—and some religious groups today erroneously believe—that Jesus was an angel, not God. Others, like the **Gnostics**, taught that he was a demi-god, meaning halfway between man and God—more powerful than human, less powerful than God. Or, He was a person so outstanding as to appear to approach divinity.

None of these categories fit the Bible's claims for Jesus. He is no halfway, lowercase god. He is not an angel. He is much more! His rise to the place of power at God's right hand reveals His supremacy over the greatest of the angels, and His special oneness with God.

## Hymn to the Greatness of the Son

key point

The Hebrew language has a word for "preaching" which literally means "stringing pearls." In verses 5–13, the author of Hebrews strings three strands of Old Testament "pearls" to show Jesus's superiority over angels. Mostly he quotes from the Psalms, the hymnbook used in Jewish **synagogue** worship for hundreds of years. Early Christianity adopted the same hymnbook for use in its house churches.

The author knew the verses he quoted would ring a bell with his readers. The words were already singing their way through Christian minds and hearts because they were part of a set of Hebrew songs to the greatness of God.

In addition to his primary goal to lift up Jesus in his readers' minds to His rightful place of honor and authority, the author of Hebrews hopes to redirect readers' hopes *away* from angels to the Son, so that angels find their proper place in Christian thinking as God's created servants, not secondary "gods" or objects of reverence. It's great fun to watch the writer do this, because he does it so powerfully yet gently with the verses of an early Christian song.

## All Hail the Power of Jesus Name!

**HEBREWS 1:4–5** *[The Son] having become so much better than the angels, as He has by inheritance obtained a more excellent name than they. For to which of the angels did [God] ever say:*
*"You are My Son,*
*Today I have begotten You"?*
*And again:*
*"I will be to Him a Father,*
*And He shall be to Me a Son"? (NKJV)*

The first "string of pearls" focuses on the excellence of the Mediator's **name**.

*To which of the angels did He ever say, "You are My Son, today I have begotten You"?*

The plain answer is "God has never said anything like that to an *angel*!" But He said it to Jesus. <u>Repeatedly</u>. The *name* God gives Jesus, which declares Him higher and better, more important than the most illustrious angel, is *"My Son!"*

what others say

**F. F. Bruce**

The angels may be called collectively "the sons of God," but no one of them is ever called the son (singular) of God in terms like these, which single out the person addressed and give him a status apart.[10]

## The Day God's Son Came into His Own

The Bible teaches that **Christ** has *always* been God's Son and God has *always* been Christ's Father . . . eternally . . . even <u>before creation</u>. So what is this "today" business?

go to

**repeatedly**
Matthew 3:17;
Mark 1:11;
Luke 1:32; 9:35

**My Son**
Hebrews 1:5;
Psalm 2:7

**before creation**
John 1:1–3; 17:5;
1 Corinthians 8:6;
Colossians 1:15–17;
1 John 1:1

**name**
biblical usage often includes character, position, reputation, accomplishments

**Christ**
Greek: "Anointed One," Messiah, King

**rose from the dead**
John 19:38–42

When he said "today" the Hebrews author was not thinking of a 24-hour day, but was using that word in a figurative sense to represent an exceptional time in history, which corresponded to Jesus's time on earth as God-man. In God's way of seeing time (2 Peter 3:8), those three-plus decades of the Son's earthly life were an eye blink—a brief period involving dramatic events that proved Christ's relationship to His Father as Son beyond reasonable doubt. The "Today Period" of Jesus Christ includes such phenomenal events as:

- *Christmas*—Jesus was born in Bethlehem as God in human flesh, fulfilling promises made to Israel (Isaiah 7:14; 9:6–7; 53), King David (2 Samuel 7:14), and the sin-weary world (Hebrews 1:5–6).

- *Good Friday*—Jesus died on the cross at Jerusalem, providing purification for human sin (Hebrews 1:3).

- *Easter*—Jesus <u>rose from the dead</u>, busting out of Joseph's garden tomb three days after His crucifixion in a demonstration of power so awesome it can only clinch the claim that He is God's Son (Romans 1:4).

- *Ascension Day*—Jesus assumed His rightful place as co-ruler of the universe, at "the right hand of the Majesty on high" (Hebrews 1:3 NKJV; Acts 1:9–11).

**what others say**

**F. F. Bruce**

He who was the Son of God from everlasting entered into the full exercise of all the prerogatives implied by his Sonship when, after his suffering had proved the completeness of his obedience, he was raised to the Father's right hand.[11]

## A Deal with David

**HEBREWS 1:5**
*"I will be to Him a Father,*
*And He shall be to Me a Son"?* ( NKJV)

That's a line from an Old Testament section called "the Davidic Covenant," a set of commitments God made to King David about 1000 BC, promising that a son from David's bloodline would one day sit on the throne of an everlasting kingdom established by God, which would rule the world in peace (2 Samuel 7:5–16; 1 Chronicles

17:3–14). The promised "Son of David" would also be known as "Son of God." Centuries of rabbis taught that the promised Son of David/Son of God would also be revered as the Messiah, Christ the King.

In the years just before Jesus was born, Jews looked forward with special eagerness to the coming of David's son, the Deliverer-King. Tired of oppression and occupation by foreign military forces, Jews were often heard wistfully repeating the words of 2 Samuel 7:14 (Hebrews 1:5).

When Jesus was born (**BC 4**), a special excitement filled His mother as the angel told her that her soon-to-be-born son would be the One everyone was looking for (Luke 2:32–33). Mary expressed the longings of the entire nation in the poem we know as "the Magnificat" (Luke 1:46–59).

**BC 4**
miscalculation caused the AD calendar to miss the birth of Jesus by four years

**what others say**

**William L. Lane**

Although Jesus was the pre-existing Son of God, he entered into a new dimension in the experience of sonship by virtue of his incarnation, his sacrificial death, and his subsequent exaltation. The enthronement at the Father's right hand was the occasion when the name, "God's Son," was conferred upon Jesus. Although angels are sometimes designated as 'sons of God' in the OT (Job 1:6), Jesus alone is recognized by God as his unique Son."[12]

## Let Angels Prostrate Fall!

HEBREWS 1:6 *But when [God] again brings the firstborn into the world, He says:*
*"Let all the angels of God worship Him." (NKJV)*

Some early Hebrew Christians mistakenly believed angels were so great they should be worshiped. Worshiping angels, they thought, would assure their continued function as go-betweens for people and God.

"No way, Jose!" (or in words to that effect) counters Paul in Colossians 2:18–19.

Angel worship is condemned by Scripture as a disastrous muddy-road, dead-end, spiritual detour. It's a form of idolatry. To turn that error on its tin ear, in Hebrews 1:6, the writer, building his case for

angels worship
Luke 2:13–14;
Revelation 5:6–14

worship
to acknowledge
worth, admiration,
dependence, sub-
mission; literally, to
bow and kiss the
hand

Father
God; first person of
the Holy Trinity—
comprising Father,
Son, and Holy Spirit

Jesus's excellence over angels, cites an Old Testament verse from the Septuagint version, in which God instructs His angel army (Psalm 97:7): "Let all God's angels *worship* [*the Son*]" (Deuteronomy 32:43, Septuagint, Dead Sea Scrolls).

## A Tribute to God's Firstborn

Calling Jesus God's "firstborn" (Hebrews 1:6 NKJV) does not mean Jesus is not God, but a created being, as some cults argue. Ancient rabbis used to speak of *God* as "firstborn of the world," meaning that He is supreme, greater than the whole world!

*"Firstborn"* is a legal title like *"heir"* (Hebrews 1:2 NKJV). In the Bible the word was used in four ways:

- To designate the first son born to his parents (Luke 2:7)
- To designate status in the family based on relationship with the father
- To indicate supremacy or headship of a spiritual family (Hebrews 1:6; Romans 8:29)
- To identify the first person in history to accomplish a thing (Colossians 1:18)

When used of Jesus, "firstborn" usually indicates supremacy. It can also mean He is the first person in human history to accomplish a thing.

For example: "firstborn from the dead" (Colossians 1:18 NKJV) means Jesus is the first person in history to be raised from the dead in a resurrected body (1 Corinthians 15:35–49). The fact that Jesus is God's firstborn means that no one is more important or more worthy to be worshiped than He is.

Obediently, all God's holy angels worship Jesus the Son, acknowledging that He is as worthy of allegiance, admiration, and obedience as His Father (John 5:23).

what others say

Johnson Oatman
Holy, holy, is what the angels sing,
And I expect to help them make the courts of heaven ring!
But when I sing redemption's story, they will fold their wings,
For angels never felt the joys that our salvation brings.[13]

Because Jesus is God's Son, He is worthy of worship, just as the Father is.

True worship *always* leads to obedience. In fact obedience *is* true worship.

**Jewish rabbis**
Jewish teachers

## Angel Wind, Angel Fire

HEBREWS 1:7 *And of the angels [God] says:*
*"Who makes His angels spirits,*
*And His ministers a flame of fire." (NKJV)*

The Greek word for "spirits" is sometimes translated "winds." Wind and fire are often associated with angelic activity. Angels are, without question, some of the most exciting life forms to emerge from the imagination of the Creator. Angels are wild and wonderful beings.

- Some are covered with thousands of eyes (Revelation 4:6–8).

- Some have multiple faces capable of looking in all directions at once (Ezekiel 1:4–10).

- Winged angels called cherubim oversee administration of God's justice and mercy (Exodus 25:17–22).

- Most powerful of all are archangels such as Michael (Jude 9; Revelation 12:7–8).

- Many angels, like Gabriel, stand in the presence of God, ready to serve at a moment's notice, awaiting God's orders (Luke 1:19).

English poet John Milton wrote:

> Thousands at [God's] bidding speed
>
> And post o'er land and ocean without rest:
>
> They also serve who only stand and wait.[14]

According to Hebrews 1:7, God can even transform angels into "winds" or "flame[s] of fire" (Psalm 104:4 NKJV). Talk about razzle dazzle! Wind? Fire? Holy thunderbolts, Batman! What does it mean? Interpretations are all over the map:

- *Jewish rabbis*—Angels are made of an "ethereal fiery substance like blazing light."[15] In fact, one order of angels is called, *seraphim*, which literally means *"fire"* (Isaiah 6:1–6).[16]

- *Billy Graham*—Wind and fire represent the role of God's angel-messengers in judgment. "The flaming fire suggests how awful are the judgments of God and how burning is the power of the angels who carry out God's decisions."[17]

- *Henry Alford, Dean of Canterbury*—God causes his angels to *act like* wind and fire when it suits his purposes.[18]

- *F. F. Bruce*—Perhaps [refers to the way angels execute God's purposes with the swiftness of the wind and the strength of fire. Or, perhaps, it pictures the "evanescence of the angels" compared with the eternity of the Son.[19]

- *William Lane*—Flames and wind emphasize "the unchangeable eternal character of the Son, by contrasting it with the changeable nature of angels."[20]

- *Robert Jameison*—*"Wind"* implies angels' wind-like velocity and subtle nature; *"fire"* expresses their burning devotion and intense, all-consuming zeal.[21]

*Angel Wind*—To fulfill God's purpose, angels sometimes take on the nature of a tornado, tearing up the landscape of human lives in judgment, vengeance, or discipline. Or they touch some overwhelmed pilgrim like a cooling breeze, with fresh inspiration to go on.

*Angel Fire*—Sometimes angels roar from God's presence like blasts of a flamethrower, to burn down useless or rebellious structures erected in human minds and hearts against God's will. Or they may go to a war-weary saint to reignite spiritual fire about to go out.

**what others say**

### Madeleine L'Engle

Cherubim, seraphim, all the angelic host as they are described in Scripture, have a wild and radiant power that often takes us by surprise. They are not always gentle. They bar the entrance to Eden, so that we may never return home. They send plagues upon the Egyptians. They are messengers of God. They are winds. They are flames of fire. They are young men dressed in white. They are God come to tell us something. To be visited by an angel is to be visited by God. To be touched by an angel is to be touched by God, and it is a terrifying experience. When the angel smote him in the thigh, Jacob limped forever after. Daniel, who had braved lions, trembled and fainted at the appearance of God's angel. And John, on the Isle of Patmos, fell down as though dead. I believe in angels.[22]

# Angels Were There in Wind and Fire!

It's a pretty good bet that angels were present doing their wind-and-fire thing at the following places and times. Look up Scriptures and read:

- Sodom and Gomorrah—Judgment by fire and brimstone destroys both cities (Genesis 19).
- Mount Horeb (Sinai)—Moses meets Yahweh ("I Am") in the burning bush (Exodus 3).
- Red Sea—East wind piles up sea waters so Israel can cross on dry land (Exodus 14).
- Mount Sinai—Erupts in fire and smoke as God gives Israel the Ten Commandments (Exodus 19–20).
- Mount Carmel—Elijah confronts 400 prophets of Baal. He prays. Fire falls from heaven (1 Kings 18).
- Jordan River—Elijah taken to heaven in a whirlwind and chariot of fire (2 Kings 2).
- Jerusalem—Isaiah cleansed, called; a flaming angel touches his lips with a burning coal (Isaiah 6).
- Jerusalem—Jesus's disciples hear wind roaring, see balls of fire, as Holy Spirit comes (Acts 2).

# As God Is My Witness

**HEBREWS 1:8** *But to the Son [God] says . . .* (NKJV)

The Hebrews author continues to build his case for the supremacy of the Son by simply asking a few well-chosen questions and quoting a few well-chosen Scripture verses. He lets the Bible speak for itself. If the reader's heart is open the message will hit home.

key point

The only witness called to testify is God, whom Hebrews 1:1 told us "spoke . . . by the prophets." The words of spiritually gifted men and women rang too true for them to be mere human inventions. Their prophetic predictions were too accurately fulfilled to be dismissed as educated guesses. The conviction became imbedded in the Jewish mind that the prophets' messages were **"breathed out"** by God and were, in fact, the *"Word of God."*

When Hebrews 1 says "God says" something, it's based on the

belief that the Old Testament Scriptures—especially those prophesying the coming of the Savior-King (Messiah)—represent things *God most certainly said!*

## Okay, God, Tell Us What You *Really* Think of Jesus

HEBREWS 1:8–9 *But to the Son [God] says:*
*"Your throne, O God, is forever and ever;*
*A scepter of righteousness is the scepter of Your kingdom.*
*You have loved righteousness and hated lawlessness;*
*Therefore God, Your God, has anointed You*
*With the oil of gladness more than **your companions**."*
*(NKJV)*

In Hebrews 1:8–12, we eavesdrop on a conversation in which the Greatest Father in the universe tells His Son how wonderful He is. Verses 8–9 are lines from a Jewish worship song celebrating a Royal Wedding (Psalm 45). Jews sang these lyrics in anticipation of Messiah's coming. Early Christians sang them to celebrate the majesty of Jesus, whom they saw as Messiah-King, already arrived.

## Jesus Is *God!*

Perhaps the most startling aspect of these verses is that, without missing a beat, the writer of Hebrews applies to Jesus a section of the song in which the Son-Bridegroom-Messiah-King is twice addressed as *"God!"* (Hebrews 1:8–9).

Jesus of Nazareth is not just *any* man. The man Hebrews addresses as "God" is the very same one Hebrews 1:3 calls "the brightness of His [God the Father's] glory" and "the express image of His person" (NKJV). Early Christians believed, and their writings insist, that Jesus Christ *is* God. (Or, as Christians often say to distinguish Him from God the Father and God the Holy Spirit, Jesus is "God the Son.")

## Jesus Is King of *Righteousness!*

*Jesus rules forever* (Hebrews 1:8). He was born to be Messiah. As Messiah He was destined for kingship. In fact, "Messiah" is another title for a particular kind of king. Like God's reign, Jesus's reign is eternal. In fact, Messiah's throne is God's throne.

*Jesus's scepter is righteousness* (Hebrews 1:8–9). Like God's, Jesus's power to reign is solidly based on the pure righteousness and justice personified and visible in His character and life. He dared His enemies to point out sin in His life (John 8:46). They could not do it! His personal righteousness and justice drove His enemies crazy with envy and hate. Jesus was so just and so right it built a fire in their bellies that drove them to kill Him! Which they did. But the power of His holy character overruled the grave!

Note two words in verse 9:

*"anointed"*—The word "anointed" means "smeared with oil." Anointing was a traditional ceremony announcing God's choice of a king, priest or prophet. To be "anointed" means "chosen," "preferred," or "special." The word "Christ" literally means "Anointed One." With anointing goes authority.

*"oil of gladness"*—The "oil" that anoints Jesus is different from the oil of initiation into a new office. It's the oil of gladness! According to Hebrews 12:2, as Jesus measured the cross where He would die to provide purification from humanity's sins, one thing that kept Him going was the expectation that after the suffering, there would be joy.

As reigning King, Jesus is never pictured grieving, heartbroken, or burdened by the difficulties of office. He is sitting. At rest. He has <u>successfully completed</u> His work. He's delighted with how it's going.

Everything is moving along according to the Master plan. Sad? Never! Sadness ended when He busted out of the crypt. Dead? Sad? Not on your life! And He invites His friends to join Him in the festivities (see Hebrews 2:12; 4:9–11).

## Changeless World Changer

HEBREWS 1:10–12 *And:*
*"You, Lord, in the beginning laid the foundation of the earth,*
*And the heavens are the work of Your hands.*
*They will perish, but You remain;*
*And they will all grow old like a garment;*
*Like a cloak You will fold them up,*

**successfully completed**
John 19:30;
Hebrews 10:12–14

**righteousness**
inner moral conformity to the character of God; acts that flow from righteous moral character; justice, goodness, godliness

**LORD**
Acts 2:35;
Romans 10:9–10

**sovereignty**
absolute right to
govern all things,
without limitations
imposed by circum-
stances or human
choices[23]

*And they will be changed.*
*But You are the same,*
*And Your years will not fail."* (NKJV)

In another astounding choice of words, God calls His Son "LORD." Among Christians and Jews, "LORD" is interchangeable with "God." It's what the early Christians believed about Jesus—He is *LORD!*

In this passage (Hebrews 1:10), calling Jesus "LORD" acknowledges His deity and identifies Him with the God of the Old Testament. During His earthly life, many people called Jesus, "LORD," not out of faith in His deity but as a common courtesy, meaning nothing more than our use of "sir" (John 20:15). But as they came to realize who He really was, the same word became their confession of faith. Finally convinced that Jesus had risen from the dead, Thomas fell to his knees before Him and called Him "my Lord and my God!" (John 20:28 NKJV).

Lordship implies **sovereignty**.

- The Son is Lord over the spiritual universe (Ephesians 1:21; 1 Peter 3:22).

- The Son is Lord (Head) of the church (Ephesians 1:22–23).

- The Son is Lord in the physical universe (Hebrews 1:3; 11:3).

- The Son is Lord over the circumstances of believers' lives, working all things together "for good to those who love God" (Romans 8:28 NKJV).

- The Son will ultimately rule the nations of the world "with a rod of iron," bringing judgment and restoring justice under His title, "KING OF KINGS AND LORD OF LORDS" (Revelation 19:15–16 NKJV).

In Hebrews 1:10–12, the writer quotes another stanza from the song Jewish Christians sang to confess confidence in Jesus as Lord. It's from Psalm 102:25–27.

Psalm 102 starts as a poetic "Woe is me!" from a guy painfully aware of how fragile life is. He can't sleep at night. He can't eat. He's lonely. Life is slipping away and he can do nothing about it. But after eleven woeful, "I'm-at-the-end-of-my-rope" verses, the composer looks beyond his "here-today-gone-tomorrow" existence and remembers the forever-ness of the Lord.

Along about the twenty-fifth chorus of his dirge on the brevity of life, the composer is inspired to hope by a disturbing discovery: Not only he himself but every created thing, from "the foundation of the earth" to "the heavens," is designed for obsolescence. It's all going to "grow old," "perish" (Hebrews 1:11 NKJV). The one thing he can count on is that everything is going to pot. Everything is changing!

And yet, in the middle of an impermanent, wishy-washy cosmos, only *one thing* remains dependable, unchanging, and secure: *Someone* is at the controls. The Creator of everything is also the cosmic demolition engineer changing everything! He made it, and He alone decides when to roll it all up and toss it all away, like a worn-out shirt.

The Someone in charge of change is the "LORD" (Hebrews 1:10 NKJV). When everything else goes down the tubes, the Lord (alias "the Son") will "remain" (Hebrews 1:11 NKJV). He'll be "the same," His years "will not fail" (Hebrews 1:12 NKJV). When heaven and earth start to go to pieces, look up! The Lord, "through whom also [God] made the worlds" (Hebrews 1:2 NKJV), the Son who is "upholding all things by the word of His power" (Hebrews 1:3 NKJV), will be there overseeing the shaking, rattling, rolling, yet ever-renewing rumble.

The theological term for this steadfast quality of the Son of God, "immutability," is a ten-dollar word meaning Jesus, the Son, never changes and never fails just like God (see Hebrews 13:8; 6:17–18).

key point

what others say

**James Radford**

God is complete and that which is complete needs no change in order to be made perfect. God already is who He always will be. He is the "I AM." He is the only one who can say, "I do not change." God does not change because that which is perfect needs no improvement.[24]

## Jesus the Conqueror

HEBREWS 1:13–14 *But to which of the angels has [God] ever said:*
*"Sit at My right hand,*
*Till I make Your enemies Your footstool"?*

**flames of hell**
Isaiah 66:24;
Matthew 25:41;
Jude 7

**to Jesus**
Mark 12:35–37;
14:61–62;
Acts 2:33–36

*Are they not all ministering spirits sent forth to minister for those who will inherit salvation? (NKJV)*

All that Hebrews 1 tries to communicate concerning the Son of God comes down to this question: Why is Jesus's superiority over angels such a big deal? The issue is brought into focus by the last word in chapter 1: *salvation*. Hebrews 1:13 hints at the meaning of that word with the picture of King Jesus sitting on His royal seat with His royal feet resting unceremoniously on His enemies' necks!

## Why Is the Red Neon Sign on the Rescue Mission Blinking "Jesus Saves"?

The word *salvation* is based on a Hebrew word meaning "to be wide or roomy" in contrast to "narrow or restricted." Old Testament Jews primarily saw *salvation* as deliverance from oppression by their enemies and freedom to enjoy God's blessings. New Testament Hebrew Christian readers understood it that way too, but would have added that salvation meant being rescued from *spiritual* distress and danger, and set free from a "restricted," personally limiting spiritual condition from which they were powerless to free themselves.

The big idea that runs like a river through the Bible, from Genesis to Revelation, is that God's enemies are committed to do anything they can to make human life generally miserable and wretched (1 Peter 5:8) and, if possible, to destroy human beings altogether (John 10:10)—including dragging them down with the devils themselves into the <u>flames of hell</u> reserved for enemies of God. But God, in His incredible kindness, has devised a plan by which miserable human beings, trapped in their own cycle of sin, on the brink of destruction, may yet be rescued, set free, and healed of spiritual and emotional sicknesses. God's Son, Jesus, is pivotal in this rescue operation.

Hebrews 1 verse 13 quotes Psalm 110, which both Jews and Christians consider a prophetic "Messiah Song." The New Testament always applies this psalm <u>to Jesus</u>. The verse contains three pictures of His royal position:

- *The Position of Power.* Jesus is told to "sit at [God's] right hand. "Sit" means to take the throne. "[God's] right hand" means Jesus is Co-Ruler of the universe.

- ***The Position of Supremacy.*** The "footstool" was a low support for the feet of a royal person, necessary because the throne was raised to keep the ruler's head higher than his standing subjects. This represents Jesus's dominance over His enemies.

- ***The Position of Conquest.*** It was the custom for an Eastern conqueror to make a "footstool" of a vanquished enemy, by literally planting his foot on the defeated foe's neck (Joshua 10:24)!

These pictures of a <u>Conquering King Jesus</u> stand in stark contrast to the powerlessness of sin-oppressed people needing rescue and liberation. The book of Hebrews will detail the specific ways Messiah Jesus fills these three positions to bring us "so great a salvation" (Hebrews 2:3 NKJV).

**Conquering King Jesus**
Matthew 28:18;
1 Corinthians
15:24–28

**exist to help**
Exodus 23:20–23;
Isaiah 63:9–10

## Seraphs at Your Service

In Hebrews 1 we've made important discoveries about angels. Angels are not mediators between people and God. Angels cannot reveal God like Jesus can (verses 1–3). Angels cannot provide purification for human sins (verse 3). Angels do not rule the universe from the right hand of God (verses 3, 8–13). Angels are inferior to the Son of God (verse 4). No angel ever rose to the position of "Son of God" (Hebrews 1:5). Angels must never be objects of worship. Even the angels are under God's orders to worship the Son (Hebrews 1:6).

Then what are angels for?

The author of Hebrews pulls together what angels do under one all-important category: "Are they not all ministering spirits sent forth to minister for those who will inherit salvation?" (Hebrews 1:14 NKJV).

Angels are not the Savior. They are "*assistants* in salvation." They <u>exist to help</u> people who by putting their faith in Jesus are destined to inherit everything that is meant by the term "salvation."

*A thumbnail definition of salvation:* God, in His incredible kindness, has devised a plan by which miserable human beings, trapped in their own cycle of sin, on the brink of destruction, may be rescued, set free, healed of their spiritual and emotional sicknesses, and set at peace.

key point

That definition is a bridge to the rest of Hebrews, where the concept of "salvation" will be looked at from many different angles.

## Chapter Wrap-Up

- Jesus won purification for human sins and ascended back to the heavenly dimension, where He sits at God's right hand as Co-Regent of the universe. He, not angels, is the Mediator between people and God. He is superior to the angels. (Hebrews 1:3–4)

- Using lyrics of a Judeo-Christian hymn, the writer contrasts Jesus with angels, showing that God calls Jesus "Son." Jesus fulfills the covenant God made with David. Angels are commanded to worship Him. (Hebrews 1:5–6).

- The Hebrews author makes his point about the supremacy of Jesus by using Scriptures in which God addresses the Son as "God" and "Lord," recognizes his kingship, and acknowledges the Son's control of the processes of the universe. (Hebrews 1:7–12)

- Jesus is the conqueror over His enemies. He makes a footstool of their necks. Angels do not usurp His rule or role as Savior, but are on a mission to help people struggling against oppression, especially those destined for salvation. (Hebrews 1:13–14).

## Study Questions

1. What was the main Jewish misconception about angels the Hebrews writer challenged in chapter 1? Why is it so important that this error be corrected?

2. Name three important times in Jesus's life when angels served Him.

3. Of the facts stated in The Scoop on Angels list, which is most surprising to you personally? Which is most encouraging? Why?

4. How does God address the Son in Hebrews 1:8 and 9? In Hebrews 1:10? What does that say about who Jesus is?

5. Name three characteristics of Jesus's kingdom, according to Hebrews 1:8–9.

6. What are angels for? (Hebrews 1:14)

# Hebrews 2:1–4 Rescue at Sea

**Chapter Highlights:**
- My Ship Is Adrift
- Forks in the Sea Lane
- Throwing Out a Life Jacket
- Airborne Express

## Let's Get Started

What *does* the neon sign over the rescue mission mean as it blinks over and over again, "Jesus Saves"? Saves what? Saves who? From what? What for? Who cares?

"Salvation" is a giant theme in the Bible. In fact, it's the whole point of the whole book! Salvation, rescue, or, as some people refer to it, "being saved," is the experience of being rescued, recovered, delivered, restored, healed, and liberated from life-and-peace-threatening, fulfillment-robbing danger—past, present, and future.

Human beings, by their <u>independence</u> from and rebellion against the Creator God, always make a royal mess of their lives and their world. As the New Testament (including Hebrews) tells it, Jesus the Christ was sent by God to pick up the pieces, to lift humans willing to trust God and follow Christ's way back to the pinnacle of abundant life (John 10:10), back to the healthy, <u>loving relationship</u> with God and each other for which they were created.

In the situation into which the Letter of Hebrews was dropped, people were being sorely tempted to turn back from the *Shalom* they'd found in Christ to the stale, toothless rituals of first-century Judaism and the BC way of life. The writer intends from start to finish of his letter to remind waffling believers, in most urgent terms, that if they turn away from Christ they will be discarding the best God offers for something of infinitely less value and power.

go to

**independence**
Proverbs 14:12;
Isaiah 53:6

**loving relationship**
Deuteronomy 6:5;
Luke 10:25–37

**Shalom**
peace, good health, success, prosperity, wholeness, satisfaction, contentment

what others say

**Revell Bible Dictionary**

Salvation then is God's work, by which He completely changes the moral condition of the believer, not only releasing him or her from sin and the prospect of divine wrath, but even making the believer able to do truly good works.[1]

# My Ship Is Adrift

**HEBREWS 2:1** *Therefore we must give the more earnest heed to the things we have heard, lest we drift away. (NKJV)*

The author suddenly spouts seamen's salty jargon to grab his readers' attention. Two Greek nautical terms urge Christians to stop drifting like anchorless vessels and get serious about what God has said.

1. *"Give the more **earnest** heed,"* (Greek: *prosechein*) to ancient Greek seamen, meant "to hold the ship toward port, or to fasten the anchors to the sea bed."[2]

2. *"Drift away"* (Greek: *pararrein*) meant "to slip or drift away." In Greek literature, this word was sometimes used to describe a ship aimlessly drifting beyond safe harbor and headed for shipwreck because her sailors forgot to take into account the direction and speed of wind and tides.[3]

*"Therefore . . ."* An old Bible teachers' cliché says, "When studying the Bible, and you come upon a *therefore*, stop and see what it's *"there for."*

key point

The *therefore* in Hebrews 2:1 points back to all the wonderful stuff we read about the Son of God in Hebrews 1—his super-revelation of God's splendor, His superiority over angels, His supreme authority and power as Co-Creator of the universe, and His victory over His enemies. *"Therefore"* (Hebrews 2:1) is like saying, "Considering all that, stop being an ignorant landlubber when it comes to what you've heard about the Son. 'Give the more earnest heed.'" In other words, "NOW HEAR THIS!"

Evidently, some Hebrew Christians' personal commitments to Christ were compromised by apathy. They were in a spiritual situation as dangerous as that of a ship cut loose and drifting beyond safe harbor. They failed to keep a tight hold on the truth and, through carelessness and neglect, were losing sight of the vitality of salvation.

The original word for "give the more earnest heed" meant not only to *see* the danger but to *do* something about it!

Spiritual laziness and indifference toward the word of God, half-heartedness in personal responsiveness to Him, leaves a Christian believer anchorless, in deep water—over his head—and headed for shipwreck. He may be doing the Christian things, talking the Christian talk, paying little visits to God now and then (when it's convenient). But he's drifting—almost undetectably at first, but most certainly—*away* from God. Intense times, like the late first century and ours, demand intensive, concentrated attention to your faith and your spiritual progress.

## Caught in the Crosscurrents

**the big picture**

**Entire Book of Acts**

Across the Roman Empire, the Jesus movement faced sporadic, terrifying local persecutions. The imperial government was engaged in a systematic attempt to establish Caesar worship everywhere. Refusal to offer the required, daily pinch of incense to Caesar as god could cost you your job—even your life!

In AD 64 Emperor Nero launched his infamous assault on Christians in and around Rome, accusing them of being the **arsonists** responsible for starting the fire that destroyed much of the capital city—even though many historians believe he started that fire himself, so he could rebuild Rome into a more glorious city. Either way, many Roman believers died horrible deaths rather than renounce Jesus. Apostles Paul and Peter, in Rome at the time, both lost their lives in this campaign of anti-Christian terror.

**arsonists**
people who start fires on purpose

**Pharisees**
ultra-orthodox Jews, many of whom had opposed Jesus

**orthodox**
conforming to established teachings and practice

How could this perilous situation develop in the *New Testament* church, which we've believed was such a dynamite community of Christ-followers? Not to make excuses for waffling faith, but perhaps it will help us understand the presence of less-than-heroic attitudes if we remember that their lives were regularly disrupted by pressures designed by enemies of Jesus to force them to break ranks with the community of faith.

> **what others say**
>
> ### H. T. Andrews
> The supreme peril of the church under the stress of persecution was the peril of relapse, and the primary object of the Epistle to the Hebrews is to face this peril and stem the tide of desertion. There is hardly a chapter in the epistle which does not contain an appeal or a warning to those whose faith is faltering.[6]

The pressure to drift from the Christian ranks took its toll on church attendance, membership, and morale.

## When You Think Everybody Likes You, Duck!

Meanwhile, in Jerusalem, overt persecution came side-by-side with more subtle pressures, all of which led to spiritual drifting. At times, especially during the early days of the movement, Christians were held in high esteem by their non-Christian Jewish neighbors (Acts 2:47; 5:13), who stopped short of joining the movement but were impressed by the way the Christians lived. Even "a great many of the priests" became believers (Acts 6:7 NKJV), along with some **Pharisees** (Acts 15:5).

key point

In Jerusalem, Jesus's people were hard to tell from "regular" Jews because the Christians were so—well—Jewish! Just like their **orthodox** counterparts, Jewish Christians kept the law of Moses, observed the Sabbath and other holy days, and enthusiastically participated in regular worship at the temple—in most aspects of their lives "fitting in." But popular acceptance has its pitfalls. Christian Judaism was so closely tied, historically, emotionally, and religiously, to regular Judaism, and Christian Jews fit so well into synagogue life, that the Jewish Jesus movement sometimes seemed at risk of being reabsorbed and lost in institutional Judaism.

## what others say

### Paul Johnson

The impression we get is that the Jerusalem Church was unstable, and had a tendency to drift back into Judaism completely. Indeed, it was not really a separate Church at all, but part of the Jewish **cult**. It had no sacrifices of its own, no holy places and times, no priests. It met for meals—and had readings, preaching, prayers and hymns....Thus, we are told, it attracted a good many people. Many of them must have regarded it as little more than a pious and humble Jewish sect, keen on charity, sharing goods, revering an unjustly treated leader, and with an **apocalyptic** message. Thus the whole movement was in danger of being first contained, then reabsorbed.[7]

**only**
John 14:6;
Acts 4:11–12

**cult**
system of religious beliefs and ritual

**apocalyptic**
containing supernatural revelations and emphasis on end-time events

## The Flickering Lantern of Commitment

Dangerous rationalizations sometimes infect Christian thinking when Christians are under pressure to fit in rather than to suffer society's rejection. Jerusalem Jewish Christians knew Jesus was the Messiah (Christ), the Son of God. But open confession of their faith was costly. Intensifying rejection, terrorism, impending expulsion from the temple, and questions regarding their patriotism all worked together to create the temptation to blend in, to go secret, to become "closet" Christians but with no intention of drifting away.

It seemed reasonable. With a few "minor" adjustments—a softening of insistence on the messiahhood of Jesus (Acts 2:36), toning down the message of His death on the cross, less-confrontational public expression of beliefs and practices—the faith of Jesus could be made almost respectable—or, at the very least, a little less irritating to the neighbors.

Sometimes drifting away was a very attractive option. Worn down by the pressures and weary of rejection, some Hebrew Christians reasoned that perhaps it would be smart to ease away from identification with their unpopular leader, Jesus, and return to the religion of their youth and family. After all, don't Christians and Jews worship the same God?

As the Gospel spread across the Empire, their belief that Jesus is the supreme revelation of God and that access to God can only come about through believing in Christ, brought charges that Christians

**international trouble-makers**
Acts 17:16

**anti-intellectual**
1 Corinthians
1:18–26

were <u>international troublemakers</u>, <u>anti-intellectual</u> dinosaurs left over from a less-enlightened age!

Weary and afraid, to find relief from the pressure, sometimes real Christians *will* cave in to such unjustified slander and quietly "drift away" (Hebrews 2:1 NKJV), with barely a thought of the great salvation they are leaving behind.

- *Jerusalem, AD 30–70*—Christian Jews were drifting away from a living faith in Jesus because of social pressure, slander, and dilution of their faith through constant intellectual bombardment and ridicule.
- *Tempe, Arizona, 2002*—A Christian psychology major at a state university, under pressure from professors and fellow students who belittled her evangelical faith and prodded her to engage in what she believed was sinful activity, finally rejected the fundamental beliefs and moral standards by which she had been raised.

## "When You Come to a Fork in the Road, Take It!"

The wisdom of baseball great Yogi Berra, if you think about it too deeply, can make you dizzy. For example, he once advised his ballplayers, "When you come to a fork in the road, take it!"

First-century Christian Hebrews were at a fork in the road. They'd stood there for 30 years, doing everything they could to put off choosing between Judaism and Christ. But the time had arrived to bite the bullet, make the tough choice, and head down the Glory Road.

The Letter to the Hebrews was written precisely because Israel—and especially the Christians there—were at a time of decision that often faces young believers: The issue being forced on them by the times was whether to go on with Jesus or to turn back to non-Christian Jewish orthodoxy. How did they get to this dizzy place? Blame God.

## Forks in the Sea Lane

HEBREWS 2:2–3a *For if the word spoken through angels proved steadfast, and every transgression and disobedience received a just reward, how shall we escape if we neglect so great a salvation . . . ? (NKJV)*

**Mount Sinai**
Exodus 19;
Hebrews 12:18–21

**Ten Commandments**
Exodus 20;
Deuteronomy 5

Over the course of Jewish history and the lives of the Hebrew believers, God, in His wisdom, had brought them to many crucial moments of decision. Two of these "forks" (or crosscurrents) in the sea lane centered around two great Middle Eastern mountains— Mount Sinai and Mount Golgotha.

## Sinai—Mountain of Fear

The first crucial moment of decision happened at <u>Mount Sinai</u> in the wild Wilderness of Sin, on the Sinai Peninsula, between the Red Sea and the Gulf of Aqaba. As the people waited in terror at the foot of what was then a rumbling volcano, Moses scaled its craggy face to talk with God. He returned from the summit with a most amazing document, inscribed on tablets of stone "with the finger of God" (Exodus 31:18 NKJV). This historic document moved mankind's understanding of God light years ahead of where it had been before the Sinai encounter. The stone tablets contained the <u>Ten Commandments</u>. As a free offer in the same package (Moses's heart and memory) came a meticulously designed system for relating to a God of high morality, absolute justice, and mercy. The document became known variously as "the Mosaic Covenant," "the Old Covenant," "the Law," or "the Old Testament" (or, in more perverse circles, "Ye Olde Fun-Killer!").

key point

Israel made its decision. With a pinch of childish faith mixed with a mountain of fear and a ton of bravado, the people shouted with one voice: "All that the LORD has spoken, we will do" (Exodus 19:8 NKJV).

## Airborne Express

According to Hebrews 2:2, the Sinai message ("the Old Covenant") had two noteworthy characteristics:

**angels**
Deuteronomy 33:2;
Psalm 68:17;
Acts 7:53;
Galatians 3:19

1. The word God spoke to Israel at Sinai was a "word spoken through <u>angels</u>" (Hebrews 2:2 NKJV). (Now we understand why so much space is given to angels in the first chapter of Hebrews!) Jews believed that the Old Testament Law, the constitution and bill of rights of the Hebrew Nation, was delivered to Moses by a squadron of <u>angels</u>.

2. The message from God at Sinai was a *legal document*. Hebrews 2:2 describes it in judicial terms.

- *"proved steadfast"*—This is legal terminology, meaning that the Sinai document "proved legally valid."[8] Time and experience provided plenty of precedents which made it crystal clear: This is the law. It must be obeyed. If not, specific consequences apply.

- *"transgression"*—In Greek, this judicial term means infringement, trespass, stepping across a line into forbidden territory, physically or spiritually. The Sinai contract sets forth rules and regulations establishing parameters for moral and just action. To cross these lines is to commit immorality or injustice and violate the will and character of God, which they reflect.

- *"disobedience"*—The original word means "imperfect or careless *hearing*"—Under the Sinai pact this legal term boils down to "unwillingness to listen to the voice of God."[9]

- *"just reward"*—This means unwillingness to listen to God, refusal to obey the rules, or deliberate lawbreaking. It demands punishment to fit the crime. The Hebrew writer coins a new word, *misthapodosia*, which only he uses, meaning "punishment as earned wages" or "punishment as reward." The punishments prescribed in the Sinai document are completely appropriate, precisely the paycheck each dirty deed has earned in the economy of God.

The consequences that resulted when the Old Testament Law's precepts and principles were ignored or disobeyed demonstrated that it was God's legally binding message.

## Sinai Plan Validated by Salvation and Disaster

Israel's historical landscape is cratered with events which proved the legality and legitimacy of the Sinai system. Again and again, when the people obeyed the provisions of the Sinai contract they experienced *salvation* according to the Old Testament understanding of the term. That is, they had good health, peace, and prosperity. They were also miraculously protected and cared for by God, and they were saved from their enemies—as one great passage from the Law clearly promises (see Deuteronomy 28:1–14).

On the other hand, when the people and leaders disobeyed the Sinai commandments and drifted into rebelliousness against God and His law there was no *salvation*. There was disaster, disease, war, poverty, rampant immorality, marital unfaithfulness, miscarriage, violence, slavery—a raw, inner sense that God had abandoned them, leaving them to reap the national and personal consequences of their national and personal wickedness, just as promised in the rest of the passage from Deuteronomy 28:15–68.

## Grace in the Sinai Ultimatum

*"The word spoken through angels"* was a legal plan for relating to God by living up to His righteous requirements. If humans were able to bring it off, it is a formula for salvation by **good works**, a roadmap to being good enough to please God. Fifteen centuries of life under the law vividly demonstrated one disturbing truth: No one can be or has ever been saved by perfectly performing the moral expectations of the Sinai plan (Galatians 3:10–11). Instead, it was and is a plan to <u>help people understand</u> the justice and morality of God *and* the extent of human spiritual inadequacy and proneness to sin. We shall never find salvation by being good enough or by doing enough good works. Because of the residual effects of sin it's simply not in us to bring off such a feat!

However, even though no one has ever found salvation by perfectly keeping God's law, by the grace of the Lawgiver, built into the Sinai system was a program of **offerings** and **sacrifices** by which, at regular occasions, admitted sinners could **atone** for their failure to keep the law.

There was, however, one humongous hitch in the Old Testament system: The offerings and sacrifices brought the worshiper no lasting sense of peace with God (Hebrews 10:1).

*Factoid:* The best of human efforts always fall short of the moral and spiritual perfection required to win God's approval (Hebrews

**help people understand**
Romans 7:7;
Galatians 3:24–25

**good works**
moral or righteous acts performed by human beings

**offerings**
rituals in which possessions of worshipers are presented to God

**sacrifices**
rituals in which animals are killed and their blood given to God to cover personal sins

**atone**
make amends, restore harmony between persons, cover sins, purify

9:9; 10:1–4). So what good was the Sinai system? Sounds like a failure to me! But was it?

- The Sinai system revealed that God was righteous, just, and loving.
- The Sinai system disclosed the basic nature of sin.
- The Sinai system demonstrated, over 1,500 years from Moses to Christ, the fundamental inability of human beings to keep God's laws and to do right, naturally.
- The Sinai system serves as a "picture album" containing carefully composed images helping to predict and explain the great spiritual transactions Jesus Christ would accomplish to implement the "great salvation" He offers to those who trust Him.
- Sinai was a prelude to the second "Mountaintop Experience" God arranged.

## Golgotha—Mountain of Grace

HEBREWS 2:3b–4 *[so great a salvation,] which at the first began to be spoken by the Lord, and was confirmed to us by those who heard Him, God also bearing witness both with signs and wonders, with various miracles, and gifts of the Holy Spirit, according to His own will?* (NKJV)

Sinai was an eye-opening, life-changing, nation-building "mountaintop experience." The Hebrews author, an ethnic Jew steeped in the Ten Commandments and the Sinai system, does not mean to belittle in any way what happened there. But he cannot resist comparison of the old system with the new way of relating to God, as signed, sealed, and delivered on the second summit. He's compelled to call what was arranged on the second mountaintop "so great a salvation" (Hebrews 2:3 NKJV).

key point

After 1,500 years of seeking to relate to God under the terms of the Law (the Sinai document) God brought Israel to another summit. However, Golgotha (also called "Calvary") is not a high mountain. It's a hill west of the Old Jerusalem wall, on a main road into the city, now overlooking an abandoned marble quarry,[10] whose cutaway side, with caves, suggested the shape of a human skull. It was the site where the Romans executed their criminals by **crucifixion**.

Some commentators imagine the hilltop was littered with human skulls, where the bodies of crucified criminals had been left to be eaten by wild dogs. Golgotha was a miserable place associated with death.

Jesus of Nazareth, God's Son, died on that hill and rose from the dead three days later from a nearby garden tomb (John 19:41–42), having "purged our sins" (Hebrews 1:3 NKJV).

Hebrews 2:3, in comparing the impact of Mount Sinai with what happened at Golgotha, makes no mention of the hill or the gruesome events of 30 years before. Instead the writer focuses on the "great . . . salvation" Jesus Christ won there, from which the Hebrew Christians of Jerusalem were at risk of drifting away, through neglect.

## Authenticating the "Great Salvation"

As noted, the Sinai contract was proved legally valid by the fact that violating its rules was "rewarded" with well-earned chastisement. The truth and consequently the believability of the "great . . . salvation" won by Jesus at Golgotha is validated by **grace** and **spiritual gifts**. The author lists three personalities and a group through which the "new and improved" plan of salvation was introduced, affirmed, rated superior to "the word spoken through angels," and stamped as "this you can believe."

1. *The Lord Jesus Himself.* The great salvation "first began to be spoken by the Lord" (Hebrews 2:3 NKJV).

The better plan for relationship with God was not the invention of clever minds struggling to find a better way! "It does not consist of guessing and groping after God; it is the very voice of God Himself which comes to us in the person of Jesus Christ."[11] The source of superior deliverance and the news about it is the Lord <u>Jesus Himself</u>, the Son of God, His life, teachings, death, resurrection, and ascension to the right hand of God as told in the four Gospels—Matthew, Mark, Luke, and John.

God occasionally speaks to His people through angels, but not often. He reveals His plans and will for us through the Lord—Jesus—God's unique Son[12]—specifically, through what is written of

**go to**

**Jesus Himself**
Matthew 4:12–17, 23–25;
Mark 1:14–15;
Luke 4:14–22;
Acts 10:36

**grace**
God's lovingkindness and mercy toward people who do not deserve it

**spiritual gifts**
graces, spiritual abilities which equip a person to help others

**apostle**
specially called and appointed "ambassador" sent to spread the good news

Him in the New Testament books and letters, and what He communicates to us personally through His Spirit, all of which always agree (see John 16:12–15).

what others say

**F. F. Bruce**

The great salvation proclaimed in the gospel was brought to earth by no angel, but by the Son of God Himself. To treat it lightly, therefore, must expose one to sanctions even more awful than those which safeguarded the law. . . . Our author was afraid that his readers, succumbing to more or less subtle pressures, might become liable to those sanctions—if not by renunciation of the gospel then possibly by detaching themselves increasingly from its public profession until it ceased to have any influence upon their lives.[13]

2. *Eyewitnesses.* The great salvation "was confirmed to us by those who heard Him" (Hebrews 2:3 NKJV).

"Confirm" means "to guarantee accuracy." The Hebrews to whom the letter was written were second- and third-generation Christians. They'd never met Jesus in the flesh. Like us, they encountered Him after the fact. News of His exploits came to them from eyewitnesses—men and women who had seen and heard Jesus in person. The truthfulness of the great salvation was validated by the testimony of people simply telling their personal, face-to-face experiences with the Lord.

It's interesting that the writer does not say this verification came through church "officials"—theologians, professional clergy, or other leadership types. Ordinary "Mr." and "Ms." Christian Believer—"just folks" who have met Jesus—share what they know. Their personal testimonies and eyewitness stories authenticate the great salvation news!

what others say

**William L. Lane**

It is significant that in Hebrews the office of **apostle** is reserved for Jesus alone (Hebrews 3:1). The highest office the writer acknowledges within the larger Christian community is that of a "hearer," i.e. one who could testify concerning the truth that Jesus had declared because he had heard the Lord.

By speaking of "the hearers," all interest is concentrated on the message, not the office, of those who brought the word of **redemption** to the community.[14]

**bunched miracles**
Matthew 4:23–24; 8:16–17

**Acts**
Acts 2:43; 4:32–34; 5:12–16

**redemption**
paying the price to free someone from sin's captivity

This is the first hint in Hebrews of the existence and indispensable ministry of a universal ministerial class, made up of *all* Christians. The salvation message is powerfully corroborated by the testimony of ordinary believers.

3. *The Seal of God.* The great salvation was ultimately certified as real and true because of "God also bearing witness," using His unique arsenal of documentation "weapons" (Hebrews 2:4 NKJV).

*"Signs."* Convincing proofs to back up the claim that salvation comes through Jesus. For example, the Gospel of John identifies Jesus's miracles as "signs" (John 2:1–11; 4:46–54; 5:1–18; 6:1–14; 6:16–21; 9:1–41; 11:1–44.) In each case someone became convinced Jesus was who He claimed to be and experienced change in his or her life.

*"Wonders."* The Greek word originally was a spooky pagan term for "something unnatural or monstrous." On the tongues of Jews and Christians the word was converted. It came to indicate astonishing events God used to reveal Himself, supernatural incidents by which He assured people of His presence.

*"Various miracles."* The apostle John says if every miracle Jesus did were recorded, "even the world itself could not contain the books that would be written" (John 21:25 NKJV). Sure, it's a hyperbole. But nearly every page of the four "life stories" of Jesus (Gospels) reports the wonderworks He performed. Sometimes, so many amazing things happened in a short time that His biographers <u>bunched Jesus miracles</u> like bananas! This redundancy of remarkable happenings continues in the book of <u>Acts</u> to validate the church as a genuine work of God.

*"Signs and wonders"* is a standard biblical phrase describing extraordinary events that "cannot be explained from the known laws of nature,"[15] which demonstrate that God is with His people. It is probably significant that this "signs and wonders" duet appears mainly (though not exclusively) around two decisive periods of

key point

**go to**

**enters**
John 14:15–20;
Revelation 3:20

**equips**
Romans 12:6–9;
1 Corinthians 12, 13,
14;
Ephesians 4:11; 1
Peter 4:10

**identifiable**
Acts 4:13;
2 Corinthians
2:14–16

**Holy Trinity**
One God existing
and expressing
Himself in three dis-
tinct personalities—
God the Father, God
the Son, and God
the Holy Spirit

Israeli history (1) the Exodus—when God delivered Israel from Egyptian slavery, and (2) the Gospels and Acts—when salvation through Jesus was introduced and the Jesus movement was launched.

4. *The Holy Spirit, the Giver.* The third personality whose activity confirms the authenticity of the great salvation is the "Third Person of the **Holy Trinity**," "the Holy Spirit" and "gifts of the Holy Spirit, according to His own will" (Hebrews 2:4 NKJV). The Spirit of the Lord <u>enters</u> the lives of those who trust Jesus for emancipation from their sins. The Spirit <u>equips them</u> to share God's grace. Through them, God expresses His graciousness in attitudes and actions clearly <u>identifiable</u> as from the Lord. The final proof of the authenticity of this salvation, "which at the first began to be spoken by the Lord" (Hebrews 4:3 NKJV) is visible in the changed lives of the "saved."

**what others say**

### William Barclay

The ultimate object of Christianity is to make bad men good; and the proof of real Christianity is still the fact that it can change the lives of men. The moral miracles of Christianity are still plain for all to see.[16]

### Ravi Zacharias

At the age of 17, while living in New Delhi, India . . . I realized that I really didn't have any meaning in life. So I attempted to take my own life by poisoning myself. When I was recovering in a hospital the Scripture read to me was John 14, where Jesus said to His apostles, "Because I live, you shall live also" (John 14:19).

I said, "This is the life that I have yearned for." I made my commitment to Jesus Christ and have never looked back, except to remember how he rescued me and put a new song in my heart—new hungers, new desires, new life. He put a new hunger in my heart for God himself. Prior to that I was more concerned about success, good grades, good jobs. I was constantly thinking about what others thought of me. God refocused my attention on himself. I knew that this was not some kind of motivational therapy but a new kind of relationship."[17]

# Throwing Out a Life Jacket

**New Covenant**
New Testament revelation; contract for relating with God in Jesus Christ

**HEBREWS 2:3a** *How shall we escape if we neglect so great a salvation?* (NKJV)

Introduction of the new, improved, better-than-Sinai plan to rescue mankind from its cycle of shame and separation from God begins with a warning, which might be paraphrased: "If the Sinai Covenant proved legally binding and disobedience earned certain punishment, do you really think you are going to get away with letting God's 'great salvation'—the **New Covenant**—slip through your fingers from neglect? Think again!"

Once captivated by the good news about Jesus Christ, there is no way life can go blissfully back to what it used to be. Once you've "heard"—really heard with your heart—God's message (Hebrews 2:1), you can no longer neglect, without serious consequences, what has come to you as light from God.

> what others say
>
> **F. F. Bruce**
>
> Our author is warning Christian readers, who have heard and accepted the gospel, that if they yield to the temptation to abandon their profession (of faith) their plight is hopeless.[18]

## Escape? Where To? *Who* To?

In conversations near the Sea of Galilee, Jesus made revolutionary claims concerning who He is (John 6:25–65), in language calculated to separate uncommitted hangers-on from His true followers. Unable to accept the new information, many of His Galilean disciples drifted away, disillusioned. As the crowds dwindled, an emotional exchange took place between Jesus and the twelve men He had chosen as His apostle-ambassadors.

"Do you also want to go away?" Jesus asked (John 6:67 NKJV). Simon Peter answered for the others, "Lord, to whom shall we go? You have the words of eternal life. Also we have come to believe and know that You are the Christ, the Son of the living God" (John 6:68–69 NKJV).

The Twelve did not understand everything Jesus was teaching. They still struggled with many of His ideas. But they had been cap-

tured by Him and His message. He had saved them from dreary, nowhere existences. They knew what the writer to the Hebrews was insisting in Hebrews 2:3—once captured by Christ, once having tasted His salvation, there is *no escape* from Him without grave consequences.

We will discover some of those consequences as we make our way through this letter:

- Restlessness (Hebrews 3:18; 4:9)
- No confidence in approaching God (Hebrews 4:15–16)
- Falling away from Christ (Hebrews 6:4–6)
- No mediator by which to come to God (Hebrews 7:22–28; John 14:6)
- Settling for religious traditions and symbols rather than experiencing the real relationship with God to which the symbols point (Hebrews 8:5–12; 10:1; Mark 7:1–8; 1 Corinthians 10:6)
- No assurance of forgiveness for sins (Hebrews 9:11–14, 22; 10:1–4, 17)

The Sinai contract, Old Testament worship, and sacrifices and rituals were given to Israel, not only as a means of approaching God but also as a sort of "photo album." It was a manual of temporary dramatizations, pointing ahead to Jesus, His life, His death, His resurrection and ascension, and what His experiences would accomplish for us. To cling to the old pictures once the person depicted had arrived would be like romancing a shadow.

Yet it is exactly this kind of decision with which the Christian disciples of Israel were faced in the AD 60s. Thus the Letter to the Hebrews was written to warn and encourage them to drop anchor and weather the threatening storm of persecution—to remain firm in their commitment to the "great salvation."

## The Day I Decided to Be an Atheist

In my mid-forties, caught in the clutches of a terrible "midlife crisis," crazy with disillusionment and grief over things in my life that disappointed me—the church, the ministry, my inability to live the way a Christian should live, my dreams of success—I decided faith wasn't working. My "cherished beliefs" were a club with which I bludgeoned myself daily. Tired and angry, I made a brilliant "executive decision"—I would throw my faith away with the rest of the trash in my life.

Faith in the existence of God, the saviorhood of Jesus, the hope of salvation—I decided to walk away from it all and be free from the responsibility those beliefs represented.

So I did. I gave it up. I didn't "drift away," I stormed away!

My brave rejection of God lasted only a few days. I found Him confronting me around every corner. Every angry **epithet** I flung into His teeth was met with forgiving grace. It was as if He said, "Whenever you finish being an atheist, I'll be here."

Most devastating of all out there in my new, **emancipated** world of unbelief was the feeling of hopelessness that came with being an atheist. What finally brought me back to sanity and faith was the dreadful awareness that if there is no God, this whole world and life itself has no meaning. Nothing makes sense. Without Him, there is no reason whatever to go on living day after meaningless day. I might as well blow my brains out and get it over with!

I discovered that the truth that God loves me and rescues me from abysmal hopelessness represents a salvation only <u>a fool</u> would want to escape.

Escape from Jesus is a flight to nowhere.

Jesus said: "I am the way, the truth, and the life. No one comes to the Father except through Me" (John 14:6 NKJV).

The early Christians said of Jesus: "Nor is there salvation in any other, for there is no other name under heaven given among men by which we must be saved" (Acts 4:12 NKJV).

If I had managed to escape the salvation offered through Christ, I would exist in a meaningless vacuum—lost and hopeless—a million miles from God and anything that matters. Apart from the great salvation in Jesus, there is *no* salvation.

**a fool**
Psalm 14:1; 53:1

**epithet**
strong language;
often includes
swearing

**emancipated**
set free

# Chapter Wrap-Up

- Using the jargon of a Greek sailor, the author of the book of Hebrews warns his readers they are in danger of drifting away from the good news of salvation. The church in the AD 60s faced secular and religious pressures calculated to force them to give up their faith. (Hebrews 2:1)

- The author compares Israel's two "mountaintop experiences," both of which were key points of decision on the road to salvation. On Mount Sinai, angels helped reveal the Law to Moses; breaking the law brought punishment. On Mount Golgotha, the Lord Himself brought the message through His crucifixion, which was authenticated by the witness of those who saw it, plus that additional signs and wonders that God gave. (Hebrews 2:2–4)

- Once a person hears and accepts the message of salvation through Jesus Christ, he or she discovers there is no escape from it without serious consequences. Apart from the great salvation offered by Jesus, life is meaningless. (Hebrews 2:3a)

# Study Questions

1. What was happening to the Hebrew Christians that caused the author of Hebrews such concern? Why was he concerned? (Hebrews 2:1)

2. What is "the word spoken through angels" (Hebrews 2:2 NKJV)? Why is it called that?

3. Can you identify three of the four judicial terms in Hebrews 2:2 that proved the validity and truthfulness of the Mosaic law? Define them.

4. Four things mentioned in Hebrews 2:3–4 authenticate the "great salvation" through Jesus Christ. Identify three of them.

5. What is the answer to the rhetorical question in Hebrews 2:3— "How shall we escape if we neglect so great a salvation?" (NKJV). Identify four consequences of ignoring the great salvation offered through Christ.

# Hebrews 2:5-18 Point Man

**Chapter Highlights:**
- What's This World Coming To?
- Magnificent Expectation
- Family Snapshot

## Let's Get Started

The front-page story in Hebrews is *not* how to squelch ambitious angels who want to be boss, or how to keep from snoozing while your boat of life washes out to sea. The super theme on the author's mind is "the world to come" (Hebrews 2:5 NKJV). Specifically— Who's in the driver's seat in "the world to come"?

His conclusion may surprise you. Like Star Trek's Scottie with hands on the controls of the Enterprise transporter, the author beams his readers into the future to show them where God's "great salvation" program is taking them, what "salvation" means, and what to expect when God is finished getting us "saved." God's heart is set on our *"Super Salvation."*

The surprise "salvation focus" of Hebrews 2 is on what the Son of God has done to piece together their broken crowns and restore Jack and Jill of planet Earth to the lost splendor of being *human*!

## What's This World Coming To?

**HEBREWS 2:5** *For He has not put the world to come, of which we speak, in subjection to angels.* (NKJV)

*"The world to come"* is a catch phrase early Christians and Jews used to refer to the future kingdom and reign of God, the as yet unexplored world in which everybody and everything finally acknowledges its rightful Ruler and experiences renewal. Other terms for this future world are "the age to come" (Hebrews 6:5 NKJV), a "city . . . to come" (Hebrews 13:14 NKJV), and what Hebrews 12:28 refers to "a kingdom which cannot be shaken" (NKJV).

The final word on Jesus's superiority over angels: [God] has not put the world to come in subjection to angels (Hebrews 2:5). Currently angels play a role in managing the universe. For example:

- Angels are assigned responsibility over certain nations—i.e., "prince of Persia," "prince of Greece" (Daniel 10:20–21 NKJV).

- Michael, the "arch (chief) angel," serves as God's prime minister, with special responsibility to protect Israel (Daniel 10:21; 12:1). He is commanding general of heaven's troops, at war against angels who revolt against God (Revelation 12:7–12).

- Gabriel ("God's hero") stands at God's throne ready to serve. God's top ambassador, he carries strategic messages (Daniel 8:15–26; 9:20–27; Luke 1:11–20, 26–37).

- Seraphim (flaming angels) and cherubim lead the universe in praise of God's splendor, and help cleanse His people from sin (Isaiah 6:1–7; Ezekiel 10).

- Paul does not define their specific roles but lists these slots in the angelic pecking order: "principalities powers . . . spiritual hosts . . . rulers" (Ephesians 3:10; 6:12 NKJV).

Nonetheless, in the future world, angels do not rule. Instead, they "answer to a higher power."

## Who's the Boss?

In Hebrews 1, the "higher power" in the God-honoring future world is identified as God's "Son" and "heir" (Hebrews 1:2 NKJV). He already occupies the place of highest authority at God's right hand (Hebrews 1:3). His conquest of His enemies is happening even as we speak (Hebrews 1:8–13)!

In Hebrews 2, we discover the astonishing fact that God's Son holds His supreme position, "Ruler of the Universe," *as a human being*! Christ ascended (Acts 1:9–11) to the throne at God's right hand and reigns today *as a man*. This revelation is a wonderful clue to what "salvation" means.

**HEBREWS 2:6a** *But one testified in a certain place, saying: (NKJV)*

key point

The brilliant theologian of Hebrews can't remember the location of the Bible reference! There's hope for me. Aha! I looked in my exhaustive concordance, which lists every word in the Bible and where to find it, and discovered the "place" this quote is from is Psalm 8:4–6; and the "someone" who said it was Israel's favorite king, David. Actually, the author of Hebrews had a good reason for being vague. As a **devout** Hebrew, he believed that the entire Old Testament, while penned by human writers, was in fact *God speaking.*

what others say

**William L. Lane**

Precisely because it is God who speaks in the OT, the identity of the person through whom he uttered his word is relatively unimportant. A vague **allusion** is sufficient. It is the substantial authority of what is said, not its source, which is of primary importance.[1]

## Magnificent Expectation

HEBREWS 2:6b–7
*"What is man that You are mindful of him,*
*Or the son of man that You take care of him?*
*You have made him a little lower than the angels;*
*You have crowned him with glory and honor,*
*And set him over the works of Your hands.* (NKJV)*

*"Man"*—the generic term for male and female people—is the focus of attention in the remainder of Hebrews 2. This quotation from the Eighth Psalm pulls back the curtain to show how God sees human beings, and who's in charge of *"the world to come."* Psalm 8 is King David's awestruck song expressing amazement that the Lord God, being who He is, should give man-and-woman-kind, being who they are, such an exalted place in His plan for the universe.

Here in Hebrews 2:6, both "man" and "the son of man" refer to humanity. Here's the amazing idea:

"You have made [man] a little lower than the angels; You have crowned him [and her] with glory and honor . . . You have put all things in subjection under his [their] feet" (Hebrews 2:7–8).

That's *humans* he's talking about! Male and female *people*. You and me, etc. In His master plan for the universe, God has designed human beings for splendor, honor, and authority. Wow!

But . . . wait a minute.

## Me? A *"Little Lower"* Than *Who?*

"A little lower than *the angels*" (Hebrews 2:7) is an accurate translation of what the author of Hebrews wrote in perfect Greek, quoting from the best available Greek version of the Old Testament, the Septuagint. But a deeper look reveals that there's a zinger to end all

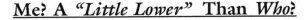

zingers hidden in the original Psalm 8, as it appears in the Hebrew Old Testament. The song's original composer, King David, writing the original lyrics of Psalm 8 in the original Hebrew language, uses a word that makes that statement so unbelievable, the Septuagint translators evidently couldn't bring themselves to let it say what it says. The Hebrew Psalm 8:5 reads: "A little lower you made him [mankind] than *Elohim* [God]."

"Elohim" is the regular Hebrew name for *God*! Are you ready for this? On the organizational chart of the universe, human beings were created to occupy a place just a notch below the Almighty, "a little less than *God*."

## King Me! King Me!

HEBREWS 2:8a
*You have put all things in subjection under his [mankind's] feet."* (NKJV)

In the Creation Hymn with which the Bible begins, God states His purpose in creating mankind:

Then God said, "Let Us make man in Our image, according to our likeness; let them have dominion over the fish of the sea, over the birds of the air, and over the cattle, over all the earth and over every creeping thing that creeps on the earth." So God created man in His own image; in the image of God He created him; male and female He created them. Then God blessed them, and God said to them, "Be fruitful and multiply; fill the earth and subdue it; have dominion over the fish of the sea, over the birds of the air, and over every living thing that moves on the earth" (Genesis 1:26–28 NKJV).

Using terms like "have dominion" (twice) and "subdue," the Bible reveals the destiny the Creator had in mind for humans from the very beginning. God gave men and women dominion over everything! Men and women were designed for kingship and queenship! The writer of Hebrews can't say it enough. In case you missed it the first time, the words are rearranged for emphasis and repeated. "For in that He put all in subjection under him, He left nothing that is not put under him" (Hebrews 2:8 NKJV).

## Pardon My "Yetting" In

**HEBREWS 2:8b** *For in that He put all in subjection under him, He left nothing that is not put under him. But now we do not yet see all things put under him. (NKJV)*

At the same time there's still another very important thing to consider. Here, in quick succession, are two huge "buts"!

Verse 8—The "But" of Broken Dreams.

Verse 9—The "But" of Hope.

Behind the three-letter simplicity ( *"yet" or "but"*) in the third sentence of verse 8 is the cosmic tragedy Bible scholars call "The Fall of Man"—the sad story of mankind's plummet from the pinnacle of princedom into **sin**.

In every generation from Adam to the present, the sin that entered into mankind in the Garden of Eden has taken away the perfection that God gave us at creation and made us imperfect, rebellious against our Creator, and unable to escape death. The creature who should have been master became slave.

Still, amid the moral rags of the pauper state, fallen humanity exhibits the tarnished remains of **God's image**; God's image is distorted by human sin the imprisoned potential for dominion. Humans harness great power sources, make great medical breakthroughs, propel themselves to the moon and beyond. They think great thoughts, take noble actions, dream utopian dreams.

At that point comes the first "But." "*But* now we do not yet see all things put under him" (Hebrews 2:8 NKJV). Men and women can control the atom, *yet* struggle to keep from destroying themselves with it, because they cannot control themselves! Scientists can bring disease germs under control, *yet* stockpile the controlled germs to

**God's image**
Genesis 1:26–27;
9:6;
Romans 8:29;
James 3:9

**sin**
willful independence or rebellion against God

**God's image**
reflection of God; like God, humans think, choose, feel, respond, initiate, act

turn their enemies into stinking heaps of rotting corpses! The "communication generation" rushes to produce more and more highly sophistocated communication devices, *yet* uses its new gadgetry to polute its minds with moral filth that ravages its soul and sets its wayward feet on the road to relational insanity! I can't click on aol.com to read my e-mail without having to delete a list of uninvited invitations to indulge in adulterous fantasies!

Created for kingship and queenship, humans bow their once-regal heads in subjection before destructive passions, unharnessed appetites, and the influence of devils. Destined for the throne, they are too blinded by sin to fulfill their destiny (Romans 3:9–18). Jack's and Jill's crowns of human splendor lie buried beneath the rubble of broken promises and unfulfilled dreams. Human beings are *not* in control of their world—or even of their own minds.

*But.*

## The "But" of Hope

HEBREWS 2:9a *But we see Jesus,* (NKJV)

God has not forgotten His original design. Granted, there's plenty of cause for pessimism about the human race, but then the tiny, three-letter word *but* (Hebrews 2:9) cuts through the smoke of human destruction and floods the scene with hope. *"But we see Jesus, . . ."*

what others say

### William Barclay

So in this passage there are three basic ideas: (1) God created man, only a little less than Himself, to have mastery over all things. (2) Man through his sin entered into frustration and defeat instead of mastery and dominion. (3) Into this state of frustration and defeat came Jesus Christ, in order that by his life and death and glory, he might make man what man was meant to be.[3]

### Ronald Allen

Man is majestic—or so God made him. When God made man as male and female he crowned him with glory and honor and gave to him power and dominion over all that God had made. When Adam and Eve rebelled against God, in some measure they lost the prerogative of rule; to some extent they lost their royal mantle. But to another Man these prerogatives are given. These powers and authorities are given to the one who became the Son of Man in flesh in the **incarnation** of Jesus.[4]

go to

**a man**
Romans 5:12–19;
1 Corinthians
15:20–22, 45–49

**flesh and bones**
John 1:14, 18;
Philippians 2:5–11

**Son of Man**
Daniel 7:13–14;
Ezekiel 2:1, 3; 3:1, 3,
10, 17; 4:1

**as God intended**
Luke 3:22;
John 8:29

## The Only One Who Can Save

HEBREWS 2:9 *But we see Jesus, who was made a little lower than the angels, for the suffering of death crowned with glory and honor, that He, by the grace of God, might taste death for everyone. (NKJV)*

Faced with humanity's failures, God acted to move His plan for people back on track. To restore rulership of the future world to the right hands, God again chose *a man*—a down-to-earth, mud and muscle, <u>flesh and bones</u>, dirt-under-his-fingernails human guy—Jesus.

Jesus's favorite nickname for Himself during His earthly sojourn was "<u>Son of Man</u>." It simply means "human." Jesus was unashamedly human. Jesus is man <u>as God intended</u> man to be.

To this point in Hebrews everything has revolved around Jesus as the Son, "the brightness of [God's] glory and the express image of His person" (Hebrews 1:3 NKJV). But now, Hebrews 2:5 takes a hairpin curve. From here to the end of chapter 2, the writer strings together Old Testament Scriptures and facts of Jesus's life to show that He is indeed the Son of Man—a flesh-and-blood earthling.

## Son of Man or Son of God?

Is Jesus *God* as Hebrews contends (Hebrews 1:1–3)? Or is He *human* as Hebrews also contends (Hebrews 2:14)? The teaching of the entire New Testament is that Jesus, is *both* God *and* man. He is *the unique person* of time and eternity. Before He was conceived in the womb of the Virgin Mary through the overshadowing of the Holy Spirit (Luke 1:35), Christ **pre-existed** with God, as God's Son (John 1:1–3), Co-Creator and communicator of God in the universe.

**incarnation**
God expressing
Himself in the
person of Jesus

**pre-existed**
lived, from eternity
past, in the heavenly
dimension

But, to rescue humanity from the disaster of sin, the Son of God <u>took on</u> human nature and became also the son of the woman Mary.

**go to**

**took on**
John 1:14, 18;
Philippians 2:5–8;
1 Timothy 3:16

**equal**
1 Corinthians 12:13;
Galatians 3:28

**what others say**

**Ronald B. Allen**

He is the one whose goings forth have been from everlasting, but he was also a human baby born in the normal manner, needing the care of His mother. He created the universe; but helpless, he needed a diaper change. He placed the stars and stretched the expanse, but was now subject to colds and colic, to rash and runny nose. The omnipotent God became vulnerable; the eternal One had a new beginning. There is no mystery in all the universe to be compared with the mystery of the Incarnation.[5]

## Glory Kids

HEBREWS 2:10 *For it was fitting for Him, for whom are all things and by whom are all things, in bringing many sons to glory, to make the captain of their salvation perfect through sufferings. (NKJV)*

The objective of the "great salvation" (Hebrews 2:3) is to get the Creator's original plan on track by "bringing many sons to glory" (Hebrews 2:10 NKJV). This was the motivation for the descent of God's Son to earth.

*"Glory."* "Glory" equals reflection of God's character in people; what theologians call the *Imago Dei*, "the Image of God" (Genesis 1:26–27; 5:1). Salvation is restoration of the original splendor humans lost in the ruinous plunge into sin.

*"Sons."* In the New Testament salvation teaching, "sons" is not a male-exclusive term. All God's children are called "sons" to emphasize their solidarity with Jesus, God's special Son. Why "sons" instead of "sons and daughters"? In first-century secular families, sons held a definite advantage over daughters. Unwanted baby daughters were often left to die of exposure. Sons stood to inherit everything from the father. Daughters might inherit only if there were no sons. In many ways, daughters were second-class family members.

**key point**

But that's *not* how it is in the culture of Christ. Male and female disciples are <u>equal</u>. Regardless of gender, all share equivalent relationship with the Father, the same access in prayer, the same spiritual gifts and ministries, and the same destiny. All are co-heirs with Christ (Romans 8:17; Ephesians 1:5). No one is "second class"—on the contrary, for New Testament writers to refer to all God's children as "sons" represented a bold conceptual shift, because they were actually recognizing that women were on the same level in God's favor as men. The "sonship" concept puts a gaping hole in the gender wall.

**go to**

**gifts and ministries**
Acts 2:17–18; 20:9;
Romans 16:1–7, 12;
1 Corinthians 11:4–5

what others say

**Larry Richards**

Jesus, determined to rescue us, took a full share of our humanity and through his death released us from our slavery. In that identification with us, Jesus also identified us with Him. He, the Son of God, became a man, that you and I might become sons of God! He entered the family of man that we might enter the family of God![6]

**Irenaeus**

The glory of God is a human being who is fully alive![7]

## Just Right for God

The phrase "it was fitting" (Hebrews 2:10 NKJV) means God's strategy to save human beings from their own self-destruction is consistent with His divine character—just the kind of thing you'd expect God to do. What God does in Jesus is precisely what the God "for whom are all things and by whom are all things" (Hebrews 2:10 NKJV) should do.

God did not create the world and then retreat to some distant hiding place to see what would happen. The God of our Bible is fully involved. What's more, He *wants* to be involved! His involvement in the human dilemma is one hundred percent consistent with who He is.

So, what has God done about the human problem? God made "the captain of their salvation perfect through sufferings" (Hebrews 2:10 NKJV).

what others say

**F. F. Bruce**

There are many who are ready to tell us confidently what would and what would not be worthy of God; but in fact the only way to discover what is a worthy thing for God to do is

**go to**

**given Him**
John 5:17–30;
7:15–18; 14:10–11

to consider what God has actually done. We may be sure that all God does is worthy of himself."[8]

**William L. Lane**

God who creates and preserves all things is precisely the one who is able to act in such a way that his design for humankind will be achieved.[9]

# Jesus Christ, Captain of Salvation?

Hebrews 2:10 calls Jesus "the captain of salvation" (NKJV). The original word for "captain" is *archegos*. It means "champion" or "hero." In Greek literature, this word described mythical champions such as Hercules, who wrestles against Death, "the dark-robed lord of the dead."[13] Likewise, the writer of Hebrews hints that Jesus is that kind of Rescuer-Hero, locked as He is in mortal combat with the devil, "him who had the power of death," Jesus overcomes the Enemy to liberate oppressed people enslaved by the evil tyrant![14] (Hebrews 2:14–15).

Jesus is our savior, but Superman He was not. When His neighbors saw Him preaching in the synagogue they asked, "Isn't this Joseph and Mary's child?" (see Mark 6:3).

Three statements in Hebrews 2:9 strip away the superhero image.

**key point**

Like all men and women, our hero was made "a little lower than the angels" (Hebrews 2:9 NKJV). In His pre-existence Christ shared unlimited power with His heavenly Father. When He stepped down to earth, He temporarily laid aside those special superpowers in order to live as an earthling (Philippians 2:5–11). Theologians call this act of Jesus *kenosis*—"emptying." Life among the humans was an adventure in dependence. The superpower to do miracles and the superwisdom with which He spoke were *given to Him*, as needed, by His Father.

Furthermore, angels don't die ( Luke 20:36)! In becoming "lower than the angels," the Son of God became mortal. When He volunteered for the mission He understood that He was going *to die*.

Jesus was "crowned with glory and honor" (Hebrews 2:9 NKJV). But His sandals never left the ground. Even so, He was able to hurdle the tallest, toughest assignment God ever gave a man to do—at the crucial moment in history (Galatians 4:4), Jesus laid His life on the line for fallen human beings. Because of this heroic act, as humanity's representative, Jesus, as a man, was lifted higher than any man had gone before (Acts 1:9–11).

**death penalty**
not just physical but spiritual death experienced as separation from God

He was . . .

- *"crowned"*—mankind's ability to reign, bestowed at creation, severely damaged in the Fall, was reinstated (Hebrews 2:8; Genesis 1:26).
- *"with glory"*—the image of God, the beauty of true manhood, was restored (Hebrews 2:7; Genesis 1:26).
- *"and honor"*—the respect that goes with intimate association with God, was renewed (Ephesians 2:6–7; Hebrews 1:13).
- *"for the suffering of death crowned with glory and honor, that He, by the grace of God, might taste death for everyone"* (Hebrews 2:9 NKJV). At the crucial moment, Jesus did not outrun the bullet. The explanation of His death and its uniqueness pierces through Hebrews like a tracer bullet, starting in 1:3.

## What's All This "Death Talk"?

Some people recoil at the mention of Jesus's death. But the reality of that death—and the reasons for which it had to come about—are woven into the Bible from Genesis to Revelation. So let's pause for a mini-study on *The Connection Between Sin, Death, and Salvation in God's System of Justice.*

### Sin and the death penalty

God created the universe to reflect His splendor (Psalm 19). Two aspects of the divine nature, justice and morality, are built into the infrastructure of the universe. In God's system of justice, sin is a capital offense. Sin accumulates a debt of guilt that can only be canceled by the **death penalty**.

what others say

**Dag Hammarskjöld**

God does not die the day when we cease to believe in a personal deity, but we die on the day when our lives cease to be illumined by the steady radiance, renewed daily, of a wonder, the source of which is beyond all reason.[10]

go to

**not one**
Psalms 14:1–3;
53:1–3;
Ecclesiastes 7:20;
Romans 3:10–18

**willingly**
John 10:17–18;
Romans 5:6–11

**commandments**
moral and spiritual
principles

### Universal guilt

"For there is no difference; for all have sinned and fall short of the glory of God" (Romans 3:22–23 NKJV). All human beings are guilty of rebellion against God. Not one of us has kept the **commandments** perfectly. We rationalize that our sins can't be so bad as to deserve capital punishment. The sins of Attila the Hun, Adolf Hitler, Joe Stalin, and Saddam Hussein may be bad enough, we reason. It's not hard to see how such monstrous sinners deserve death. But *surely* not respectable delinquents like you and me!

On the contrary, every form of independence from God disrupts connectedness with Him. *All* breaches of God's law destroy the perpetrator.

### Cancellation of the sin debt

"For when we were still without strength, in due time Christ died for the ungodly. God demonstrates His own love toward us, in that while we were still sinners, Christ died for us" (Romans 5:6, 8 NKJV). The debt created by human sin can only be canceled when the death penalty has been exacted! This idea is foreign to sin-streaked human thinking. So the Bible, an inspired thousand-page book, has been written to explain it. The Book tells of God's love for lawbreakers and describes how His mercy-driven justice system not only demands the death payment, but provided a sin-free substitute to take the offender's place at the execution. At the climax of the salvation saga, the author-hero of our salvation, the Mediator, steps forward and takes the rap for the guilty.

In His dual role as High Priest and Sacrifice, Jesus willingly went to the cross. God's sinless Son gave His life to pay for the sins of every person on earth.

## Jesus Christ—Trailblazer

Another meaning of *archegos* ("captain"—Hebrews 2:10) is "trailblazer," one who goes on ahead and blazes a trail for others to follow.

What Jesus did He did as "trailblazer." Everything He attained is something into which His disciples follow Him. When you reach God's goals and are all you were created to be, you shall be nothing more nor less than *human*, which means you'll be free from the dehumanizing effects of sin! Like Jesus.

And get this: The trail over which Jesus will lead us to the goal will involve for us what it did for Him—a certain amount of suffering, including healthy doses of <u>persecution</u> because of our association with Him.

In the ultimate sense, to be "saved" from sin means to be liberated from what keeps us from being the "humans" that God intended us to be. Humanness (with its unique sensitivities, intelligences, gifted-nesses, and capacities) fulfills God's plan and prepares God's future rulers to fill our place of authority in "the world to come" (Hebrews 2:3–8).

**what others say**

### Larry Richards

What the Book of Hebrews is telling us, then, is this: "Because of Jesus you have been—and are being—restored to the experience of dominion and mastery for which God always intended man." To see yourself accurately, you need to see not the slave made impotent by sin, but the renewed [person] who has a restored capacity for dominion and who, in Christ, is master of life. You need to see yourselves as *undefeated*.[11]

### John Killinger

What does the church have to do with being human? Is it really concerned with such a question? Maybe it is more interested in making us divine, or something like that. Before we answer the question, we ought perhaps to ask what Jesus's own attitude toward it seems to have been. What was He after, anyway? Was He really interested in an institution that would proscribe rather narrowly the boundaries of human nature, and give glory to God, so to speak, by pinching man? Did He conceive of the church as a kind of ethical and creedal mold for turning out men and women who all acted and thought just alike?[12]

## Perfecting the Champion

**HEBREWS 2:10** *For it was fitting for Him, for whom are all things and by whom are all things, in bringing many sons to glory, to make the captain of their salvation perfect through sufferings.* (NKJV)

*What?* Christ, the perfect pioneer, sinless Son, model man and

**persecution**
Psalm 119:86–87;
Matthew 5:10–12, 44;
John 15:25; 16:1–3;
Acts 12:5;
1 Corinthians 12:26;
2 Thessalonians 1:4;
1 Peter 4:16

**consecration**
dedication, ordination, to be set aside

**priest**
mediator; Latin: "bridge"

taint-free saint, needs to be "perfected"? How can you make someone perfect who is without character flaws, faults, weaknesses, or intellectual gaps?

In the language of the twenty-first century, perfection is almost a foreign concept. Yet *perfect* is a favorite word of the author of Hebrews (Hebrews 2:10; 7:28; 10:14; 12:2, 23). Understanding this concept is key to understanding the letter. In Greek, "perfect" is *teleios*. The early Greeks used it to describe:

- An animal that is unblemished and fit to be offered as a sacrifice at the temple
- A scholar who is no longer at the elementary stage, but is mature
- A person who is fully developed and full grown

The basic meaning of *teleios* (perfect) is that the thing or person it describes "fully carries out the purpose or plan for which he or it was designed or intended."[20]

## Our Champion, Our Priest

The word "perfect" *(telios)* is used in the Greek Old Testament for the **consecration** of priests for service in the tabernacle or temple (See Exodus 29:9, 29, 33, 35; Leviticus 4:5; 8:33; 16:32; 21:10; Numbers 3:3). Its Hebrew equivalent literally means "to fill the hands,"[21] or to prepare, equip, and qualify the person to be a priest, a go-between able to bring God and people together.

The Hebrews writer reminds readers that Jesus is fully qualified to be their high **priest**.

## Down and Dirty

key point

Made "perfect through sufferings" (Hebrews 2:10 NKJV) was an important aspect of preparation for Jesus's priestly ministry. He got down where you and I live. He tasted the bitterness, poverty, sweat, prejudice, rejection, hatred, discrimination, name-calling, persecution, malicious gossip, injustice, loneliness, misunderstanding, torture, perjury, grief, sorrow, tears, pain, sickness, excommunication, shame, and death—the final shame.

go to

fishermen, outcasts,
sinners
Matthew 4:18–22;
Matthew 4:24;
Luke 5:29–32;
15:1–2

transcendence
beyond human
experience and
knowledge

sinners
in first-century
religious lingo,
the word referred
to people who
habitually skipped
synagogue services

## what others say

### F. F. Bruce

The perfect Son of God has become his people's perfect
Savior, opening up their way to God; and in order become
that, he must endure suffering and death. The pathway of perfection which his people must tread must first be trodden by
the Pathfinder; only so could he be their adequate representative and high priest in the presence of God.[13]

### John of the Cross

God perceives the imperfections within us, and because of his
love for us, urges us to grow up. His love is not content to
leave us in our weakness, and for this reason he takes us into
a dark night. He weans us from all of the pleasures by giving
us dry times and inward darkness. In doing so he is able to
take away all these vices and create virtues within us. Pride
becomes simplicity, wrath becomes contentment, luxury
becomes peace, gluttony becomes moderation, envy
becomes joy, and sloth becomes strength.[14]

For effective ministry, both priest and people must know He
knows what they're going through.

*Jerusalem, AD 60*—Like Christ, His followers were perfected
through suffering. Often this involves persecution.

*Palawan Province, Philippines, 2002*—The Muslim extremist
group Abu Sayyaf took hostage Martin and Gracia Burnham, New
Tribes missionaries. After a year of threats and mistreatment, when
the extremists were under attack from the Philippine army, Martin
was shot to death. "He was a good man," said his wife, "and he died
well."

## Family Snapshot

**HEBREWS 2:11** *For both He who sanctifies and those who are
being sanctified are all of one, for which reason He is not
ashamed to call them brethren. (NKJV)*

The remainder of Hebrews 2 deals with the Champion's priestly
credentials. The Son of the Almighty drops His **transcendence**,
throws carpenter arms (Mark 6:3) around smelly <u>fishermen, outcasts
and **sinners**</u>—the likes of you and me—looks into their world-weary

eyes, and with a hefty big brother squeeze around their shoulders and a huge, toothy grin, announces with pride, "Brothers! Sisters! My family!" (Hebrews 2:11).

With this declaration Jesus fulfills the first qualification for priestly ministry: "For every high priest taken from among men is appointed for men in things pertaining to God, that he may offer both gifts and sacrifices for sins" (Hebrews 5:1 NKJV). Angels need not apply. This is a job only a human being can do.

## A Family of Priests

The secret is "leaked" in Hebrews 2:11 of the existence of a special order of ministers Christians call the "universal priesthood of believers" (see 1 Peter 2:5, 9). This cadre of caregivers shares three things with Jesus:

- Common humanity ("of one [family]" "brethren"—Hebrews 2:11)
- Consecration to the priesthood ("sanctified"—Hebrews 2:11)
- Community ("the assembly"—Hebrews 2:12)

Christian believer-priests are not Lone Rangers galloping off on silver stallions to their independent ministries. Effective ministry to God and people happens in a context of fellowship with other people.

### what others say

**Bishop Desmond Tutu**

We need other human beings in order to be human. We are made for forgiveness, we are made for family, for fellowship, to exist in a tender network of **interdependence**.[15]

**Dietrich Bonhoeffer**

I have community with others and I shall continue to have it only through Jesus Christ. The more genuine and the deeper our community becomes, the more will everything else between us recede, the more clearly and purely will Jesus Christ and his work become the one and only thing that is vital between us. We have one another only through Christ, but through Christ we do have one another, wholly, and for all eternity.[16]

**interdependence** dependence that goes in all directions; "intertwined" with otherss

## Oneness with Christ

go to

with them
Matthew 18:20;
28:20;
Hebrews 13:5

church
the called-out ones
assembled

HEBREWS 2:12–13 *saying:*
*"I will declare Your name to My brethren;*
*In the midst of the assembly I will sing praise to You."*
*And again:*
*"I will put My trust in Him."*
*And again:*
*"Here am I, and the children whom God has given Me."*
(NKJV)

key point

A string of Old Testament quotations (Hebrews 2:12–13) empha-size how oneness with Christ is experienced and played out in the context of the community of believers. The locating phrase is "in the midst of the assembly" (Hebrews 2:12 NKJV). The original word for "congregation" is *ekklesia*, the main Greek word for **"church."** It means "the called-out ones assembled," the people God separates from the world and its culture to be together in His presence and service.

Ancient Hebrews believed these were the words of the Messiah revealed to the prophet Isaiah centuries before Messiah's arrival. They give assurance that when Christians gather, Jesus is <u>with them</u>, acting through them to accomplish four priestly functions:

***Declaring God's name*** (Hebrews 2:12; Psalm 22:22). In biblical terms the "name" is not just a label by which a person is identified but stands for the person's character and accomplishments. God's name is evidence of His presence.

> **what others say**
>
> **Crosspoint**
>
> God said his name was I AM (Exodus 3:12, 14), By speaking his name, God said to Moses that he was always present. He was not a God of the past or future but of the now—past and future are always present with God. By saying his name, God declared that all that exists belongs to him. The name is so awesome it is impossible to understand all the depth of its meaning.[17]

***Worshiping God*** (Hebrews 2:12; Psalm 22:22). When people gather to worship and sing, Jesus sings His Father's praise with them. If you listen you can hear His voice, singing.

**occult**
mediums, spiritists, the dead, forces of darkness—anything but God's Word

**propitiation**
making of atonement, or "paying the price"

*Trusting God* (Hebrews 2:13a; Isaiah 8:17). The emphasis in the Isaiah passage here is on *waiting for the Lord*. Waiting for God is a fundamental demonstration of faith.

*Demonstrating the presence of God* (Hebrews 2:13b; Isaiah 8:18). Christ's declaration, "Here am I and the children whom God has given Me," was originally said in a context of general unbelief and rejection. Many in Isaiah's Israel had turned for life's true answers to anti-God sources, such as the **occult**. Surrounded by unbelief, Christ and His people themselves are living, breathing "signs and symbols" testifying that God is alive in this world.

Through the set-apart lives of His priestly family, Jesus:

- declares God's name

- sings God's praises

- waits for God's actions

- demonstrates God's presence

Worship is not man-made ritual; it is Christ's Spirit revealing God's name and person, singing God's praises, and confessing faith from "called-out" hearts gathered in Jesus's name.

## Somebody Up There Understands What It's Like to Be Human

**HEBREWS 2:14–18** *Inasmuch then as the children have partaken of flesh and blood, He Himself likewise shared in the same, that through death He might destroy him who had the power of death, that is, the devil, and release those who through fear of death were all their lifetime subject to bondage. For indeed He does not give aid to angels, but He does give aid to the seed of Abraham. Therefore, in all things He had to be made like His brethren, that He might be a merciful and faithful High Priest in things pertaining to God, to make **propitiation** for the sins of the people. For in that He Himself has suffered, being tempted, He is able to aid those who are tempted. (NKJV)*

Who are these "children" God has given to Christ? They are human earthmen and earthwomen, carbon-based creatures of flesh and blood, body, soul, and spirit.

By taking on human nature, God's Son, Jesus, was able to:

- Break the devil's reign of terror (Hebrews 2:14–15).

key point

- Free believers from fear of dying (Hebrews 2:15).
- Help the physical and spiritual descendants of Abraham (Hebrews 2:16).
- Be the bridge (priest) between people and God (Hebrews 2:17).
- Make atonement ("propitiation") for sins, establishing a place for people to meet God (Hebrews 2:17).
- Help people beat temptation (Hebrews 2:8).

To accomplish these things, like His human "children," Jesus Christ had to become "flesh and blood." He had to share in their humanity (Hebrews 2:14).

Somebody up there understands what it's like to be human. Somebody "feels with" us because He is one of us. He understands temptation and trouble because, as a temptable, trouble-prone human, He has experienced it. Because He remembers the pain and feels the feelings, Jesus can *really help us!*

## Chapter Wrap-Up

- Angels have had a significant role in ruling the universe, but are not destined to rule the future. (Hebrews 2:5)
- God's vision is for human beings to occupy a place of power a little lower than angels, close to God Himself, exercising authority over everything in creation. Mankind has not yet assumed this authoritative role. (Hebrews 2:6–8)
- Mankind's fall into sin disrupted the dream and humans lost their honor; but Jesus, as God in human form, gave His life to restore humanity's splendor. (Hebrews 2:9–10)
- Jesus's identification with human beings prepared Him to serve as High Priest to those who believe in Him, and led to salvation and spiritual development of a family of priests composed of all who follow Him. (Hebrews 2:10–18)

## Study Questions

1. Where can we look to find an example of the glory for which God created humans? (Hebrews 2:9)

2. Hebrews 2:10 (NKJV) calls Jesus "captain of their salvation." Name two other meanings of the original word for "captain" and comment on what they tell you about Jesus Christ.

3. What does the Bible mean when it speaks of being made "perfect"?

4. Identify three or four priestly functions Jesus performs with His human brothers and sisters. (Hebrews 2:12–13)

# Hebrews 3
## Border Crossing to Freedom

**Chapter Highlights:**
- 10 Reasons to Obsess
- One Last Dance
- Open House
- Jesus Speaks Today
- Spy Story

## Let's Get Started

People live far below their potential. Designed to be godlike (Hebrews 2:6–8), they fall far short of their destiny. Intended to live with purpose and conviction, many drift. This can be discouraging to think about, yet into this potential "Slough of Despond"[1] the author of Hebrews interjects a flash of blazing light—"But we see Jesus" (Hebrews 2:9 NKJV).

God's "great salvation"—the grand design for restoring humanity's lost splendor and damaged authority to reign—revolves around Jesus, God's Son, who stepped down from heavenly splendor to take on human flesh and blood and reestablish humanity's royal destiny. This He did by dying on a Roman cross, rising from the dead, and then gathering around Himself a worshiping, serving community of brothers and sisters.

Since those times the family of Jesus has always lived in a world of danger, temptation, and suffering. The Christian Jews to whom the book of Hebrews is addressed knew better than most the stresses of such a world. The harassment and pressures they faced caused many to reevaluate their decision to follow Jesus. Some were tempted to forsake Jesus and return to non-Christian Judaism.

Thus it was crucial for these harassed Hebrews to understand and become more firmly persuaded concerning the new life they had adopted. How serious would it be to turn away from Christ if such a choice could relieve the tension? Can a person live without Christ? Does it really matter whether you are Jewish or Christian—or, for that matter, Hindu or Muslim—as long as you are sincere?

On this point, missionary-statesman E. Stanley Jones, in his classic book, *The Christ of the Indian Road*, tells of a conversation between the Christian **mystic**, Sadhu Sunder Singh, and a European professor of comparative religions at a Hindu college in India.

**mystic**
believes a person can experience personal consciousness of God and revelations of truth

**Incarnation**
God in human flesh; the Son of God took upon Himself true humanity in Jesus and became "Immanuel"—"God with us"

**agnostic**
one who claims we "cannot know" about God

*what others say*

### E. Stanley Jones

The professor was an **agnostic** as far as Christianity was concerned and interviewed the Sadhu with the evident intention of showing him his mistake in renouncing another faith for Christ. [The professor] asked, "What have you found in Christianity that you did not have in your old religion?"
The Sadhu answered, "I have Christ."

"Yes, I know," the professor replied, a bit impatiently, for he was hoping for a philosophical argument. "But what particular principle or doctrine have you found that you did not have before?"

The Sadhu replied, "The particular thing I have found is Christ." Try as the professor might, he would not budge from that position. The professor went away discomfited—and thoughtful. The Sadhu was right. The non-Christian faiths have fine things in them, but they lack—Christ.

But someone objects: "Aren't they getting along pretty well without Christ?" My answer is that I know of no one, East or West, who is getting along pretty well without Christ. Christ being Life is a necessity to life![2]

### Ravi Zacharias

When man lives apart from God, chaos is the norm. When man lives with God, as revealed in the **Incarnation** of Jesus Christ, the hungers of the mind and heart find their fulfillment. For in Christ we find coherence and consolation as he reveals to us, in the most verifiable terms of truth and experience, the nature of man, the nature of reality, the nature of history, the nature of our destiny, and the nature of suffering.[3]

## 10 Reasons to Obsess

**HEBREWS 3:1a** *Therefore, holy brethren, partakers of the heavenly calling,* (NKJV)

*"Therefore"* (Hebrews 3:1) signals a link between what's been said and what's about to be said. In the first two chapters, ten facts have been placed into evidence to build the case for faith and life focused on Jesus.

### Top Ten Reasons to Pay Attention to Jesus

| | |
|---|---|
| Reason 10: Jesus is able to aid tempted people. | Hebrews 2:18 |
| Reason 9: Jesus forgives sinners. | Hebrews 2:17 |
| Reason 8: Jesus breaks the devil's power. | Hebrews 2:14–16 |
| Reason 7: Jesus makes bad people holy. | Hebrews 2:10–14 |

**Top Ten Reasons to Pay Attention to Jesus (cont'd)**

| | |
|---|---|
| Reason 6: Jesus bridges the chasm between God and people. | Hebrews 2:10, 17 |
| Reason 5: Jesus restores damaged humanness. | Hebrews 2:9 |
| Reason 4: Jesus reveals God's scheme to rescue spiritual drifters. | Hebrews 2:1–4 |
| Reason 3: Jesus is greater than angels. | Hebrews 1:4–14 |
| Reason 2: Jesus is God's right hand man. | Hebrews 1:3, 8–12 |
| Reason 1: Jesus perfectly represents God; to see Jesus is to see God. | Hebrews 1:2–3 |

## Focusing Together

Those who are urged to "consider" or "fix your thoughts on Jesus" are identified three different ways in Hebrews 3:1; as . . .

- *"Holy brothers"*—members of Jesus's family (Hebrews 2:11).

- *"Partakers ("sharers") of the heavenly calling"*—Christians help keep each other marching to Jesus's beat instead of to the rebellious cadence of the world.

- *"Confessors"*—Believers who declare faith and commitment to Jesus.

key point

When Hebrews was written, pressures were building to sever Christian Hebrews from all contact with traditional Jewish society. To counteract their fear that separation from the temple and priesthood might leave them without a place to meet God, the author exhorts them, "Consider the Apostle and High Priest of our confession, Christ Jesus" (Hebrews 3:1 NKJV).

It is crucial that believers on shaky ground stay focused on Jesus. Fixing your thoughts means more than a casual nod in Jesus's direction. Words like concentration, obsession, and fascination better describe the meaning. The original Greek word is *katanoein*, "to fix attention on something in such a way that the inner meaning of the thing, the lesson that the thing is designed to teach, may be learned."[4]

There is no more fascinating person than Jesus Christ. The safety net for people dancing the high wire between Christianity on one side, tradition and family on the other, is to become absorbed in knowing and relating all of life to Jesus. Flipping through the pages, looking at pictures may be okay for *People* magazine, but it's not enough for "partakers of the heavenly calling." Knowing Jesus is a

something to ponder

**life and death**
Matthew 5:6;
John 6:68–69;
1 John 5:12

**gird up the loins**
for work or battle a
man tucked his tunic
between his legs, up
through his belt to
assure freedom of
movement

*key point*

lifetime obsession. Knowing Him—who He is, what He does, what He says, what He thinks—are <u>life-and-death</u> matters! Something Jesus said seems like a call to waffling Christians: "Blessed are those who hunger and thirst for righteousness, for they shall be filled" (Matthew 5:6 NKJV).

### what others say

**William Barclay**

If we are ever to learn Christian truth, a lack luster, disinterested, detached glance is never enough; there must be a concentrated gaze in which we **gird up the loins** of the mind in a determined effort to see its meaning for us.[5]

The central focus of Christian worship is not architecture, creeds, liturgy, music, speech-making, evangelism, or indoctrination, but concentration on the person and presence of Jesus. Done right it happens not just on Sunday but all the time, not just when Christians gather but also when they scatter. (See Romans 12:1–21; Proverbs 25:21–22.)

### what others say

**Matt Redman**

I'm coming back to the heart of worship,
and it's all about you, Jesus, all about You,
it's all about You, Jesus.
I'm sorry, Lord, for the thing I've made it,
when it's all about You,
it's all about You, Jesus.[6]

## Jesus's Double-Barreled Mission

HEBREWS 3:1b *consider the Apostle and High Priest of our confession, Christ Jesus. (NKJV)*

Jesus fills two fascinating roles in the spiritual family (Hebrews 3:1):

*Apostle*—The Greek word *apostolos* means "one who is sent forth"—an envoy, ambassador, representative. An ambassador is "clothed with all the power and authority of the country or the king who sends him. The voice of the ambassador is the voice of the king or country who sent him."[7] We would not know God without His personal representative, showing us in His person what God is like. That personal representative is Jesus (Hebrews 1:3; John 1:14, 18).

*High priest*—The Latin word for priest is *pontifex*, meaning "bridge-builder." Before the letter is finished, Hebrews connects the dots to complete the picture of priesthood the Old Testament began to sketch. As High Priest, Jesus offered the sacrifice to God which **atones** for human sin. He is Priest *and* Sacrifice (Hebrews 9:12–13; 10:8–10). He is the bridge between God and people.

go to

**atones**
Leviticus 16,
especially verses 2,
14, 15, 29–34;
1 John 2:1;
Romans 3:21–18

**food laws**
Mark 7:1–8;
Acts 10:9–15;
11:2–3;
Acts 15;
Galatians 2:11–13

**atones**
paying sin's debt
with His blood shed
on the cross, Jesus
covers human sins
with forgiveness,
open access to God

> **what others say**
>
> **Larry Richards**
>
> In his own person as true God and fully man, Jesus links God and man in indissoluble union. Thus Jesus is able to perfectly represent God to man, communicating to us by his living Word in a voice we can recognize in our every "today" (Hebrews 3, 4). At the same time he stands in God's presence to guarantee access, forgiveness and aid.[8]

As *Apostle* and *High Priest* Jesus is both God's representative among human beings and human beings' representative in the presence of God.

## One Last Dance

**HEBREWS 3:2a** . . . *who was faithful to Him who appointed Him* . . . (NKJV)

For almost 40 years Jerusalem's Christians lived side-by-side with orthodox Jews, often participating in the same synagogues, Sabbath after Sabbath. For 40 years they remained loyal to their ancient traditions while embracing Jesus as Messiah. They circumcised their sons (Acts 16:4). They kept the feasts (Acts 2; 20:6, 16). They offered the sacrifices (Acts 18:18). They attended the daily prayer services at the temple (Acts 3:1). They lived according to the Law (Acts 21:24), including the special food laws that so sharply separate practicing Jews from other people.

Receiving Christ, the ancient religion came alive and they pursued it with increased enthusiasm. They considered Jesus the best part of being Jewish.

But in the AD 60s, with Jewish nationalism snowballing, the unavoidable decision bore down on them like a battalion of Sherman tanks! Ready or not, in Jerusalem, Rome, Alexandria—in cities with large Jewish populations, and hamlets where the Gospel had gained a foothold among dispersed Jews, Hebrew Christians faced pressure to forsake Christ and return to traditional Judaism or be outcast.

By the middle of the first century AD, Hebrew (i.e., "Jewish") Christians realized that all the ancient prophecies of the coming Jewish Messiah had been fulfilled in Jesus Christ—that He indeed *was* the Heavenly One they'd waited for so long. And more important, they finally began to realize that, by His death, He had rendered their sacrificial system totally obsolete, along with all the specific laws and regulations (part of what was often called the "Mosaic Law" after the person to whom God literally "gave" it on Mount Sinai) that defined and regulated it. Forgiveness for sin no longer required the death of an innocent animal; the shed blood of Christ replaced all that and provided salvation for all who would accept it. This was the greatest "religious development" in the history of the world and took some getting used to!

**key point**

### what others say

**F. F. Bruce**

The claims of Christ and the Gospel, indeed, are foreshadowed in the ministry which was committed to Moses: Moses's ministry was designed as *"a shadow of the good things to come"* (Hebrews 10:1), the good things which now have indeed come in Christ. In some sections of Jewish Christianity Christ's role was envisaged as primarily that of a second Moses; here he is presented as being much more than that.[9]

**Merrill C. Tenney**

The members of the Jewish church still clung to the observances of the law, though they trusted for their salvation in Jesus, the Messiah. . . . [Meanwhile, official] Jewish rejection of the Christian message finally came to the point where even Paul abandoned any hope of national repentance.[10]

## Jesus vs. Moses: Fifteen Rounds or Partnership?

There is no competition. Moses and Jesus are members of the same team. Look:

- Both Jesus and Moses are *"apostles"*—representatives <u>*sent from God*</u> to fulfill aspects of His Great Salvation plan. Hebrews 3:1 (NKJV) identifies Jesus as "the Apostle of our confession." In Exodus 3:10 (NKJV) God tells Moses, "I will send you" (the Greek Old Testament reads, literally: "I will apostle you to Pharaoh."

- As God's representatives, both Moses and Jesus were "faithful to Him who appointed" them (Hebrews 3:2 NKJV).

- Both Jesus and Moses are "priests"—sharing God's Word with people and **interceding** with God for people. Moses's brother, Aaron, was first to wear the official vestments and hold the title "High Priest," but many Scriptures tell how, when the chips were down, it was Moses, not Aaron, who was Israel's true Advocate with God.[12] (Exodus 19:7; 32:11–14, 30–32; Numbers 14;13–19; Deuteronomy 5:5)

- Neither Moses nor Jesus was ever officially ordained, but both served as priests under the call of God the Father. They modeled the universal priesthood of believers, which came into being when the Holy Spirit came upon the disciples at Pentecost (Acts 2). Without official title, every Christian serves the priestly office—sharing the Word and interceding for others.

**sent from God**
Luke 4:18;
John 7:28–29; 8:16;
Exodus 3:10

**interceding**
praying for someone; pleading the cause of someone before God; being an advocate

## "Mister Law"

As we see in Hebrews 2, Jesus is a bona fide flesh-and-blood human being. But He is not your ordinary, garden-variety person. Jesus, Hebrews 3 insists, is the *greatest man* who ever lived—even greater than Moses.

Now, it's one thing to say Jesus is greater than the prophets (Hebrews 1:1–3) or Jesus is greater than the angels (1:4–14). But to say Jesus is greater than *Moses* is to claim Jesus is greater than the man Orthodox Jews believe, even today, is the *greatest man who ever lived!* You have to be a Jew to fully appreciate the unique and important place Moses has in Jewish thinking.

God spoke to Moses "face to face" (Deuteronomy 34:10 NKJV). He was the direct recipient of the Ten Commandments (Deuteronomy 5:6–21). After the "finger of God" carved the Ten Commandments in stone, God Himself gave them directly to Moses. (Exodus 31:18 NKJV). To the Jew, the greatest thing in the

**faithful**
Matthew 25:14–30;
2 Timothy 2:11–13;
4:7


**face to face**
literal Hebrew—
"mouth to mouth"

world is the Old Testament Law, also called "the Mosaic Law." In Jewish thinking, Moses and the Law are virtually the *same thing*![13] Nobody but nobody stands closer to God than Moses.

## Faithfulness—The Stuff Greatness Is Made Of

HEBREWS 3:2b *as Moses also was <u>faithful</u> in all His house. (NKJV)*

God Himself lifted Moses to the place he occupies in Jewish thinking. God Himself discloses the characteristic that, more than anything else, makes a man "great." In an incident recorded in Numbers 12:6–8, Moses's brother Aaron and sister Miriam are going around the camp badmouthing Moses because of his marriage to a Cushite (African) woman. By putting Moses down, they undoubtedly hoped to gain political clout for themselves. God took the gossips aside, looked them square in the eyes, and said, in effect, "Shut up!"

The Lord silenced Moses's two siblings by reminding them that Moses was no run-of-the-mill prophet. Other prophets got God's messages indirectly in visions or dreams. But "I speak with him **face to face**, even plainly, and not in dark sayings; and he sees the form of the LORD" (Numbers 12:8 NKJV), said God. He then underlined this glowing affirmation with a warning: Anyone who slammed Moses had good reason to shake in his boots!

Why did God hold Moses in such high esteem? Because he was "faithful in all My house" (Numbers 12:7 NKJV; Hebrews 3:2).

Moses is great because he was *"faithful"*. A thousand times he could have pulled out of the Hebrew slave emancipation program and nobody would have thought it strange. The Israelites were often grossly unfaithful, disloyal. They complained against Moses and God and just about everything else. Except for God, no one would have raised an eyebrow if Moses had packed his grip and caught the next camel back to Egypt. Instead, he chose to stay with them, bit the bullet, forgave their miserable whining, and faithfully did the job God gave him to do:

*The Job*—To communicate God's moral expectations and His temporary methods of forgiveness via the OT sacrificial system, to this company of complainers. And, to get them ready to invade the Promised Land.

But until then, "Faithful" was Moses's middle name. People who met him, if their spiritual eyes were open, realized they were in the presence of true greatness. Yet even so, it was essential that wavering first-century Jewish Christians got a grip on the rest of the story. Moses was great but Moses was *not* Jesus.

"For the law was given through Moses, but grace and truth came through Jesus Christ. No one has seen God at any time. The only begotten Son, who is in the bosom of the Father, He has declared Him" (John 1:17–18 NKJV).

Moses was the man who communicated God's Law. Jesus was God Himself in human form (John 1:14; Colossians 1:15–18; Hebrews 1:2–3; 1 John 1:1–3). Jesus, the Son of God, is "the radiance of [God's] glory and the exact representation of His being."[14] Moses proved his loyalty to the family of God. Jesus "was faithful to Him who appointed Him" (Hebrews 3:2 NKJV).

Incredible as it may have seemed to some, when first-century Jews believed in Jesus, they linked up with Someone even greater than Moses! In fact, the Letter to the Hebrews shows clearly how Jesus exceeded Moses in faithfulness.

## What Hebrews Says About Jesus's Faithfulness

| Hebrews | Promise |
| --- | --- |
| Hebrews 1:10–12 | Everything in the universe changes but Jesus remains the same. |
| Hebrews 2:17 | Jesus is our faithful High Priest, able to make atonement for our sins. |
| Hebrews 3:2 | Jesus was faithful to God, who appointed Him. |
| Hebrews 3:6 | Jesus was faithful as a Son over God's house. |

house we are
1 Peter 2:5; 4:17;
1 Timothy 3:15

## What Hebrews Says About Jesus's Faithfulness (cont'd)

| Hebrews | Promise |
|---|---|
| Hebrews 7:25a | Because He lives forever, Jesus is able to save completely all who come to God through Him. |
| Hebrews 7:25b | Jesus always lives to intercede for people. |
| Hebrews 13:5 | Jesus promises, "I will never leave you nor forsake you" (NKJV). (See also Matthew 28:20.) |
| Hebrews 13:8 | "Jesus Christ is the same yesterday, today, and forever" (NKJV). |

The first reason why Christians may meet whatever comes down the pike with confidence and an attitude of rest, is that Jesus was, is, and always will be *faithful*.

# Open House

**HEBREWS 3:3–6** *For this One has been counted worthy of more glory than Moses, inasmuch as He who built the house has more honor than the house. For every house is built by someone, but He who built all things is God. And Moses indeed was faithful in all His house as a servant, for a testimony of those things which would be spoken afterward, but Christ as a Son over His own house, whose house we are if we hold fast the confidence and the rejoicing of the hope firm to the end. (NKJV)*

In this paragraph "God's house" is not a building. The original word for "house" also means "household" or "family."

- In the OT, God's "house" is the people of Israel, Jacob's off-spring.

- In the NT, God's "house" is the people who believe in Jesus Christ as their Savior and Lord, the living church, the family of *both* Jew and Gentile followers of Jesus.

- "God's house" is not material, but spiritual. Hebrews 3:6 states: "whose house *we are*." God's "house" is, in fact, the human clan of which God is the Father, and all who have linked up with Him and each other by faith and adoption are "brothers and sisters and mothers and children" (see Mark 3:35; Luke 18:29–30). Christians are the *House of God*.

In Jerusalam around AD 65–70, Jewish Christians threatened with expulsion from the temple found hope in the fact that separation from institutional religion can never separate a true believer from the house of God, because together, Christians are the *House of God*.

### The House of God

| Scripture Passage | Aspect of God's Family |
|---|---|
| Mark 3:31–35 | Jesus's family composed of those who do God's will |
| Matthew 18:20–21 | Basic structure of God's family—2 or 3 gathered in Jesus's name. |
| Acts 2:41–47; 4:31–35 | Common, healthy everyday life of God's family. |
| Romans 8:12–17 | Members come into God's family through adoption. |
| Ephesians 2:18–20 | Foundation of God's family; the family as God's dwelling. |
| 1 Peter 2:5–9 | God's house is a house for priests. |
| Hebrews 7:25a | Because He lives forever, Jesus is able to save completely all who come to God through Him. |
| Hebrews 7:25b | Jesus always lives to intercede for people. |
| Hebrews 13:5 | Jesus promises, "I will never leave you nor forsake you" (NKJV). (See also Matthew 28:20.) |
| Hebrews 13:8 | "Jesus Christ is the same yesterday, today, and forever" (NKJV). |

**Head**
Ephesians 1:21–23;
4:15; 5:23;
Colossians 1:18

## Will the Top Dog in God's House Please Stand Up?

The critical issue for Hebrew Christians in the tug-of-war between Moses and Jesus was: Who is Head? Who has the final word? The author insists it's Jesus. Moses is a bigger-than-life presence, but in the house and family of God, Jesus is <u>Head</u>.

The following chart traces the writer's logic.

*key point*

### Who's the Greatest in God's House—Moses or Jesus? (Hebrews 3:1–6)

| Moses, the servant, because . . . | Jesus, the Son, because . . . |
|---|---|
| v. 2—Faithful to do what God sent him to do | v. 2—Faithful to do what God sent Him to do |
| v. 3—Part of God's house | v. 3—Builder of God's house<br>v. 4—Equated with God as the house Builder, thus equal with God |
| v. 5—Servant *in* God's House. | v. 6—Son *over* God's house |
| v. 5—Prophet/witness to future truth about Christ | v. 6—Present Source of security (courage/hope) |

The Hebrews author's argument is that, in God's family, Jesus is superior to Moses as surely as the son of the owner and builder of the house deserves more recognition than the butler or chamber maid. The message for waffling and uncertain Hebrew believers was

**code**
"Mosaic Law;"
"Law of Moses"—
Ten Commandments,
sacrificial system, etc.

really quite simple: Don't settle for second best! Don't seek *shalom* in Moses and the law. True peace, security, health, and salvation are found in Jesus, not Moses.

Remaining loyal to Jesus is an absolute must! Continued relationship with God and security in his family circle depends on commitment to "hold fast the confidence and the rejoicing of the hope firm to the end" (Hebrews 3:6 NKJV).

key point

---

**what others say**

**William L. Lane**

(This) is the beginning of a sustained effort to persuade the [Hebrews] to remain loyal to Christ in the presence of pressures that would encourage them to abandon their confession [of faith in Christ].[17]

**Lawrence O. Richards**

Jesus is superior to Moses, just as the person who plans, designs, builds and pays for a house is greater than the butler who serves in it. The **code** that bears Moses's name patterned all of life for the Jewish people. It should follow then, since Jesus has come with His superior message, that He will also introduce a superior way of life![18]

---

## Jesus Speaks Today

> **HEBREWS 3:7** *Therefore, as the Holy Spirit says:*
> *"Today, if you will hear His voice . . . (NKJV)*

*"Therefore"*—Once more that Bible buzzword introduces the next leap in the author's logic. Because Jesus is "the Greatest"—the next step is to listen to what He says and do it!

The writer of Hebrews now lays out a series of facts:

- First, the Bible is the primary means by which the Holy Spirit speaks to people.
- Then, the scribbler writes, "the Holy Spirit says . . ."
- Then he/she quotes from Psalm 95:7–11—the message of the Holy Spirit to people.

Here is Bible truth: Jesus, the Great One in God's family, speaks today!

The writer to the Hebrews has just established Jesus's authority to speak, to be listened to and obeyed. The first thing to note is that He speaks to people, person to person, just as God has always spoken to His believing people, by means of "the Holy Spirit" (Hebrews 3:7 NKJV). (See chart "How God Speaks" in Chapter 1.)

The Holy Spirit is also known as "the Spirit of life in Christ Jesus," "the Spirit of God," and "the Spirit of Christ," or simply "the Spirit." (Check it out in Romans 8.)

## The Day They Burned Down God's House!

As Hebrews was being written, zealot daggermen prowled the streets of Jerusalem, assassinating Roman sympathizers and Christians alike. Soon the legions of Rome would encircle Jerusalem in a terrifying siege.

Meanwhile, as the noose tightened around the neck of the city, Hebrews who rejected Jesus as Messiah become more obsessed with ridding Judaism of His influence. Hebrew Christians faced hatred and harassment. Finally, they suffered the ultimate rejection—official Judaism labeled them "heretics" and banned them from the temple.

This decade of terror ended in AD 70 with a catastrophe which, in terms of the death toll, dwarfs the fall of the World Trade Center in New York, September 11, 2001. More than half a million Jews died in the siege and final battle between themselves and the Roman army.

**Herod's temple** was sacked and burned; its treasures hauled off as the spoils of war. Hundreds of thousands of Jews in the city and surrounding territory were slaughtered or starved to death. Thousands more were carried off to Rome as slaves.

It is difficult for someone who is not a Jew to understand how spiritually devastating the destruction of Jerusalem was. For first-century Jews, religion and politics were the same thing. Religion, government, and the land were inseparably bound together as the Jew's source of identity, purpose for living, and *shalom*.

what others say

### Merrill C. Tenney

Judaism as a religion and Judaism as a political system were one, and when the political system fell so that the Jew was without a land, without a temple, and without a government of his own, he lost much of his essential system. When Judaism was forced to relinquish these means of outward expression, it became solely the worship of God through the study of the law, and consequently its legalism was strengthened.[19]

According to an **extrabiblical** report, a number of Christian Jews escaped just before the Holy City fell. Forty years earlier, Jesus had prophesied a time when Jerusalem would be "surrounded by armies" (Luke 21:20 NKJV), with "men's hearts failing them from fear and the expectation of those things which are coming on the earth" (Luke 21:26 NKJV). The prophecy included a few sentences indicating that some people might escape if they left the city quickly and headed for the hills (Luke 21:21).

As the siege developed, the report tells us that Christian prophets reminded Christians in and around Jerusalem about Jesus's warnings. As all hell broke loose in the city, a significant group of believers (some sources say most of them) fled to territory ruled by Herod Agrippa II, who gave them asylum and freedom to establish a Hebrew Christian community.

The Letter to the Hebrews was strategically timed to speak to those tumultuous times.

## Spy Story

HEBREWS 3:8–9
*Do not harden your hearts as in the rebellion,*
*In the day of trial in the wilderness,*
*Where your fathers tested Me, tried Me,*
*And saw My works forty years." (NKJV)*

At this point most people who study Hebrews begin to understand that the gut issue—both in ancient times and today—is not politics, greed, military strength, or who's running the show. The *gut*-issue is **faith**.

Do we believe God? If so we must show it by doing what God is telling us to do and trust Him to deliver on His promises. The one who writes to first-century Hebrew Christians sees their situation as spiritually parallel to the ancient Hebrews at Kadesh. Fifteen hundred years before his readers heard the call to follow Christ, a motley crowd of footsore Israelites, recently escaped from slavery in Egypt, stood next to the Promised Land, struggling with the Lord's command to invade.

So what does God say next?

**HEBREWS 3:10–19**
*Therefore I was angry with that generation,*
*And said, 'They always go astray in their heart,*
*And they have not known My ways.'*
*So I swore in My wrath,*
*'They shall not enter My rest.'"*
*Beware, brethren, lest there be in any of you an evil heart of unbelief in departing from the living God; but exhort one another daily, while it is called "Today," lest any of you be hardened through the deceitfulness of sin. For we have become partakers of Christ if we hold the beginning of our confidence steadfast to the end, while it is said:*
*"Today, if you will hear His voice,*
*Do not harden your hearts as in the rebellion."*
*For who, having heard, rebelled? Indeed, was it not all who came out of Egypt, led by Moses? Now with whom was He angry forty years? Was it not with those who sinned, whose corpses fell in the wilderness? And to whom did He swear that they would not enter His rest, but to those who did not obey? So we see that they could not enter in because of unbelief. (NKJV)*

Because He is absolutely holy, God's wrath must be viewed in the light of His grace, justice, and mercy. Dying on the cross, God's Son, Jesus, took on Himself the wrath of God, on our behalf. If we believe, trusting Jesus's sacrifice to be the sufficient substitute to purchase pardon and forgiveness for us, we will not face the wrath our sins deserve. Since God can do nothing inconsistent with His nature and character, His justice requires that people who refuse to believe, choosing rather to rebel against what His grace and mercy provide, shall of necessity face the just wrath sin and rebellion against God deserve.

There is a place of peace, security, and restoration in the thick of life's stress. The following-God-around lifestyle comes with a guarantee: Listen to God, do what He says, and your "ship of the desert" is going to be rocked! But along with a quivering skiff comes a warranty you can't refuse—God's "rest."

That's a promise.

## Chapter Wrap-Up

- The first two chapter of Hebrews very carefully build the case for developing a powerful faith and living a dedicated life, totally focused on Jesus Christ.
- Christ Himself fills two very specific roles in our "spiritual family. Indeed, the third chapter of Hebrews makes it clear that Jesus is the greatest man who ever lived, even more so than Moses.
- Throughout Hebrews we are told over and over that the main issue—the one lesson we must come away with after reading Hebrews—is an understanding that our lives must be built on faith in the power of God to direct and re-direct our lives as He sees fit.

## Study Questions

1. What ten facts are outlined in the first two chapters of Hebrews that build the case for faith and life focused on Jesus?

2. What two roles in the spiritual family does Jesus fill (Hebrews 3:1)?

3. According to Hebrews 3, who is the greatest man who ever lived?

4. What other four names is the Holy Spirit known as?

5. If it's not politics, greed, or military strength, what is the gut issue of Hebrews?

# Hebrews 4:1–13
# The Rest of the Story

**Chapter Highlights:**
- The Good News About Rest
- It's God's Rest
- Rest Today
- The Scalpel's Edge

## Let's Get Started

The community of Jewish followers of Jesus in Jerusalem was under intense pressure. Refused access to the temple and the ancient forms of worship that had thrilled the hearts of godly Jews for centuries, scorned by the fellow countrymen, and no doubt suffering economically, the Jews of the Holy Land had good reason to be discouraged.

Then, like a lifesaver thrown to a drowning man, a letter "to the Hebrews" arrived. It was quickly copied and passed from house church to house church. The letter reminded the early Jewish Christians that God had spoken to them in Jesus, His final and ultimate revelation. This Word, which had come to them in Person, invited them to experience a reality that *all prior revelation* had merely foreshadowed.

But the good news also came with a warning. To profit from this Word from God, as with His previous words, they must welcome it with an open and receptive heart. These Jewish followers of Jesus must not "harden [their] hearts as in the rebellion, in the day of trial in the wilderness" (Hebrews 3:8 NKJV). In their own day of trial these Jewish Christians must guard against "an evil heart of unbelief," and against "departing from the living God" (Hebrews 3:12 NKJV). There must be no turning back to the familiar, comfortable Old Testament faith. The Christian community, despite its own "day of trial," must follow Jesus on a path that seemed to many filled with pain and uncertainty.

In this fourth chapter of the Letter to the Hebrews, the writer powerfully expresses the significance of the choice that his generation of believers, like the Exodus generation, had to make. They can respond to the Word spoken in Christ with unbelief, incur the anger of God, and never know rest. Or they can fully trust and respond to what God is saying and experience the blessing of a rest that only God can provide.

key point

# The Good News About Rest

The key word in Hebrews chapter 4 is "rest." It occurs nine times in the 13 verses we're considering. But what is "rest"?

Three Hebrew words are used to convey the idea of "rest" in the Old Testament:

- *Sabat* implies reaching the end of an activity followed by peacefulness.
- *Nuah* indicates security and a sense of inner ease.
- *Saqat* conveys the idea of finding tranquility.

Summing up the significance of "rest" in the Old Testament, the Zondervan *Encyclopedia of Bible Words* notes that:

The words that communicate the idea of "rest" imply a wide range of benefits. There is security, an absence of danger and anxiety. There is an ease and confidence that has both outer and inner bases, each of which can be traced directly to one's relationship with the Lord. Only through a relationship with the Lord can we experience the blessing of the rest that God has for those who trust him.[1]

**what others say**

**Sally Breedlove**

From God's point of view, rest is not an accessory blessing. Our lives are meant to flow from a solid garden core of spacious inner quiet. When we turn to the Creation story we see how foundational rest is.[2]

What sudden and unexpected joy must have flooded the hearts of the fearful and troubled Jewish followers of Jesus when they read the words that open chapter 4!

# Working Your Way to Rest

HEBREWS 4:1 *Therefore, since a promise remains of entering His rest . . .* (NKJV)

Think about it for a moment. Your life is full of stress. You've lost your job and fear no one will hire you at your age. Your son has made some disastrous choices and you fear for his future. You're waiting for a test your doctor has ordered, and dread the results. Especially since, when you lost your job you lost your health insurance. As you wait, feeling overwhelmed and helpless, you can sense your blood pressure rising. You wonder how long you can bear up under the stress, and search desperately for solutions hidden in the mist of uncertainty.

At times like these—and we all experience them—you can understand how the amazing promise that Hebrews offers must have struck readers who were living under constant stress.

God offers me rest? There's some way I can actually feel secure? Tranquil? Me? In my situation? *Vos iz der chochmeh?*

The first readers of this epistle must have hesitated at these words, and read them over and over again. *"A promise remains of entering His rest."* After taking in this stunning revelation, the next question they must have asked was, "How?" How, with my stomach churning out acid as I search frantically for solutions, can I know the inner ease and confidence that I yearn for?

The writer of Hebrews has the answer, for the early Jewish Christians and for believers today. It hinges on our response to God's Word.

## "*His* Rest"

**HEBREWS 4:1–3** *Therefore, since a promise remains of entering His rest, let us fear lest any of you seem to have come short of it. For indeed the gospel was preached to us as well as to them; but the word which they heard did not profit them, not being mixed with faith in those who heard it. For we who have believed do enter that rest, as He has said:*
*"So I swore in My wrath,*
*'They shall not enter My rest,'"* (NKJV)

Let's make no mistake about it. The rest that God provides is "His" rest. We'll see in a moment the full significance of this statement. But for now simply note that it is "His" rest because God alone can provide the inner peace we need.

Many people today look for rest, for security, in wealth. Many hope to find their deepest needs met in popularity or fame. Even among those of us who believe in God, too few expect to find inner tranquility through our relationship with the Lord. Yet centuries before Christ the prophet, Isaiah reminded his readers:

The wicked are like the troubled sea, when it cannot rest, whose

the church
Acts 6:1;
1 Corinthians 16:1;
2 Corinthians 8–9

persecution
Luke 21:12;
John 15:20

Israelites
the Old Testament
name for the Jewish
people

the church
the community of
believers in Christ

waters cast up mire and dirt. "There is no peace," says my God, "for the wicked." (Isaiah 57:20–21 NKJV)

Strikingly, these words of Isaiah were not addressed to foreign idol worshipers. Isaiah spoke to God's own "wicked" people. Like the Exodus generation the writer of Hebrews refers to in chapter 3, these were **Israelites** who failed to trust God and act on the teachings of His Word. No peace or rest can exist for such people.

## Fear Will Find You Out

HEBREWS 4:1 . . . *let us fear lest any of you seem to have come short of it.* (NKJV)

The word "fear" has a number of meanings in Scripture. Fear can be:

- Dread of being harmed (Genesis 3:10; 1 Samuel 28:5)
- Worry or anxiety about circumstances (Genesis 26:7; Exodus 3, 4)
- Respect or reverence for God (Proverbs 1:7; Psalm 36:2–4)
- Amazement or wonder at God's acts (Luke 5:26; Mark 5:15)

In Hebrews 4:1 it's best to understand "fear" as worry or anxiety. These early Jewish Christians focused on their circumstances. From a purely human point of view they had every reason to worry. No doubt the needy among them were cut off from the daily dole of food provided by temple officials. This responsibility had been taken on by **the church**. But an element of the general persecution must have included refusal by traditional Jews to employ Jesus's followers or to shop at their businesses. Many early Jewish Christians must not have known where their next meal was coming from.

Yet the writer of Hebrews tells these members of the early church to be anxious lest they come short of experiencing God's rest! In other words, these Christians—and you and I as well—are not to worry about our troubles but about our *relationship with the Lord*.

key point

**what others say**

**Ray Stedman**

Failure to expect God to act caused the disobedience of Israel in the Old Testament, and a similar failure destroys thousands today.[4]

This should come as no surprise to any follower of Jesus. Christ Himself gave us the prescription to follow when we're sick with worry.

**MATTHEW 6:25–26, 33–34** *Therefore I say to you, do not worry about your life, what you will eat or what you will drink; nor about your body, what you will put on. Is not life more than food and the body more than clothing? Look at the birds of the air, for they neither sow nor reap nor gather into barns; yet your heavenly Father feeds them. Are you not of more value than they? But seek first the kingdom of God and His righteousness, and all these things shall be added to you. Therefore do not worry about tomorrow, for tomorrow will worry about its own things.* (NKJV)

God doesn't promise to change our circumstances, but to provide rest. We need to focus on entering that rest rather than on our problems. For, while rest is available, we can easily "come short of it."

apply it

## The Old Family Recipe: How to Enter God's Rest

- Hear the gospel word (Hebrews 4:2)
- Mix well with faith (Hebrews 4:2)
- Enter God's rest (Hebrews 4:3)
- Respond to God's voice (Hebrews 4:6–7)

The Hebrews prescription is deceptively simple. To profit from it we need to understand its ingredients.

**command**
Deuteronomy 1:26

**promised**
Genesis 12:7;
Numbers 14: 22, 23

**military victory**
Deuteronomy
1:29–31;
Joshua 12:17–31

**passages of Scripture**
Matthew 5:22–24;
18:15–17

# How a Fine Batch of Good News Can Go Bad

The Greek word translated "gospel" (verse 2) literally means "good news." We typically think of the gospel as the good news that everlasting life has been provided for us by Jesus. But in this passage, "gospel" describes *any* word from God. That's why the author can speak of "the gospel" preached to the Exodus generation. That gospel word wasn't God's promise to humankind made in Jesus. That gospel word was a divine <u>command</u> to go up and take the land God had <u>promised</u>. The command was good news, for God was fully able to provide the needed <u>military victory</u>. But the Israelites failed to focus on God's ability. Instead they focused on the apparent superiority of Canaanites. Ten of the spies reported that:

> NUMBERS 13:28, 32–33 *The people who dwell in the land are strong; the cities are fortified and very large; The land through which we have gone as spies is a land that devours its inhabitants, and all the people whom we saw in it are men of great stature. We were like grasshoppers in our own sight, and so we were in their sight. (NKJV)*

Terrified by this report, the Israelites viewed God's command to go up and take possession of Canaan as bad news rather than the good news it truly was!

All too often today we take the commands of Scripture as bad news rather the good news they truly are. A friend of mine was speaking at a pastor's conference. During the week a half dozen pastors approached him for advice. Each one was thinking of leaving his church because of strained relationships with an influential member of his congregation. My friend pointed them to <u>passages of Scripture</u> that tell us to go to such persons and work the conflict out. Each of the pastors shook his head and said, "That's hard." Like the people of Numbers 13, the first reaction of these pastors was to view God's command as bad news!

# Mix Well with Faith

> HEBREWS 4:2 . . . *the word which they heard did not profit them, not being mixed with faith in those who heard it. (NKJV)*

Every word of God is gospel. Every command, like every promise, is truly good news. But it only seems like good news when we receive it in faith. Without faith the good news becomes bad news, for when we fail to respond we lose our opportunity to enter God's rest.

This is especially true when the Gospel in view is the message of salvation in Jesus. This is what the apostle Paul has in mind when he writes to the Corinthians of his mission to preach Christ's gospel. In his preaching of Christ he:

> 2 CORINTHIANS 2:14–16 *diffuses the fragrance of His knowledge in every place. For we are to God the fragrance of Christ among those who are being saved and among those who are perishing. To the one we are the aroma of death leading to death, and to the other the aroma of life leading to life. (NKJV)*

Put bluntly, Paul is saying that to those who do not believe in Jesus, the New Testament promise of salvation in Christ stinks. But to those who are being saved, the story of Christ's death on the cross and His resurrection is as sweet-smelling as the most expensive perfume. The Gospel story is the same for both, but those who refuse to believe are <u>doomed</u>. For them the Gospel is bad news indeed. But for those who believe, the Gospel is the most wonderful news in the world, for it offers them forgiveness of sins and <u>eternal life</u>.

What is true of the message of salvation in Christ is true of every word spoken by God. Every word is good news. But only as long as it is *"mixed with faith"* in those who hear it.

go to

**doomed**
John 3:18–19;
1 John 5:11–12

**eternal life**
John 3:16;
1 John 5:11–12

## A Word About "Faith"

We need to be clear about what the writer of Hebrews is saying when he says a word from God must be "mixed with faith" (4:2 NKJV). Today many people would say that they "believe" in Jesus and are Christians. But a striking percentage of such people simply mean, "I think that Jesus lived and was a great moral teacher."

This falls far short of what the Bible means by "faith." A poll reported in *Christianity Today* indicates that 70 percent of Americans say that Jesus is God or Son of God.[5] Yet even this is not "faith" in a biblical sense. After all, the apostle James explains to those who claim to believe that there is one God that "even the demons believe—and tremble" (James 2:19 NKJV).

What, then, is "faith" to the writer of Hebrews? Both Old Testament and New Testament terms provide a clear definition.

## Old and New Testament Terms for Faith

| Term | Definition |
|---|---|
| 'aman | This is a Hebrew word that expresses faithfulness, certainty, firmness. In one form it is typically translated "faith" or "belief," and indicates certainty based on the reliability of what is believed. |
| batah | This Hebrew word indicates trust in a person, or reliance on him. Its focus is the impact of such trust on the believer who commits himself to God, and as a result experiences a sense of well-being and security. |
| mahseh | This Hebrew word is also related to trust, and means "to seek refuge." It portrays human helplessness and the need to seek refuge in God. |
| pistis (n) pisteuo (v) | This family of New Testament faith words builds on the Old Testament concept. In all but 12 verses Jesus is the object of New Testament faith. One unique use of this faith word is to link it to the preposition "in," something never done in **secular** Greek. This grammatical construction pictures the believer believing *into* Christ, that is, fully committing himself to Jesus. |

key point

"Faith" in a biblical sense is a commitment of oneself to God, an abiding trust in the Lord that results in full reliance on Him and His Word.

How does anyone measure the existence and reality of biblical faith? Simply by one's response to any gospel word. As the writer of Hebrews reminds us frequently, "Today, if you will hear His voice, do not harden your hearts as in the rebellion" (Hebrews 3:7–8 NKJV). Rather than treat the gospel word as bad news and draw back from it, you and I are to hear it as good news and gladly embrace it. Unlike the Israelites of Numbers 14, you and I are to *have such confidence in God that we gladly do as He tells us, no matter what our circumstances.*

## Summing Up

- Rest is something only God can give.
- God guides us into rest through His Word.
- Those who hear the Word must mix it with faith.
- Resting in His promises, respond by doing what you understand God wants you to do.

Early in the year of struggle—as told above—God spoke to me through the book of Hebrews, assuring me that if I would do what I knew was right He would take care of His promises, even if my faith-feelings were weak or nonexistent.

The writer closes this part of his teaching by reminding his Jewish-Christian readers of the wonderful position they have through their relationship with Jesus, the Son of God.

"For we who have believed do enter that rest" (Hebrews 4:3 NKJV). Through their initial faith in Jesus as <u>Savior</u> they have a personal relationship with God. Their eternal destiny is settled and sure. And now, in this relationship, they can hear the guiding Word whispered by the Holy Spirit as they search the Scriptures, respond to it, and experience rest despite their trying circumstances. Truly what they—and *you and me too*—have in Jesus Christ, the Son of God, who is higher than angels and greater than Moses, is *"so great a salvation!"*

**Savior**
Acts 16:30–31;
Romans 5:7–10

**united to Jesus**
Romans 6:5–14;
8:10–11

## It's God's Rest

**HEBREWS 4:3b–5**
*"So I swore in My wrath,*
*'They shall not enter My rest,'"*
*although the works were finished from the foundation of the world. For He has spoken in a certain place of the seventh day in this way: "And God rested on the seventh day from all His works"; and again, in this place: "They shall not enter My rest."*
*(NKJV)*

Earlier I noted that the "rest" the writer of Hebrews offers his stressed-out audience of Jewish Christians is God's rest. I suggested it was God's rest because only God can provide believers with peace and tranquility in trying circumstances. Now the writer is about to take us into a deep and wonderful mystery. The rest we are offered is not only provided by God. *It is in fact the same rest that God Himself experiences!*

In verse 3 we're told that "we who have believed do enter that rest." As Christ's own, <u>united to Jesus</u> we are now free to hear and respond to God's every word as gospel, good news. We have the potential now of experiencing that unique rest which God Himself experiences.

## The Seventh Day

**HEBREWS 4:4** *For He has spoken in a certain place of the seventh day in this way: "And God rested on the seventh day from all His works"; (NKJV)*

**consequences**
Genesis 3

**promises**
Genesis 26:2–4
Genesis 28:13–15

**sages**
scholars and inter-
preters of the Old
Testament

The "certain place" to which the writer alludes is Genesis 2:2, which tells the story of Creation. The writer of Genesis carefully traces the accomplishments of each creative day, and as he tells his story he marks each with the phrase, "So the evening and the morning" were the first day (Genesis 1:5), the second day (Genesis 1:8), the third day (Genesis 1:13), and so on. But after the sixth day this formula is abandoned and the Scripture says:

**GENESIS 2:1–2** *Thus the heavens and the earth, and all the host of them, were finished. And on the seventh day God ended His work which He had done, and He rested on the seventh day from all His work which He had done.* (NKJV)

The Jewish **sages** were quick to note that while the biblical text implies a beginning to the seventh day, no evening is mentioned. To them this indicated that God's seventh day has never ended. God is still at rest!

## God's at Rest but Not Asleep

It was clear from history that God's rest did not imply that He was inactive. In fact the Old Testament record makes it clear that God remains actively involved in human affairs. When Adam and Eve sinned, God confronted them in the Garden of Eden and laid out the terrible <u>consequences</u> of their act. God spoke to Abraham (Genesis 12:1–3, 7) and gave him wonderful <u>promises</u>, which He later confirmed to Abraham's son Isaac and grandson Jacob.

God then sent angels to destroy Sodom (Genesis 18–19), and He performed terrible miracles which forced Egypt's ruler to release His Israelite slaves (Exodus 5–11). God parted the sea so Israel could escape a pursuing army (Exodus 14), and God thundered from Mount Sinai when He gave Israel His law (Exodus 19, 20). Again and again the Old Testament portrays God acting decisively to punish or to bless His people. No, whatever God's "rest" implied, it did not indicate an inactive or uninvolved Deity.

But what, then, can the Scriptures mean when they say God *"rested from all His work"*?

# Finished!

**HEBREWS 4:3b** . . . *although the works were finished from the foundation of the world.* (NKJV)

The clue that gives us the answer is found in this verse fragment. The writer states that God's works were finished "from the foundation of the world." The Genesis account of creation is a picture of God planting a seed. Like the seed of any plant, the universe God created contained the full-grown plant. Genesis tells us of the beginning. The rest of the Bible and history itself tell us what grew from that beginning. God's "work" was to design—not just the beginning of everything—but also the end toward which history would move. God's work was to foresee every future event, and to work out ahead of time His solution to every problem. And with every problem solved, God was—and is—able to rest.

Think what this means for you and me. In any circumstance we face, any problem we encounter, God has already worked out the solution!

No wonder each word from God is gospel, good news. For the word God speaks to us guides us to the very solutions we struggle so hopelessly to discover! If we mix His word with faith—if we trust Him so completely that we follow the path He lays out—we find rest. In fact, we enter *His* rest, for only through a faith response to God's Word can we find the solutions He has worked out *"from the beginning of the world"!*

## Does God Really Know Everything?

There's a debate these days among **theologians** about God's relationship to time. Some hold that God is time-bound and works through events with us; that He has no more idea of what lies ahead than we human beings do. This kind of God is as much a captive to circumstances as we are, although He's better equipped to figure out what to do. Others hold the traditional view that God is above and outside of time. God knows what has happened, what is happening, and what will happen. God truly is **omniscient**.

The writer of Hebrews comes down firmly on the side of the traditionalists. The God who offers us rest is Himself at rest because He had the end in sight from the beginning. He is at rest because He

key point

**theologians**
those who study the nature and purposes of God

**omniscient**
knows everything

knows what will happen and has planned for every contingency. No matter what humans or **demons** may do, history moves toward God's intended end.

## Free Will?

What about **"free will"**? Many reject the idea that the path of history has been determined from the beginning. They're fearful that this would mean that human beings live without choices. Yet hasn't God **predestined** what will happen? In that case, aren't we helpless pawns, our supposed "free will" overridden by decisions God has already made?

The answer is no. Our choices are free and we are responsible for them. The gospel word comes to us, but whether we take it as good news or bad news is up to us. God knows what decision we will make, but He does not coerce us.

The reason can be found in the view that God is outside of and above time. You and I are locked in the flow of time. We remember the past. We experience the present. And the future remains unknown. Each present moment we make choices, and those choices are real; they do determine what lies ahead for us.

But to God, outside of time, our past, present, and future are all present! God doesn't know our future because He has robbed us of free will. God knows what seems to us to be the future because for God it's the present.

An illustration may help. You're in a canoe on a winding river. You don't know what lies around the next bend, whether a quiet pool or raging rapids. But you have a friend with a cell phone on a high hill who can see the whole stream. He can see those rapids because, while they're future to you, they are present to him. So he calls your cell phone and warns you. "You better come ashore here. There are rapids ahead."

Now, you might ignore his warning, and plunge into the rapids. Or you might heed the warning and follow his suggestion. But the point is, his knowledge of what lurks around the corner didn't determine your choice. You made the choice freely and without coercion.

Similarly, God sees the rapids that lie ahead for His people, and He knows what will take us to safety. God speaks to us—in His Word, by His Spirit, or in any of those ways we look at elsewhere in this book. But we are the ones who choose. We respond with faith, taking His Word as good news—or with rebellion, taking His Word as bad news. The fact that God knew what was ahead, or even that He knows the choices we will make, in no way determines what we will do. We have free will. We are responsible for our choices—and for their consequences.

## Entering God's Rest

God is at rest because He knows what will happen, and has worked out solutions to every problem. God invites us to enter His rest—to experience the solutions He's had worked out from before the foundations of the world. Only those who have believed in Jesus (Hebrews 3a) can experience His rest. Believers experience His rest by continuing to trust Him so completely that we do as He says when we hear His voice.

Those who take any gospel word as bad news, like the generation that refused to obey God's command to enter Canaan, "shall not enter My rest" (Hebrews 4:5 NKJV).

## Rest Today

> HEBREWS 4:6–10 *Since therefore it remains that some must enter it, and those to whom it was first preached did not enter because of disobedience, again He designates a certain day, saying in David, "Today," after such a long time, as it has been said:*
> *"Today, if you will hear His voice,*
> *Do not harden your hearts."*
> *For if Joshua had given them rest, then He would not afterward have spoken of another day. There remains therefore a rest for the people of God. For he who has entered His rest has himself also ceased from his works as God did from His. (NKJV)*

Here the writer makes a significant point. He has been arguing from Psalm 95. That psalm was written in the time of David, long after the Exodus generation was dead and gone. Yet in the psalm the inspired writer speaks about "today." The implication is clear. If the promise of rest was only for the Exodus generation, a psalm written hundreds of years later in David's time, would not have said "today." To the Old Testament scholar who wrote Hebrews the application

was clear. The promise of rest is still valid! "There remains therefore a rest for the people of God" (Hebrews 4:9 NKJV).

In every "today" God's people are invited to listen for a word from God and, mixing that word with faith, to experience God's rest.

## <u>Original Rest</u>

We've seen that the word "rest" suggests peace and tranquility. It has a slightly different emphasis in the book of Numbers. God promised Abraham that his offspring would possess Canaan, the Promised Land. They would live there, in a land that "flows with milk and honey" (Numbers 13:27 NKJV). Despite the richness of the land, that first generation of freed slaves refused to obey <u>God's command</u> to take it. Forty years later, when that first generation died out, their children were given an even more detailed promise:

> DEUTERONOMY 8:7–10 *For the LORD your God is bringing you into a good land, a land of brooks of water, of fountains and springs, that flow out of valleys and hills; a land of wheat and barley, of vines and fig trees and pomegranates, a land of olive oil and honey; a land in which you will eat bread without scarcity, in which you will lack nothing; a land whose stones are iron and out of whose hills you can dig copper. (NKJV)*

Once again the Israelites were given the command to go over the Jordan River to dispossess "nations greater and mightier than yourself" (Deuteronomy 9:1 NKJV), and this time the Israelites trusted God and did as He said. The record of their victories is found in the book of Joshua, and the land God had promised became theirs. They entered His rest—finding peace and security in the Promised Land.

In this first instance, the "rest" that God provided was material and physical as well as emotional. For a time Israel was secure, in possession of a prosperous land and unchallenged by any enemies.

But Israel's occupation of Canaan only partially fulfilled God's promise of rest. The promise of rest was still available to those who lived in David's *"today."* Then, too, whoever heard God's voice and welcomed what He said with an open heart could experience God's rest for themselves. That rest might involve a change of circumstances. Or, it might simply be emotional and spiritual, the experience of inner peace despite difficult or even desperate circumstances.

**God's command**
Deuteronomy 1:26

The voice of God, that personal word to individuals, guides believers to solutions that God in His wisdom and love has already worked out to all their problems. And such solutions do not always mean that our problems go away.

thorn in the flesh
2 Corinthians 12:7

## Resting with a Thorn

The experience of the apostle Paul illustrates this. The great first-century missionary and writer of thirteen books of the New Testament experienced a debilitating illness, which he calls his "thorn in the flesh." Paul tells us:

> 2 CORINTHIANS 12:8–9 *Concerning this thing I pleaded with the Lord three times that it might depart from me. And He said to me, "My grace is sufficient for you, for My strength is made perfect in weakness." Therefore most gladly I will rather boast in my infirmities, that the power of Christ may rest upon me.* (NKJV)

In other words, God didn't change Paul's circumstances by answering his prayer for physical healing. Instead, God gave Paul grace and enabled him to minister in spite of his infirmity. And with that grace He gave His apostle inner peace.

## David's Responses to the Voice of God

The life of David, Israel's greatest king, teaches us additional lessons about the nature of rest and the significance of responding when we hear God's voice. David usually heeded the voice of God—but not always!

key point

Each of the following charts deals with a different event in David's life. As they demonstrate, at times David hardened his heart and rebelled. Read through each one carefully to follow the ebb and flow of David's fortunes, and those who were affected by what he did.

### Main Events in David's Life

**David and Goliath (1 Samuel 17)**

| | |
|---|---|
| **Situation** | A giant Philistine challenges an Israelite army to send out a champion to fight him. All the Israelites are terrified. |
| **God's Voice** | David knows God is the the "living God" and fights for his people. |
| **Response** | David goes out to meet the giant Philistine warrior. |
| **Outcome** | David kills Goliath, the Philistines flee, and the Israelites win a great victory. David is given officer rank in Saul's army. |

# Main Events in David's Life (cont'd)

### David and the Priests of Nob (1 Samuel 21)

| | |
|---|---|
| **Situation** | Saul is intent on killing David. David flees, and asks the priests of Nob for food and a weapon. |
| **God's Voice** | David sees a man named Doeg there, and realizes that Doeg will report the priests to Saul |
| **Response** | In spite of the danger to the priests, David lies about being on a mission for King Saul and receives their help. |
| **Outcome** | Saul orders the murder of the priests. David confesses to the one surviving priest that he knew he was putting the priestly family in danger. |

### David at Keilah (1 Samuel 23)

| | |
|---|---|
| **Situation** | The Philistines attack the Israelite city of Keilah. David asks God whether he should try to help. Later, when Saul sends an army unit to capture David, David asks if the people of Keilah will surrender him. |
| **God's Voice** | David seeks answers from a priest who asks God for guidance using a special instrument God provided to Israel's high priest. Through the high priest God tells David to go to Keilah's aid, and later that the citizens of Keilah will hand him over to Saul. |
| **Response** | David obeys God's word and goes to help Keilah. |
| **Outcome** | The people of Keilah are saved. Later David flees the city and escapes Saul's forces. |

### David and Abigail (1 Samuel 25)

| | |
|---|---|
| **Situation** | David is angered by an insult from a man named Nabal. He hurries toward Nabal's ranch, intending to murder him. On the way Abigail, Nabal's wife, intercepts him. |
| **God's Voice** | Abigail reminds David that it's wrong to avenge yourself "with your own hand" and urges David to rely on God to avenge him. |
| **Response** | David heeds Abigail's advice and lets Nabal and his men live. |
| **Outcome** | Nabal has a stroke and dies. David, impressed with Abigail's strength and wisdom, marries her. |

### David and Ziklag (Samuel 29, 30)

| | |
|---|---|
| **Situation** | David has become discouraged and leads his men to Philistia, where he promises to fight for one of the Philistine kings. The king gives David and his men the city of Ziklag. David conducts raids against Israel's enemies, but tells the Philistine king he's been raiding in Israel. When a war between the Philistines and Israel is about to start, David is expected to fight against his own—and God's!—people. |
| **God's Voice** | The other kings of the Philistines don't trust David and force the king to whom David swore allegiance to send David home. |
| **Response** | David returns to Ziklag to find his city has been attacked by raiders and his men's families taken captive. Now David asks God what to do, and is told to follow the raiders and recover the women and children, which he does. |

## Main Events in David's Life (cont'd)

### David and Ziklag (Samuel 29, 30) (cont'd)

| | |
|---|---|
| Outcome | David is saved from having to fight against his own people. When he follows God's guidance and pursues the raiders he recovers the captive family members and takes much booty. |

### David and Bathsheba (2 Samuel 11, 12)

| | |
|---|---|
| Situation | From the top of his palace David sees a beautiful women taking a bath at night in her own courtyard. David's passion is aroused. |
| God's Voice | David knows very well the Old Testament's prohibition against having sex with another man's wife (Leviticus 18:20). |
| Response | David hardens his heart and violates God's command. He sends men to bring her to him and has sex with her. When later she notifies him that she's pregnant, David arranges for her husband to be killed so his rape will remain a secret. |
| Outcome | David is confronted by the prophet Nathan and forced to confess his sin. The child he has fathered dies in infancy. Because David's sin had become public David has to make a public confession, which he does by writing Psalm 51. |

Many other stories of David further illustrate how God spoke to David in his "today," and the consequences of David's response or rebellion. The few that I've included illustrate two important truths:

**1.** God's "today" word comes to us in various ways.

**2.** How we respond to God's voice has an impact on us and on others.

## How God's "Today" Word Comes to Us

God spoke to David in various ways. He spoke to David:

- through what David already knew about the Lord (David and Goliath)
- through David's conscience (David and the priests of Nob)
- through an Old Testament priest (David at Keilah, and Ziklag especially)
- through a godly woman's advice (David and Abigail)
- through the moral commands of Scripture (David and Bathsheba)

In all these cases, David recognized the voice of God even though he failed at times to respond to the message with faith.

the solution
1 Corinthians 10:13;
Matthew 7:24;
James 1:22–25

# The Impact of Response to God's Voice

Disaster followed when David rebelled against the voice of God, not only for David but also for others. If David had heeded his conscience the priests of Nob would have survived. If he had heeded God's written commandments he would have overcome his lust, and Bathsheba would not have been raped or her husband murdered. The consequences of rebelling against God's voice are exactly as Isaiah described: "There is no peace . . . for the wicked" (Isaiah 48:22 NKJV).

On the other hand, when David welcomed God's Word and responded to it, both he and others were blessed. An Israelite army was saved when David trusted God and fought Goliath. David saved an Israelite city when he drove the Philistines from Keilah, and he won a wise wife when he recognized God's voice and heeded Abigail's advice. David failed to seek guidance from God when he took his men to Philistia and settled in Ziklag.

The point the writer to the Hebrews makes is a vital one. God speaks to believers in every era. He spoke to the Exodus generation. God spoke to their children. God spoke to David and David's contemporaries. And God speaks to you and me in our own time. The challenge now, as then, is not so much to recognize God's voice as to be committed to respond when He speaks to us.

what others say

### Jerry Vines

The Holy Spirit explores the deep treasures of God and the truths which God has in store for those who love Him. Spiritual revelation is not something we achieve; it is something we receive.[6]

The good news is that "there remains therefore a rest for the people of God" (Hebrews 4:9 NKJV). When we enter that rest, we too cease from our works "as God did from His" (Hebrews 4:10 NKJV). Rather than struggle constantly to find our own way through difficult circumstances ("our works"), we look to God to lead us. Then we hear His voice, and mixing His Word well with faith, we find the solution He has already worked out for us. And we enter into God's rest.

**Wilda Green**

Never does God force acceptance of his promises upon us. Instead we are urged to a boldness of belief, and a daring trust which leads to experiences we can have in no other way. For the follower of Christ, his promises are not optional. We cannot refuse God's gifts and still have a life which is enriched and nourished by his gifts. God's promises challenge our faith to accept and to make them the aim of our lives.[7]

## The Scalpel's Edge

**HEBREWS 4:12–13** *For the word of God is living and powerful, and sharper than any two-edged sword, piercing even to the division of soul and spirit, and of joints and marrow, and is a discerner of the thoughts and intents of the heart. And there is no creature hidden from His sight, but all things are naked and open to the eyes of Him to whom we must give account. (NKJV)*

As he concludes this section of his teaching, the author of the book of Hebrews reminds us that the word of God is "living and powerful." The word of God is not simply the ancient texts whose translations we read. Nor as we face challenges in our lives will we hear God's voice only in some specific verse. After all, David recognized God's voice speaking to him through his general knowledge about God, through his conscience, and through the advice of a godly woman as well as through the Leviticus 18:20 prohibition of adultery.

Nor are we to expect God to direct each individual down the same path. Should you homeschool your children? For some Christian families the answer will be "Yes." For others the answer will be "No." Should you accept the promotion at work even though it means you have to move your family? Again, for some the answer will be "Yes" and for others "No." Should a young person dedicate his or her life to be a missionary? Some definitely should. But others definitely should not. While Scripture makes it clear that some choices are always morally wrong, it doesn't speak directly to every individual with questions about life choices he or she is facing now.

That's why it's so important to recognize that God speaks to us in various ways, and that each individual believer is to hear and recog-

key point

nize God's voice speaking to him personally. That's why we are told in Hebrews 4:12 that the word of God "is living." God is able to communicate with each believer and point out the path that is best for him or her.

## God Really Knows Us

**HEBREWS 4:12** . . . *sharper than any two-edged sword and is a discerner of the thoughts and intents of the heart. (NKJV)*

key point

The image here is not of a weapon, but a surgical instrument. God's living word is a scalpel, capable of dissecting even to the division of soul and spirit. God's living word knows us better than we know ourselves, for the Lord is aware of every thought and intent of our hearts.

What a blessing this is! When we hear God's voice directing us, we can be sure that He has taken everything about who we are into account. He knows our deepest needs, our greatest weaknesses, our fullest potential. And so, when we hear His voice we can welcome it as gospel, for it is a word just for us as individuals. For example:

- Kelly and Jennifer each want to go to secular colleges. Their moms are worried that going to a state school may involve temptations they're not ready to meet. Both girls have been active in church youth groups and are professing Christians. Only God knows Kelly and Jennifer so well that He can guide the girls and their families to the choice that is right for each of them.

- Barry lives in Southern California. He's been offered a job in the Midwest by a Christian organization. But Barry is concerned about his three young children. It's winter now, and he doesn't have enough money to buy them warm clothing if they should move. What choice should Barry make? Only God knows the best choice.

- Celeste is eager to get married. She wants children desperately. But is Frank the right person? Is she mature enough at twenty to handle the pressures of married life? Should she wait for a different man, or wait until she matures more?

No Bible proof text provides specific guidance to any of these people. But the word of God is "living and powerful." God can and will speak to each and will offer guidance. But it will still be up them, when they hear His voice, to accept the word they hear as good news and follow Him, or to hear His word as bad news and rebel.

The truly good news is that "all things are naked and open to the eyes of Him to whom we must give account" (Hebrews 4:13 NKJV). God is omniscient. He knows all things, and He knows what is best for us. And just as wonderful, God's word is "living and powerful." God can and does speak words of guidance to believers—living words that are directed to us individually—powerful words that we recognize as His, whatever agency He may use to speak them.

And so it's no wonder that the author, so eager to encourage and exhort his fellow believers in Jesus in Jerusalem, repeats it again and again: "Today, if you will hear His voice, do not harden your hearts."

No, open your hearts. Listen for God's word to you. And when you recognize His voice, welcome His guidance as the gospel, the good news that it is.

Obey His living word.

And find rest.

# Chapter Wrap-Up

- God invites believers to experience His rest, an inner peace and tranquility that we can know whatever our circumstances.
- When we hear God's voice we have the choice of responding to it with faith, or rebelling against the One who speaks to us.
- God has a contemporary "voice" and speaks to believers in their "today."
- God's "living and powerful" word provides guidance to believers shaped to their circumstances and individual characteristics.

# Study Questions

1. What are several **synonyms** for rest?

2. In what two ways is the rest God promises "His rest"?

3. What should be our focus when we experience trials or difficult circumstances?

4. How is God able to guide us in the best possible path for our lives?

5. What is the significance of "today" in Hebrews 4?

6. Why must each individual believer listen for and heed God's voice?

# Part Two
# HEBREWS 4:14-7
# THE BRIDGE

# Hebrews 4:14–5:11 Jesus Priest!

**Chapter Highlights:**
- The Bridge
- Jesus's Credentials
- The New/Old Order of Melchizedek
- Eternal Salvation

## Let's Get Started

The first four chapters of Hebrews gave persecuted first-century Christian Jews plenty to think about. Many in Jerusalem were tempted to abandon Jesus and rely again on the older revelation. Thus the writer confronts them with the fact that in Jesus, God's Son, they have a revelation far more wonderful and complete than the one given by angels and through Moses. Rather than drift back into an Old Testament way of life, they need to hold fast to the hope they have in Christ. They must not follow the example of the Exodus generation, which rebelled when God commanded them to enter Canaan. That hard-hearted generation refused to trust God, and so missed the rest God had prepared for them.

At this point the author discussed in the previous chapter: *The God who spoke to ancient Israel speaks to His people in every "Today."*

If only these Jews remain committed to Jesus, God will speak to them as well. They will hear His voice, and God's voice will guide them through their own difficult circumstances. God, who knows all, also has an intimate knowledge of each individual and will speak living words of guidance to each believer. Responding to God's voice, even the most harassed will find rest.

With this first theme developed, the writer of Hebrews now turns to a point-by-point comparison of Old and New Testament faiths. He looks at critical elements of the religious system God gave to Israel. He shows how Old Testament religion was but a shadow of the real thing. He then shows us the real thing—Christ—who, unknown to Israel, was portrayed in the shadow images all along. How foolish these early Jewish Christians would be if they abandoned reality in favor of mere copies of heavenly truths!

As we read this stunning New Testament letter today, we're instructed on the significance of Old Testament practices of which we may have been unaware. Far more than that, we're reminded of the unimaginable blessings that you and I have in Jesus Christ.

**go to**

**430 years**
Galatians 3:17

**Hebrew people**
Israelites, Jews

## The Superiorities of Christ in Hebrews 4:14–10:18

| Fact | Hebrews | Blessing |
|---|---|---|
| Jesus is a superior priest. | 4:14–5:11 7:1–8 | He provides eternal salvation. |
| Jesus administers a superior covenant. | 8:1–13 | The New Covenant transforms from within. |
| Jesus offers a superior sacrifice. | 9:1–10:18 | His blood purifies us from all sin and gives us access to God. |

# The Bridge

HEBREWS 4:14–16 *Seeing then that we have a great High Priest who has passed through the heavens, Jesus the Son of God, let us hold fast our confession. For we do not have a High Priest who cannot sympathize with our weaknesses, but was in all points tempted as we are, yet without sin. Let us therefore come boldly to the throne of grace, that we may obtain mercy and find grace to help in time of need.* (NKJV)

These verses plunge us into one of the most significant elements in Old Testament religion: the priesthood. What was the priesthood and why was it necessary? We know it is significant, for the Hebrew word for "priest," *kohen (cohen)*, occurs over 700 times in the Old Testament. In the structure of traditional Hebrew religion, a priest and his sacrificial offerings were every Hebrew's bridge over which to enter into fellowship with God. But to better understand that we need to review some Old Testament history.

# Roots of the Priesthood

For some <u>430 years</u> the descendants of Abraham, Isaac and Jacob lived in Egypt. Welcomed at first, as the **Hebrew people** grew in numbers they were later enslaved by the Egyptians. During these centuries their knowledge of God was limited. They knew that God had spoken to their forefathers. They knew that God had promised that Abraham's offspring would be given the land of Canaan. But beyond stories and folktales they knew little about their God.

Then around 1450 BC an aged man trudged out of the Sinai desert with a stunning message. The God of their forefathers was about to win their freedom and lead them to the Promised Land! The old man, Moses, was welcomed by the suffering slaves and ridiculed by Egypt's ruler. But a sequence of powerful miracles that devastated Egypt forced Pharaoh to free the Hebrews. Some two and a half million Israelites (or more!) then set out across the desert, following Moses.

God personally led this multitude with a pillar of fire, and after additional miracles brought the whole company to a mountain in the Sinai peninsula. There God called Moses up to the top of the mountain, and while thunder clouds and lightning shrouded the peak He gave Moses the Ten Commandments and additional laws that the Hebrews were to follow.

The awed multitude, waiting at the base of the mount, then committed themselves to worship the Lord who had freed them, and to keep His rules and commandments. With this **Law Covenant** ratified, God committed to bless those generations of Israelites that were obedient and to punish any generations that broke the Law.

But what about the individual who **sinned**? Violating God's commands or rules breached the relationship a person had with the Lord. How could that relationship be mended? What could a person do to get back into a harmonious relationship with the Deity?

## Contract for Building a Bridge to God

It is here that the priesthood enters. When God gave the Israelites His moral law and other rules for living. He also provided them with a priesthood. It was the duty of the priests to represent flawed human beings before God, by offering sacrifices and offerings that would restore or enrich an individual's personal relationship with Israel's God.

At the same time the priests were to represent God to the people, communicating His teachings and showing the Israelites how to live a **holy** life. Those offerings and sacrifices are shown on the chart below.

**powerful miracles**
Exodus 5–11

**pillar of fire**
Exodus 13:21

**additional miracles**
Exodus 14:21–31;
15:25; 16:11–18

**thunder clouds and lightning**
Exodus 19:16–19

**committed**
Exodus 24:1–3

**bless**
Deuteronomy
28:1–14

**punish**
Deuteronomy
28:15–68

**sinned**
James 2:10–11

**breached the relationship**
Isaiah 59:2

**Law Covenant**
a legally binding agreement that spelled out rights and responsibilities of God and His Old Testament people

**sinned**
broke the law

**holy**
obedient, blameless

### Old Testament Sacrifices and Offerings

| Offerings | Contents | Significance |
| --- | --- | --- |
| Burnt offerings Lev. 1; 6:8–13 | An unblemished bull, ram | A voluntary offering symbolizing complete surrender to God |
| Grain (meal) offering Lev. 2; 6:1–23 | Grain, flour, or bread, with olive oil and salt | A voluntary offering made with burnt offerings, symbolizing devotion to God |

**ritual uncleanness**
Numbers 5:1–4;
9:6–12;
Leviticus 13:45–46

**for causes see**
Leviticus 11–15

**atonement**
Leviticus 6:24–30;
12:6–8

**all sinned**
Romans 3:23;
Ecclesiastes 7:20

**ritual uncleanness**
a condition in which
a person could not
participate in the
community's life or
worship

**atonement**
a sacrifice that deals
with guilt so that a
person is brought
back into right rela-
tionship with God

**guilty**
has in fact violated
God's command and
is due punishment

### Old Testament Sacrifices and Offerings (cont'd)

| Offerings | Contents | Significance |
|---|---|---|
| Fellowship (peace) offering Lev. 3; 7:11–36 | An unblemished animal from flock or herd | The meal following symbolizes fellowship with God and thanksgiving |
| Sin offering Lev. 4:1–5:13 | The very poor could offer fine flour | A required offering for **ritual uncleanness** symbolizing **atonement** |
| Guilt offering Lev. 5:14–6:7; 4:12–18 | Unblemished ram or lamb | A required offering when a person steals or in another way violates another individual's rights |

## But There's a Problem

LEVITICUS 4:13, 22, 27; 5:15 *Now if the whole congregation of Israel sins unintentionally and they have done something against any of the commandments of the LORD in anything which should not be done, and are guilty; When a ruler has sinned, and done something unintentionally against any of the commandments of the LORD his God in anything which should not be done, and is guilty; If anyone of the common people sins unintentionally by doing something against any of the commandments of the LORD in anything which ought not to be done, and is guilty. If a person commits a trespass, and sins unintentionally in regard to the holy things of the LORD. (NKJV)*

Each of these verses, which introduce the sin offering to be officiated at by Israel's priests, has one important thing in common. Each specifies that the sacrifice is for *unintentional* sins! If an Israelite sinned willfully, knowing what he was about to do was a violation of God's will, no sacrifice made by any ordinary priest could cover that sin. There might be hundreds or even thousands of priests in Israel at any given time, but they were all powerless to provide atonement for intentional sins. And, unfortunately, the position of Scripture is that "all have sinned."

## "I Did It My Way!"

The Old Testament vocabulary of sin is a rich one. The most common word for "sin" is *hata'*, a word which pictures the sinner falling short of the standards God sets for human beings. While the other Old Testament words for sin each imply actions measured against a divine standard, the actions are different. The Hebrew word *pesa'* portrays a sin which is a conscious revolt against the standard. And the Hebrew word *'awon* describes deviation from or twisting of the divine standard. Tragically, we human beings are prone to react to the standards God has set in each of these ways. And so the psalmist says:

PSALM 14:1b–3
*They are corrupt,*
*They have done abominable works,*
*There is none who does good.*
*The LORD looks down from heaven upon the children of men,*
*To see if there are any who understand, who seek God.*
*They have all turned aside,*
*They have together become **corrupt**;*
*There is none who does good,*
*No, not one. (NKJV)*

And the prophet Isaiah adds, "All we like sheep have gone astray; we have turned, every one, to his own way" (Isaiah 53:6 NKJV).

If the Old Testament priests were truly powerless to atone for intentional sins, then no Israelite could have hoped to remain in touch with God. So God provided a unique, once-a-year solution.

## One and Only High Priest

While many Old Testament priests might serve at the same time, there was only one high priest. His ministry in Israel's religion was unique. While ordinary priests might offer sacrifices for unintentional sins, the high priest, and then only once a year, offered a sacrifice for the nation and its people that made atonement "for all their sins" (Leviticus 16:34 NKJV).

This sacrifice took place on Israel's most holy day, the Day of Atonement (Yom Kippur). On that day the high priest entered the most sacred room in the temple—a room-inside-a-room, both of which were hidden from view by thick curtains. Only the priests could go into the first room, and only the high priest himself could go beyond the final curtain into the inner room, sometimes called the "Holy of Holies" or the "Most Holy Place." And even the high priest could enter that room only on the Day of Atonement.

**legal**
according to
God's system of
jurisprudence
revealed in the Law
of Moses—Leviticus
16, for example

# The Mercy Seat

Within the most sacred room was an object called the Ark of the Covenant. On the box-like Ark was a gold cover, bearing the figures of two golden angels whose wings were outspread and whose gazes were fixed on the center of the cover. The place where their gaze met was the symbolic location where God met with human beings and accepted the annual sacrifice of blood as the covering (atonement) for their sins. This meeting place was called the "mercy seat."

The high priest entered the sacred room carrying a basin filled with the blood of a bull that had been killed as a sin offering. Carefully, reverently, the high priest sprinkled the blood on and around the mercy seat. The theological word for the **legal** transaction taking place between God and people at the mercy seat is "propitiation" (1 John 2:1–2 NKJV); the act of appeasing another person's anger by the offering of a gift, in this case a sacrifice (see Hebrews 9:4–5).

> **what others say**
>
> **D. R. W. Wood**
>
> "Propitiation" is a reminder that God is implacably opposed to everything that is evil, that his opposition may properly be described as "wrath," and that this wrath is put away only by the atoning work of Christ.[1]

# O Happy Day!

The chapter describing events of the Day of Atonement concludes with these words:

> **LEVITICUS 16:33–34** *and he shall make atonement for the priests and for all the people of the assembly. This shall be an everlasting statute for you, to make atonement for the children of Israel, for all their sins, once a year. (NKJV)*

Two things are vitally important in Leviticus 16: First, God does provide atonement for intentional as well as unintentional sins. There is a blood sacrifice that covers "all" sins. And second, only one person in all of Israel was qualified to make that sacrifice—the high priest.

All this was clear immediately to first-century Jewish Christians. In stating, "We have a great High Priest" (4:14 NKJV), the writer of

Hebrews thus made it crystal clear that Jesus was the one and only person who could provide cleansing from all sin. The only hope these first-century Jewish believers had for forgiveness of all their sins was to rely on Jesus Christ. Go back to the old system? Never! Rather, "Let us hold fast our confession" (Hebrews 4:14 NKJV).

**go to**
with God and as God
John 1:1–14

## Jesus's Credentials for High Priesthood

The writer lists several things that are special about our High Priest, Jesus:

- He has passed through the heavens (4:14)
- He is the Son of God (4:14)
- He can sympathize with our weaknesses (4:15)
- He dispenses mercy (4:16)
- He is the source of grace to help in our time of need (4:16)

The high priests of the old system were mere humans, earthbound creatures born on our planet who lived out their lives here, died, and were buried. But our High Priest comes from heaven. He was a man and lived a human life, but His origin and destiny are heavenly. He "passed through the heavens" (Hebrews 4:14 NKJV), both in His descent into our universe and in His return to take His rightful place in glory.

The writer of Hebrews has underscored this in chapters 1 and 2. Our High Priest is no mere man. He is God in the flesh, the second person of the Holy Trinity who, from the beginning, has existed <u>with God and as God</u>. Later in this letter the writer will point out that human priests die (Hebrews 7:23–24) but the Son of God lives forever, and His endless life guarantees our salvation (Hebrews 7:25). This man did it all, including dying and rising again from the dead (1 Corinthians 15:3–4).

something to ponder

## Sympathizes with Our Weaknesses

Our High Priest lived a true human life. In this verse "weaknesses" are not moral flaws or fallen nature. The weakness the writer has in mind is our vulnerability to all those pressures and stresses we human beings experience. As humans we're subject to hunger and thirst, to physical

go to

**as a "man"**
Matthew 4:4

**angels would keep**
Psalm 91:11–12;
Matthew 4:6–7

**fast**
to go without food

pain and exhaustion. As humans we are emotionally vulnerable. We hurt when we're ridiculed. We suffer when those we love fail to love us in return. We feel the ache of rejection, the sting of unfulfilled dreams, the grief of loss. Because Jesus was a real human being, He experienced all these pressures and knows what it means to be human.

## In All Points Tested/Tempted

As the writer says, Jesus was "in all points tempted as we are, yet without sin" (Hebrews 4:15 NKJV). The Greek word translated "tempted" also means "tested." The word "tempt' in English has an unhealthy connotation. "Temptation" seems subjective; it suggests that something in us is being drawn toward doing wrong. We think of someone who is "tempted" as attracted to some supposedly delightful sin. The "temptress" of literature is a woman who entices, and every man can imagine the pull of her allure. But "test" connotes something entirely different. A test is something objective, outside of us. A test may be difficult, but "test" doesn't imply the person being tested has any evil intent.

In this passage the phrase "tempted as we are" may be read "tested as we are." The mere fact of being human, of having human physical needs and human emotions, means that we will be tested all the time. And Jesus too was tested. We see this clearly in the account of Christ's temptation [testing] by Satan (Matthew 4:1–11; Luke 4:1–13). Each of the Gospel accounts tells us Jesus was famished after a 40-day **fast**. When Satan challenged Him to use His powers to turn stones into bread, Jesus refused. His Father had sent Him to live a truly human life. He would meet life's challenges as a "man," not as the Son of God.

Another of Satan's temptations [tests] focused on emotions. Satan suggested that Christ leap from the top of a temple wall. Since God had promised angels would keep Him from dashing a foot against a (pavement) stone. The appearance of angels to save Him would win Jesus instant acceptance by the people. Why should Christ spend futile years teaching and preaching, only to be rejected and crucified in the end? Each of us knows how much rejection hurts. It hurt Jesus too, for Christ was a true human being. Yet Jesus chose the will of God over expedience (Matthew 4:10). During His years on earth

Jesus experienced every test that human nature forces upon us, and He passed each one "without sin."

## Tempted but Without Sin

I struggled for many years with doubt that Jesus, as Matthew and Luke describe His temptation, had the foggiest idea how I experience temptation. He had it easy. The devil appeared to Him, and tried to entice Jesus with "temptations" that were so obvious even a *nebbish* like me could see through them.

In paintings, movies, and other depictions of the temptation event, the devil is invariably pictured approaching Jesus in some visible humanoid or reptilian form. Yet nowhere in the New Testament stories does it say the Tempter appeared. The NKJV correctly translates it from the original Greek, "The tempter came to Him" (Matthew 4:3 NKJV) and "The devil said to Him" (Luke 4:3 NKJV). If Jesus was tempted like I am, the enemy never showed his actual face.

The tempter didn't have to bring up the subject of food. Jesus was already thinking about food. Temptations like these had plagued Him for almost six weeks (Luke 4:2). Most, apparently, having to do with Jesus's commitment to do His Father's will and the completion of His mission. The master plan led through the cross. If there was any way to bypass that ghastly experience and still do the right thing, humanly speaking, any sane flesh-and-bones earthling could be expected to hope for a way around it.

Without bread the man Jesus could die of starvation. It was not an evil thought nor was it lust. It was simply what every human being would be thinking after 40 days of hunger. But, as noted above, He was on earth to live life as a man, a fully human man. Furthermore, if His mission for the Father was to be completed, everything in His life, including every decision and motivation, must be in full harmony with the master plan of God. The temptations, as told by Luke and Matthew, were all calculated to entice Jesus to take an easier, quicker, less painful path to save the world He loved.

If Jesus had to walk with God and interact with the spiritual world like you and I do—by faith, not by sight (2 Corinthians 5:7)—it is probable that temptation came to Him like it does to us—not as an outward struggle with an easily identifiable enemy, but as a some-

**Satan's highway**
Ephesians 2:2

**forgive**
1 John 1:8–2:2;
John 18:24–27 with
John 21:15–19

**sympathy**
compassion, love,
pity

**grace**
that attitude of
acceptance and love
God displays toward
us in Jesus

times confusing war raging inside the mind, involving emotions and imagination.

Personally, the devil has never appeared to me by laying his enticements before me like a tray of exotic hors d'oeuvres. With me the tempter sneaks up behind and tiptoes through my imagination. If your mind is in tune with God's Word and is spiritually sensitized by experience in applying biblical principles to the situations of your life, you are more likely to know it right away when a suggestion is contrary to the nature of God and His way of doing and thinking. To the person used to seeking to do God's will, spiritual and moral baloney is easier to spot and avoid. With experience comes the knowledge that every idea that pops into a believer's mind is not necessarily something God is saying.

Knowing that in Jesus we have a God who fully understands the human condition, and is filled with **sympathy** for us, the writer of Hebrews invites us to come boldly to the "throne of **grace**." There we will find "mercy and . . . grace to help in time of need" (Hebrews 4:16 NKJV).

## Mercy

Mercy is the loving compassion that moves God to come to a human being's aid. The New Testament tells us that "God, who is rich in mercy, because of His great love with which He loved us, even when we were dead in trespasses, made us alive together with Christ" (Ephesians 2:4–5 NKJV). God reached down to helpless sinners who by nature traveled <u>Satan's highway</u> and shared His life with them. Even as now mercy moves our Savior to <u>forgive</u> our failures, to lift us up, and to set us on His path again.

## Grace to Help

Our High Priest dispenses grace as well as mercy. As He overcame the tests human nature imposes on every individual, so He is able to help us overcome. God promises that the One who "raised Christ from the dead will also give life to your mortal bodies" (Romans 8:11 NKJV), enabling us to meet and to pass life's tests.

The author of Hebrews will have more to say about this in chapter 8. For now he is intent on demonstrating to his Jewish readers that, even under rules laid down by Moses, Jesus is fully qualified to be our "great High Priest."

## So You Want to Be the High Priest?

**HEBREWS 5:1–4** *For every High Priest taken from among men is appointed for men in things pertaining to God, that he may offer both gifts and sacrifices for sins. He can have compassion on those who are ignorant and going astray, since he himself is also subject to weakness. Because of this he is required as for the people, so also for himself, to offer sacrifices for sins. And no man takes this honor to himself, but he who is called by God, just as Aaron was. (NKJV)*

Not just anyone could serve the Israelite community as an ordinary priest, much less as High Priest. One of the first questions an early Jewish Christian would ask when told that Jesus holds the position of High Priest was: Is He qualified? The writer of Hebrews answers this question by reminding his readers that a high priest must:

- Be a human being
- Be called to the priesthood by God

## A Human Being

Hebrews' statement that high priests are "taken from among men" and are appointed "for men" is significant (5:1 NKJV). There is no parallel priesthood in the spiritual universe, for angels or demons. The whole system of sacrifices and offerings was devised by God specifically for humankind. Angels do not sin and require no priests or sacrifices. And demons are wholly committed to evil. As the writer of Hebrews stressed in chapter 2, the Gospel of Christ is for humanity alone. Christ came to:

key point

**HEBREWS 2:15–16** *release those who through fear of death were all their lifetime subject to bondage. For indeed He does not give aid to angels, but He does give aid to the seed of Abraham. (NKJV)*

worship system
Exodus 20;
Leviticus 9

**worship system**
a way of relating
God that included
laws and rules for
holy living, a central-
ized gathering place
for worship [the tab-
ernacle, and later
the temple], a
priesthood, sacri-
fices, and a fixed
religious calendar

Salvation is therefore a matter between God and human beings only. And that's why Hebrews 2:17 continues "in all things He [Jesus] had to be made like His brethren, that He might be a merciful and faithful High Priest" (NKJV).

Only by becoming a human being could the Son of God become the sacred bridge on which sinful human beings and a holy God might meet.

It is no slight matter that the prime requirement for selection into the priesthood is that a priest must be a human being. His sympathies must be with *people*. God doesn't need sympathizers. But people will never touch God without the aid of a mediator to argue for their acquittal. A priest must be committed to God and his fellow strugglers.

# The Call

But it took more than being human to become high priest. The one who would serve as high priest had to be called to this position by God Himself.

**what others say**

**Philip Edgcumbe Hughes**

Indeed, if one thing is stressed throughout the New Testament it is that, assuming the office of savior and high priest, so far was the Son from exalting and glorifying Himself that he accepted it knowing full well that meant Him the experience of the darkest depths of humiliation, rejection, agony and death. His office-bearing was the furthest possible from self-glorification.[2]

When Moses established the Old Testament **worship system** under God's personal supervision, Moses, under God's instructions (Exodus 28:1) appointed his brother, Aaron, to serve as high priest. At the same time Aaron's sons were appointed to serve as ordinary priests. Other members of the clan descended from Jacob's son Levi (the Levites) were set aside to assist at the worship center. But only a direct descendant of Aaron was qualified to serve as priest or high priest. God called only Aaron's family out of all the families in Israel to the priesthood. No member of any other Hebrew family line was qualified to be a priest.

So the question these Jewish Christians must have asked the author of this letter when he presented Christ as our "great High Priest" (Hebrews 4:14 NKJV) was: Where in Scripture is Jesus, a descendant of the clan of Judah—not Levi—called by God to serve as High Priest?

To this challenge the writer of Hebrews has an unexpected answer.

## The New/Old Priestly Order of Melchizedek

> HEBREWS 5:5–6 *So also Christ did not glorify Himself to become High Priest, but it was He [God] who said to Him:*
> *"You are My Son,*
> *Today I have begotten You."*
> *As He also says in another place:*
> *"You are a priest forever*
> *According to the order of Melchizedek";* (NKJV)

In answering the challenge the writer of Hebrews first quotes a line from Psalm 2. God is speaking in verse 7. The Psalm does not imply that Jesus is a secondary God, created by the Father. Instead, these words constitute the official proclamation that Jesus is God's "*Anointed*," the one the Father has chosen to rule from heaven and on earth (Psalm 2:4, 6). The same Jesus whom God appointed King, He also appointed a "priest forever."

The second quote is from Psalm 110. Again there is no question that God is speaking, or that He is speaking to the Son. Like Psalm 2 this is a psalm that predicts and celebrates **Messiah**'s triumph. And imbedded among images of the Messiah's rule over earth's nations is His divine appointment to the priesthood.

## Melchizedek?

> PSALM 110:4 *The LORD has sworn and will not relent, "You are a priest forever according to the order of Melchizedek."* (NKJV)

Of all the Old Testament characters we might expect to show up in the New Testament, Melchizedek is one of the least likely. He briefly touches the <u>life of Abraham</u> and surfaces again only in Psalm 110. Peeking out only twice from among the thousands of verses in the Old Testament, we would hardly expect him to be as significant as he really is.

go to

**Anointed**
Psalm 2:2

**life of Abraham**
Genesis 14:18

**anoint**
to pour or smear oil on someone to signify that he or she has been officially chosen, consecrated and empowered for a particular office or ministry; the "Anointed One" is "Christ"

**Messiah**
the Christ, the Anointed One

**tithe**
tenth, ten percent

Genesis 14 tells the story of a raid on Palestine by a coalition of northern kings. The raiders penetrated the South all the way to the plains city of Sodom, where Abraham's nephew Lot had settled (Genesis 13:10–12). When Abraham realized his nephew had been captured he followed with his servants. Attacking by night, Abraham drove off the raiders and rescued Lot. He also freed the other inhabitants of Sodom and recovered all the spoils the raiding kings had taken.

On the way back, Melchizedek, the king of Salem (later Jerusalem), who was also "the priest of God Most High" (Genesis 14:18 NKJV) fed and blessed Abraham. Abraham responded by dedicating to Melchizedek a **tithe** of the spoils. Abraham then went on his way and returned to his tents. Later in Hebrews the writer will carefully dissect this passage and find surprising significance in every detail. For now, however, the writer hurries on, having established a vital point.

Jesus's priesthood isn't like the priesthood held by Aaron and his sons. It finds its source not in Aaron, but in another priest entirely. Jesus is a priest "according to the order of Melchizedek" (Hebrews 5:6 NKJV).

## Garden of Tears

HEBREWS 5:7–10 *who, in the days of His flesh, when He had offered up prayers and supplications, with vehement cries and tears to Him who was able to save Him from death, and was heard because of His godly fear, though He was a Son, yet He learned obedience by the things which He suffered. And having been perfected, He became the author of eternal salvation to all who obey Him, called by God as High Priest "according to the order of Melchizedek." (NKJV)*

Having established Jesus's call by God to the High Priesthood, the writer of Hebrews shifts his focus to the man Himself, and focuses on an incident that was critical in Christ's ability to fulfill His High Priestly mission. Earlier we saw that Jesus passed the tests that Satan designed at the beginning of Jesus's ministry (Matthew 4; Luke 4). Now the writer focuses our attention on a test that God designed, which took place near the end of Jesus's life on earth. The language of these verses, with their references to "supplications, with vehement

key point

cries and tears" (Hebrews 5:7 NKJV), makes it clear the writer is referring to what happened in the Garden of **Gethsemane** the night before Christ was crucified. Let's look again at the familiar story.

**Gethsemane**
"olive oil press"

Jesus has just finished sharing a last meal with His disciples. During the meal, Judas, one of the twelve men who had been with Christ since He began to preach and teach, left before the meal was over. Judas had agreed with Christ's enemies to turn Him over to them for thirty silver coins. After the meal was over Jesus led the remaining eleven to a hill outside Jerusalem where they often stopped to rest and pray. Christ was obviously disturbed, and went a little way off to pray. Luke describes the scene:

LUKE 22:40–45 *When he came to the place, He said to them, "Pray that you may not enter into temptation." And He was withdrawn from them about a stone's throw, and He knelt down and prayed, saying, "Father, if it is Your will, take this cup away from Me; nevertheless, not My will, but Yours, be done." Then an angel appeared to Him from heaven, strengthening Him. And being in agony, He prayed more earnestly. Then His sweat became like great drops of blood falling down to the ground. When He rose up from prayer, and had come to His disciples, He found them sleeping from sorrow.* (NKJV)

what others say

**David R. Anderson**

The second qualification of any priest was that he be sympathetic. Somehow he had to be able to identify with those he served. The Levitical priests could do this simply because they too had their weaknesses and sins, just like their constituency. But the Son had no weaknesses or sins, so how could he sympathize with those he served? The answer to this question is found in the suffering of the Son described in Hebrews 5:7–9. Like any great leader, the Son did not ask His followers to do anything he was not willing to do. He too suffered undeservedly for His convictions, just as the Hebrews were undoubtedly doing. And it hurt.[3]

**Robert H. Smith**

Although he was a Son, in spite of his absolutely unique ranking among all the children of God, in spite of his superiority to angels and Moses, he was not exempt from the severest discipline of pain and suffering.[4]

*something to ponder*

It's common to take the "cup" Jesus prays about as His coming crucifixion. And the prospect of death on the cross truly was terrifying. The victim hung with outstretched arms nailed to a crossbar, his knees bent and a spike driven through his ankles. As his body sagged his chest compressed painfully as he struggled for breath. Only by lurching upward and bearing the agonizing stabs of pain in his ankles could the victim relieve the great pain in his chest and catch a breath. Many struggled for hours or even days before surrendering to their fate. Clearly, crucifixion was terrible enough to cause most human beings to tremble and cry out at the prospect.

Others have seen a deeper concern reflected in Jesus's cries at Gethsemane, a terror of the moment when Christ would cry out from the cross, "My God, My God, why have You forsaken Me?" (Mathew 27:46 NKJV).

**what others say**

**Lawrence O. Richards**

As terrible as the physical suffering was, it did not compare with the spiritual anguish that Jesus experienced. How could it be that in this awesome moment the Godhead itself was torn apart, Son separated from the Father, and spiritual death experienced by he who is the source of eternal life?[5]

We could certainly understand this "awesome moment" being the cup that Jesus begged the Father to take from Him. But the writer of Hebrews gives us a fresh perspective on Gethsemane. For he tells us Christ prayed to God as "Him who was able to save Him from death" and, significantly, that Christ's prayer "was heard" (Hebrews 5:7 NKJV).

*key point*

The Old Testament scholar who wrote the book of Hebrews was fully aware of the significance of the word "hear" in the Hebrew Scriptures. The verb, translated both "hear" and "listen," occurs some 1,050 times there, not to mention its many derivatives. While at times "hear" simply describes the physical act, when the Scripture speaks of humans "hearing" God the word implies an obedient response. And when God's people ask God to "hear" their prayers they are asking Him to answer them, not simply take note. When Hebrews asserts that Jesus's prayer "was heard" the writer is saying unequivocally that Jesus's Gethsemane prayer was answered! God did as His Son requested.

If this is the case, then the cup Jesus begged not to drink could hardly have been crucifixion, or even the moment that Jesus became "sin for us" (2 Corinthians 5:21 NKJV) and the Father forsook Him. The cup must have been death, not as momentary separation from God but as an everlasting doom. For when Jesus bowed His head and took on Himself the sins of the world, He was incapable of raising Himself.

Jesus's prayer was answered. And on that first Easter Sunday the power of God the Father flowed into the inert body of Jesus Christ. And His Spirit returned. His body was transformed by a <u>surge of divine power</u>, and Jesus Christ exited His tomb.

> **ROMANS 1:3–4** *Jesus Christ our Lord declared to be the Son of God with power according to the Spirit of holiness, by the resurrection from the dead.* (NKJV)

Gethsemane was the ultimate test for Jesus. In spite of the possibility of endless death, Jesus submitted, praying, "Nevertheless, not as I will, but as You will" (Matthew 26:39 NKJV).

Gethsemane established once and for all that the man, Jesus, acted at all times out of *"godly fear"*—a reverence for God that moved Him to be ever-obedient to the voice of God. It also established another important fact. *God answers Jesus's prayers!* We'll see how vital this is later when the writer reminds us that Christ "always lives <u>to make intercession</u>."

As High Priest the living Jesus prays for us, and His prayers are always answered. No wonder He is able to "save to the uttermost those who come to God through Him" (Hebrews 7:25 NKJV).

## Author of Eternal Salvation

> **HEBREWS 5:8–9** *though he was a Son, yet He learned obedience by the things which He suffered. And having been perfected, He became the author of eternal salvation to all who obey Him.* (NKJV)

Nothing that happened on earth changed Jesus in His essential deity. Taking on humanity didn't alter the fact that the Son was as much God as the Father and the Holy Spirit. Yet the writer tells us that He "learned obedience by the things which He suffered" (Hebrews 5:8 NKJV).

**surge of divine power**
Romans 8:11;
1 Corinthians
15:40–49

**to make intercession**
Hebrews 7:25

There are some things that a person can only learn by personal experience. We may see others riding a bicycle. We may read about riding a bicycle. A bicycle rider may explain how a person rides a bicycle. But we *learn* to ride a bicycle only by getting on a bike and riding it.

"Obedience" is the same. We may know that obedience means acting as another instructs or commands us. We may see others do it. We may read about people who were obedient. We may even read "how to" books designed to help us obey. But we only *learn* obedience by being obedient. What's more, we only learn obedience by the things that we suffer!

Suppose a parent tells his or her child, "Eat this ice cream cone." Or that the same parent says, "Forget your homework. Go play with your friends." Or "Stay up late tonight and watch TV." Do you think that child is learning obedience? Hardly, for each of these commands is in complete harmony with what the child already wants to do!

But what if the parent says, "Eat your spinach. It's good for you." Or if the parent says, "Finish your homework before you go out to play." Or "No more TV. It's time for bed." These commands are different. They conflict with what the child wants to do. It's going to hurt to obey these commands.

But learning to obey commands to do something you don't want to do is the only way a person really learns obedience.

Jesus didn't want to be hungry after His fast. But it was God's will for Him to live among us as a human, willingly setting aside His divine powers to live with our human limitations. Jesus didn't enjoy being rejected by His friends and neighbors and countrymen. But He chose to be subject to human weaknesses in obedience to His Father.

Most of all, Jesus didn't look forward to the physical or spiritual pain of crucifixion, or the dark chasm that yawned before Him after death. But Jesus submitted to God's will, and obeyed. Jesus truly "learned obedience by the things which He suffered" (Hebrews 5:8 NKJV).

In the book of Philippians the apostle Paul describes Christ's attitude and urges us to adopt it. He writes:

**obey**
here, believe in,
respond appropriately to

**PHILIPPIANS 2:4–8** *Let each of you look out not only for his own interests, but also for the interests of others. Let this mind be in you which was also in Christ Jesus, who, being in the form of God, did not consider it robbery to be equal with God, but made Himself of no reputation, taking the form of a bondservant, and coming in the likeness of men. And being found in appearance as a man, He humbled Himself and became obedient to the point of death, even the death of the cross.* (NKJV)

None of us like to suffer. Too often the prospect of some kind of a "hurt" will make us hesitate to obey God. But we need to follow Jesus's example and learn obedience by being obedient. Only then will we be equipped for whatever service God intends for us.

At the same time, *only then will we receive the wonderful things that God has planned for us!* For Philippians 2 takes us beyond the suffering to the true outcome of obedience.

**PHILIPPIANS 2:9–11** *Therefore God also has highly exalted Him and given Him the name which is above every name, that at the name of Jesus every knee should bow, of those in heaven, and of those on earth, and of those under the earth, and that every tongue should confess that Jesus Christ is Lord, to the glory of God the Father.* (NKJV)

## Salvation to the Max

**HEBREWS 5:9–10** *And having been perfected, He became the author of eternal salvation to all who obey Him, called by God as High Priest "according to the order of Melchizedek . . ."* (NKJV)

We've commented on the idea of "perfection" before. The Greek word carries the idea of being full grown, mature, of achieving full potential. Here Jesus is pictured as having been fully qualified through His obedience to the Father, for the task the Father set before Him—to be the author (source) of salvation for all who themselves **obey** Him.

key point

Jesus is our High Priest. He alone is able to provide forgiveness for all our sins and bring us into a personal relationship with the Father. How tragic it would have been if these early Jewish Christians had turned back to a priesthood that, as we will see, has now been set aside.

## And Now, a Digression

**HEBREWS 5:10–11** *"according to the order of Melchizedek," of whom we have much to say, and hard to explain, since you have become dull of hearing.* (NKJV)

We can sense the writer's frustration here. He wants to communicate so much. But because the Jewish Christians are so dull of hearing he finds it increasing difficult to explain. He wants to say much more about the Melchizedekian (There's a three-dollar word!) priesthood. But will these foolish Christians ever understand?

So, before he goes on about Melchizedek, the author is going to insert another warning, a personal exhortation addressed to believers who are spiritually immature. We'll look at that warning in the next chapter.

## Chapter Wrap-Up

- Old Testament priests offered God gifts and sacrifices on behalf of the people.
- Only the high priest could offer the Day of Atonement sacrifice that atoned for unintentional and intentional sins.
- Jesus, a true human being, was called by God to serve as High Priest and provide those who believe in Him with an "eternal salvation."

## Study Questions

1. Why was the Old Testament priesthood instituted?

2. What kinds of sins or violations of the law couldn't an ordinary priest deal with?

3. What does the word "atonement" mean in relation to Old Testament sacrifices?

4. What are several special things about the Old Testament high priesthood?

5. Why is it that Jesus can sympathize with our weaknesses?

6. What does Hebrews 4:15 mean when it says Jesus was "tempted"? What doesn't it mean?

7. What two qualifications for the high priesthood does the writer emphasize?

8. What is the name of the Old Testament priest Jesus's priesthood is modeled on?

# Hebrews 5:12–6:20
# Stop Being a Big Baby and Grow Up!

## Let's Get Started

The writer of Hebrews is a passionate person. He teaches carefully and logically. But he can't resist inserting fervent **exhortations** and warnings. "Beware, brethren" (Hebrews 3:12 NKJV), he warns in one place. "Consider" (Hebrews 3:1 NKJV), he pleads. He urges his readers, "Let us hold fast" (Hebrews 4:14 NKJV) and "Let us therefore come boldly to the throne of grace" (Hebrews 4:16 NKJV).

This writer is more than a teacher. He's an old-fashioned preacher. He can't help getting excited about his message, and he passionately appeals to the people to whom he is preaching to act on the truths he's explaining. And like the old-fashioned preacher, he doesn't hesitate to spell out the painful consequences if his listeners don't respond!

This is why several large sections of Hebrews are called "warning" passages. In them the writer bluntly states what will happen if we don't listen.

We've already worked through one of these longer "exhortation" or "warning" sections. In Hebrews 1:1–3:6 the writer presents Jesus as God's ultimate revelation, His final Word to human beings. In 3:7 through 4:13 he issues a stern warning: "Today, if you will hear His voice, do not harden your hearts" (Hebrews 3:7, 15; 4:7 NKJV).

In other words, if the Christian Jews to whom he is writing harden their hearts now, they will never experience God's rest. Disobedience to God's living word in Christ means years of emptiness and emotional wandering, even as the Exodus generation was forced to wander in the desert for forty years until every one of them died (Numbers 14:22–34)!

The most important message the writer of Hebrews brings is the truth that, in Jesus Christ, God has given believers—which would include modern Christians, first-century Gentile converts, and first-century, once-Jewish-but-now-fulfilled-through-Jesus-the-Messiah Jews—their one and only "great High Priest" (Hebrews 4:14 NKJV).

**exhortations**
encouragement, guidance, urgings

**Annas 1, etc.**
all the high priests
from time of Jesus
through AD 48

**oracles**
revelations, truths

Now, you and I might at first puzzle over what a high priest should mean to us, and perhaps some of the early Gentile Christians did too. But the Jewish believers in Christ in Jerusalem instantly knew—at least in a traditional "Jewish" sense.

Turning to Christ as their Messiah left "Jesus Jews" without access to the high priest and his sacrificial ministry. Probably nothing involved in the conversion process was more confusing. After more than three decades as followers of Jesus, you'd think they'd have understood that Jesus now filled the role of High Priest for them. Think of it. Three decades! And still in the dark! Hello?

I don't know how long it took for a letter from Italy to get to Judea, but it was urgent. Hurting brothers and sisters needed its message. In the nick of time! Just when it looked like everything was dark, "To the Hebrews" arrived with great news that was on the brink of slipping away. Lift up your heads, wounded soldiers:

*Jesus is our one and only High Priest and bridge to God*

You no longer need **Annas 1, Caiphas, Jonathon, Ananias, and Annas 2**, or any of that family of spiritual shysters appointed by Rome, not according to Mosaic Law.[1] Let 'em go! Jesus is all the High Priest you will ever need from now on! None other!

Just as he begins to explain, the writer breaks off in frustration to launch into an extended exhortation; a warning that spells out what many have taken as the most terrible consequence of all. It's this powerful and frightening passage that we explore in this chapter.

## It's High Time You Grew Up!

HEBREWS 5:12–14 *For though by this time you ought to be teachers, you need someone to teach you again the first principles of the **oracles** of God; and you have come to need milk and not solid food. For everyone who partakes only of milk is unskilled in the word of righteousness, for he is a babe. But solid food belongs to those who are of full age, that is, those who by reason of use have their senses exercised to discern both good and evil.* (NKJV)

We sense the author's frustration in verse 11; a verse that serves as a bridge between his introduction of Christ as High Priest and his extended exhortation.

**HEBREWS 5:11** . . . *of whom [Christ, the great High Priest] we have much to say, and hard to explain, since you have become dull of hearing.* (NKJV)

Like a schoolteacher struggling to get bored teens to pay attention, the writer of Hebrews seems almost at the end of his rope. How can he get through to these people? It's usually not a good teaching strategy, but the writer can't help confronting his readers.

- You don't *listen* ("dull of hearing")
- You're way *behind* ("by this time you ought to be teachers")
- You need to go back to *kindergarten*! ("you need someone to teach you *again* the first principles" [italics added])

## Political Correctness Can't Cut It Here

Some people today think it's simply not politically correct to confront students who fail to learn. After all, we might damage their fragile self-esteem. Never mind that failing to learn in school is likely to result in a lifetime of minimum-wage jobs.

But the writer of Hebrews doesn't hesitate to confront. His students are in far greater danger than simply sentencing themselves to life of poverty. They are in danger of turning away from Christ for a religious system that has served God's purposes but has now been replaced. So the Hebrews author speaks bluntly and plainly, to shock his readers into paying attention. "Hang on to your high chairs, kiddies! It's time to grow up!"

key point

## The First Principles

In Greek philosophy the "first principles" were the most difficult. The first principles were the realities that lay beneath what human beings could see and experience. The Greeks were convinced that underneath this world of flux and change there must be *something* that was stable and unchangeable. For centuries they thought and studied and tried to imagine what these fundamental building blocks might be, and many candidates were suggested. But the writer of Hebrews isn't a Greek philosopher, and his first principles aren't hidden truths at all. His first principles are the most basic starting points in coming to know God.

something to ponder

Imagine that you've been invited to share a meal with a person from a different culture who knows nothing of the Christian God. What would you tell him first? What are the basic truths he'd need to grasp to make sense of the rest? Here are a few ideas:

key point

- "God" is the Person who created everything that exists, including human beings.
- Human beings are in rebellion against God. This rebellion separates us from the Creator and makes us selfish and hostile in our relationships with each other.
- God continues to love us. He is eager to restore our broken relationships with Him, and to heal the damage we do to ourselves and to others.
- To accomplish these purposes, God Himself became a human being and died on a cross, taking the punishment we rebels deserve.
- God invites us to have personal relationships with Him, and to be healed within, if we will simply trust the God who, in dying, paid the price for our rebellion.

There's much more to say about each of these first principles, and God has revealed many, many additional wonderful truths. But these five are the basic truths a person needs to understand to commit himself to Jesus.

The Jewish Christians to whom Hebrews was written *did* understand the first principles. They knew God as Creator. Israel's history was evidence of the impact of humankind's rebellion, as well as evidence of God's continuing love. And these Jews had accepted Jesus as Son of God and Messiah; they had committed themselves to Christ as Savior.

So what does the writer mean when he says someone needs to "teach you" these first principles "again"? Simply this—he is saying, "You know the first principles, but *you still don't get it!* If you'd gotten it, you'd never have given a second thought to going back to classic Judaism without Jesus Christ as your Head Priest."

something to ponder

## Milk-Fed Babies

HEBREWS 5:12–13 *you have come to need milk and not solid food. For everyone who partakes only of milk is unskilled in the* *word of righteousness, for he is a babe. But solid food belongs to those who are of **full age**. (NKJV)*

**full age**
mature, grown up

Once again the writer of Hebrews is using a familiar word, *teleios* (in the noun form, or *teleioo* in the verb form), which we have already encountered in chapter 4 of this book. As we indicated earlier, the word emphasizes *completion* and is translated in a variety of ways in both Hebrews and other books of the New Testament.

- A *teleios* person is one who is "mature," "full grown" or "of full age" (Hebrews 5:14; 6:1).

- A *teleios* love is "perfect love," complete and whole-hearted (1 John 4:18).

- A *teleios* power is one that is completely, fully expressed (1 Corinthians 12:9).

- A sacrifice that makes the believer "perfect" (*teleios*) is one that has completed the task set for sacrifices (Hebrews 7:19).

- Jesus was "perfected" (*teleios*) in that His sufferings as a man fully equipped Him for His High Priestly ministry by enabling Him to sympathize with human beings (Hebrews 5:9).

- A *teleios* Christian is one who is experienced with living the teachings of Christ, applying His principles to the situations of life as it unloads its surprises, a believer who is becoming discerning, that is, able to tell right from wrong. She/he is becoming skilled in avoiding evil choices and making good ones (Hebrews 5:14).

In the present passage the reference to "of full age" indicates that the first readers of this Letter to the Hebrews were *immature* believers. They'd never grown up. Why? Because they were fixated on "milk" and were "unskilled in the word of righteousness" (Hebrews 5:13 NKJV).

## Bridge Construction—How Priests Are Made

Suffering through thirty-some years of human experiences—the kind of rough-and-tumble experiences that make strong men cry—

**believer priests**
Exodus 19:5–6;
1 Peter 2:5, 9;
Revelation 1:5–6

prepared Jesus to serve as High Priest and Author of eternal salvation (Hebrews 5:7–10). Meanwhile, His followers' application of Scripture, which teaches them to make good choices and thus helps them survive life's tough stuff, also uniquely equips them to serve as <u>believer priests</u> for one another.

**what others say**

### John MacArthur

Jesus knew first hand the drive of human nature toward sin. It is here that Jesus faced and fought sin. He was victorious, but not without the most intense temptation, grief and anguish.[2]

## Pablum Passages?

Some have misunderstood parts of Hebrews and have tried to divide Scripture into "milk" and "meat" passages. They've suggested that prophetic or other hard-to-understand passages are the "meat" of Scripture, while less-difficult passages are the "milk." But this isn't the Hebrews writer's point. He's saying they're "unskilled in the word of righteousness" (Hebrews 5:13 NKJV).

The phrase "word of righteousness" can be taken in more than one way.

*key point*

*It may mean that the word itself is righteous.* This idea is as old as the grassy hills around Bethlehem. David, shepherd king of Israel, composer of most of the Psalms, sings to the Lord about His word in Psalm 119:105–106:

> *Your word is a lamp to my feet*
> *And a light to my path.*
> *I have sworn and confirmed*
> *That I will keep Your righteous judgments. (NKJV)*

and in Psalm 119:137:

> *Righteous are You, O LORD,*
> *And upright are Your judgments. (NKJV)*

Another possible meaning of "word of righteousness" is that the Word of God *produces* righteousness. The Word that the writer of Hebrews has already described as "living and powerful" (Hebrews 4:12 NKJV) works within the believer to yield a righteous and godly life. Thus in the Old Testament's great poem in praise of God's Word, David sings:

PSALM 119:99–104
*I have more understanding than all my teachers,*
*For Your testimonies are my meditation.*
*I understand more than the ancients,*
*Because I keep Your **precepts**.*
*I have restrained my feet from every evil way,*
*That I may keep Your word.*
*I have not departed from Your judgments,*
*For You Yourself have taught me.*
*How sweet are Your words to my taste,*
*Sweeter than honey to my mouth!*
*Through Your precepts I get understanding;*
*Therefore I hate every false way.* (NKJV)

David was skillful in applying God's Word to his own life. His meditation on the life-meaning of Scripture gave him wisdom, helped him restrain his feet "from every evil way," taught him to hate "every false way," and kept him from "[departing] from" God's judgments. Because of the good results of applying the Word in his life, David takes genuine delight in God's Word. Hearing, studying, and meditating on it are like eating rich dessert! "Sweeter than honey," insists Israel's singing king.

It is right here that these early Christian Jews have fallen short. They know the "first principles," but they simply aren't "skillful" in seeing their implications. They need to be taught all over again, for they've never seen what these basic Gospel realities have to do with their daily lives. They are spiritual babes. But spiritual maturity comes through a rough-and-tumble process involving facing every circumstance of life with the question, "Where are You trying to lead me, Lord?"

## Use It or Lose It

HEBREWS 5:14 *But solid food belongs to those who are full age, that is, those who by reason of use have their senses exercised to discern both good and evil.* (NKJV)

This verse makes it very clear. These Jewish believers are wavering between going on with Christ or going back to Judaism because they aren't "of full age." They've never grown up spiritually. They have missed the blessing Jesus provides His people because they haven't applied what truths they know, in dealing with their own circumstances. Truth is to be used or else we never grow up.

Every Christian is to meditate on, and **keep** God's Word daily.

## Discerning Good and Evil

A believer matures as David did. He exercises his ability to discern between "good" (*kalos*) and "evil" (*kakos*). The implication is that when a believer comes to any fork in his path, he will use the Word of God to distinguish the good way from the evil one.

There are two Greek words translated "good" in the New Testament, *kalos* and *agathos*. While the two are often treated as synonyms, there are shades of difference between them. Typically, when moral issues are involved, New Testament writers choose *agathos*, which implies that the right thing to do is also the most beneficial. On the other hand, *kalos* tends to represent the ideal and the beautiful. *Kalos* good is in full harmony with God's ideal in every respect.

It's significant that the writer chose to use *kalos* here. Too often Christians tend to think of Scripture as a divinely inscribed list of moral do's and don'ts. But many of the decisions we make have no moral implications. Should I go to work here, or there? Should I propose now, or wait until later? Is this local church right for my family, or is it that one? These decisions aren't moral ones, but they're important. And we want to make *good* choices; choices that are in fullest harmony with God's ideal will for our lives. In such cases we can't look to the obvious do's and don'ts of Scripture. But we are to meditate on God's Word and search for principles that may guide us to choose the *kalos*-good.

We're to use God's Word to discern His will, and we're to make choices that are *good*.

Similarly, the writer's choice of *kakos* for evil rather than another Greek word, *poneros*, [pronounced pone-a-ros] is significant. *Poneros*, the stronger word, has definite moral implications and is often translated "wicked." On the other hand, *kakos* depicts that which is flawed, which falls short of God's best.

The problem, then, isn't that the recipients of this New Testament letter have no concept of the "first principles" of their Christian faith. The problem is that they don't apply what they know to help them make the choices their situation forces on them. Our author has no choice but to try to shock them back to their senses by confronting them with their failure.

But what the writer has just said isn't nearly as shocking—or perhaps as frightening?—as what he is about to say.

## You Can't Go "Home" Again

**HEBREWS 6:1–6** *Therefore, leaving the discussion of the elementary principles of Christ, let us go on to perfection, not laying again the foundation of repentance from dead works and of faith toward God, of the doctrine of baptisms, of laying on of hands, of resurrection of the dead, and of eternal judgment. And this we will do if God permits. For it is impossible for those who were once enlightened, and have tasted the heavenly gift, and have become partakers of the Holy Spirit, and have tasted the good word of God and the powers of the age to come, if they fall away, to renew them again to repentance, since they crucify again for themselves the Son of God, and put Him to an open shame. (NKJV)*

Before we explore this passage, there are several things we should note.

The writer assumes his readers are Christians. They don't need to be saved. They need to "go on to perfection" (Hebrews 6:1 NKJV), i.e., maturity. They don't need to re-lay foundational truths again. They already accept and rely on them.

The writer's concern here, as has been spelled out in verses 12–14, is his readers' immaturity. They simply haven't grown as Christians. If they had, they never would have considered going back "home" to Judaism.

Both Christianity and Judaism rest on the same foundation.

- Each faith calls for "**repentance** from **dead works**."
- Each faith requires "**faith toward** God."

**repentance**
change of heart and behavior

**dead works**
here, self-effort that can lead only to death rather than life

**faith toward**
trust in

- Each faith has its own **doctrine** about baptism and laying on of hands.
- Each faith looks forward to a literal "resurrection of the dead."
- Each faith teaches "eternal judgment."

In Christ, while we build on truths also found in the Old Testament revelation, we "go on to perfection." In Christ, all the promises of the Old Testament are fulfilled, and we are to find our fulfillment in Him.

what others say

**Philip Edgcumbe Hughes**

Alienation from God, who is the source of all life . . . can result only in death; hence the necessity of repentance from dead works and, beyond repentance, of the atonement made available to us by the blood of Christ which purifies the conscience from dead works to serve the living God.[3]

## Don't Just Lie There! Build on It!

It's as if these first Jewish Christians are lying flat on a foundation of cement reinforced with steel rods that have been laid down on solid rock, desperately digging in their fingernails in fear they'll fall off. The frustrated writer of Hebrews is shouting to them, "Get up and build!" They don't need to lay the foundation again—it's super solid and will never give way. They simply need to trust the foundation, build their lives on it, and "go on to perfection" (maturity).

I noted that there are several "exhortation" or "warning" passages in Hebrews. It's helpful before we go on in Hebrews 6 to compare the first two, point by point.

A quick look at this chart makes several things clear. First, two warnings have a similar structure. Each is based on the immediately previous teaching. Each assumes that the readers are believers. Each focuses on a specific concern that the writer has for his audience. Each calls for a specific response. And each warning spells out what will happen if the readers do respond, and if they do not.

key point

## The First Two Warnings

| Passage | Hebrews 3:7–4:13 | Hebrews 5:12–6:20 |
|---|---|---|
| Basic Truth | Jesus is the full and final revelation of God (1:1–3:6) | Jesus is our great High Priest (4:14–5:11) |
| Recipients | Holy brethren, partakers of the heavenly calling (3:1) | Babes (5:13); beloved (6:9) |
| Author's Desire | Do not harden your hearts (3:8); be diligent to enter God's rest (4:11) | Go on to perfection (6:1); show the same diligence to the full assurance of hope until the end (6:11) |
| Negative Response | They harden their hearts when they hear God's voice and do not obey (3:13) | Not go on to maturity |
| Result | They do not enter God's rest (3:11; 4:3) | Bear thorns and briers (be unfruitful, 6:8), become sluggish (6:12) |
| Positive Response | Welcome God's voice, obey and enter God's rest (4:10) | Apply truth (5:14); go on to perfection (maturity, 6:1); show diligence until the end (6:11) |
| Result | Rest; cease from our works as God did from His (4:10) | Bear "useful" herbs; (be fruitful, 6:7); inherit the promises (6:12) |

The first warning is addressed to those who do hear God's voice, urging them to respond. The second warning is addressed to those who are still babes, urging them to apply what they know in their daily lives and go on to maturity. We need to keep the subject of these warnings clearly in view, and to remember that the writer's concern in the second warning is the immaturity of these Jewish Christians.

## Then What About *This*?

> HEBREWS 6:4–6 *For it is impossible for those who were once enlightened, and have tasted the heavenly gift, and have become partakers of the Holy Spirit, and have tasted the good word of God and the powers of the age to come, if they fall away, to renew them again to repentance, since they crucify again for themselves the Son of God, and put Him to an open shame. (NKJV)*

This paragraph has jolted many and led them to fear for their salvation. Can a Christian really "fall away"? And if so, can such a person ever go back and become a Christian once again? This is an issue that theologians debate, with one side arguing that "once saved, always saved," and the other holding that a believer can choose not to believe and pass from a "saved" to a "lost" state. Some have tried to avoid the question by arguing that the people described in this paragraph haven't yet made a final decision about Christ. They are only partially "enlightened" and have merely "tasted" God's heavenly gift, in contrast to eating and digesting it. But this view simply won't stand up.

In Psalm 34:8 David invites, "Taste and see that the LORD is good" (NKJV). Here as always in both the Old and New Testaments, "taste" is used in the sense of "experience." Come, get to know God. Experience Him, and you'll find that the Lord truly is good. In fact "taste" is never used in contrast to "partake." In Hebrews 6, "tasted the heavenly gift" as well as the other descriptive phrases make it clear that the people in view truly have accepted the Gospel message.

But it is hardly clear that "if they fall away" (Hebrews 6:6 NKJV) refers to losing one's salvation. The Greek word *perapipto*, literally, "to fall aside," is used only here in the New Testament. This leaves us with only one option. We must interpret "falling away" within and by its **context** here in Hebrews. And what is that context?

The writer has paused in an exposition of Christ's High Priesthood to warn his readers, who've been considering a return to Judaism, and is about to contrast the High Priesthood of Jesus with the ministry of the Old Testament high priest. His readers must make a choice between the priests of the Old Testament religious system and Jesus—and only High Priest Jesus offers an "eternal salvation" (Hebrews 5:9 NKJV). In this context, "falling away" is going back to rely on the priests of the Old Testament rather than continuing to rely on Jesus alone. Somehow these Christian Jews felt that going back was going "home," where they'd been comfortable.

But this makes no sense at all!

The author's indignation is captured by a **paraphrase** of Hebrews 6:4–6. In these verses the author of Hebrews asks a **hypothetical question**.

"What would you do? Return to Judaism? How then would you ever be restored to your present relationship with the Lord—you who have been enlightened, tasted the heavenly gift, shared in the Holy Spirit, and known the flow of resurrection power? Would you crucify Jesus all over again, and through a new sacrifice be brought back to repentance? Shame! How dishonoring to God to even suggest that Christ's death on the cross isn't sufficient!"

The truth is that Christ's death is sufficient. There's no way that a Christian Jew could abandon Jesus and return to his roots without shaming the Savior. In posing the hypothetical, the writer of Hebrews confronts his readers with something they've failed to think of. It's not an issue of how falling away would affect *them*. The issue is how their turning back to Judaism would reflect on the Savior! Rather than bringing Him honor and glory, abandoning Jesus now would dishonor and shame their great High Priest.

So we must go elsewhere in Scripture to find texts to debate on whether a Christian can be "lost." Here in the second great warning passage in Hebrews the issue is not salvation, but maturity. And this "frightening" paragraph isn't about the impact on those who turn back, but about the impact on God's reputation!

---

**what others say**

**James Thompson**

Jesus Christ died once-for-all (9:26). This "onceness" of Christ's sacrifice has its counterpart in the uniqueness of conversion. The Christian has been once enlightened just as Christ died once. Thus to repeat one's conversion would be to repeat Christ's crucifixion: literally, "to recrucify" the Son of God.[4]

---

## Truth Has Consequences

**HEBREWS 6:7–8** *For the earth which drinks in the rain that often comes upon it, and bears herbs useful for those by whom it is cultivated, receives blessing from God; but if it bears thorns and briers, it is rejected and near to being cursed, whose end is to be burned.* (NKJV)

There are real consequences to the readers of the choice they must now make. And the writer casts those consequences in terms of maturity and immaturity. Will they "go on to perfection" (maturity)? Or will they remain babes? Will their lives be fruitful, or barren? This is a familiar analogy, found frequently in Scripture. God has seeded a field and provided rain. He expects fruitfulness. Land that produces fruit is blessed. But land that produces thorns and briers is useless, its vegetation burned off. The choice the first readers of

key point

Hebrews make, concerning whether they will grow toward perfection, will not determine whether they remain "saved." But it will determine if they experience God's blessing or if their lives will be barren and empty.

## Three Examples

• *Sour Grapes*

ISAIAH 5:1–7 *My Well-beloved has a vineyard on a very fruitful hill. He dug it up and cleared out its stones, and planted it with the choicest vine. He built a tower in its midst, and also made a winepress in it; so He expected it to bring forth good grapes, but it brought forth wild grapes. And now, O inhabitants of Jerusalem and men of Judah, judge, please, between Me and My vineyard. What more could have been done to My vineyard that I have not done in it? Why then, when I expected it to bring forth good grapes, did it bring forth wild grapes? And now, please let Me tell you what I will do to My vineyard: I will take away its hedge, and it shall be burned; and break down its wall, and it shall be trampled down. I will lay it waste; it shall not be pruned or dug, but there shall come up briers and thorns. I will also command the clouds that they rain no rain on it. For the vineyard of the LORD of hosts is the house of Israel, and the men of Judah are His pleasant plant. He looked for justice, but behold, oppression; for righteousness, but behold, a cry for help.* (NKJV)

key point

There's no doubt that the reference to fruitfulness in Hebrews immediately brought this passage to the minds of Jews steeped in the Old Testament. And its implications must have been immediately clear. God would bless them only if they continued on and grew in their Christian faith. While the Lord had never totally abandoned their Old Testament forebears, His judgments on the Israelite generations that failed to produce fruit had been painful indeed.

• *Well Connected*

Jesus used the analogy in a different context, but in the same way.

JOHN 15:1–8 *I am the true vine, and My Father is the vinedresser. Every branch in Me that does not bear fruit He takes away; and every branch that bears fruit He prunes, that it may* *bear more fruit. **Abide** in Me, and I in you. As the branch can-not bear fruit of itself, unless it abides in the vine, neither can you, unless you abide in Me. I am the vine, you are the branches. He who abides in Me, and I in him, bears much fruit; for with-out Me you can do nothing. If anyone does not abide in Me, he is cast out as a branch and is withered; and they gather them and throw them into the fire, and they are burned. By this My Father is glorified, that you bear much fruit; so you will be My disciples.* (NKJV)

When Hebrews was penned the apostle John hadn't yet recorded this teaching of Jesus. Yet it's likely that Christ's words about fruit-fulness were known by many Jerusalem Jews. Here again the impli-cations are clear. Stay close to Jesus and you will bear fruit that glo-rifies God. Cut yourself off from Him and you'll wither. You'll pro-duce no fruit and, like withered and stringy grape vines that have no value and are burned by farmers, you'll reflect no glory on God.

### • Trial By Fire

The apostle Paul uses an analogy similar to the above. After liken-ing the church at Corinth to a field he has planted and another teacher has watered, he shifts focus slightly, telling the Corinthian believers, "You are God's field, you are God's building" (1 Corinthians 3:9 NKJV). Jesus is the foundation of this building, and Paul continues:

**1 CORINTHIANS 3:12–15** *Now if anyone builds on this foun-dation with gold, silver, precious stones, wood, hay, straw, each one's work will become clear; for the Day will declare it, because it will be revealed by fire; and the fire will test each one's work, of what sort it is. If anyone's work which he has built on it endures, he will receive a reward. If anyone's work is burned, he will suffer loss; but he himself will be saved, yet so as through fire.* (NKJV)

Each of these three illustrations makes the same point. After we become believers we are to produce fruit that will glorify God. An unfruitful Christian life is empty and of no value to the Lord. Nor is an unfruitful life rewarded with divine blessing, either in our life on earth or in Eternity.

No wonder the writer of Hebrews urges his readers to go on to maturity. They need to grow up and be fruitful, not remain helpless babes who do nothing to bring glory to God.

**saints**
literally "set apart ones," in the New Testament every Christian is a "saint"

**minister**
serve, support, give aid to

**sluggish**
lazy

what others say

**James Thompson**

It is important in understanding the author's stern warning that he is not dealing with a situation where there are apostates wanting to return to the church. Instead, he is pointing out the danger that threatens the community in order to encourage steadfastness. He is looking forward to the potential apostate, not backward to the actual penitent.[5]

**Oliver Cromwell**

(a motto written in Latin in his pocket Bible):
*He who ceases to be better ceases to be good.*[6]

# Brethren, Hang in There!

HEBREWS 6:9–12 *But, beloved, we are confident of better things concerning you, yes, things that accompany salvation, though we speak in this manner. For God is not unjust to forget your work and labor of love which you have shown toward His name, in that you have ministered to the **saints**, and do **minister**. And we desire that each one of you show the same diligence to the full assurance of hope until the end, that you do not become **sluggish**, but imitate those who through faith and patience inherit the promises. (NKJV)*

Here the writer suddenly softens his tone. He wants to shake up his readers, not turn them off. He doesn't consider these Jewish Christians a lost cause, for he knows that they have already produced *some* fruit. They have shown their love for God in ministering to other believers, and this is something God will not forget. It's just that the writer of Hebrews wants them to display their hope in God "until the end" (Hebrews 6:11 NKJV) rather than become lazy. What will motivate them to keep on serving? The key is the phrase "the full assurance of hope" (6:11 NKJV).

# Hope? What Hope?

In casual conversation, "hope" has an uncertain sound. A friend's "I hope I can make it there on time" is more likely to cause doubt than confidence. But in Scripture, "hope" rings with confident expectation. While Old Testament words translated "hope" imply waiting for something that is yet future, they also <u>focus attention on God</u> who guarantees the future. As David writes,

**PSALM 119:49–50** *Remember your word to Your servant, upon which You have caused me to hope. This is my comfort in my affliction, for Your word has given me life.* (NKJV)

In both Testaments "hope" is a relational term, for any believer's confidence is rooted in personal relationship with the Lord. But in the New Testament there is a slight change in the "future" emphasis. Many of the blessings for which God's people **hope** are to be experienced now. For instance, because the Holy Spirit is at work in believers, the apostle Paul can speak of a "hope of <u>righteousness</u>" (Galatians 5:5 NKJV). Many of the blessings to which ancient Israel could only look forward, Christians can hope to experience here and now!

And the writer of Hebrews urges his readers to continue to show diligence "to the full assurance of hope until the end" (6:11 NKJV). Rather than become lazy in their faith they can "through faith and patience" actually "inherit the promises" (6:12 NKJV).

## When God Promises

**HEBREWS 6:13–18** *For when God made a promise to Abraham, because He could swear by no one greater, He swore by Himself, saying, "Surely blessing I will bless you, and multiplying I will multiply you." And so, after he had patiently endured, he obtained the promise. For men indeed swear by the greater, and an oath for confirmation is for them an end of all dispute. Thus God, determining to show more abundantly to the heir of promise the **immutability** of His **counsel**, confirmed it by an oath, that by two immutable things, in which it is impossible for God to lie, we might have strong consolation, who have fled for refuge to lay hold of the hope set before us.* (NKJV)

Looking back into history the writer of Hebrews points to a pivotal event. God gave Abraham promises, several of which hinged on his having a son with his wife Sarah. This promise was an essential element in carrying out God's plan for humankind. But for decade after decade Abraham and Sarah were childless. During these years the <u>promise was repeated</u>, the last time when Abraham was 99 years

**focus attention on God**
Psalms 31:23–24;
39:7; 71:14

**righteousness**
Romans 8:3–4, 11;
Galatians 5:22–23

**promise was repeated**
Genesis 12:1–3;
15:1–6; 17:1–7

**hope**
confidently expect

**immutable**
unchangeable, sure
and certain

**counsel**
here, God's purpose, his plan

**go to**

**presence rested**
Exodus 29:42–46;
Leviticus 16:2

old! Through it all Abraham continued to believe the God who had promised him a child. Finally, at age 100, the promised son was born (Genesis 21:1–5)!

During these years of waiting, to encourage Abraham's faith God confirmed His promise "by an oath." Genesis 15 relates how God caused Abraham to fall into a deep sleep, and then God passed between the divided halves of sacrificial animals. In Abraham's time this act marked the sealing of the most binding of legal **covenants**. God not only gave Abraham His word; God had His promise "put in writing!" God's purpose in doing this was "to show more abundantly to the heirs of promise the immutability of His counsel" (Hebrews 6:17 NKJV).

There is to be no mistake. When God makes promises, He commits Himself 100 percent. Our God is a promise-making and promise-keeping God!

**key point**

God did keep His promise to Abraham. Yes, there were long years of waiting. But the promised child was born, and God's announced purposes were advanced. What the Christian Jews in Jerusalem don't seem to realize is that God has also made promises to them—and has kept them!

## This Hope

> HEBREWS 6:19–20 *This hope we have as an anchor of the soul, both sure and steadfast, and which enters the Presence behind the veil, where the forerunner has entered for us, even Jesus, having become High Priest forever according to the order of Melchizedek.* (NKJV)

The **institution** of Israel's priesthood was in itself a promise; a promise of access to God. Yet that access was denied by a thick curtain, or veil, that cut everyone off from the Holy of Holies where God's <u>presence rested</u>. Then, centuries later, God confirmed His intention to provide access by swearing an oath to the Son, "You are a priest forever according to the order of Melchizedek" (Psalm 110:4 NKJV). In Christ, God has kept His promise, for Jesus has entered "the Presence behind the veil" (Hebrews 6:19 NKJV) where He serves as our High Priest forever. Through Jesus we now have guaranteed access to God the Father, and are free to "come boldly to the throne of grace" (Hebrews 4:16 NKJV)!

**covenants**
contracts,
commitments

**institution**
inauguration, the
setting up, the
establishment

God's promise has been made—and kept! And we have *this hope*, this settled confidence in our present access to God through Jesus, as *an anchor of the soul, both sure and steadfast.*

what others say

**Robert H. Smith**

Hope, with eyes uplifted and hearts fixed upon the eternal order, is a spiritual anchor. The material world offers no safe harbor for ourselves. Our hope is in a sure and steadfast anchor cast into the heavenly sanctuary, mooring our lives to the unshakeable inner shrine behind the curtain or veil of the Holy of Holies. No storm can shake believers so anchored.[7]

But the significance of Jesus's High Priesthood hasn't been realized by the Jerusalem church. So in the next chapter the writer of Hebrews will go on to explain what Christ's High Priesthood means to them, and to us.

The writer has warned his readers. You can't go "home" again. Now he's about to show them why they shouldn't *want to* go back to their ancestral faith.

## Chapter Wrap-Up

- Immature Jewish Christians are considering turning back to Judaism.

- These believers are immature because they haven't applied Christian truths in their daily lives.

- Nor have they realized the consequences of turning back; namely, to bring dishonor to Christ's reputation and to doom themselves to unfruitful lives.

- These Jewish Christians aren't a total disaster. They do love God and minister to others. But they need to show more diligence.

- They also need to remember God is a promise-keeping God, who has kept the promise of providing them access to Him through Jesus, our great High Priest.

## Study Questions

1. What basic problem does the writer of Hebrews address in 5:12–6:20?

2. How does a believer grow to maturity?

3. How do we know the persons addressed in 6:4–6 are true Christians?

4. Why is the writer so upset with Jewish believers who consider going back to Judaism?

5. What consequence will the readers experience if they do go back?

6. What do they know about God that should give them continuing confidence in Jesus?

7. What promise implicit in the Old Testament priesthood does Jesus now fulfill?

# Hebrews 7:1-28
# The Power of an Indestructible Life

## Let's Get Started

The writer of Hebrews interrupted his discussion of Christ's priesthood (4:14–5:11) to issue what began as a stern warning (5:12–6:8), but quickly softened into words of encouragement (6:9–20). Now he's ready to get on with his teaching about Christ's High Priesthood.

Now he has to show that the High Priesthood of Jesus is consistent with Old Testament revelation. On the surface this seems an impossible task. God Himself set the tribe of Levi apart (Numbers 4, 8) to serve Him, and selected Aaron's family, and <u>only Aaron's family</u>, to serve as priests. But, as the writer is about to show, unexpected truths are imbedded in the Old Testament—truths that even the most insightful of **Jewish sages** have missed!

**only Aaron's family**
Exodus 28;
Numbers 16:40

**Jewish sages**
revered experts in the Old Testament

## Remember Mel?

**HEBREWS 7:1–3** *For this Melchizedek, king of Salem, priest of the Most High God, who met Abraham returning from the slaughter of the kings and blessed him, to whom also Abraham gave a tenth part of all, first being translated "king of righteousness," and then also king of Salem, meaning "king of peace," without father, without mother, without genealogy, having neither beginning of days nor end of life, but made like the Son of God, remains a priest continually. (NKJV)*

> what others say
>
> **John MacArthur**
>
> Melchizedek is also a type of Christ. Types are frail illustrations at best. They are analogies, and, like all analogies, they correspond to the person or thing to which they are compared only in certain ways—perhaps only in one way. Though Melchizedek is in no way an equal of Christ, his unique priesthood and even his name typify Christ and his work in a number of significant ways.[1]

**exegesis**
to explain, to high-
light significance of

**scepter**
symbol of royal rule

**Branch**
a title of the
Messiah-king

At first glance the writer seems simply to remind his readers of the incident described in Genesis 14. Melchizedek met Abraham after he had rescued his nephew Lot from raiding kings, blessed Abraham, and Abraham gave him a tenth of the spoils. But the writer is laying a foundation for his argument by **exegesis** the Old Testament text.

## What's in a Name?

Names in Scripture are more than labels. They're expected to communicate something of the character or essence of the person or thing named. The name Melchizedek is, literally "king" (*melech*) of "righteousness" (*tzdek*), and he rules Salem (*shalom*) peace. His names overflow with significance, for righteous rule is intimately associated with God and with His Messiah.

> PSALM 45:6 *Your throne, O God, is forever and ever; a **scepter** of righteousness is the scepter of Your kingdom.* (NKJV) (also Hebrews 1:8)

> ISAIAH 32:1 *Behold, a king will reign in righteousness, and princes will rule with justice.* (NKJV)

> JEREMIAH 23:5–6 *"Behold, the days are coming," says the LORD, "that I will raise to David a **Branch** of righteousness; a King shall reign and prosper, and execute judgment and righteousness in the earth. In His days Judah will be saved, and Israel will dwell safely; now this is His name by which He will be called: THE LORD OUR RIGHTEOUSNESS."* (NKJV)

> JEREMIAH 33:14–16 *"Behold, the days are coming," says the LORD, "that I will perform the good thing which I have promised to the house of Israel and to the house of Judah: 'In those days and at that time I will cause to grow up to David a Branch of righteousness; He shall execute judgment and righteousness in the earth. In those days Judah will be saved, and Jerusalem will dwell safely. And this is the name by which she will be called: THE LORD OUR RIGHTEOUSNESS.'"* (NKJV)

Prophecy

## King of Righteousness, City of Peace

In pointing out the meaning of the name Melchizedek, the writer of Hebrews is preparing to provide a stunning interpretation of the Genesis passage. But first he goes on to similarly emphasize the name of the city which this "King of Righteousness" rules. That name is Salem, meaning "peace." Bible scholars have suggested that we know the city, Salem, better as Jerusalem. But the writer of Hebrews fixes our attention on the significance of the city's name rather than its location. Like the phrase "King of Righteousness," the city named "peace" is also intimately linked with the Messiah-King.

**servant David** frequently a reference to the Messiah, who was to be a descendant of King David

## Governor Christ

ISAIAH 9:6–7
*For unto us a Child is born,*
*Unto us a Son is given;*
*And the government will be upon His shoulder.*
*And His name will be called*
*Wonderful Counselor, Mighty God,*
*Everlasting Father, Prince of Peace.*
*Of the increase of His government and peace*
*There will be no end,*
*Upon the throne of David and over His kingdom,*
*To order it and establish it with judgment and justice*
*From that time forward, even forever.*
*The zeal of the LORD of hosts will perform this.* (NKJV)

## "David" and His Sheep

EZEKIEL 34:23–25 *"I will establish one shepherd over them, and he shall feed them—My **servant David**. He shall feed them and be their shepherd. And I, the LORD, will be their God, and My servant David a prince among them; I, the LORD, have spoken. I will make a covenant of peace with them, and cause wild beasts to cease from the land; and they will dwell safely in the wilderness and sleep in the woods."* (NKJV)

## Everlasting Ruler

MICAH 5:2, 5a
*But you, Bethlehem Ephrathah,*
*Though you are little among the thousands of Judah,*
*Yet out of you shall come forth to Me*
*The One to be Ruler in Israel,*
*Whose goings forth are from of old,*
*From everlasting.*
*And this One shall be peace.* (NKJV)

**go to**

**genealogical records**
Genesis 11:10;
11:27; 25:12; 36:1;
Ruth 4:16;
1 Chronicles 1–10

# King *and* Priest!

In Old Testament law the roles of king and priest were separated. Priests were taken only from the tribe of Levi and the family of Aaron. After David, legitimate kings had to be David's descendants (2 Samuel 7:12–16), and David was from the tribe of Judah. The Messiah, a descendant of David, was to come from the tribe of Judah. How, then, could Jesus, whom these Christian Jews acknowledged as the promised Messiah, be a High Priest?

The writer of Hebrews finds the answer in Psalm 110. There God announced His intention to provide a priest "after the order of Melchizedek" (Psalm 110:4 NKJV). And Melchizedek was both a king and "priest of God Most High" (Genesis 14:18 NKJV; Hebrews 7:1). God never intended that the Messiah would carry on the priesthood established in Old Testament law, but that he would be a priest of an even more ancient and honorable order: An order in which one man not only could be but was both priest and king!

# One More Shocker

The author has one more shocking thing to draw from the Old Testament's brief account of the unexpected appearance of Melchizedek. Melchizedek symbolizes an *endless* priesthood.

To Jewish scholars of the Old Testament, every detail of a text was filled with sometimes unexpected significance. To the writer of Hebrews it's particularly significant that Melchizedek appears unexpectedly, with no reference to his birth or parents, and that he disappears from the text with no reference to his death. This is particularly impressive when we realize the emphasis the Hebrew people placed on genealogies.

# I Dream of Genealogies

We find <u>genealogical records</u> scattered throughout the Old Testament, carefully locating key individuals and their descendants in family lines. The genealogies are evidence that the Scriptures truly are historical documents, not fables, and that the heroes of the Bible were real, flesh-and-blood people. Genealogies gave individual Jews a sense of their own place among God's people, serving as a title-deed to their membership in the chosen race.

# The Melchizedek Factor[2]

When the writer of Hebrews highlights the *omission* of any record of Melchizedek's birth or death, first-century Jewish Christians would have agreed that this was significant. But what did the absence mean? The writer of Hebrews concludes that this man, "without father, without mother, without genealogy, having neither beginning of days nor end of life remains a priest continually" (Hebrews 7:3 NKJV). Since Scripture records no end to his life, he symbolizes a continual, endless, priesthood. In this too, Melchizedek is the prototype for Jesus's High Priestly ministry, for the resurrected Jesus "continues forever" (Hebrews 7:24 NKJV), and "always lives to make intercession for them" (Hebrews 7:25 NKJV).

The failure of Scripture to record a "beginning of days" for Melchizedek is another indication that he was "**made like** the Son of God," for Jesus had no beginning, but has existed forever with God and <u>as God</u>.

All this has caused some biblical scholars to speculate. Was Melchizedek entirely a human being in all respects, or does Genesis 14 describe a **preincarnation** appearance of Jesus Himself? There's no definitive answer to this question.

Nor is an answer relevant to the writer's argument. What counts for him is that the biblical account of Melchizedek's meeting with Abraham, along with God's oath recorded in Psalm 110, provides a solid foundation on which Jesus's High Priesthood can rest! Those who honored the Old Testament as God's revealed word simply *had to have* a biblical basis for the Christ's High Priesthood. And the Melchizedek incident provides it!

**as God**
John 1:1–11;
1 John 1:1–3

**made like**
intended to
represent

**preincarnation**
before the Son of
God entered history
as a true human
being

**tithes**
ten percent

# The Ten-Percent Solution

**HEBREWS 7:4–10** *Now consider how great this man was, to whom even the patriarch Abraham gave a tenth of the spoils. And indeed those who are of the sons of Levi, who receive the priesthood, have a commandment to receive **tithes** from the people according to the law, that is, from their brethren, though they have come from the loins of Abraham; but he whose genealogy is not derived from them received tithes from Abraham and blessed him who had the promises. Now beyond all contradiction the lesser is blessed by the better. Here mortal men receive tithes,*

**Levitical priesthood**
the priesthood God
established in Old
Testament law

*but there he receives them, of whom it is witnessed that he lives.*
*Even Levi, who receives tithes, paid tithes through Abraham, so*
*to speak, for he was still in the loins of his father when*
*Melchizedek met him.* (NKJV)

The writer has now established four critical points:

1. The **Levitical priesthood** is not the only priesthood the Old Testament validates. Melchizedek too was a priest of God Most High.

2. Unlike the Levitical priesthood, the Melchizedekian priesthood unites the roles of priest and king in one person. As a Melchizedekian priest, Jesus can be both the Messiah-King and the believer's High Priest.

3. Melchizedek's likeness to Jesus can be established (a) from his name, which means "king of righteousness," (b) from the city he rules, "peace," and (c) from his lack of beginning or end (implied in the Genesis text).

4. Finally, Jesus's Melchizedekian priesthood is established by God's oath sworn to the Messiah and recorded in Psalm 110:4: "The LORD has sworn and will not relent, 'You are a priest forever according to the order of Melchizedek'" (NKJV).

## A Better Priesthood

But suppose that Jesus does have a right to the High Priesthood. There's another question that must be answered: "Which priesthood is *superior?*" The Levitical priesthood functioned satisfactorily in Israel for well over a millennium. How could this "new" priesthood of Jesus be better?

It's a fair question. So the writer of Hebrews suggests, "Consider how great this man was" (Hebrews 7:4 NKJV). If he can establish that Melchizedek was greater than Levi, it will be clear to his readers that Jesus's present Priesthood is superior to that of the priests who still labored daily in the Jerusalem temple.

# Follow the Money

**HEBREWS 7:5** . . . *those who are of the sons of Levi, who receive the priesthood, have a commandment to receive tithes from the people according to the law.* (NKJV)

Priests were vital in the Old Testament system. They had to be available to offer sacrifices and offerings, and to teach the people. So the Old Testament required members of every other tribe to set aside 10 percent of what their land produced to support the Levites. And the Levites then set aside 10 percent (Numbers 18:21–32) of what they received to support the priests. In this way the Levites would be free to maintain the place of worship and perform other duties, and the priests would be free to teach God's law and offer sacrifices on the people's behalf. This practice didn't set the Levites above the other tribes, for they were all brothers, the offspring of Father Abraham (Hebrews 7:5). Even the tribes were inferior to Abraham, for in the biblical world the ancestor was always viewed as superior to his descendants.

But what happened when Abraham met Melchizedek? Melchizedek blessed Abraham, and Abraham *gave Melchizedek* a tithe of all the spoils he had just won! In bowing to receive the blessing and in paying the tithe, Abraham acknowledged Melchizedek as his superior, for "beyond all contradiction the lesser is blessed by the better" (Hebrews 7:7 NKJV).

What does this have to do with the Levitical priesthood? Everything. For Levi, "who receives tithes, paid tithes through Abraham" (Hebrews 7:9 NKJV). The logic seems strange to us, but it was a perfectly reasonable argument.

# Levi's Secret Tithe

Because Levi was potential in Abraham's DNA, when Abraham received Melchizedek's blessing and paid him tithes it was *as if* Levi paid tithes too, thus acknowledging Melchizedek's superiority. It follows that if Melchizedek is superior to Levi, then Melchizedek's priesthood is superior to the Levitical priesthood!

This argument was convincing to the first-century Jewish Christian readers. But it is admittedly an abstract, theoretical argument. It might win the author debating points, but what the writer of Hebrews yearns to do is win the hearts of his readers. So as he continues to write about Jesus's High Priesthood he will bring out practical implications of having a Melchizedekian High Priest.

## Now Everything Has Changed!

**HEBREWS 7:11–14** *Therefore, if perfection were through the Levitical priesthood (for under it the people received the law), what further need was there that another priest should rise according to the order of Melchizedek, and not be called according to the order of Aaron? For the priesthood being changed, of necessity there is also a change in the law. For He of whom these things are spoken belongs to another tribe, from which no man has officiated at the altar. For it is evident that our Lord arose from Judah, of which tribe Moses spoke nothing concerning priesthood.* (NKJV)

what others say

**J. Vernon McGee**

The New Testament priesthood is centered on Christ. This is a revolutionary departure from Old Testament law, thus calling for special, detailed handling by the writer of Hebrews. His readers, steeped in the Mosaic Law concerning priesthood, would wonder on what legal ground Christ could possibly be a priest. But priest he is, and such a real and sufficient priest that all the Aaronic privileges and responsibilities are completely abolished and swept away by him. They are now completely obsolete and redundant.[3]

This time when the writer uses the word *telios,* "perfection," it's with the basic meaning of bringing something to completion. In reference to plants or people "perfection" is maturity. But here the reference is to the priest's ministry, which was to offer sacrifices that gave a sinful nation and sinful individuals access to God. But while the priests opened the door a crack, they couldn't throw it wide open. The descendants of Aaron couldn't complete (bring to perfection) the task set assigned to the priesthood.

The writer of Hebrews makes two more important points.

- First, if the priesthood established in the Old Testament could have done the job, there would have been no need for God to speak later of a priest "according to the order of Melchizedek."

- Second, the fact that God has changed the priesthood means that the whole Old Testament system under which Israel lived is now obsolete!

This is a critical point, for the religion of the Old Testament is an organic whole. Its laws, its ways of worship, its temple, its sacrifices and offerings, its priesthood, its holy days and festivals, are all elements of an integrated system.

## Jumpin' Jupiter!

It's somewhat like our solar system. Each planet takes its own orbit around our sun, held in place by gravitational and other forces that interact with every other planet. What would happen if, say, Jupiter, were suddenly removed? The orbit of every other planet would be thrown off, and the whole once-stable system would be changed forever.

This is the point that the writer of Hebrews makes. Change one element in the system given by Moses and every other element is affected as well. The change from Levitical to Melchizedekian priesthood means "of necessity there is also a change of the [whole] law [system]" (Hebrews 7:12 NKJV). And there has been a change in the priesthood, for "it is evident that our Lord arose from Judah, of which tribe Moses spoke nothing concerning priesthood" (Hebrews 7:14 NKJV).

## A Word About "Law"

What does the writer mean when he says "of necessity there is also a change of the law" (Hebrews 7:12 NKJV)? The Hebrew word for

**teaching young people**
Deuteronomy 6;
Proverbs 3:1; 13:14

**God's instruction**
Deuteronomy 4:5–8

key point

"law" is *torah*. The basic meaning of the word *torah* is "teaching" or "instruction," and it's used in that sense in passages that refer to <u>teaching young people</u> or <u>God's instruction</u> of His people. It's not surprising then that the Old Testament itself is considered, and called, *torah*. The problem is that in reference to Scripture, *torah* can have a variety of meanings:

- Any revelation of God is *torah*.
- The books of Moses, the first five in the Old Testament, are *torah*.
- The entire Old Testament is *torah*.
- The Ten Commandments are *torah*.
- All the moral commandments and instructions of God are *torah*.
- All the ceremonial or ritual rules in the Old Testament are *torah*.
- Any specific set of commands, such as commands concerning religious festivals, is *torah*.
- The Old Testament religious system as a whole, with its temple, priesthood, sacrifices, etc., is *torah*.

So it's tough when we come across the word "law" in New Testament references to the Old Testament. Which meaning does the writer have in mind?

However, as the writer goes on in Hebrews to analyze changes in the other elements of Old Testament religion, it becomes more and more clear that the "law" which Christ's High Priesthood changes is the then-existing religious system as a whole.

## System Failure

HEBREWS 7:15–19 *And it is yet far more evident if, in the likeness of Melchizedek, there arises another priest who has come, not according to the law of a fleshly commandment, but according to the power of an endless life. For He testifies:*
*"You are a priest forever*
*According to the order of Melchizedek."*
*For on the one hand there is an annulling of the former commandment because of its weakness and unprofitableness, for the law made nothing perfect; on the other hand, there is the*

*bringing in of a better hope, through which we draw near to God. (NKJV)*

**annulled**
canceled, became invalid, null, and void

## Does God Change His Mind?

The idea of discarding the entire Old Testament system was shocking to first-century Jewish Christians. But this is what the writer of Hebrews calls for. When Jesus stepped forward to take up the High Priesthood the "former commandment" was **"annulled."** But how could a system commanded by God be set aside? Does God change His mind?

To answer that, the writer reminds us that the function of the Old Testament system was to provide a way "through which we draw near to God" (Hebrews 7:19 NKJV). God hasn't changed His mind about *this*. What God has done is to replace a system which could barely hold open the door into His presence a crack, with a system which throws the door open wide! Look at the chart below to get a clearer view of the difference.

### The Two Priesthoods

| Characteristic | Old Testament Priesthood | Christ's Priesthood |
|---|---|---|
| Basis | A command given through Moses | An oath sworn by God Himself |
| Authority | External, based on birth into Aaron's family | Intrinsic, based on the power of an endless life |
| Extent | Limited; priests die and are replaced by others | Unlimited, for Christ is a Priest forever |
| Evaluation | Made nothing perfect; couldn't complete its mission | Successful through Christ |

When we compare the characteristics of the two priesthoods it's clear that in Christ we have a far "better hope." So, God's purpose hasn't changed. What's changed is the way in which he's going about achieving it.

## A Better Covenant?

HEBREWS 7:20–22 *And inasmuch as He was not made priest without an oath (for they have become priests without an oath, but He with an oath by Him who said to Him:*
*"The LORD has sworn*
*And will not relent,*
*'You are a priest forever*

**Canaan**
Israel, Palestine

*According to the order of Melchizedek'"),*
*by so much more Jesus has become a surety of a better covenant.*
*(NKJV)*

It's perhaps more important to understand the Old Testament concept of "covenant" than any other concept in Scripture. Basically, a "covenant" is a contract or agreement which spells out how almost any relationship between two or more parties is to work. In business a "covenant" is a "contract." In international relations a "covenant" is a "treaty." In the life of a nation a "covenant" is a "constitution." In the settling of a dispute a "covenant" is an "agreement" or "settlement." In each of these uses the covenant is considered a legally binding document. It is the basis for the relationship it covers, and typically spells out the rights and duties of each party, as well as spelling out the consequences of keeping or breaking the agreement.

The biblical covenants define relationships between God and human beings. There are two basic types of biblical covenant: unconditional covenants, often called Promise Covenants, and one conditional covenant.

## Promise Covenants

**key point**

The unconditional covenants are called "Promise Covenants" because they spell out what God is firmly committed to do in His ongoing relationship with human beings. There are three major unconditional covenants: the Abrahamic Covenant; the Davidic Covenant; and the New Covenant.

1. *The Abrahamic Covenant* (Genesis 12:1–3, 7; 15:1–6; 17:1–8). This is a Covenant between God, Abraham, and Abraham's descendants. God stated that He would bless Abraham, make him a great nation, make his name great, and bless all the families of the earth through him. God also promised that Abraham's descendants would inherit the land of **Canaan**.

These promises were made unconditionally. That is, there was nothing Abraham had to do to receive the promises, and nothing that he might do could void them.

History records God's faithfulness to these commitments. Abraham was blessed during his lifetime. His descendants have multiplied and the Jewish people have survived through the centuries. The promise to make Abraham's name great is reflected in the respect paid to him by adherents of three world religions—Judaism, Islam, and Christianity. All nations have been blessed through Abraham, for his descendants gave us the Scriptures and the Savior was born a Jew. Finally, students of prophecy look forward to a future time when a converted Israel will possess the promised land.

genealogies
Matthew 1:1–17;
Luke 3:23–38

2. *The Davidic Covenant* (2 Samuel 7:12–15; Psalm 89:3–4). God promised David that his descendants would be the only rightful kings of God's people. During the years the Israelites maintained a kingdom, a descendant of David continuously occupied the throne of Judah. Two New Testament <u>genealogies</u> demonstrate that Jesus was from David's family. Many Old Testament prophecies concerning the Messiah portray Him as a coming King who will reign forever.

This promise too is unconditional. There was nothing David had to do to receive the promise, and nothing he might do could void it.

3. *The New Covenant* (Jeremiah 31; Hebrews 8). Through Jeremiah God promised to one day make a New Covenant with the Israelites. This covenant would not be like the "covenant that I made with their fathers in the day that I took them by the hand to lead them out of the land of Egypt" (Jeremiah 31:32 NKJV). The unique feature of the new covenant was that it promised complete forgiveness and an inner transformation. The promised New Covenant was initiated by Jesus's death and resurrection. As Christ said, "This is My blood of the new covenant" (Mark 14:24 NKJV; see also Matthew 26:26).

Once again the promise is unconditional. There was nothing God's people had to do to receive the promise, and nothing they might do could void it.

In these three covenants God revealed His purposes in human history. He intends to bless all peoples. The full blessing will be experienced when a descendant of David appears to establish an eternal kingdom. That full blessing involves forgiveness of sin and the transformation of sinful human hearts. The complete fulfillment of the promises awaits the return of Jesus to rule. But the New Covenant

**apostasy**
abandoning of God
and His ways

was "made" when Jesus died on the cross and rose again, and today those who trust in Jesus live under the New Covenant, not the old.

# The Only Conditional Covenant

*The Law, or Mosaic Covenant* (Exodus–Deuteronomy). This is the "old" covenant. It laid down moral and other rules that God's people were to follow. It too contains promises. If any generation of God's people remained faithful and obeyed Him, God promised to bless them (Leviticus 26:1–13; Deuteronomy 28:1–14). But if any generation was unfaithful and disobeyed Him, God promised to punish them severely (Leviticus 26:14–46; Deuteronomy 28:15–68).

These promises are conditional, not unconditional. What happens to any generation *does* depend on what they do! And Old Testament history is filled with reports of the Israelites' **apostasy**, and is just as filled with reports of the national disasters that followed. The problem with the old covenant wasn't a flaw in the system God gave to His people. In the words of the writer of Hebrews, the flaw lay in "the law of a fleshly commandment" (7:16 NKJV). That is, that Moses's law was addressed to weak and sinful human beings, who simply couldn't keep it!

# The Ironclad Guarantee!

Against this background we can sense the power of the writer's conclusion: "by so much more Jesus has become a surety of a better covenant" (Hebrews 7:22 NKJV). The word translated "surety" here is *engyos*. This is the only place this word is used in the New Testament. It was a common business term in the first century, meaning "bond" or "collateral." A person who signed on a surety bond pledged his resources to guarantee the fulfillment of the contract.

Why, then, is New Covenant priesthood so much superior to the Levitical? Simply because the promises contained in the Old depended on the actions of flawed and weak human beings. The promises made in the system of which Jesus Christ is High Priest are *guaranteed by Him!*

key point

Our access to God no longer depends on our actions or on the ministry of any Old Testament priest. Our access to God depends on Jesus, and on Jesus alone!

## We Have It So Much Better

HEBREWS 7:23–28 *Also there were many priests, because they were prevented by death from continuing. But He, because He continues forever, has an unchangeable priesthood. Therefore He is also able to save to the uttermost those who come to God through Him, since He always lives to make intercession for them. For such a High Priest was fitting for us, who is holy, harmless, undefiled, separate from sinners, and has become higher than the heavens; who does not need daily, as those high priests, to offer up sacrifices, first for His own sins and then for the people's, for this He did once for all when He offered up Himself. For the law appoints as high priests men who have weakness, but the word of the oath, which came after the law, appoints the Son who has been perfected forever. (NKJV)*

There are two respects in which we have it so much better than Old Testament believers. First, our High Priest is better than the Old Testament's priesthood. And second, our High Priest's ministry is *effective*.

### The Two Priesthoods

| Old Testament Priests | High Priest Jesus |
|---|---|
| Were many | There is only One |
| Were prevented by death from continuing | Jesus continues forever |
| Sacrificed for their own sins | He is holy<br>He is harmless [innocent]<br>He is undefiled<br>He is separate from sinners<br>He has become higher than the heavens |
| Needed to make daily sacrifices | He sacrificed "once for all" |
| Were men who had weaknesses | He has been "perfected" [is fully equipped] for His task |

## Sweet Success

As striking as the contrasts are between the Old Testament priests and our High Priest, Jesus, the contrast between the effectiveness of

**intervene**
mediate, get
involved

their ministries is even more so. Later, looking at the sacrifices offered under the Old and the New Covenants, the writer of Hebrews will point out that the "blood of bulls and goats" could never truly cleanse the worshipper (Hebrews 9:13–14 NKJV). But now he focuses on the present ministry of Jesus for believers. As our High Priest, Jesus is "able to save to the uttermost those who come to God through Him, since He always lives to make intercession for them" (Hebrews 7:25 NKJV).

what others say

**Philip Edgcumbe Hughes**

It is quite possible that the recipients of this epistle were being enticed to look to angels as their intercessors instead of Christ. Whether this was so or not, our author makes it perfectly plain that as Christ is the sole mediator of the new covenant so also he is our sole intercessor, for intercession is itself an activity of mediation. To rely upon angels or saints or any other finite beings for their intercessions is not only futile; it also betrays a failure of confidence in the adequacy of Christ as our intercessor, and it is to honor the creature rather than him who is our Creator and Redeemer.[5]

**Wilda Green**

The Christian has mainly three points of view. Looking back to the cross, he sees his salvation accomplished in the Atonement made by Jesus as his High Priest. Looking forward, he envisions Christ's return when he will come to rule (Heb. 9:28); and this view gives meaning to all things. Looking upward between these two, he beholds his High Priest interceding continually on his behalf.[6]

## Your Personal Intervention Specialist

There are many different words for "prayer" in Hebrew, and several in Greek. Forms of two Old Testament words that are translated "intercede" or "intercession" help us better understand this ministry of Jesus. The one, *palal*, indicates intervening or interposing. The second, *paga'*, indicates a meeting or encounter. The one who intercedes goes to meet someone to **intervene** on behalf of another. The Greek word used here in Hebrews 7:25 has a similar meaning: "to plead on behalf of someone."

## Surefire Salvation

As our High Priest Jesus is able to "save to the **uttermost**" (Hebrews 7:25 NKJV) because the ever living Savior pleads for us. Simply put, the fact that Jesus now ministers as our High Priest <u>guarantees</u> our salvation!

This is hard even for believers to grasp. Suggest that a person's salvation is guaranteed and someone is sure to object, "But then he can commit any sin he wants!" The objection shows a basic misunderstanding of the nature of the believer's relationship with the Lord. What keeps a believer from sinning is not fear of punishment, but <u>love for the Lord</u>.

Jesus's ministry of intercession, and the assurance that should we sin the Savior will intercede for us, is explored by the apostle John.

## What If You Sin?

*1 JOHN 1:8–2:2 If we say that we have no sin, we deceive ourselves, and the truth is not in us. If we confess our sins, He is faithful and just to forgive us our sins and to cleanse us from all unrighteousness. If we say that we have not sinned, we make Him a liar, and His word is not in us. My little children, these things I write to you, so that you may not sin. And if anyone sins, we have an **Advocate** with the Father, Jesus Christ the righteous. And He Himself is the **propitiation** for our sins, and not for ours only but also for the whole world. (NKJV)*

John, writing to believers, urges us to acknowledge the fact that we remain flawed and vulnerable to sin. He urges us come to God when we sin and acknowledge that what we've done was wrong. He wants us to know that even when we sin Jesus is on our side, sponsoring us before God, pleading His sacrifice for us as the basis on which we can be forgiven.

## Halt! Stop Sinning! Now!

If John is speaking for God (and he is) it sure sounds like God wants His people to cease and desist their wicked, disobedient ways. How to stop them from continuing their sinful patterns? Punishment? Exile? Shame? Grudge-bearing? Withdrawal of love?

**go to**

**guarantees**
Hebrews 7:22;
John 10:27–28

**love for the Lord**
Deuteronomy 11:13;
John 15: 23–24, 31

**uttermost**
absolutely, completely, for all time, forever

**Advocate**
a supporter, a sponsor, someone to intercede for us

**propitiation**
the one who satisfies the justice of a holy God and averts punishment

**apply it**

Solitary confinement? These are the typical responses human society has to those who break the rules.

God's outrageous scheme to get people to stop sinning, however, is to *forgive* their sin and to cleanse them from the unrighteousness which moved them to act as they did. He expunges the record of their sins and even provides as their Defense Advocate the very person (Jesus Christ) who laid His life on the line to make it legal for God to be so generous and forgiving. God has arranged it, through the bloody death of Christ on the cross, to justify His spendthrift response.

This plan to change sinners is shocking in the eyes of polite society. Many find it unbelievable. "When does God lower the boom?"

If the disobedient sinner confesses (agrees with God about the sin and the wrongness of it), God forgives and accepts him or her, without penalty.

## No Ticket to Sin!

John's motive isn't to hand out free passes that *encourage* sin. His motive in writing is "that you may not sin" (John 2:1 NKJV). He realizes that the more we grasp the depth of God's forgiving love in Jesus, the less we will *want* to displease Him.

What greater love could God possibly have for us? And how could we respond, except with a love for the Savior that motivates us to please Him?

## Chapter Wrap-Up

- As a Priest "after the order of" Melchizedek, Jesus can serve as both Priest and King.

- The Melchizekian priesthood is both more ancient than and superior to the Levitical priesthood.

- When God replaced the Levitical priesthood with Jesus as Melchizedekian High Priest, He annulled the entire system of worship laid out in the Old Testament.

- The High Priesthood of Jesus is vastly superior to the old system, for through Jesus we can now "draw near to God" (Hebrews 7:19 NKJV).

- The High Priesthood of Jesus is vastly superior to the old system, for our eternal High Priest is able to save us "to the uttermost" (completely and forever) (Hebrews 7:25 NKJV).

## Study Questions

1. Who was Melchizedek?

2. What three things about Melchizedek does the writer of Hebrews develop?

3. What is the significance of Melchizedek's blessing Abraham and receiving tithes from him?

4. What does the word "perfection" in 7:11 imply?

5. What does the change from a Levitical to a Melchizedekian priesthood imply?

6. Although there has been a change in the priesthood, what hasn't changed (7:19)?

7. What is the meaning and significance of "surety" in 7:22?

8. Describe the present ministry of High Priest Jesus for you.

# Part Three
# HEBREWS 8–10
# BLOOD BROTHERS

# Hebrews 8:1-13 The New Covenant—Operation Intimacy

**Chapter Highlights:**
- Copies and Shadows
- A Fault-Finding God?
- What Will You Do for Us, God?
- Fade to Black

## Let's Get Started

By this point in the Letter to the Hebrews the earliest readers must have almost been convinced. In Jesus they did have a superior revelation. And in Jesus they did have a better High Priest.

But there was something about the religion these Jewish Christians had practiced from childhood that was so familiar and comforting. The writer has argued that a change in priesthood meant that "of necessity there is also a change of the law" (Hebrews 7:12 NKJV). But was that really true? After all, God Himself had given Israel the *torah*, with all its detailed prescriptions for worship and holy living. Would God totally abandon everything He had said in His earlier word?

This is a question that troubles modern **Messianic Jews**. The community of Jesus's followers in Jerusalem had maintained the practices they'd always followed. Outwardly, they would be hard to distinguish from their orthodox Jewish neighbors. What was the writer of Hebrews calling for? Abandonment of the old and trusted ways?

Some years earlier there had been a council in Jerusalem, called to debate whether non-Jewish followers of Jesus should be required to adopt a Jewish lifestyle. See Acts 15. The answer was, "No." A person didn't have to live like a Jew to be a dedicated follower of the Lord.

So what was the writer to the Hebrews suggesting? That now Jewish Christians should be required to abandon Jewish ways and live like Gentiles?

Thoughts like these must have swirled through the minds of the first readers of the unknown author's letter. This letter was intended to encourage a persecuted Jewish Christian community not to abandon the Messiah and make a full return to Judaism. But what was it really saying?

**Messianic Jews**
Jewish Christians who worship Jesus as the Messiah, but also maintain a Jewish way of life

**Ray Stedman**

This has been the penchant of Hebrews all along. To cling to the shadows of the past and not to move on to the clear light of the great salvation in Christ. To delay, in fact, to be in danger of drifting into a total apostasy. But the tabernacle and sacrifice lose its standing in our eyes. Go on to the reality to which the Holy Spirit is pointing—the full forgiveness of sins of the new covenant and the resulting intimacy with God.[1]

## Copies and Shadows

prophecy

HEBREWS 8:1–5 *Now this is the main point of the things we are saying: We have such a High Priest, who is seated at the right hand of the throne of the Majesty in the heavens, a Minister of the sanctuary and of the true tabernacle which the Lord erected, and not man. For every high priest is appointed to offer both gifts and sacrifices. Therefore it is necessary that this One also have something to offer. For if He were on earth, He would not be a priest, since there are priests who offer the gifts according to the law; who serve the copy and shadow of the heavenly things, as Moses was divinely instructed when he was about to make the tabernacle. For He said, "See that you make all things according to the pattern shown you on the mountain." (NKJV)*

Before the writer moves on to answer the pressing question of lifestyle he provides a summary and a preview. The "main point" that he's been making is that our High Priest functions in heaven itself, representing those who believe in Him in the "true tabernacle." This theme of reality versus "copy and shadow" will continue to be developed through the next two chapters of the Letter to the Hebrews.

### Copies vs. the Real Thing

| Passage | On Earth | In Heaven |
| --- | --- | --- |
| 8:2; 9:14 | Levitical priests minister in a copy of the true Tabernacle | Christ our High Priest ministers in the true Tabernacle itself |
| 8:2, 5; 9:24 | The copy Tabernacle is of human construction | The true Tabernacle is in heaven, constructed by God |
| 8:3–4; 9:12–15 | Levitical priests offer the blood of bulls and goats | Christ offers His own blood |
| 8:3–4; 10:14 | Their repeated offerings can't take away sin | Christ's one offering for sins makes us "perfect forever" |
| 8:5, 10–13 | Operates under a covenant God gave through Moses | Operates under the New Covenant God made in Christ |

Typically, even the opening paragraph of this development in the author's **argument** is packed with significance.

## God's Right Arm

**HEBREWS 8:1** . . . *who is seated at the right hand of the throne of the Majesty in the heavens.* (NKJV)

There were no seats for the priests in the Jerusalem temple. The writer accurately notes that "every priest stands ministering daily and offering repeatedly the same sacrifices, which can never take away sins" (Hebrews 10:11 NKJV). There was no rest for the Levitical priests because their work was never finished. But Jesus is seen "seated" at the right hand of God. Why is He seated? Because "after He had offered one sacrifice for sins forever, [He] sat down at the right hand of God" (Hebrews 10:12 NKJV).

Furthermore Christ is seated "at the right hand" of the Majesty in the heavens. "Right" and "left" often have symbolic significance in Scripture. The right hand is specifically linked to the exercise of God's power, especially on behalf of His people. It was by the power of God's right hand that He brought the Israelites (Exodus 15:6), and the psalmist says confidently, "Now I know that the LORD saves His anointed; He will answer him from His holy heaven with the saving strength of His right hand" (Psalm 20:6 NKJV).

The fact that Jesus is now seated at the right hand of God is <u>consistently emphasized</u>, in the New Testament. Paul explains the significance of this position in First Peter. The fact that Jesus "has gone into heaven and is at the right hand of God" means that "angels and authorities and powers [are] made subject to him" (1 Peter 3:22 NKJV; see also Ephesians 1:20–22). Jesus not only is our High Priest. He exercises authority over the entire visible and invisible universe!

## Rabbit Shadows on the Wall

**HEBREWS 8:2** . . . *a Minister of the sanctuary and of the true tabernacle which the Lord erected, and not man.* (NKJV)

One of the activities children enjoyed BTV (before television) was making animals appear on the wall. All it took was a dark night, a flashlight, a wall, and some nimble fingers. You pointed the light

go to

**consistently emphasized**
Matthew 22:44;
Mark 14:62; 16:19;
Acts 2:33–34; 5:31;
Romans 8:34;
Hebrews 1:3, 13;
8:1; 10:12;
1 Peter 4:19

**argument**
line of reasoning,
the case he's making

key point

toward the wall and then used your fingers to cast shadow animals. A player could make an elephant or a cat or a dog appear. The shadow elephant could even wave its trunk, and the dog could open its mouth and seem to bark.

A good player could also cast a shadow that looked just like a rabbit, with its bunny ears waving. Of course, shadow animals weren't truly like the real thing. They were just insubstantial shadow outlines cast by fingers.

The writer of Hebrews now asserts that the Old Testament worship system was itself a "copy and shadow" (8:5 NKJV). While the shadow was cast by an authentic, heavenly tabernacle, the Old Testament worship center was insubstantial, at best a blurred silhouette. If a person looked closely at the Old Testament tabernacle and what happened there, he or she might catch a glimpse of what lay beyond. But the earthly sanctuary should never be mistaken for the real thing.

The Levitical high priests were shadows cast by One destined from eternity to be our High Priest. Their offerings were frail and flimsy phantoms compared to the ultimate sacrifice Christ would offer on our behalf. God had told Moses, "See that you make all things according to the pattern shown you on the mountain" (Hebrews 8:5 NKJV). The earthly tabernacle was built by mere men, and all the construction details were provided by God.

Yet those details were important, and so God had said "make all things according to the pattern shown you on the mountain." The earthly tabernacle and ancient Israel's worship had never been the real thing, but the pattern had to be authentic. Everything about the tabernacle, and later the Jerusalem temple, must accurately portray spiritual realities.

## The Glory Road Paved with Good Intentions?

The story of the construction of the **tabernacle** fit naturally into the flow of Old Testament history. God had exercised the power of His right hand and had freed His people from slavery in Egypt. He had led them to Mount Sinai, and there offered a covenant that showed them how to live in fellowship with Him. The covenant spelled out both moral and ceremonial rules they were expected to follow. It also defined God's commitment to bless obedience and punish disobedience.

There, beneath the shadow of the mighty mountain, the children of Israel shouted their acceptance of the offered agreement: "All the people answered with one voice and said, 'All the words which the LORD has said we will do'" (Exodus 24:3 NKJV). Early the next morning, representatives of each of Israel's tribes presented blood offerings and again the people said, "All that the LORD has said we will do, and be obedient" (Exodus 24:7 NKJV). In an act that sealed the relationship between God and Israel, Moses sprinkled the blood of the sacrifices on the altar.

It was done. Israel was now committed to God, and God committed to deal with His people according to the newly established law.

The following morning Moses went up to the top of Sinai to meet with the Lord. There God gave him detailed instructions for the construction of a worship center and for the **vestments** of both ordinary priests and the high priest (Exodus 25–31).

## Idle Worship

Meanwhile at the base of the mountain **Aaron**, who was to become the high priest, was pressured by the people to make an idol (Exodus 32). This was direct disobedience to the commands the people had just promised to obey! Giving in to the people, Aaron cast the image of a calf from gold and presented it to the people as "your God that brought you out of the land of Egypt" (Exodus 32:4 NKJV).

This rebellious act was the first of many. And truly, rebellious acts and subsequent punishments are a <u>hallmark</u> of Old Testament history. But this was something that God had known very well would happen.

## Cleaning Up After the Bull

Even while the Israelites gathered to worship the idol at the foot of Mount Sinai, on its top the Lord was giving Moses instructions for a system of worship that would provide covering for His people's sins <u>until Jesus appeared</u> to provide complete forgiveness.

go to

**hallmark**
Leviticus 26:41;
Acts 7:51–53

**until Jesus appeared**
Romans 3:23–26;
5:6;
Galatians 3:22–25

**vestments**
special clothing
worn by priests
when they
ministered

**Aaron**
Moses's brother

**mediator**
a go-between, a
third party, interme-
diary

# Sanctuary of Shadows

In the details of the tabernacle and of the worship there we see glimpses of truths about personal relationship with God that the New Testament makes clear. In the Old Testament tabernacle system these truths appear as shadows; in the New Testament we're shown the solid realities, the central truths of authentic Christian faith.

> **what others say**
>
> ### J. Vernon McGee
>
> Old Testament saints had only the shadows; we have the substance. They had good tidings; we have better. Their sphere and horizon were earthly; ours is heavenly.[2]

The writer of Hebrews doesn't explore the significance of every detail of tabernacle worship. Nor will we. But there are several details that are especially significant:

- There was only *one door* in the courtyard wall, through which a worshipper had to pass to approach the tabernacle (Exodus 16:27; John 10:9).

- The *altar of sacrifice* was the first object inside the courtyard. No one could approach the Lord without a sacrifice (Exodus 40:6; Hebrews 9:22–24).

- *Only the priests* could enter the tabernacle itself, and then only to go into the outer room, the holy place. It was necessary for people to have a **mediator** to represent them before God (Exodus 17:20–21; Hebrews 9:11–15).

- *A curtain* through which only the high priest could pass, and then only once a year, blocked entrance into the inner room, the Holy of Holies. The curtain symbolized the fact that the way to full access to God was not yet open (Exodus 26:31–33; Hebrews 9:6–8).

Students of the Old Testament have found shadows of New Testament truth in every detail of the tabernacle's construction. But the writer of Hebrews focuses our attention on shadows that express the most critical spiritual realities. While the significance of these elements of Old Testament worship might not have been understood in earlier times, their meaning became clear when Jesus initiated the New Covenant by dying for us and rising from the dead to become our High Priest *"forever."*

## A Fault-Finding God?

*HEBREWS 8:6–9 But now He has obtained a more excellent ministry, inasmuch as He is also Mediator of a better covenant, which was established on better promises. For if that first covenant had been faultless, then no place would have been sought for a second. Because finding fault with them, He says: "Behold, the days are coming, says the LORD, when I will make a new covenant with the House of Israel and with the house of Judah—not according to the covenant that I made with their fathers in the day when I took them by the hand to lead them out of the land of Egypt; because they did not continue in My covenant, and I disregarded them, says the LORD." (NKJV)*

The writer of Hebrews is well aware that he's walking a fine line. Who is he—or who is anyone—to find fault with the covenant God gave Israel through Moses? As the Lord said to Job when that suffering saint questioned His ways, "Where were you when I laid the foundations of the earth? Tell Me, if you have understanding" (Job 38:4 NKJV).

key point

But now the writer points out that it's *God Himself* who finds fault with the old covenant! If there was nothing wrong with the old covenant, then why would God promise a new covenant? And it's clear from the words of Jeremiah the prophet, quoted in the Hebrews passage above, that God intended to set aside the old covenant and replace it with a new one. What's more, the new was to be a very different kind of covenant; one that is "not according to the covenant that I made with their fathers in the day when I took them by the hand to lead them out of the land of Egypt" (Hebrews 8:9 NKJV).

## What's Wrong with the Old Covenant?

The writer of Hebrews isn't the only one who explores the question of what's wrong with the Mosaic Covenant. Jewish opponents challenged Jesus on similar grounds. "We know that God spoke to Moses; as for this fellow, we do not know where He is from" (John 9:29 NKJV). Later they challenged the apostle Paul, who was quick to respond to every such challenge. Paul's response is typically to turn the question upside down and so confound his critics.

key point

In the book of Romans, Paul argues that righteousness can come only by faith. When accused of being an enemy of Old Testament law he replies, "Do we then make void the law through faith? Certainly not! On the contrary, we establish the law" (Romans 3:31 NKJV).

Paul is saying that salvation by faith is necessary to give law its proper place. Paul develops this argument in his letter to the Galatians, in a dialogue with the Old Testament itself (Galatians 3:10):

### New Testament Vs. Old Testament

| Galatians 3:10 Concepts | OT Counterpoint |
| --- | --- |
| Rely on works required by law? | Then you're under the curse, for it is written (Deuteronomy 27:26): "Cursed is the one who does not confirm all the words of this law" (NKJV). |
| No one is **justified** by [keeping] the law. | For "the just shall live by his faith" (Habakkuk 2:4 NKJV). |
| But the law isn't of faith. | "You shall therefore keep My statutes and My judgments, which if a man does, he shall live by them" (Leviticus 18:5 NKJV). |
| Christ **redeemed** from the curse a curse for us. | (For it is written), "He who is hanged is accursed of God" (Deuteronomy 21:23 NKJV). |

## *Quo Vadis?* Where Are You Going?

Asked for a road map to heaven, orthodox Jewish critics of Christianity would quickly reply, "Follow the Law." To which Paul replies, "That road doesn't go there!"

When Paul wrote to the Romans and said that the gospel of faith in Jesus "establish[es]" the law (Romans 3:31 NKJV), he was making a vital point. Faith puts law in perspective. Faith "establishes" the law by clarifying its true purpose. Law wasn't intended to be a dead-end road. God always intended it to go somewhere. But where? Paul explains more fully in Galatians.

**justified**
declared righteous in God's sight

**redeemed**
delivered, saved us

**Seed**
Jesus

GALATIANS 3:19, 21–22 *What purpose then does the law serve? It was added because of transgressions, till the **Seed** should come to whom the promise was made. Is the law then against the promises of God? Certainly not! For if there had been a law given which could have given life, truly righteousness would have been by the law. But the Scripture has confined all under* *sin, that the promise by faith in Jesus Christ might be given to those who believe. (NKJV)*

A person who takes the road of law is intended to come to the place where he realizes that he is a sinner and needs to be saved. In this there is "no difference" between those who have God's Law and those who do not. For "all have sinned and fall short of the glory of God" (Romans 3:22–23 NKJV). But the Law was a great gift to Israel, because "by the law is the knowledge of sin" (Romans 3:20 NKJV) (we come to realize that we are sinners)!

## Don't Blame the Law!

If we go back and look more closely at the fault-finding passage above, we note something important. God doesn't find fault with the old covenant itself. He promised a new covenant because He was "finding fault *with them*" (Romans 8:8 NKJV). The flaw wasn't in the law; it was in the *people* who received the law.

In a sense, God dropped an anchor that would moor His people securely to Him. The anchor was solid and serviceable. But the stubborn hearts of God's people were like a hard sea bottom, which no ship's anchor can grip.

The weakness of the law was inherent in the sinfulness of the human heart (Jeremiah 17:9). No law could change human nature, and so no law could provide the righteousness a person needs to establish a personal relationship with God.

## Detour! There's a Muddy Road Ahead!

But the Israel of Jesus's day had a second weakness. Misunderstanding the real function of the law, they thought that rigorously seeking to keep every detail would win them favor with God. They foolishly thought that the highway marked "law" would bring them to Salvation City. And so they missed the highway marked "faith" and failed to reach the destination they eagerly sought. They forfeited salvation "because they did not seek it by faith, but as it were, by the works of the law" (Romans 9:32 NKJV).

**Fred Wood**

Those who insist on viewing their religious life from a legal state must understand implications of this decision. If one sets up the requirements of the law as a standard for his salvation, he immediately becomes a miserable creature, because he must face the fact that he violates the law continuously. The old cliche "no one is perfect" is descriptive of his spiritual state. Paul puts it stronger. According to him, those who do not do all that the law requires are cursed. This means they stand in a state of condemnation. The law, of course, had value. Properly understood, its function was essential. The law was given in order that man might be reminded not only of his obligation to live right in the sight of God but also of his complete inability to fulfill this obligation. Understanding this purpose of the law, the law is valuable to him. When, however, he attempts to evaluate how much of the law he has kept and concludes he has merit in God's sight because his record is good, then the law becomes a stumbling block to him and even a curse.[3]

key point

No wonder a loving God promised His people a New Covenant. The New Covenant would supersede the Old, and where the Old Covenant emphasized what man was *supposed* to do, the New Covenant would emphasize what God was willing and able to *do for us!*

## What Will You Do for Us, God?

HEBREWS 8:10–12 *For this is the covenant that I will make with the house of Israel after those days, says the LORD: I will put My laws in their mind and write them on their hearts; and I will be their God, and they shall be My people. None of them shall teach his neighbor, and none his brother, saying, 'Know the LORD,' for all shall know Me, from the least of them to the greatest of them. For I will be merciful to their unrighteousness, and their sins and their lawless deeds I will remember no more." (NKJV)*

**Vern S. Paythress**

The Mosaic covenant includes all the elements just listed above, but prominently among them it includes law. The new covenant, "I will put my laws in their minds and write them on their hearts." "My laws" in this verse refers back to the laws of the Mosaic covenant, which had been violated by Israel. The new covenant thus continues the standards of righteousness of the Mosaic covenant. Yet radical transformation is also in view.[4]

### Leo the Great

Thus says the Lord, I will put my laws in their hearts and on their hearts I will write them. He who before had spoken to Moses, spoke to the apostles, and the swift hand of him who wrote deposited the secrets in the disciples hearts. There thick clouds surrounding him of old, the people frightened off from watching the mountain by frightful sounds and lightening. Rather, quietly and freely he has reached the ears of those who stood by, that the harshness of the law might give way before the gentleness of grace.[5]

## God's "Do for" List

Here Hebrews lists, in reverse order, what God does for human beings through Jesus:

- God no longer remembers our sins and lawless deeds.
- God enables us to know Him.
- God maintains a personal relationship with us.
- God puts His law in our hearts and minds.

Understanding these wonderful gifts hinges on grasping the meaning of key words in the phrases. These include "remember," "know," "be their God," and "write [my laws] on their hearts." By examining these words and phrases, we come to better understand the salvation Jesus provides for us. Indeed, unless you grasp the significance of these key words, you will not understand "salvation" at all!

## Surfing the Sea of God's Forgetfulness

**HEBREWS 8:12 . . .** *I will be merciful to their unrighteousness, and their sins and their lawless deeds I will remember no more." (NKJV)*

It's sometimes difficult for us to remember that we saints are also sinners. Too often we pretend to be something we're not. We show up in church, dressed in our Sunday best, enthusiastically join in singing the morning hymns, and piously praise the pastor's sermon.

**remember God, His commands**
Numbers 15:39–40;
Deuteronomy 5:15;
24:9, 18, 22

**failed to remember**
Ezekiel 16:43–63

**act on their behalf**
Numbers 13:14;
Psalm 25:6; 74:18

We carefully disguise the anger that flares during the week with Sunday smiles, and tithe money we've gained at the expense of the needy.

We never let other churchgoers hear the cruel words and criticism we use to control family members, or the gossip we engage in at the office. We hide the jealousy and envy that poison our hearts, the selfish ambition that drives us, and the repressed hostility that's driven a wedge between us and our spouse.

We never let anyone catch a glimpse of the lust that turns others into sex objects, or the pride that drives us to waste God's bounty on possessions whose only purpose is to impress our neighbors. We even hide our failings from ourselves, and try to convince ourselves that, if we're not perfect, at least we're better than most in our congregation.

We forget that God says, "I will be merciful to their unrighteousness, and their sins and their lawless deeds I will remember no more" (Hebrews 8:12 NKJV). God knows us better than we know ourselves. He's aware of all our sins. In Christ He has chosen to be merciful, and promised not to *"remember"* them.

## Scatterbrains Need Not Apply

This promise not to remember our sins doesn't mean that God is unaware of our flaws. It doesn't mean that God literally forgets the wrongs we do. After all, God is omniscient and knows everything. What it does mean is that God has chosen, because Christ died to pay for our sins, to be merciful and *not act to punish us* for the wrongs we do.

In Scripture, *"remember"* is often used in this sense. Calls for Israel to <u>remember God and His commands</u> are, in fact, calls to obey Him; to act in accord with His Word. Likewise, to charge that Israel has <u>failed to remember</u>, is to charge the nation with disobedience.

When God's people beg the Lord to remember them, their appeal isn't for the mental process of recalling, but for God to intercede and <u>act on their behalf</u>. And when it's reported that God "remembered His covenant" (Exodus 2:24 NKJV), the meaning is that God is about to act to keep His promises.

Thus the phrase "not remember their sins" in Jeremiah's New Covenant, now in force through Christ's death, means that the believer's sins will not be punished by God.

Can this be true? Do sinners who continue to sin just walk away Scot free? Does God just wink and say, "Boys will be boys"?

go to

Law of Sowing and Reaping
Hosea 10:12–13;
Psalm 26:6;
Proverbs 22:8

## What Goes Around Comes Around

Let's not misunderstand this feature of the New Covenant. It does *not* mean that there will be no consequences when we sin. It does mean that the consequences aren't divine punishment.

Say that Jack, for whatever reason, robs a convenience store. God's promise that "their sins and lawless acts I will remember no more" is not a guarantee that Jack will get away with it. And, when Jack is caught and sent to prison, he shouldn't say, *"God* is punishing me." The simple fact is that the government is punishing him for breaking the law. The Bible clearly states that one purpose of government is to punish evildoers (Romans 13:3–4).

something to ponder

A person who because of gossip loses a friend isn't being punished by God. Broken relationships are a natural consequence of gossip.

No one trusts a person who lies. But the failure of others to trust such a person isn't divine punishment. It's a natural consequence of being untrustworthy.

No one truly "gets away with" any sin. We live in a moral universe, and the wise Creator has woven consequences into the fabric of the universe. All the choices we make have consequences, whether for good or evil.

The ancient <u>Law of Sowing and Reaping</u>, which declares, "Whatever a man sows, that he will also reap," still applies (Galatians 6:7–9 NKJV).

The principle also applies that "we know that all things work together for good to those who love God, to those who are the called according to His purpose" (Romans 8:28 NKJV). Which means that God is at work in and through the natural harvest (consequences) of my choices, using them to change me until I stop making destructive choices and am progressively reshaped into the image and likeness of Jesus (Romans 8:29).

When Jack, the "robber believer," is thrown into the hoosegow for his crime, he may cry, "God is punishing me!" But he would be better served to say, "Lord, what are You trying to teach me? How do You want to use this painful experience to work Your likeness into me?" If Jack has indeed welcomed Christ into his life (we are assuming he has), it isn't a question of being lost, saved, or loved by God, but it is a rare opportunity to cooperate with God in the extreme moral makeover He's working out in Jack.

Nonetheless, the reality is that because we have Jesus as our High Priest, He speaks up for us when we sin and God is merciful to us. He does not hold the sin against us, nor does He punish us for it. In the idiom of the Scripture, *He remembers our sins no more*. Wow!

## Forgiveness—Launching Pad of the New Covenant

This is a good place to start when seeking to understand salvation. It begins with forgiveness of all our sins. In Jesus we have "**redemption** through His blood, the forgiveness of sins, according to the riches of His grace" (Ephesians 1:7 NKJV; cf. Colossians 1:14).

No wonder the heavens ring with praise to Jesus, "who loved us and washed us from our sins in His own blood" (Revelation 1:5 NKJV). In Jesus we have been saved, now and forever.

what others say

**F. W. Dillistone**

It is significant that one of the earliest, if not the earliest, doctrinal statements incorporated in a creed is the simple confession, "I believe in the forgiveness of sins." From the beginning the Church has held fast to the conviction that in some way the cross is the place of full and complete forgiveness.[6]

## The Jewel of the New Covenant—Knowing God

**HEBREWS 8:11** *None of them shall teach his neighbor, and none his brother, saying, 'Know the LORD,' for all shall know Me, from the least of them to the greatest of them. (NKJV)*

**redemption**
God's rescue of helpless human beings from the power and outcome of sin

There's an old spiritual that says, "Everybody talkin' 'bout heav'n ain't goin' there." We might paraphrase it, "Everybody talking about God doesn't know Him."

Actually, most people know something about God. They believe He exists. Most accept the idea that God somehow created everything. There's a general acceptance of the idea of heaven, and a slightly less general acceptance of the idea of hell. There's also a general acceptance of the idea that God rewards good people and punishes bad ones. But in a rather pointed comment the apostle James notes that even demons believe in God (James 2:19)—and He scares them!

Thus there's a vast difference between knowing *about* God and *knowing God*. A person can study the Bible and have quite accurate knowledge about God without knowing Him at all!

The Hebrew word for "know" is *yada'*. It's found some 950 times in the Old Testament, and used pretty much in the same ways that we use "know" in English. In both languages "knowing" may refer to sensory experiences, to information and facts, to the learning of skills, to mere acquaintance with other persons. "Knowing" can also involve the process of thinking about, classifying, and organizing all sorts of information. While "knowing God" may incorporate all of these elements, a special aspect of knowing God underlies the New Covenant promise. For knowing God involves an experience of God's work in and for us. Welcoming God and His wisdom (revealed in the Holy Scriptures) into all the aspects of our lives can lead to genuine intimacy with Him. Knowing God is the most precious jewel in the New Covenant treasure chest.

## Intimacy's Power Play

Exodus tells the story of powerful miracles (Exodus 5–14) God worked in Egypt in order to free His people. But why bring such devastation on Egypt? The Lord explained that Moses was to tell the Israelites:

**EXODUS 6:6–7** *I am the LORD; I will bring you out from under the burdens of the Egyptians, I will rescue you from their bondage, and I will redeem you with an outstretched arm and with great judgments. I will take you as My people, and I will* *be your God. Then you shall know that I am the LORD your God who brings you out from under the burdens of the Egyptians. (NKJV)*

The Israelites as a people came to know God through the experience of His power at work for them. In the New Covenant the promise is made that every individual believer will "know Me," not in the abstract but as a Person who is actively at work in his or her life. This is the experience the apostle Paul seeks for his converts in Ephesus, praying that:

EPHESIANS 1:18–19 *The eyes of your understanding being enlightened; that you may know what is the hope of His calling, what are the riches of the glory of His inheritance in the saints, and what is the exceeding greatness of His power toward us who believe, according to the working of His mighty power. (NKJV)*

God is at work in each believer's life. This is our heritage under the New Covenant. All we need is eyes to recognize what He is doing. When we do, we will know that we truly are being saved.

## Dear God with His Dear People

HEBREWS 8:10b *I will be their God, and they shall be My people. (NKJV)*

God acts in our lives because now we belong to Him and He belongs to us. In affirming "I will be their God, and they shall be My people," God acknowledges us as His own. We are family now, loved and treasured. He is our Father; we are His children.

In one of the most stunning of biblical affirmations, the apostle Paul reminds believers that as sons of God now we are privileged to cry out to God, "Abba, Father" (Romans 8:15; Galatians 4:6 NKJV). The word "abba" in Aramaic is the same as "daddy" in English. It's one of the first words a child learns as he stretches out his arms, eager to be picked up and held by the one he knows as his daddy.

"Abba" expresses something of the personal relationship that exists between the follower of Jesus and the King of the heavens. He is the Almighty, the Creator, the Holy One, the Righteous Judge. He is the most awesome figure in the universe; a figure before whom angels fall prostrate in admiration and respect. Yet to us He is also "Daddy," to whom we can come at any time, assured of His welcome and attention.

This too is guaranteed under the New Covenant promise, "I will be their God, and they shall be My people" (Hebrews 8:10 NKJV).

## King of Hearts

HEBREWS 8:10 *I will put My laws in their mind and write them on their hearts. (NKJV)*

There was a problem with the old covenant mediated by Moses. It revealed something of the righteousness God expected in His people. But while the words describing righteousness were posted on a billboard in letters so large anyone might read them, the hearts of those who did read them were hard and unresponsive. Generation after generation of Israelites knew what they *should* do, but that knowledge didn't change their rebellious attitude. The people of God consistently fell short of His standards. Or they rebelled against Him and His standards. Or they twisted the standards, shaving something off here and adding a bit there so they could pretend they were living God's way.

key point

The Old Testament prophets expressed the problem plainly. "The heart is deceitful above all things, and desperately wicked" (Jeremiah 17:9 NKJV). The "evil heart of unbelief" displayed by the Exodus generation (Hebrews 3:12 NKJV) has characterized human beings from **the Fall**.

The prophets not only understood the problem, they conveyed a message of hope. Jeremiah speaks of a day when "I will give them a heart to know Me" (Jeremiah 24:7 NKJV), and Ezekiel looks forward to a day when "I will put a new spirit within them, and take the stony heart out of their flesh that they may walk in My statutes and keep My judgments and do them; and they shall be My people, and I will be their God" (Ezekiel 11:19–20 NKJV).

## Extreme Moral Makeover

The law was useless as long as it was engraved in stone and written on parchment. There it might serve as a mirror in which an honest person came face-to-face with the fact of his own sinfulness, but the written law could not give life, or change twisted and bent human hearts. What God would have to do was to transform sinners from within. God would have to give human beings a moral makeover, until their hearts themselves were righteous.

This too God has done for us in Christ. He has given us a thirst for righteousness, a desire to please Him, and the promise that in the resurrection each of us will be completely renewed. In this the New Covenant's promise is that we will be saved. Completely.

## New Covenant Salvation, in Every Tense of the Word

I mentioned earlier that we only understand salvation when we understand the elements of the New Covenant God has executed in Christ. Like the covenant, salvation comes to us in three tenses: the past, the present, and the future.

- *Past tense* salvation is expressed in the phrase "their sins and their lawless deeds I will remember no more" (Hebrews 8:12 NKJV). God has acted in Christ to win forgiveness for us. We have been saved through Jesus's death for us on Calvary. When we place our trust in Jesus as Savior the transaction is complete; salvation is ours. We have been saved, now and forever.

- *Present tense* salvation is expressed in the phrases "all shall know Me" and "I will be their God" (Hebrews 8:11, 10 NKJV). Right now, today, Christians have an intimate personal relationship with God, a relationship so intimate that we can call on Him as "Abba, Father." Within the context of that relationship God Himself is at work in our lives. His Spirit energizes us so that despite our frailty we have the possibility of living righteous lives here and now (Romans 8:1–4)! We'll never achieve perfection in this life. But we can and will grow to become more and more like Jesus (2 Corinthians 3:17–18) as we walk with Him. Through the relationship that Jesus provides us with the Father and Spirit, God is at work building righteousness into our character and lifestyle. We are being saved, day by day.

- *Future tense* salvation is expressed in the phrase "I will put My laws in their mind and write them on their hearts" (Hebrews 8:10 NKJV). The process of inner transformation these words express has already begun. It continues situation after situation in our lives. Inscribing or implanting God's principles in our hearts and minds is the work of the Holy Spirit. Jesus promised that when His Spirit enters our lives He will remind us of the things Jesus taught (John 16:4–15). When Jesus returns the transformation will <u>be complete</u>. We will experience the fullness of salvation when we have been made righteous through and through and God's laws become an "inside job."

**be complete**
1 Corinthians
15:42–44, 53–55;
1 John 3:1–3

**Nazirite vow**
vow of service and dedication to God; involves shaving the head and then not cutting hair again, and abstaining from all products of the grape

## The Consummate Ambassador

**HEBREWS 8:13** *In that He says, "A new covenant," He has made the first obsolete. Now what is becoming obsolete and growing old is ready to vanish away. (NKJV)*

This glimpse of the glories of the New Covenant must have shaken those who seemed about ready to return to the old religion. Especially now that the writer has proven from the Old Testament that it was God who set aside the old ways, not men. But has the writer answered the implicit question about lifestyle? In view of the initiation of the New Covenant, should the Jews who have trusted Jesus stop following the old ways?

There are two answers to this question. The first is hinted at by Paul's actions when he returned to visit Jerusalem. Some of the Jerusalem Christians encouraged Paul to undertake a **Nazirite vow** (Numbers 6:1–21) and the ritual purification laid down in Old Testament law. This was to counter rumors that Paul was teaching the Jews who lived outside the holy land "to forsake Moses, saying that they ought not to circumcise their children nor to walk according to the customs" (Acts 21:21 NKJV). Without any hesitation Paul agreed. While with Gentiles he had lived like Gentiles, not following Jewish dietary or other rules. But in Jerusalem he found no reason not to fit into that community.

In one of his letters Paul had written, "To the Jews I became as a Jew, that I might win Jews; to those who are under the law, as under the law, that I might win those who are under the law; to those who are without law, as without law (not being without law toward God, but under law toward Christ), that I might win those who are without law" (1 Corinthians 9:20–21 NKJV).

Paul explained further in another place, "One person esteems one day above another; another esteems every day alike. Let each be fully convinced in his own mind" (Romans 14:5 NKJV). Relationship with God is no longer a matter of externals! If an ethnic Jew wishes to honor God by living a Jewish lifestyle and observing what were known as *halakha*, which often involved days of traditional fasting or feasting, then he or she is not to be judged. If a Gentile chooses to ignore such days, or to observe his own traditions, that's up to him. The new covenant weans us away from any emphasis on externals, to focus on seeking to know and serve the Savior in whatever culture we may find ourselves.

The lesson of the New Covenant for the early Jewish community—and for us—was never to rely on anything we might do for God, but rather to rely totally on what Jesus has done for us.

And then express the gratitude and joy that wells up in our hearts by listening for God's voice, and gladly responding every day.

## Fade to Black

**HEBREWS 8:13** *Now what is becoming obsolete and growing old is ready to vanish away. (NKJV)*

The hostility of Jerusalem Jews to their Christian brothers was only one issue stirring Jewish passions in the middle of the first century. The Jews were passionate by nature, and the resentment of Palestinian Jews against Roman rule was building. In the late 60s resentment burst into the flame of an armed rebellion. But Rome knew how to deal with rebellion. By the end of the decade the holy city was surrounded by a Roman army. Inside the city people starved while armed mobs fought fierce hand-to-hand battles for control. Finally the Romans struck. The city walls were breached, the defenders, along with women and children, were butchered. Survivors were forced into camps to be sold later as slaves. Then, wall by wall and stone by stone the city buildings were dismantled and the building materials removed. Finally the mounds of raw dirt that remained were covered with salt, to kill anything that might try to grow, and the Roman general decreed that no Jew should come within miles of their holy city's site.

And the Jewish Christians? Tradition tells us that they were warned by prophets in the community of believers to flee the city before the siege began. Flee they did, and found refuge in Pella in Perea in the territory ruled by Herod Agrippa II. There they must have realized that God Himself had protected them not just from loss of life but also from the danger of turning back to the old faith. With the razing of the city the temple, where the priests had offered sacrifices and the high priest had once a year slipped behind the curtain blocking off the Holy of Holies, had also been destroyed.

## Vanishing Faith

With the temple gone the religion of the Old Testament could no longer be practiced. There remained the moral code and many ritual regulations. But there was no altar on which a priest might burn a sacrifice. There was no blood for a high priest to carry into God's presence to provide a covering of the people's sins for another year. Without the temple there truly was no religion.

As Jewish scholars struggled to find a solution to what was in fact the end of Old Testament ways, they fastened on a unique concept. One could no longer offer sacrifices. There was no priesthood to hold open the door to God even the smallest crack. All they had were descriptions of the sacrifices that God required. And so the scholars decided that to *study* the sacrifices was the same as actually offering them. And so it has been for nearly 2,000 years, as God's ancient people hold fast to a way of life which became obsolete, was withered with age, and in fact has vanished away.

## Chapter Wrap-Up

- Christ is now seated as our High Priest, ministering in heaven.
- The Old Testament worship system merely symbolized heavenly realities which are available to us now under the New Covenant that God promised in the time of the prophet Jeremiah.
- Under the New Covenant, believers in Jesus experience many benefits:
  - God no longer "remembers" our sins.
  - We have full and complete forgiveness.
  - We come to know God and experience His work in our lives.
  - We have the promise of a complete moral makeover.
  - The New Covenant has made the Old Covenant obsolete and irrelevant.

## Study Questions

1. In what way was Old Testament worship a "copy and shadow"?

2. Why were the details of tabernacle construction so important?

3. What was wrong with the Old Covenant [Mosaic Law]?

4. What are the major superiorities of the New Covenant?

5. What happened to the Old Covenant when the New Covenant was inaugurated?

# Hebrews 9
# Sprinkled with Blood

**Chapter Highlights:**
- Back on Earth
- Once and for All
- Where There's a Will There's a Death
- Packed Up

## Let's Get Started

The writer of Hebrews has shown that God has replaced the old covenant He made with Israel with a brand-new one, just <u>as He promised</u>. The law covenant, made in the time of Moses, defined what God's *people must do.* The new covenant lays out what *God has done.* God has saved us, forgiving our sins. He is saving us, planting His laws in our hearts and empowering us to live in harmony with it. And He will save us, completing the process and making us like Himself in our resurrection.

It's as if God took your Model-T Ford, which didn't run, and gave you the latest model, fully equipped and ready to go. The Model-T was great as long as you were satisfied to just sit there, imagining you were on the road. But the new model will really take you places!

And it didn't cost you a cent! Not that the new model's cheap, or that the Model-T was of equal value. In fact, the old junker was so rusted out that it was ready "to vanish away." And what it cost to give you the new model was far more than anyone had imagined. Even though there had been <u>hints in Scripture</u> all along.

**go to**

**as He promised**
Jeremiah 24:7;
31:31–34;
Ezekiel 11:19–20

**hints in Scripture**
Psalm 22:6–8;
Isaiah 53:1–6;
Zechariah 12:10

**sanctuary**
the holy place

## Back on Earth

HEBREWS 9:1–5 *Then indeed, even the first covenant had ordinances of divine service and the earthly sanctuary. For a tabernacle was prepared: the first part, in which was the lampstand, the table, and the showbread, which is called the* **sanctuary**; *and behind the second veil, the part of the tabernacle which is called the Holiest of All, which had the golden censer and the ark of the covenant overlaid on all sides with gold, in which were the golden pot that had the manna, Aaron's rod that budded, and the tablets of the covenant; and above it were the cherubim of glory overshadowing the mercy seat. Of these things we cannot now speak in detail. (NKJV)*

golden table
Exodus 25:35;
40:22–23;
Numbers 4:7

**Mosaic Covenant**
covenant made at
Mount Sinai
between God and
the Israelites; some-
times called "Sinai
Covenant"

# Any Color, As Long As It's Black

There are many stories about the early Ford cars from the early twentieth century. Henry Ford reportedly remarked that customers could get any color they wanted as long as it was black. He's also said to have told one supplier he'd get Ford's business if he shipped his parts in a crate that Henry designed. The supplier agreed—and when Henry's workmen took the crates apart, the pieces fit to make up the car's floorboards. Henry figured out lots of ways to cut corners with those early, mass-produced Fords.

Given even the briefest of looks, the tabernacle associated with the **Mosaic Covenant** is hard to compare with any out-of-date car. The tabernacle was one-of-a-kind, with so much wealth lavished on it that it would have been too expensive to duplicate (Exodus 38:24–29).

# It Was a Cadillac

Immediately inside the outer perimeter was a room, called the "sanctuary" or "holy place." It was furnished with three pieces of furniture, perhaps the most impressive of which was a six-foot tall, seven-branched, oil-burning lampstand whose seven flames, always kept burning, caused the gold of which it was made to literally glow (Exodus 25:31–35). The seven-branched lampstand is now known as a menorah and has become the official symbol of the modern State of Israel. Modern Judaism also uses a nine-branched menorah in connection with Hanukah, which is a man-made, commemorative Jewish "festival" also known as the Feast of Dedication, which Christ Himself honored by going to the Temple celebration in John 10:22–23. The same light burnished the golden table on which fresh loaves of bread (called *showbread*) were placed once a week, and a golden incense altar. But what was even more impressive were the contents of the inner room, the Holy of Holies.

Only the high priest could enter the Holy of Holies, and then only once a year (Leviticus 16:11–19). Everything within this inner room was also rich in gold. This included the gold-covered Ark (Exodus 25:10–16), made in the form of a box with a thick cover of solid gold, over which two golden angels bowed (Exodus 25:17–22). In the Ark was a golden pot filled with manna (Exodus 16:33), and Aaron's wooden rod from which sprouted a branch laden with fruit (Numbers 17:1–10). And there were two stone tablets which God Himself had engraved (Exodus 34:1–2).

Every one of these items shouted, "This place is special." It was not just the gold or the artistry each creation displayed. Each item was a reminder of God's personal involvement in the life of His people.

**represented the prayers**
Revelation 5:8; 8:3–4

**God supplied every need**
Exodus 16:31–35; Deuteronomy 8:3

- *The Ark of the Covenant.* This object represented the presence of God among His people. The Ark was so holy that it was not to be touched or even looked at (Exodus 6:1–7). When the people traveled the Ark was covered. Those who carried it touched only poles that were thrust through golden rings attached to the sides of the Ark.

- *The Mercy Seat.* The removable top of the Ark was made of solid gold. Two golden angels, whose wingtips almost touched, seemed to focus their gaze on the spot at its center where once a year the high priest sprinkled the blood of a sacrificial bull, thus covering another year of sins for God's people.

- *The golden censer.* When the high priest entered the Holy of Holies he carried a censer filled with burning coals from the altar. The coals were sprinkled with a special incense that was used only in the worship (Exodus 30:34–37) of the Lord. This incense <u>represented the prayers</u> of God's people, and its fragrance—which tradition tells us could be discerned up to three miles away—reminded Israel that the Lord welcomed their worship and their requests.

- *The golden pot of manna.* For forty years <u>God supplied every need</u> of His people, despite their rebellion. The manna kept in the Ark, as fresh as the day it fell from heaven, was a vivid reminder of God's grace and His continuing concern for His frequently straying people.

- *Aaron's rod that budded.* When other Levite families jealously demanded the right to worship God directly rather than accept Aaron and his sons as mediators, fire fell from heaven and destroyed the rebels (Numbers 16). Then members of the other tribes were challenged to bring staffs and lay them beside the staff of Aaron. Overnight Aaron's staff budded and bore fruit (Numbers 17:1–10). The miracle authenticated God's call of Aaron's descendants to a perpetual priesthood.

- *The stone tablets of the law.* God did much more than simply tell Moses the Ten Commandments. Later God personally engraved them on stone tablets. These "ten words" served ever after as a revelation of God's own moral character, and the way He expects human beings to treat Him and each other.

Even so, for all its splendor and majesty the tabernacle was essentially a tent that could be torn down and raised as the people moved on.

## From Luxury Wheels to the Salvage Yard

Yet the writer of Hebrews speaks dismissively of the Tabernacle as "becoming obsolete and growing old" and "ready to vanish away" (8:13 NKJV). At best it was a "copy and shadow" (8:5 NKJV) of heavenly things. It was in fact an "earthly sanctuary" (9:1 NKJV), and though its every feature was rich in spiritual significance, the writer of Hebrews can't be bothered to "speak in detail" (9:5 NKJV) of these things.

After all, the old system, despite its apparent splendor, was a vehicle that never carried God's people to the goal of direct access into God's presence.

> **what others say**
>
> **J. Vernon McGee**
>
> In the Old Testament era, the Israelites had only shadows. The substance is in Christ. The shadow of a key cannot unlock a prison door; the shadow of a meal cannot satisfy the hungry; the shadow of Calvary cannot take away sins.[1]

What the writer of Hebrews wants his readers to concentrate on isn't the familiar old covenant system with its powerful symbols. The writer wants his readers to focus on the new covenant system and what it actually delivers for them and for all followers of Jesus Christ.

## The Drama of Redemption

**HEBREWS 9:6–8** *Now when these things had been thus prepared, the priests always went into the first part of the tabernacle, performing the services. But into the second part the high priest went alone once a year, not without blood, which he offered for* *himself and for the people's sins committed in ignorance; the Holy Spirit indicating this, that the way into the Holiest of All was not yet made manifest while the first tabernacle was still standing. (NKJV)*

While the tabernacle seemed spectacular to the early Israelites, it's important to see it primarily as a stage on which a significant drama was to be acted out. Thus the writer says "when these things had been thus prepared," and goes on "the priests always went into the first part of the tabernacle, performing the services."

## "Break a Leg!"

If the tabernacle was a stage the priests were the performers. Outside the tabernacle the priests made required daily sacrifices (Leviticus 9:17) and slaughtered animals (Leviticus 7:1–5) provided by worshippers. Every day some priest entered the tabernacle, but "always went into the first part of the tabernacle" (Hebrews 9:6 NKJV). He trimmed the wicks and made sure there was oil in the lampstand so the light never went out. Once a week he replaced the loaves of bread laid on the golden table that stood before the thick curtain separating the inner and outer rooms. He faced the barrier curtain and burned incense before the Lord. But no matter which priest was chosen for these services at any particular time, the curtain that blocked access to the Holy of Holies hung, unmoving and unmoved.

what others say

### Wilda Green

The Day of Atonement was observed in the seventh month of each year and on the tenth day of that month. It was the most solemn day in the lives of the Israelite people, a time of repentance and of remembrance of their great need for forgiveness.[2]

## The Big Scene

An observer who watched day after day might well have wondered at the endless repetition. But then when Yom Kippur, the Day of Atonement (Leviticus 16), arrived "once a year," a new actor

**God was present**
Exodus 25:22; 29:43

appeared on the stage. This was the high priest, who "went alone" into the inner room, but "not without blood" (see Leviticus 16:14). As a fasting nation waited, the high priest entered with a basin of blood, fresh from an animal sacrifice. Careful not to spill any of the blood, he moved the heavy curtain aside. Inside the Holy of Holies, filled with awe, he sprinkled the fresh blood on the Mercy Seat and on the sides of the Ark of the Covenant, offering the blood as a covering for his own and the people's sins.

When the high priest was done he backed away from the Ark, again moved the heavy curtain, and retreated from the one place on earth where <u>God was present</u> in a special way.

## Once More, with *Chutzpah!*

The next day an ordinary priest resumed the regular, daily service. A service that was repeated the following day. And the next. And the next. Until a year passed and once again the high priest brought the blood of an animal sacrifice into the Holy of Holies, before retreating again. And this too was repeated. Year after year after year after year.

In this way a never-ending drama was acted out on the stage God had directed His people to construct; a never-ending drama whose author was God Himself. A never-ending drama worth far more than the thousand words a single, still photograph is reputed to convey.

## Time to Retire the Old Bucket o' Bolts

What did God's repetitious stage play communicate? The writer of Hebrews is about to spell out truths that tabernacle worship should have ingrained in Israel's soul, preparing them to grasp the significance of Jesus's death. Truths that should have been abundantly clear from the pattern of tabernacle worship.

It should have been abundantly clear *that the Old Testament priesthood was not doing the job.* Despite hundreds of years of ministry, no ordinary priest could pierce the barrier between the outer and inner rooms of the tabernacle. And if priests had no access into God's presence, what hope was there for ordinary men and women?

It should have been abundantly clear that *the annual sacrifice offered by the high priest was inadequate*. No matter how many centuries the sacrifice of the Day of Atonement was repeated by a series of high priests, the curtain hung there unmoved. It would take more than the ministry of a Levitical priesthood to provide God's people with direct access to Him.

**report the same event**
Mark 15:38;
Luke 23:44

The high priest could never enter God's presence without the blood of a sacrifice. Yet while that blood sacrifice provided a temporary covering for the sins of God's people, the annual repetition made it absolutely clear that *whatever forgiveness the blood won was only temporary*, and not complete. Blood was necessary. But the blood of animals was not enough to satisfy the justice of God.

What the Old Testament worship system revealed was that God's people needed access into God's presence, and that as long as the Mosaic system existed that access was impossible! As the writer tells us, the Holy Spirit was indicating "that the way into the Holiest of All was not yet made manifest while the first tabernacle was still standing" (Hebrews 9:8 NKJV).

key point

## Calvary Curtain Call

The Gospel of Matthew reports an amazing happening. At the moment of Jesus's death, "then, behold, the veil of the temple was torn in two from top to bottom" (Matthew 27:51 NKJV). Mark and Luke <u>report the same event</u>. The Gospel writers fail to develop the significance of this event, for its significance should have been clear to any reader with knowledge of Old Testament religion. In His death Jesus dealt with the barrier that had existed between human beings and God. Jesus opened the way into the holiest of all for you and me!

Even the fact that the curtain was torn "from top to bottom" speaks to us. The veil of the temple was woven according to the pattern given in Exodus. It was "woven of blue, purple, and scarlet thread, and fine woven linen. It shall be woven with an artistic design of cherubim" (Exodus 26:31 NKJV). The temple veil was reputedly loosely woven and several inches thick. No number of men could have torn that curtain apart. But to make it even more clear that God Himself had torn the veil, when Jesus died it was ripped from "top to bottom."

It took an act of God to get rid of the barrier that cut humans off from His presence.

Tradition tells us that the high priest hurriedly had the torn veil stitched together. It would never do for the people or for ordinary priests to associate the tearing of the temple curtain with the crucifixion of Jesus. The repair made no difference. Within thirty years the temple itself was destroyed by the Romans, and the failed Old Testament system of worship was gone.

The never-ending play God had staged for His people, first at the tabernacle and later at the Jerusalem temple, was over.

## Once and for All

HEBREWS 9:9–14 *It was symbolic for the present time in which both gifts and sacrifices are offered which cannot make him who performed the service perfect in regard to the conscience—concerned only with foods and drinks, various washings, and fleshly ordinances imposed until the time of reformation. But Christ came as High Priest of the good things to come, with the greater and more perfect tabernacle not made with hands, that is, not of this creation. Not with the blood of goats and calves, but with His own blood He entered the Most Holy Place once for all, having obtained eternal redemption. For if the blood of bulls and goats and the ashes of a heifer, sprinkling the unclean, sanctifies for the purifying of the flesh, how much more shall the blood of Christ, who through the eternal Spirit offered Himself without spot to God, cleanse your conscience from dead works to serve the living God? (NKJV)*

what others say

**Andrew Murray**

The blood of a man is of more worth than that of a sheep. The blood of a great general is counted of more value than hundreds of common soldiers. The blood of the Son of God—it is in vain the mind seeks for some expression of its value; all we can say is it is His own blood, the precious blood of the Son of God.[3]

Placed side by side as in the following chart, we see the parallels Hebrews 9:9–14 draws between Christ's High Priestly ministry and the ministry of Levitical high priests. And we see the vast differences.

——————— The Smart Guide to the Bible ———————

## Two High Priestly Ministries

| Point of Comparison | Levitical High Priests | Our High Priest, Jesus |
| --- | --- | --- |
| Where | In earthly tabernacle | In heaven itself |
| Nature | Symbolic | Real |
| Extent | Temporary, until reformation | Eternal |
| Concerned with | Foods and drinks, various washings, fleshly ordinances | Perfecting the conscience |
| Offerings | Blood of goats and calves | His own blood |
| Accomplishments | Purifies the flesh | Cleanses the conscience |
| Final Result | None | Enables worshipper to serve God |

## That "Bloody Religion"

HEBREWS 9:12 *Not with the blood of goats and calves, but with His own blood He entered the Most Holy Place once for all, having obtained eternal redemption.* (NKJV)

what others say

### Tom Fettke and Camp Kirkland

They saw the bloody woven thorns with which His head was crowned; they watched the bloody cross of wood be dropped into the ground. The soldiers gambled for His clothes; they watched them win and lose; they saw the sign above His head that said, "King of the Jews." "It is finished!" and the sky grew black as the night. "It is finished!" and the people scattered in fright. The work had been done; redemption had been won; the war was over without a fight. "It is finished!"[4]

More than one modern theologian has wrinkled his lips in distaste over the notion that somehow blood sacrifice could play a part in anyone's relationship with God. Such "primitive" notions don't fit with the more enlightened concept of a God so kind that He can wink at sin and will eagerly welcome anyone who bothers to nod in His direction. After all, didn't Jesus tell His followers not to judge, and to forgive?

The Bible's consistent emphasis on blood sacrifice is ignored by some who purport to speak for God, or it's dismissed with mumbled explanations about how the contemporary concept of God is so much "more advanced" than that of the ancients. If an enlightened modern human doesn't feel comfortable with the idea of blood sacrifice, it's hard to imagine that God would be comfortable with it

key point

go to

terrible consequences
Genesis 3:16–19;
Ephesians 2:1–3

either. It's much more pleasant to re-create God in our image than to let God be God and accept His view of what justice calls for.

# The Long, Long Trail of Blood

It's not that the idea of blood sacrifice was invented by Moses, or that it was taken over from pagan cultures. Blood sacrifice has its roots in the very beginning of man's relationship with God. Genesis 3 tells the story of the first sin. First Eve and then Adam disobeyed God and ate fruit from a forbidden tree.

Immediately following history's first sin, Adam and Eve were filled with shame and guilt. With them came fear of the Creator. The man and the woman tried desperately to hide from each other by fashioning coverings of leaves, and when they heard the Lord moving in the garden they ran from Him, stricken by suddenly awakened consciences.

But it was impossible to hide. God found and confronted them. Although each tried to shift the blame for committing the sin, God held each accountable and explained terrible consequences which must now follow. Then God did something amazing: "For Adam and his wife the LORD God made tunics of skin, and clothed them" (Genesis 3:21 NKJV).

Thus it was God Himself who initiated blood sacrifice. The humans' frantic effort to cover themselves failed. It took the shedding of the blood of an innocent animal to provide coverings for the two whose choices brought the idyllic Eden existence to a whimpering end.

# A Tale of Two Brothers

Later Adam and Eve had children. The first two recorded were named Cain and Abel. Their story is familiar. When "in the process of time" the two brothers approached God, each brought an offering. Abel brought a lamb while Cain offered "of the fruit of the ground" (Genesis 4:3 NKJV). God accepted Abel's blood offering and told Cain that "if you do well, will you not be accepted?" (Genesis 4:7 NKJV).

Jewish sages have suggested that Cain's offering was rejected because he brought rotted fruits and vegetables. Some scholars suggest that Cain was aware that a blood sacrifice was required, a knowledge he would have gained from his parents. To others, however, the text seems more strongly to suggest that Cain was arrogant, angry, and rebellious in his heart toward God and his brother Abel. Rather than "do well" and trade with his brother for a lamb, Cain took out his anger at God's rejection on Abel and murdered him.

The story underlines two vital truths. The sad reality of original sin was transmitted by Adam and Eve to their children. And from that moment onward a blood sacrifice like the one God made in order to cover the first pair was required from anyone who sought to approach God.

Likewise, from that same moment onward the ancient world's most primitive—and its most complex religions as well—all found a role for blood sacrifice.

## Why Blood?

In most ancient religions the role of sacrifice was distorted. It came to be viewed as a bribe that might win a deity's favor, or as a gift of some value that might placate a deity's wrath. But in the religion that God established for Israel, the original role and significance of sacrifice was reestablished. Leviticus 17:11 explains, "For the life of the flesh is in the blood, and I have given it to you upon the altar to make atonement for your souls; for it is the blood that makes atonement for the soul" (NKJV).

key point

Blood represents life. And God chose to temporarily accept the life of an animal in place of the life of a sinner. The death of an animal substitute provided a temporary covering that allowed God to accept and forgive sinners.

Even the process that a worshipper went through in offering a sacrifice for sin taught this lesson. The sacrificial animal was brought to the priest. Then the worshipper "shall lay his hand on the head and kill it at the place where they kill the burnt offering before the LORD" (Leviticus 4:24 NKJV). In laying hands on the animal the sinner identified himself with it, symbolically acknowledging that he deserved death and offering the animal's life in place of his own.

## The Show Goes On and On and On

Generations of Old Testament believers brought the required sacrifices. They laid hands on the sacrificial animals' heads and offered them in their own place. Again and again they acted out a scene that foreshadowed Christ's offering of Himself on Calvary.

In images worth far more than a thousand words, Israel and the world were being prepared to recognize the significance of Jesus's death on Calvary. His shed blood represented His life, given freely for us. In surrendering up His life, Jesus took our place and bore the punishment that we deserve. But in so dying Christ satisfied forever the requirements of justice; that sin merits the death penalty and that that penalty must be paid.

But God didn't rely simply on the acting out of this spiritual truth. He communicated the truth in words as well. No clearer Old Testament word picture exists than that sketched by the prophet Isaiah some seven hundred years before the birth of Jesus.

ISAIAH 53:4–6, 10 *Surely He has borne our griefs and carried our sorrows; yet we esteemed Him stricken, smitten by God, and afflicted. But He was wounded for our transgressions, He was bruised for our iniquities; the chastisement for our peace was upon Him, and by His stripes we are healed. All we like sheep have gone astray; we have turned, every one, to his own way; and the LORD has laid on Him the iniquity of us all. Yet it pleased the LORD to bruise Him; He has put Him to grief. When You make His soul an offering for sin, He shall see His seed, He shall prolong His days, and the pleasure of the LORD shall prosper in His hands. (NKJV)*

## He Is Our Offering for Sin

Christ's blood was shed, His life was given, in exchange for ours.

The prophecy God Himself acted out for Adam and Eve at the beginning of time, that He commanded be acted out again and again on history's stage; has in Christ at long last been fulfilled.

# What About Those Old Testament Saints?

**justified**
declared "not
guilty" and set free

What happened to those Old Testament saints who believed in God? All they had were animal sacrifices. As Hebrews reminds us, those sacrifices could only purify material things. How, then, could God forgive those who trusted Him before Christ appeared? The apostle Paul deals with this question in Romans:

> **ROMANS 3:24–26** *being **justified** freely by His grace through the redemption that is in Christ Jesus, whom God set forth as a propitiation by His blood, through faith, to demonstrate His righteousness, because in His forbearance God had passed over the sins that were previously committed, to demonstrate at the present time His righteousness, that He might be just and the justifier of the one who has faith in Jesus. (NKJV)*

Looking back, Paul notes that God "passed over" (i.e., seemed to ignore) the sins of Old Testament saints. But in the death of Jesus we see that God didn't ignore sin at all. Jesus's death was a propitiation. That is, in dying Christ satisfied the demands of justice. Jesus's cross is a demonstration of the righteousness of God. Sending Jesus to die in our place was the only thing God could do if He were to declare sinners "not guilty" and still do what justice demands.

key point

At the same time, in the death of Jesus we at last see that the righteousness of God, as demonstrated in His pre-Christ's-death forgiveness of the Old Testament saints, was something God could offer *only because He always operates in the "present," even though the death of His own Son was—by earthly reckoning—still several centuries in the future.*

To put it another way, on the basis of Jesus's still-future death, God was able to righteously forgive *all sins* prior to His Son's actual death. And He is able to do so in the present, and will do so in the future as well, but based in these last two cases on what has already happened—not what He alone knew would *eventually* happen.

# Is Jiminy Cricket Always Right?

> **HEBREWS 9:9, 13–14** *It was symbolic for the present time in which both gifts and sacrifices are offered which cannot make him who performed the service perfect in regard to the conscience. For if the blood of bulls and goats and the ashes of a*

*heifer, sprinkling the unclean, sanctifies for the purifying of the flesh, how much more shall the blood of Christ, who through the eternal Spirit offered Himself without spot to God, cleanse your conscience from dead works to serve the living God? (NKJV)*

The Greeks invented the word for "conscience." They weren't happy with the term or with what it described. Originally, "conscience" was simply "remembrance of past acts," but it soon involved evaluation of those acts in terms of "good" and "evil." The trouble was that this kind of evaluation tends to end up with more counts of "evil" than anything else.

Paul describes the plight of sinners forced to face their past failures. He notes that their "consciences" bear witness to the moral nature of the universe, so that they struggle, "their thoughts accusing or else **excusing them**" (Romans 2:15 NKJV).

Today we tend to think of conscience as the moral faculty we're to use when looking ahead at moral choices. But while Jiminy Cricket might urge Pinocchio to "always let your conscience be your guide," we all know that conscience still drags our eyes backward. We all know what it means to have a "guilty conscience" or a "bad conscience." We all have moral standards, whether those standards are biblical or not. And every human being violates the standards he or she holds, even those who act as if they had no conscience at all.

## The Trouble with a Troubled Conscience

What we may not understand is how past acts that trouble our conscience affect our lives. It's not just that we struggle to excuse ourselves or that we tend to blame others. Awareness of past failures is like a bunch of ropes wrapped around our limbs, immobilizing us.

We'd like to step out in faith and respond to God's voice. But just as we're ready to tentatively extend one foot, conscience shouts a reminder of our past failures and drains away our confidence. Being the kind of persons we are, how can our future be any different from our past? And so the testimony of our conscience as to "the kind of person we are" robs us of hope for the future.

What we desperately need is a cleansed conscience; one emptied of the residue of past sins and failures. A conscience that will neither nag us nor trip us up as we try to follow Jesus. And this is just what the writer of Hebrews promises his readers. The sacrifices of the Old Testament provided an external, temporary purification. "How much more," he asks, "shall the blood of Christ cleanse your conscience from dead works to serve the living God?" (Hebrews 9:14 NKJV).

## I'm Really Forgiven!

King David knew the relief that floods a person's soul when he or she realizes, "I'm forgiven!" David expressed this joy in Psalm 32:1–2: "Blessed is he whose transgression is forgiven, whose sin is covered. Blessed is the man to whom the LORD does not **impute** iniquity" (NKJV). But there is more to forgiveness than not being held accountable for one's sins and failures.

Three different Greek words are translated "forgive" in English versions of the New Testament.

- *Charizomai.* This word means "to be gracious to." It was used in business to describe canceling a debt (Luke 7:42–43), a usage that's similar to David's praise of God for not holding him accountable for his iniquity. When Christians are urged to forgive one another, this is the word that's used to indicate <u>not holding some sin against</u> a brother or sister.

- *Aphiemi.* This verb is used 146 times in the New Testament. It's used in the sense of "forgive" 49 times. But the basic meaning is "to dismiss or release." When Jesus told a paralytic, "Your sins are forgiven" (Mark 2:5 NKJV), He was not saying that his past sins would not be held against him. Jesus was claiming the right to dismiss, or send away, the sins themselves. You and I may be gracious to others who sin against us, but we have no power to rid them of the sins themselves. But this is exactly what God's forgiveness does!

- *Aphesis.* This word is used 17 times in the New Testament, most expressing divine forgiveness or **remission** of sins. Again the emphasis is on removal of the sins themselves, not simply dismissing the charges.

Christ's death did more than deal with our guilt. In dying, Christ paid for our sins and removed them. Objectively speaking, our sins are literally *gone*!

**go to**

**not holding sin against**
2 Corinthians 2:7–10;
Colossians 3:13;
Ephesians 4:32

**remission**
Luke 1:77;
Acts 2:38;
Ephesians 1:7;
Colossians 1:14;
Hebrews 9:22

**impute**
charge with, hold accountable for

**remission**
cancellation

# That Smoke-Filled Room

Have you ever gone into a motel room and immediately been overwhelmed by the odor of smoke? You wrinkle your nose, and start to cough. There's no one smoking in the room, of course. It's empty. But the odor from the past lingers on to plague the next non-smoker who enters.

It's a lot like this with forgiveness. Christ has taken away our sins. Objectively speaking our sins are gone. But somehow they linger in our awareness, clogging our consciences and robbing us not only of joy but also of hope for our future. Subjectively we've never claimed the cleansing God has provided; a cleansing by Christ's blood that purged our consciences from those "dead works" that have taken root and attempt to define for us the "kind of person we are."

That definition may be accurate for "the kind of person we *were*." But remembered sins no longer define the person we are *becoming*. The sins that once defined us are gone, forgiven, sent away. The conscience that condemned us, based on what we did in the past, has been cleansed. We no longer need to look back and see ourselves reflected in our sins. Now we can look ahead and see ourselves in what we are becoming.

The apostle Paul draws a powerful contrast between what believers were without Christ and what we're becoming in Him. He uses the imagery of fruit.

## With and Without Christ

| The Works of the Flesh (who we were) | The Fruit of the Spirit (who we're becoming) |
| --- | --- |
| Adultery, fornication, uncleanness lewdness, idolatry, sorcery, hatred, contentions, jealousies, outbursts of wrath, selfish ambitions, dissensions, heresies, envy, murders, drunkenness, revelries, and the like (Galatians 5:19–21 NKJV) | Love, joy, peace, longsuffering, kindness, goodness, faithfulness, gentleness, self-control (Galatians 5:22–23 NKJV) |

Any of those sins in the list on the left that you've committed are forgiven in Christ. They're gone, washed away by His blood. And they no longer define who you are or determine what you'll do in the future.

All of those qualities in the list on the right may not characterize you right now. But they do define the person you're becoming in Christ. They define who you *will* be, and they free you to step out in faith and live God's way. In the words of the writer of Hebrews, with your conscience "cleansed . . . from dead works" you are free "to serve the living God" (9:14 NKJV).

**testament**
a will

## Clean Clear Through and Deodorized Too

How can we experience the cleansing that Scripture affirms that Christ has provided? We simply take God's Word for our cleansing. When old thoughts and attitudes rear up to discourage us, we trust in God's promise and refuse to be dominated by them. We claim by faith the person God will help us become, and we choose to act in harmony with what we are becoming. This is how we experience the joy of our salvation, and find freedom from our past.

That's some inheritance! And it's ours. All ours.

## Where There's a Will There's a Death

**HEBREWS 9:15–21** *And for this reason He is the Mediator of the new covenant, by means of death, for the redemption of the transgressions under the first covenant, that those who are called may receive the promise of the eternal inheritance. For where there is a **testament**, there must also of necessity be the death of the testator. For a testament is in force after men are dead, since it has no power at all while the testator lives. Therefore not even the first covenant was dedicated without blood. For when Moses had spoken every precept to all the people according to the law, he took the blood of calves and goats, with water, scarlet wool, and hyssop, and sprinkled both the book itself and all the people, saying, "This is the blood of the covenant which God has commanded you." Then likewise he sprinkled with blood both the tabernacle and all the vessels of the ministry. (NKJV)*

Our inheritance as believers under the new covenant is truly amazing. We've been forgiven. Our consciences have been cleansed. At last we can set out confidently to serve our God. But now the writer of Hebrews reminds us that what we have truly is an inheritance. Shifting to another image, he portrays the new covenant as a will. He makes the point that for a person to inherit anything under a will, the one who draws up the will must first die.

Who is the Mediator, the One through whom the new covenant blessings come? Jesus. Then obviously Jesus had to die for us to inherit its blessings.

Even the old covenant required death to institute it, though the blood shed then was that of "bulls and goats." Again, without specifically saying it, the writer points up the superiority of the new covenant. The new covenant was instituted through blood shed by the Son of God. No wonder its blessings are so superior to any benefits the old covenant might provide! But, was the death of Christ truly *required*?

key point

what others say

**John MacArthur**

Blood is a symbol of death, and there follows closely the idea of a testator's having to die in order for a will to become effective. But blood also suggests the animal sacrifices that were marks of the Old Covenant, even, in fact, of the Abrahamic covenant. In the Old Covenant, the death of animals was typical and prophetic, looking forward to the death of Christ that would ratify the second covenant. Even before the old priestly sacrifices were begun, the Abrahamic covenant was inaugurated, or ratified, with blood (Genesis 15).[6]

## Packed Up and Put Away

GOD AT WORK

HEBREWS 9:22–28 *And according to the law almost all things are purified with blood, and without shedding of blood there is no remission. Therefore it was necessary that the copies of the things in the heavens should be purified with these, but the heavenly things themselves with better sacrifices than these. For Christ has not entered the holy places made with hands, which are copies of the true, but into heaven itself, now to appear in the presence of God for us; not that He should offer Himself often, as the high priest enters the Most Holy Place every year with blood of another—He then would have had to suffer often since the foundation of the world; but now, once at the end of the ages, He has appeared to put away sin by the sacrifice of Himself. And as it is appointed for men to die once, but after this the judgment, so Christ was offered once to bear the sins of many. To those who eagerly wait for Him He will appear a second time, apart from sin, for salvation. (NKJV)*

**Tom Fettke and Camp Kirkland**

In Christ alone my hope is found; He is my light, my strength, my song. This Cornerstone, this solid ground, firm through the fiercest drought and storm. In Christ alone, who took on flesh, fullness of God in helpless Babe. This gift of life and righteousness, scorned by the ones He came to save. 'Till on that cross, as Jesus died, the will of God was satisfied; for ev'ry sin on Him was laid, here in the death of Christ, I live. No guilt in life, no fear in death, this is the power of Christ in me; from life's first cry to final breath, Jesus commands my destiny. No power of hell, no scheme of man can ever pluck me from His hand; till He returns or calls me home, here in the power of Christ I stand.[7]

Every day the Levitical priests sharpened their knives and brought out their basins to collect the blood of sacrificial animals. Every evening they washed their equipment in preparation for the next day. There was no end to their task of outwardly purifying those who violated some law or regulation, for purification and the remission of sins called for repeated shedding of blood. But that was here on earth, where everything was a copy of "the heavenly things" (Hebrews 9:23 NKJV).

To purify heavenly things a far better sacrifice was required—"the sacrifice of Himself" that Christ offered. That sacrifice was a one time event, for by the sacrifice of Himself Jesus "put away sin" (Hebrews 9:26 NKJV). There was no need for another sacrifice. Christ accomplished what the Old Testament system could not do.

It was time at last to pack up and put away the Levitical priest's tools. Jesus completed the work He was assigned, "now to appear in the presence of God for us" as our High Priest (Hebrews 9:24 NKJV). Men die once, and afterward face God's judgment. Jesus died once, to bear the sins of many.

Once was enough. When on the cross Jesus cried, "It is finished," He told the absolute truth.

## The Sacrifice Returns

And so the writer of Hebrews ends this section of his teaching with a good word: "To those who eagerly wait for Him He will appear a second time, apart from sin, for salvation" (9:28 NKJV).

Jesus died but He isn't dead. He lives today, seated at the right hand of the Father, speaking up for us as our High Priest. This same Jesus is coming again. When He comes it will not be to deal with sin. It will be to bring us the full and complete salvation His blood won for us.

What a glorious thing this is for "those who eagerly wait for Him" (Hebrews 9:28 NKJV).

## The Final Strokes of Justice

But not everyone is eager for Christ to appear. Not everyone trusts the Savior and has his or her sins forgiven. For such persons the future is bleak rather than bright. For the writer's words are true. It is "appointed for men to die once." Everyone dies. "But after this the judgment" (Hebrews 9:27 NKJV). Death isn't the end for any human being. And what awaits us is either salvation or judgment.

**REVELATION 20:11–15** *Then I saw a great white throne and Him who sat on it, from whose face the earth and the heaven fled away. And there was found no place for them. And I saw the dead, small and great, standing before God, and books were opened. And another book was opened, which is the Book of Life. And the dead were judged according to their works, by the things which were written in the books. The sea gave up the dead who were in it, and Death and Hades delivered up the dead who were in them. And they were judged, each one according to his works. Then Death and Hades were cast into the lake of fire. This is the second death. And anyone not found written in the Book of Life was cast into the lake of fire. (NKJV)*

Trust the blood of Christ and look eagerly for Jesus to return. Or refuse to trust and be afraid.

## Chapter Wrap-Up

- Ministry in the Old Testament tabernacle and temple conveyed important spiritual truths, such as the necessity of blood sacrifice.

- But the ministry of the Old Testament priesthood was unable to provide forgiveness or access to God.

- Jesus opened the door of access to God when He offered Himself as sacrifice for us.
- Blood sacrifice has its roots in Genesis, and its significance is reflected in the Old Testament sacrificial system.
- Jesus's one sacrifice of Himself won forgiveness for us, and with forgiveness cleansing of our conscience.
- We Christians are no longer defined or limited by our past, but we are defined and freed by what we are becoming in Christ.
- Jesus has dealt with sin completely. When He returns it will be to complete our salvation.

## Study Questions

1. In what way was the Tabernacle a stage?

2. What lessons might be drawn from the never-ending enactment on that stage of the script God had written for the priests to act out?

3. What was the significance of the veil or curtain that hung between the Tabernacle Holy Place and the Holy of Holies? What was the significance of its tearing when Jesus died?

4. When was blood sacrifice first initiated, and by whom?

5. What does blood stand for?

6. What are two functions of the conscience. Why was it vital that Christ's death "cleanse your conscience" (Hebrews 9:14 NKJV)?

7. In what way is the new covenant like a will?

8. What's the difference between the forgiveness we might offer another person and the forgiveness God provides for us?

9. How do we break the bonds that conscience imposes on us?

Chapter Highlights:
• Back in Shadowland
• Cease Fire!
• Your Verdict, Please
• Going AWOL—Not
  Your Style!

# Hebrews 10
# The X-treme Volunteer

## Let's Get Started

The writer of the Letter to the Hebrews has made his case. God's revelation in Jesus is superior to that given through Moses. Jesus's High Priesthood is superior to that of the Levitical priesthood. The new covenant that Jesus administers is superior to the old covenant made with Israel in Moses's day. As our High Priest Jesus serves in the heavenly temple, while Israel's priests minister in a mere copy and shadow of the true. And Jesus's sacrifice of Himself has accomplished what the blood of sacrificial animals could never do.

But as the writer is about to move on to Christian lifestyle, like a good attorney, he closes this section of the book by going over key points once again. If what we read in Hebrews 10 sounds familiar, it's because it is familiar. But it's also vital. And the writer wants to be sure that there's no mistake about the core truths he's taught. After all, our life depends on them.

## Back in Shadowland

> **HEBREWS 10:1–4** *For the law, having a shadow of the good things to come, and not the very image of the things, can never with these same sacrifices, which they offer continually year by year, make those who approach perfect. For then would they not have ceased to be offered? For the worshipers, once purified, would have had no more consciousness of sins. But in those sacrifices there is a reminder of sins every year. For it is not possible that the blood of bulls and goats could take away sins.* (NKJV)

This is one of the writer's most powerful arguments. The very nature of the old system is proof of its inadequacy. The tabernacle system was supposed to deal with sins and provide access to God, but that whole system simply could not do the whole job. If the sacrifices had really worked and cleansed the worshippers, they would not have had to be repeated. If the worshippers had been fully cleansed, they wouldn't have remained so aware of their transgres-

**perfect**
complete the task of
making them
acceptable to God

sions. In reality, what the repeated sacrifices did was remind the worshippers that they were sinful!

**what others say**

**Vern S. Paythress**

Animal sacrifices are ultimately inadequate. Israel goes on sinning year after year, and new animals must be presented year after year in the same repetitious ceremonies in a process that never ends. The process never suffices. Animals could never be an adequate substitute for human beings made in the image of God The very inadequacy of these sacrifices confirms the inadequacy with the tabernacle structure. They are only copies of the heavenly realities.[1]

It's something like a person whose kidneys are failing, who has to go on a dialysis machine three times a week. The treatments cleanse the blood temporarily and keep the patient alive. But the fact that the treatment must be repeated over and over is a constant reminder of how ill he truly is.

In the same way, the fact that Old Testament sacrifices had to be repeated over and over again was a constant reminder to Old Testament believers that they were sinners, the animal sacrifices provided temporary relief—in a sense they kept the sinner alive. But they were no cure. It would take more than the blood of bulls and goats to "make those who approach **perfect**" (Hebrews 10:1 NKJV). It simply wasn't possible "that the blood of bulls and goats could take away sins" ( Hebrews 10:4 NKJV). At best, the Old Testament sacrificial system was a hint of good things to come!

## So Jesus Stepped Forward

HEBREWS 10:5–10 *Therefore, when He came into the world, He said:*
*"Sacrifice and offering You did not desire,*
*But a body You have prepared for Me.*
*In burnt offerings and sacrifices for sin*
*You had no pleasure.*
*Then I said, 'Behold, I have come—*
*In the volume of the book it is written of Me—*
*To do Your will, O God.'"*

Septuagint
an early Greek trans-
lation of the Old
Testament

*Previously saying, "Sacrifice and offering, burnt offerings and offerings for sin You did not desire, nor had pleasure in them" (which are offered according to the law), then He said, "Behold, I have come to do Your will, O God." He takes away the first that He may establish the second. By that will we have been sanctified through the offering of the body of Jesus Christ once for all. (NKJV)*

In quoting from Psalm 40:6–8 (Hebrews 10:5–8, above) the writer asks us to see in the familiar verses a commitment made by God the Son to the Father. The quote doesn't exactly match the NKJV version of the Psalm. Remember, the author of Hebrews always quotes from the Bible version with which Greek-speaking Jews are most familiar, the **Septuagint**.

### Sacrifices—Neither Desired Nor Required

| Psalm 40:6 | Hebrews 10:5–6 |
| --- | --- |
| Sacrifice and offering You did not desire | Sacrifice and offering You did not desire |
| Burnt offering and sin offering You did not require | In burnt offerings and sacrifices for sin You had no pleasure |

The psalm and Hebrews make the same point. God never wanted sacrifices and offerings in the first place! The psalm goes so far as to say God didn't "require" them. What God did want, and what He required, was that His people live godly lives, loving Him and keeping His commandments. The sacrificial system was instituted only because the Israelites sinned and failed to do what God really desired. If they had remained faithful, that would have pleased the Lord a lot more!

key point

## No Kick from Pop-Guns or Burnt Offerings

When I was about eight I wanted a BB gun. I was thrilled when I saw a gun-shaped package under the Christmas tree at my grand-parents' house. But when I opened the package I found a pop-gun that shot corks! It was terribly hard for me to pretend to be happy. I'd yearned for the real thing and had received what I considered a worthless substitute.

I must have felt something like God did as He yearned for His people's love and obedience, yet all He received were sacrifices and

**awl**
sharp-pointed metal
tool for making
holes

offerings that underlined how tragically they had failed Him. No wonder Scripture says of the sacrifices, "You had no pleasure" (Hebrews 10:6 NKJV).

There was an additional reason why God had no pleasure in offerings and sacrifices. Although they demonstrated His mercy, centuries of sacrifices and offerings never succeeded in truly changing the hearts of His people.

## Servant—The One with His Ear Nailed to the Door!

**PSALM 40:6**—*My ears You have opened. (NKJV)*
**HEBREWS 10:5**—*But a body You have prepared for Me. (NKJV)*

The Septuagint translation points back to a law concerning servants that's found in Deuteronomy 15. When a Hebrew sold himself as a servant/slave to a fellow Israelite, his servitude was limited to six years. In the seventh year the servant was to be freed, and supplied with essentials so he could get a fresh start.

But the law also provided for a situation where the slave/servant did not want to leave "because he loves you and your house" (Deuteronomy 15:16 NKJV). In this case the owner "shall take an **awl** and thrust it through his ear to the door, and he shall be your servant forever" (Deuteronomy 15:17 NKJV).

This is the image that the writer of Hebrews sees in Psalm 40:6. The Son of God chooses to accept the role of the Father's servant. He says, "My ears You have opened [pierced]" (Psalm 40:6 NKJV).

The apostle Paul parallels this understanding when he writes in Philippians of Jesus, "who, being in the form of God, did not consider it robbery to be equal with God, but made Himself of no reputation, taking the form of a bondservant, and coming in the likeness of men" (Philippians 2:6–7 NKJV).

key point

### Getting a Kick from Doing God's Will

| Psalm 40:7–8 | Hebrews 10:7 |
|---|---|
| Then I said, "Behold, I come; in the scroll of the book it is written of me. I delight to do Your will, O my God, and Your law is within my heart." (NKJV) | Then I said, "Behold, I have come—in the volume of the book it is written of Me—to do Your will, O God." (NKJV) |

This Old Testament quotation looks ahead to a time when the Son will enter the human race ("I come"). The Septuagint translation, from which the writer of Hebrews quotes, changes the tense ("Behold, I have come"). This focuses our attention on the two covenants. The older covenant given to Moses that was ineffective is now obsolete. God's will was for Jesus to initiate the promised new covenant.

And so Jesus, committed to do the will of the Father, stepped forward. He volunteered to be born into our world as a true human being, to die for our sins, and to be raised again to become our great High Priest.

what others say

**J. Dwight Pentecost**

The father was the One who offered His Son as the sacrifice (Psalm 22:15; Isaiah 13:10) Jesus Christ became a sacrifice by submitting to the will of His Father."[2]

## The Only Sacrifice That Makes You Holy

HEBREWS 10:10 *By that will we have been sanctified through the offering of the body of Jesus Christ once for all.* (NKJV)

The Greek word translated "sanctified," *hagiazo*, means "to make holy." The word is used in the Bible to indicate at least two spiritual realities:

- *Set aside*—In the Old Testament someone or something was "made holy" or "sanctified" when it was isolated from every ordinary use and set apart solely for the service of God. Under this meaning, the priests, the tabernacle (later the temple), and its furnishings were "holy."

- *Changing*—In the New Testament the idea of separation yields to a new emphasis. Sanctification is now dynamic and vital; the infusion of life-changing, Holy Spirit power. *Hagiazo* has to do with *condition* as well as use. The emphasis is on change of quality. "To cause someone to have the quality of holiness" (see 1 Thessalonians 5:23).[3] When the Spirit of God sanctifies someone, it's not just that the person's name has been moved from the Devil's team roster to the Lord's. To have been "sanctified" is to be "separated from the common condition." To put it

**go to**

**holy in God's sight**
Acts 20:32;
Romans 15:16;
1 Corinthians 1:2;
6:11

**a process**
1 Thessalonians
5:23–24;
Romans 8:3–4;
2 Corinthians 3:18

another way—*changed*. The quality of what the person now is and is becoming marks her/him as the Lord's.

## The Process of Becoming

Like salvation, sanctification has past, present, and future aspects:

- *Past.* Hebrews 10:10. Because of Christ the believer *has been* sanctified (made <u>holy) in God's sight</u>.

- *Present.* Hebrews 10:14. Because of Christ the believer *is being* sanctified (made holy). It's in the Greek aorist tense: *Past completed action continuing in the present.* Sanctification is also <u>a process</u>.

- *Future.* At the same time sanctification is something that we will experience fully only in our resurrection:

1 CORINTHIANS 15:51–52 *"Behold. I tell you a mystery: We shall not all sleep [in death] but we shall all be changed—in a moment, in the twinkling of an eye, at the last trumpet. For the trumpet will sound, and the dead will be raised incorruptible, and we shall be changed."* (NKJV)

1 JOHN 3:2 *"When He [Christ] is revealed, we shall be like Him, for we shall see Him as He is."* (NKJV)

## Incredible!

The writer of Hebrews doesn't focus on these aspects of sanctification. He simply makes it clear that our hope of holiness doesn't depend on anything that we might do. In offering Himself "once for all" (Hebrews 10:10 NKJV), Jesus has done all that needs to be done! We stand before God robed in a holiness Jesus has provided. We experience the dynamic and transforming power of the Spirit, who enables us to live holy lives only because this too is something Jesus had provided.

As with salvation, our positive response—**repent** and trust in Jesus—clears the way for the holiness process to begin. Jesus has provided that His holy life and character may increasingly pervade your life, your lifestyle, and your actions. And when you are raised from the dead, purified from every taint of sin, this too will be something Jesus has provided for you.

And He provided all this in His one sacrifice of Himself in the body that God the Father prepared for His Son.

JERUSALEM. *Circa* AD 64—An edict from the authorities has placed the Temple off-limits to Hebrew Christians. Animal sacrifices on which, all their lives, they had counted for forgiveness and peace with God were now impossible. The teaching of the letter *"To the Hebrews"* that Jesus's *"once for all"* sacrifice is sufficient for access to God must have been a great relief. Believable truth about a way to constant fellowship with God, free from the blood of bulls and goats, made early Jewish Christians willing to die rather than renounce faith in Jesus.

KABUL, AFGHANISTAN—Associated Press, March 26, 2006— An Afghan court dismissed charges against Abdul Rahman, a 41-year-old convert to Christianity, angering Muslim clerics who insist, according to Islamic law, he should be killed. His family had reported him to authorities. His wife and daughters believed he was mentally ill. Before his arrest Rahman worked in Pakistan for a Catholic humanitarian organization. "I read the Bible and it opened my heart and my mind," Rahman said. The Italian newspaper, *La Repubblica*, after an interview with Rahman reported that he said, "I am serene. I have full awareness of what I have chosen. If I must die, I will die." Then he added, "Somebody, a long time ago, did it for all of us."[6]

## The Sacrifice to End All Sacrifices

HEBREWS 10:11–14 *And every priest stands ministering daily and offering repeatedly the same sacrifices, which can never*

go to

repent
Matthew 4:17;
Luke 3:3, 7–14

repent
turn around, "do a 180," confess and renounce your sins

*take away sins. But this Man, after He had offered one sacrifice for sins forever, sat down at the right hand of God, from that time waiting till His enemies are made His footstool. For by one offering He has perfected forever those who are being sanctified. (NKJV)*

key point

This too is familiar territory. The writer of Hebrews is like the old southern preacher who was asked how he preached. "I tells what I'm going to tell 'em. Then I tells 'em. And then I tells 'em what I told them." The Hebrews preacher too believes in repetition and in contrast.

## Earthly Sacrifices Don't Even Compare to Jesus's Sacrifice

| Old Testament Sacrifices | New Testament Contrast |
| --- | --- |
| Earthly priests offer repeated sacrifices. | Jesus offered one sacrifice. |
| They *stand*, their work unending. | Jesus *sits*, His work complete. |
| They labor on earth. | Jesus is seated at God's right hand, in power and glory. |
| Their sacrifices can never take away sins. | His sacrifice achieved its goal and made us holy forever. |

## The Conqueror's Footstool

The author adds one more powerful image. Jesus is seated, "waiting till His enemies are made His footstool" (Hebrews 10:13 NKJV). This image, quoted from Psalm 2, is drawn from another Old Testament incident:

JOSHUA 10:22–25 *Then Joshua said, "Open the mouth of the cave, and bring out those five kings to me from the cave." And they did so, and brought out those five kings to him from the cave: So it was, when they brought out those kings to Joshua, that Joshua called for all the men of Israel, and said to the captains of the men of war who went with him, "Come near, put your feet on the necks of these kings." And they drew near and put their feet on their necks. Then Joshua said to them, "Do not be afraid, nor be dismayed; be strong and of good courage, for thus the LORD will do to all your enemies against whom you fight." (NKJV)*

Early in the campaign to take the Promised Land, the Israelites—with Joshua as their general—defeated a coalition of five kings. After the defeat the five kings hid in a cave, which Joshua's men had sealed with rocks. The rest of the story is in Joshua 10.

## "I'll Be Back!" (Jesus)

**consecrated**
set aside

**house**
household, family

REVELATION 6:15–17 *And the kings of the earth, the great men, the rich men, the commanders, the mighty men, every slave and every free man, hid themselves in the caves and in the rocks of the mountains, and said to the mountains and rocks, "Fall on us and hide us from the face of Him who sits on the throne and from the wrath of the Lamb! For the great day of His wrath has come, and who is able to stand?"* (NKJV)

Earlier the writer of Hebrews had mentioned Jesus's return, promising that He would "appear a second time, apart from sin, for salvation" (Hebrews 9:28 NKJV). Here he expands on that return. When Christ comes back He will do more than complete our salvation. When Jesus returns He will crush all opposition and His enemies will be "made His footstool" (Hebrews 10:13 NKJV).

This promise of total victory is drawn from Psalm 2 and foreshadowed by the event in Joshua's time. That victory is more fully described in the book of Revelation, where one passage seems to reflect the terror that must have been felt by the five kings. There John describes his vision of the sky torn apart and mountains and islands jolted from their place (Revelation 6:15–17).

What a message for the harassed Jewish Christians of Jerusalem, and throughout the Roman Empire! In that fragment from Psalm 2 there was an echo of Joshua's word of encouragement to his troops: "Do not be afraid, nor be dismayed; be strong and of good courage, for thus the LORD will do to all your enemies against whom you fight" (Joshua 10:25 NKJV).

## Cease Fire!

HEBREWS 10:19–25 *Therefore, brethren, having boldness to enter the Holiest by the blood of Jesus, by a new and living way which He **consecrated** for us, through the veil, that is, His flesh, and having a High Priest over the **house** of God, let us draw near with a true heart in full assurance of faith, having our hearts sprinkled from an evil conscience and our bodies washed with pure water. Let us hold fast the confession of our hope without wavering, for He who promised is faithful. And let us consider one another in order to stir up love and good works, not forsaking the assembling of ourselves together, as is the manner*

**go to**

**Knowledge of Himself**
Jeremiah 9:23;
Hosea 6:6

**exhorting**
encouraging,
supporting

**Day**
hrist's return and
final victory

**summation**
outline, summary

*of some, but **exhorting** one another, and so much the more as you see the **Day** approaching. (NKJV)*

**David R. Anderson**

This completed work of the King-Priest also completely perfected forever those being sanctified. That is completely perfected in the sense that their sins have been completely removed for all time. They never have to crawl again; now they can come boldly throne of grace. The inaugurator of a better priesthood, and a better covenant, and a better sacrifice, is also the inaugurator of better access to God.[7]

The truths that the writer of Hebrews has emphasized in his **summation** aren't abstract philosophical concepts with no implications for our daily lives. When we take hold of these key truths by faith, we find that all our relationships change.

## In Good with God

Whoever thought we would be invited to "barge in" with boldness to the friendly presence of God with our needs and our desires to talk to Him about? At last we can feel totally comfortable, and we can even delight in God's presence. After their sin Adam and Eve ran to hide from their Creator. After Christ's sacrifice we run to Him, eagerly searching Him out to share our joys and sorrows, to ask for "grace to help in time of need" (Hebrews 4:16 NKJV) and apply for cleansing when we sin.

## What a Change!

**James I. Packer**

What were we made for? To know God. What aim should we set ourselves in life? To know God. What is the "eternal life" that Jesus gives? Knowledge of God. . . . (John 17:3). What is the best thing in life, bringing more joy, delight, and contentment than anything else? Knowledge of God. What of all the states God ever sees man in, gives him most pleasure? <u>Knowledge of himself.</u>[8]

We now draw near to God "in full assurance of faith" (Hebrews 10:22 NKJV). Our **hearts** have figuratively been sprinkled from an evil conscience and our bodies **washed with pure water**.

We've spoken of the conscience before. Our conscience was evil in that it was both a storehouse for remembered sin and a mass of tangled chains that kept us from acting in faith. But now, just as the Old Testament priests cleansed worshipers outwardly by sprinkling sacrificial blood and washing with water, Christ's blood has cleansed us inwardly, changing our hearts and wiping out our sins.

**go to**

washed with pure water
Ezekiel 36:25–27;
Hebrews 9:12–14

heart
the essential "me,"
the person as a
whole

washed with pure
water
figurative for cleansing the conscience,
not baptism

> **what others say**
>
> **Andrew Murray**
>
> True religion is a thing of the heart, an inward life. It is as the desire of the heart is fixed upon God, the whole heart seeking for God, giving its love and finding its joy in God, a man can draw near to God. Faith believes that God can be found: that He can and will make Himself known; that He cares for everyone who truly longs for Him.[9]

## I'm Okay with Me

We're no longer bound by our *evil consciences.* We can now look at ourselves in a new way. We are no longer merely sinners condemned by our own thoughts and fearful of God. We are "sanctified sinners" who have been cleansed and who are being transformed. In the words of the hymn, "I'm not what I wanta be, I'm not what I'm gonna be, but thank God, I'm not what I was!"

We're members of God's family now, loved by the Father, saved by the Son, empowered by the Spirit. God has given us a hope to hold on to, a new identity. And "He who promised is faithful" (Hebrews 10:23 NKJV).

## Siblings of Grace

What's more, we're no longer alone. We're members of God's family. We have others who care about us, and about whom we care. Rather than focusing on outsiders who criticize and pressure them, these early Jewish Christians are encouraged to "consider one another" (Hebrews 10:24 NKJV). They are to focus on the relationships they have with Christian brothers and sisters, and they are to make positive contributions to their lives, stirring up "love and good works" (10:24 NKJV).

Instead of letting persecution drive them away from other followers of Jesus, these early Jewish Christians need to let persecution drive them together. They—and we—need each other's encouragement. And especially, the writer adds, in view of the fact that the day of Jesus's return is approaching.

That Day has been approaching for almost two millennia. And we can be sure that it is closer now than it was then. For all we know, that Day is just around the corner, and we may wake up tomorrow to hear the trumpets blowing, to see the dead in Christ rising from their graves, and to join them in the air to "always be with the Lord" (1 Thessalonians 4:17 NKJV).

## Your Verdict, Please

HEBREWS 10:26–31 *For if we sin willfully after we have received the knowledge of the truth, there no longer remains a sacrifice for sins, but a certain fearful expectation of judgment, and fiery indignation which will devour the adversaries. Anyone who has rejected Moses' law dies without mercy on the testimony of two or three witnesses. Of how much worse punishment, do you suppose, will he be thought worthy who has trampled the Son of God underfoot, counted the blood of the covenant by which he was sanctified a common thing, and insulted the Spirit of grace? For we know Him who said, "Vengeance is Mine, I will repay," says the Lord. And again, "The LORD will judge His people." It is a fearful thing to fall into the hands of the living God. (NKJV)*

The writer of Hebrews has argued his case. Now he calls on his readers to register their verdict.

The warning in chapter 6 posed a clearly hypothetical case. The author was speaking to Jewish believers in Jesus, and he pointed out how ridiculous it was to go back to a system whose repeated sacrifices had proved ineffective. He asked what they would do if they returned to Judaism and then later changed their minds and wanted to identify themselves as Christians. Would they crucify Jesus all over again?

Now, after having clearly explained the significance of Christ's one sacrifice—and that of the new covenant relationship with God that Jesus won for His followers—the writer is much more blunt. They need to reach a verdict about Jesus and stick with it. There must be no more wavering between Jesus and the old system. It's time to *choose.*

go to

**sinned unintentionally**
Leviticus 4:13, 22, 27

## No Way Around the Cross

**HEBREWS 10:26** *For if we sin willfully after we have received the knowledge of the truth, there no longer remains a sacrifice for sins. (NKJV)*

The writer is referring to a feature of Old Testament law that we examined earlier. A sin offering was available only to a person who sinned unintentionally. The only provision the law made for intentional sins was the sacrifice offered by the high priest on the Day of Atonement "for all their sins" (Leviticus 16:34 NKJV).

It's as though the writer of Hebrews is saying to his readers, "You think you want to go back to the Law Covenant? Well, you know the truth now. And look what the law says about those who know the truth and still sin!" What it says is, for them "there no longer remains a sacrifice for sins" (Hebrews 10:26 NKJV).

Go back if you must. But if you do go back, realize that the law makes no provision for the sin of rejecting the Savior!

key point

> what others say
>
> **Calvin Miller**
>
> The blood of Christ is the witness of God to the triumph of love. The blood of Christ is God's signature on His new agreement with us. Blood means that God means business and the agreement is valid. God asks only that we look on the cross and believe.[10]

## The Fiery Decree

**HEBREWS 10:27** *but a certain fearful expectation of judgment, and fiery indignation which will devour the adversaries. Anyone who has rejected Moses' law dies without mercy on the testimony of two or three witnesses. (NKJV)*

If the readers choose to go back, the law offers no hope of a sacrifice that might even temporarily cover their willful sin. What it does offer is judgment. And the phrase "fiery indignation" recalls several Old Testament incidents:

When Aaron and his sons were commissioned as priests the Lord gave them explicit instructions about how they were to present sacrifices and offerings. But two of the sons, Nadab and Abihu, ignored God's instructions. They offered "**profane** fire before the LORD, which He had not commanded them. So fire went out from the LORD and devoured them, and they died before the LORD" (Leviticus 10:1–2 NKJV).

Shortly after receiving the law at Mount Sinai, the people "complained" and it "displeased the LORD and His anger was aroused. So the fire of the LORD burned among them, and consumed some in the outskirts of the camp" (Numbers 11:1 NKJV).

Still later, after leaving Sinai, Korah led a rebellion against God's choice of Aaron's family to serve as priests. When he and his followers appeared to offer incense before the tabernacle, "a fire came out from the LORD and consumed the two hundred and fifty men who were offering incense" (Numbers 16:35 NKJV).

Not only was there no hope of a sacrifice to cover intentional sins. The Old Testament recorded what happened to those who went against the law!

Even those who didn't directly affront God as those in the three examples did could expect no mercy. Anyone who committed a capital crime, observed by two or three witnesses, was to be condemned to death (Deuteronomy 17:6). And that law required "the hands of the witnesses shall be the first against him to put him to death, and afterward the hands of all the people. So you shall put away the evil from among you" (Deuteronomy 17:7 NKJV).

## Trust Jesus or You're Toast!

**HEBREWS 10:29** *Of how much worse punishment, do you suppose, will he be thought worthy who has trampled the Son of God underfoot, counted the blood of the covenant by which he was sanctified a common thing, and insulted the Spirit of grace? (NKJV)*

In a series of images the writer sums up what it would be like should a follower of Jesus turn back to the old covenant:

- He or she would be treating Jesus with utter contempt, as if they had "trampled the Son of God underfoot."

- He or she would be showing disrespect for the blood that makes believers holy.

- He or she would be insulting God's Spirit.

So, he challenges, "how much worse punishment, do you suppose," one who deserts Jesus would deserve?

The author of Hebrews is pulling no punches. What some of the Jerusalem Jewish Christians were considering was unthinkable! How could they even consider treating the Christ that way? And with this said, he concludes with a pointed warning:

**HEBREWS 10:30–31** *For we know Him who said, "Vengeance is Mine, I will repay," says the Lord. And again, "The LORD will judge His people." It is a fearful thing to fall into the hands of the living God. (NKJV)*

Hello? Are you listening?

## Well Now, What's Your Verdict?

In this powerful warning section the writer of Hebrews challenges everyone who has heard the Gospel, not just wavering Jewish Christians of the first century. The promise of all the good things we are offered in Jesus is set against dire divine warnings of what awaits those who reject Him. Hebrews reminds us that each man and woman has a choice to make, and that choice is between life and death. Between blessing and judgment. For judgment is just as certain as grace, and that expectation of judgment is fearful indeed.

So, what's your choice, pilgrim? Will you trust the Savior, and "draw near with a true heart in full assurance of faith" (Hebrews 10:21 NKJV)?

Or, will you show contempt for the Savior who shed His blood for you, and continue to live "with a certain fearful expectation of judgment, and fiery indignation which will devour the adversaries" Hebrews 10:27 NKJV)?

key point

*The fact that such terrifying warnings are here, on the heels of the good news of the great sacrifice of love, indicates that God has no taste for devouring troublemakers. His desire is to receive with open arms every rebel who accepts His offer of grace.*

## Going AWOL—Not Your Style!

HEBREWS 10:32–39 *But recall the former days in which, after you were illuminated, you endured a great struggle with sufferings: partly while you were made a spectacle both by reproaches and tribulations, and partly while you became companions of those who were so treated; for you had compassion on me in my chains, and joyfully accepted the plundering of your goods, knowing that you have a better and an enduring possession for yourselves in heaven. Therefore do not cast away your confidence, which has great reward. For you have need of endurance, so that after you have done the will of God, you may receive the promise:*

*"For yet a little while*
*And He who is coming will come and will not tarry.*
*Now the just shall live by faith;*
*But if anyone draws back,*
*My soul has no pleasure in him."*

*But we are not of those who draw back to perdition, but of those who believe to the saving of the soul. (NKJV)*

Just as in chapter 6, here the writer's tone changes. He has called for his readers to register their verdict concerning Christ. But he doesn't want them to feel that he views them as deserters. So now the tone is comforting, as the writer recalls shared experiences. He lets them know that he places them in that same group of the faithful among whom he places himself, and says that "we are not of those who draw back to perdition, but of those who believe to the saving of the soul" (Hebrews 10:39 NKJV).

Implicit in the writer's words is something many believers experience. Perhaps you have? You were excited and enthusiastic when you first come to faith. Nothing seemed to deter you. You "joyfully accepted" the "plundering of your goods" (Hebrews 10:34 NKJV). Ridicule didn't intimidate you. You weren't daunted by persecution or frightened by sufferings.

something to ponder

Yet as the months and years go by, the constant struggle seems to wear you down. Gradually, so slowly you hardly noticed, you've lost your enthusiasm. Your once-bright outlook is shrouded in clouds, and you've become indifferent.

This is what happened to the Christian Jews in first-century Jerusalem. In time they wondered if they had made the right choice. Surely, if they were really God's chosen, things would go better for them.

## Hebrews Rx for Potential Deserters

1. First, remember what it was like at the beginning. That's the way it should continue to be.

2. Second, don't "cast away your confidence" (Hebrews 10:35 NKJV).

3. Third, what you need is "endurance, so that after you have done the will of God, you may receive the promise" (Hebrews 10:36 NKJV).

"Endurance" is something that's difficult in any era. It's particularly difficult here in the twenty-first century, where our culture promises instant gratification of every desire. Dating but not ready for the commitment of marriage? Just move in together. Want to go on a cruise you can't afford? Use your credit card. Credit card debt grown too big to handle? Take out a loan against your home. Don't worry about the future. Grab all the pleasure you can, now.

But God never has been in the instant gratification business. He calls on us to do His will in our today that *afterward* we may "receive the promise." And that *afterward* isn't in a few months or years or even in our lifetime. That "afterward" is when Jesus comes again. And He *is* coming. "For yet a little while, and He who is coming will come and will not tarry" (Hebrews 10:37 NKJV).

## Chapter Wrap-Up

- Like a lawyer, the writer of Hebrews now presents a summation of the key points in the case for Jesus.
- After the summation he calls for his readers to register their verdict. Will they stick with Jesus, or return to their old faith?
- Arguing from events and rulings in the Old Testament, the writer shows that a person who truly turns back has no hope.
- Despite confronting his readers so harshly, the writer remembers their early enthusiasm and is convinced they will remain faithful to Jesus.
- They will endure until Jesus returns, doing the will of God now, and when Christ comes they will "receive the promise" (Hebrews 10:35 NKJV).

## Study Questions

1. Why do the themes in Hebrews 10 seem so familiar?

2. How many of these themes can you list without looking at the text?

3. When calling on his readers to make a firm decision, the writer refers to Old Testament events and principles. Why?

4. What were the initial readers of this letter like when they first became Christians?

5. Why and how have they changed?

6. What three things make up the writer's prescription for those who have become discouraged? Which do you think is most important?

# Part Four
# Hebrews 11–13
# A LONG WALK OUTSIDE THE CAMP

# Hebrews 11
# The Visionaries

**Chapter Highlights:**
- The Trail of the Ancient God-Seekers
- Off to See the City
- The Case of the Unbelieving Believers

## Let's Get Started

Old Testament Law was a system of clearly established rules. There were unmistakable do's and unmistakable don'ts. When a person was uncertain about what God expected, he could check with a priest or, by the time the Letter to the Hebrews was written, with a great body of explanatory rules developed by Israel's rabbis and sages. There was always some expert in the law who'd be delighted to tell an inquirer just what God's will was.

The problem for the early Jewish Christians—and for many Christians today—is that the New Covenant instituted at Jesus's death doesn't work the way the Old Covenant did. Instead of listing rules, the writer of Hebrews tells his readers to listen for God's voice in their today (Hebrews 4:3–11).

They—and we—know the moral and spiritual principles imbedded in God's revelation. Those principles haven't changed. But now, rather than having rules to guide the application of moral principles in specific situations, we're to expect the Lord to speak to us and give us His personal guidance. To a people whose lives before Jesus were patterned by rules governing every aspect of daily life, the idea of abandoning the rules must have seemed terrifying.

What, then, does the writer of Hebrews have to offer in the place of life by rules? What he offers is a life of faith. And in this chapter he's about to demonstrate why his earliest readers—and you and I—should accept the life of faith.

key point

## Confidence in the Unseen

**HEBREWS 11:1–3** *Now faith is the substance of things hoped for, the evidence of things not seen. For by it the elders obtained a good testimony. By faith we understand that the worlds were framed by the word of God, so that the things which are seen were not made of things which are visible. (NKJV)*

**future resurrection**
Acts 2:26; 24:15;
26:6–7;
1 Thessalonians 4:13

**working today**
Galatians 5:5;
Colossians 1:27;
Philippians 2:13

The Greek word *hypostasis* is translated "substance" here. The Greek word can also be translated as "assurance" or "being sure." Faith, the writer tells us, is "being sure" of the "things hoped for." The word "hope" also rings with a sense of positive expectation. All the promises God makes to us in Christ will be fulfilled. Our hope isn't limited to a <u>future resurrection</u> but includes God <u>working in our lives today</u>.

In essence, faith is being sure that God is at work in us now and will work in us in the future.

But faith is also defined as "the evidence of things not seen" (Hebrews 11:1 NKJV). This phrase repeats and emphasizes the thought of its first occurence. The word translated "evidence" also means "confidence." Faith, which involves being sure of things hoped for but not yet realized, calls for having confidence in the unseen.

what others say

**Bede Frost**

Faith makes the hoped-for heavenly realities (which are extant and real independently of our faith) real to us.[1]

## Faith Lives in Unseen Realities

Earlier the writer contrasted the earthly tabernacle constructed in the time of Moses with the "true" worship center that exists in heaven. The visible tent and its furnishings were merely "copy and shadow" (Hebrews 8:5 NKJV). What these early Jewish Christians needed to learn was to abandon confidence in the detailed laws and the visible religious structures they had relied on all their lives, and to commit themselves fully to live by unseen realities.

What's more, the writer wants us to understand that a "by faith" way of life isn't as great a step away from the old religion as it might seem. The fact is that the "elders" also lived by faith, and it was by faith that they "obtained a good testimony" (Hebrews 11:2 NKJV). That is, the Old Testament saints we revere provide vivid testimony to the primacy and the effectiveness of living by faith in the unseen!

In arguing this point in Romans 4, the apostle Paul looks back at Genesis 15:6. There the Scripture reports that Abraham "believed in the LORD, and He accounted it to him for righteousness" (NKJV). Abraham's relationship with God was based on his trust in the God who promised him a son, despite Abraham's advanced age.

Humanly speaking, what God promised was impossible. But Abraham "did not consider his own body, already dead (since he was about a hundred years old), and the deadness of Sarah's womb. He did not waver at the promise of God through unbelief, but was strengthened in faith, giving glory to God" (Romans 4:19–20 NKJV).

A law that had not yet been given had no bearing on Abraham's relationship with God. Everything depended on Abraham's reliance on God's promise.

In Galatians 3 Paul makes this same point. The Law of Moses came some four centuries after the promises were given to Abraham. The Law, with its call to obedience, can't erase or supersede promise, which is claimed by faith. Faith had precedence in history, and faith has priority in the believer's life.

## Faith Generates Obedience Better Than Law

First-century Judaism placed its emphasis on obedience to God's law. A Jew sought to win God's favor by striving to keep the Law, for keeping the Law was assumed to be the key to maintaining a relationship with the Creator (Romans 9:30–32). It was a challenge for first-century Jewish Christians to shift their focus from living law-abiding lives to living life by faith. But the writer of Hebrews has earlier demonstrated that faith has priority.

In Hebrews 3 the writer analyzed the disobedience of the Exodus generation. They were told to enter the land of Canaan and to take it. But the spies sent out by Moses reported that the men of Canaan were like giants, and their fortified cities were impregnable. Terrified at the prospect of invading, the Israelites disobeyed God and were condemned to four decades of wandering in the desert.

Why did they fail? Because of "unbelief" (Hebrews 3:19 NKJV). They gave more weight to the enemy they could see than to the God they could not see. Despite the miracles the Lord had performed to win their freedom, these ex-slaves were still unwilling to place their faith in God when crunch time came. The writer sums it up, saying, "The word which they heard did not profit them, not being mixed with faith in those who heard it" (Hebrews 4:2 NKJV). It's clear from this exposition that faith in the unseen must have precedence, if for

**translated age**
Matthew 13:39;
28:20;
1 Corinthians 10:11;
Hebrews 9:26

no other reason than the fact that faith alone can generate true obedience!

## Seeing the Unseen Hand That Shapes the Ages

**HEBREWS 11:3** *By faith we understand that the worlds were framed by the word of God, so that the things which are seen were not made of things which are visible. (NKJV)*

This verse is frequently taken to refer to the creation of the universe. Certainly the details fit. God did call the universe into being by speaking the word (Psalm 33:4–11). And the physical universe was not fashioned of preexisting matter. It was not "made of things which are visible."

But it's likely that the writer is making a different point here.

The word translated "worlds" is *aion*. This word appears over one hundred times in the New Testament, and is normally <u>translated "age"</u>. It refers to a period of time of undetermined extent; an epoch or "era" marked by distinctive characteristics.

If this is the intended meaning, here the writer is telling us that God is acting behind the scenes to frame the various ages or epochs of human history. Rather than being able to explain past events in terms of causes and consequences ("the things which are seen" [Hebrews 11:3 NKJV]), faith enables us to understand that God's unseen hand has framed the ages and even now is shaping the era in which we live. We may not know our role in this present age, but we do know that God is at work in it and in us.

For at least these three truths we must learn to live by faith:

1. Faith in the unseen has priority in Scripture, for promise came long before law.

2. Faith in the unseen has priority in our experience, for faith produces obedience to God's voice.

3. Faith in the unseen provides the perspective we need to fit into God's plan for us in this present age.

All these are summed up in the principle laid down by the writer in Hebrews 4:7: "Today, if you will hear His voice, do not harden your hearts" (NKJV). The life of faith is lived by listening attentively for God's voice and responding to His leading in our today.

## The Trail of the Ancient God-Seekers

**HEBREWS 11:4–7** *By faith Abel offered to God a more excellent sacrifice than Cain, through which he obtained witness that he was righteous, God testifying of his gifts; and through it he being dead still speaks. By faith Enoch was taken away so that he did not see death, "and was not found, because God had taken him"; for before he was taken he had this testimony, that he pleased God. But without faith it is impossible to please Him, for he who comes to God must believe that He is, and that He is a rewarder of those who diligently seek Him. By faith Noah, being divinely warned of things not yet seen, moved with godly fear, prepared an ark for the saving of his household, by which he condemned the world and became heir of the righteousness which is according to faith. (NKJV)*

If we define faith by what we learn in this chapter, we discover that people of faith are not merely people believing the record of history. They are men and women possessed by a vision of realities not yet experienced. They live in hope that the best is ahead and they keep reaching for it. They see things the rest of the world cannot see, and that keeps them moving along a totally different trail from the road the rest of the world is following. True faith tends to make them aliens in this world. And *they* make history.

Now the writer of Hebrews begins listing "elders" who have "obtained a good testimony" by faith (11:2 NKJV). Interestingly, the chronological list also represents eras.

### The Pre-Flood Era
- Abel      Hebrews 11:4
- Enoch      Hebrews 11:5–6
- Noah      Hebrews 11:7

### The Patriarchal Era
- Abraham      Hebrews 11:8–10
- Sarah      Hebrews 11:11
- Abraham      Hebrews 11:12–19
- Isaac      Hebrews 11:20

- Jacob      Hebrews 11:21
- Joseph      Hebrews 11:22

### The Exodus Era

- Moses      Hebrews 11:23–28
- Israelites      Hebrews 11:29–30
- Rahab      Hebrews 11:31

### The Judges and Monarchy Eras

- Gideon      Hebrews 11:32
- Barak      Hebrews 11:32
- Samson      Hebrews 11:32
- Jephthah      Hebrews 11:32
- David      Hebrews 11:32–34
- Samuel      Hebrews 11:32–34
- Prophets      Hebrews 11:32–34

### From Every Era

- Martyrs      Hebrews 11:35–40

## Living on Postponed Promises

All of these, the writer says, "obtained a good testimony through faith" but "did not receive the promise" (Hebrews 11:39 NKJV). They lived in the confident expectation of a better future; a future they have not yet received but one that they most surely will.

The dream this list of heroes of the faith were all following, which gave them a reason to keep looking ahead, was a vision of a homeland and a vision of the Christ! It was not so clearly defined at first. But promises and pictures of these realities increased and sharpened in detail as time went on. The Old Testament prophets were given insights that clarified the vision of the Great One rising out of the Hebrew family to rule His everlasting universe-wide kingdom. Even when the picture of their fabulous future seemed sketchy, they believed enough to die rather than forsake the vision.

In contrast, the waffling Christians of Judea had just had their religious rug pulled out from under them (expulsion from temple worship); now the writer of Hebrews has explained how all those worship pictures had been fulfilled in Christ. The bridge connecting the

key point

message, "The earthbound High Priest is *passé*" and, "The ancient vision of a homeland and a Messiah is still alive" is this list of Old Testament men and women who believed the promise of God. These historic believers were kept going by the very thing the early Christian believers must live on—*faith!*

The New Testament Hebrews' advantage, of course, was that the Messiah had, in their generation, been disclosed. He was here. In and among them. To them the long-awaited promise was fulfilled. *Christ is here!*

As we read through the list, what's fascinating is to note that each of these named heroes of the faith heard God's voice in his or her own today, with a word just for him or her. In most cases, responding meant going against what could be "seen" (i.e., the "wise" choice based on human experience and understanding).

Also, the response each person made carried forward God's plan for the ages. God truly did "frame the ages" by the word He spoke to human beings; something that He continues to do in our own day, and through you and me.

But let's examine each life more closely, and see what we can discover about living our lives by faith.

## Faith to Die For

**HEBREWS 11:4** *By faith Abel offered to God a more excellent sacrifice than Cain, through which he obtained witness that he was righteous, God testifying of his gifts; and through it he being dead still speaks.* (NKJV)

The tragic tale is told in Genesis 4 of two brothers, sons of Adam and Eve, who brought offerings to the Lord. "Now Abel was a keeper of sheep, but Cain was a tiller of the ground. And . . . it came to pass that Cain brought an offering of the fruit of the ground to the LORD. Abel also brought of the firstborn of his flock and of their fat. And the LORD respected Abel and his offering, but He did not respect Cain and his offering. And Cain was very angry, and his countenance fell. (Genesis 4:2–5 NKJV).

In scene 2 Cain kills his brother Abel when they are in the field together.

**depravity**
spiritual and moral corruption, wickedness, willful lack of conscience

Why was Cain's offering *not respected*? And why, to complicate matters, was Abel's respected?

- *The traditional view* is that God had taught Adam and Eve that blood sacrifice was required to cover their sins (Genesis 3:21). They passed this lore on to their children (although the Bible doesn't mention this), and a tradition of blood sacrifice became imbedded in every human culture. Abel heard God's voice through the instruction of his parents, and "by faith" offered the "more excellent" sacrifice of the firstborn of his flock (Hebrews 11:4 NKJV). His brother Cain probably received the same parental instruction, but offered "the fruit of the ground to the LORD" (Genesis 4:3 NKJV). Cain's offering was rejected, yet God spoke to Cain and encouraged him. If Cain would "do well" (do what was right, that is, bring a blood sacrifice), he too would be accepted (Genesis 4:7 NKJV).

- *Another way to look at it* is that the issue was not so much the difference between the two offerings as it was a heart issue: "faith." Abel had it; Cain did not. Nothing is said in Genesis or Hebrews about blood sacrifice or parental instruction. Genesis 4:4–5 clearly states that the Lord's respect was not just for Abel's gift, but for "Abel and his offering" (NKJV). The withholding of respect was not just because of Cain's bloodless grain offering, but because of "Cain [the man] and his offering" (NKJV). The person is in focus, not just his worship. And acceptance or rejection hinged on the attitude of each man.

Abel came with an attitude of faith (Hebrews 11:4). Cain's attitudes included anger at God (Genesis 4:5–6), failure to resist ("rule over") sin, hatred of his brother, murder, evasion of personal responsibility ("Am I my brother's keeper?" [Genesis 4:9 NKJV]), and blaming God ("You have driven me out" [4:14 NKJV]). Abel is noted among the heroes because of his faith—the attitude of his heart.

Cain's vicious response set the consequences of humankind's response to God's voice in stark contrast. Human beings can respond and be accepted by God or can rebel and take a path to greater and greater **depravity** The Lord "respected Abel and his offering" (Genesis 4:4 NKJV), and this phrase the writer of Hebrews takes as evidence that Abel "obtained witness that he was righteous" (Hebrews 11:4 NKJV). Despite becoming a murder victim, Abel's act of faith speaks volumes today.

**used figuratively**
Deuteronomy 8:6;
Colossians 3:7;
2 John 4, 6

**Stuart Briscoe and Lloyd Ogilvie**

It is tempting to read into the differing offerings some suggestion that one contained blood and was therefore acceptable and the other did not and was therefore unacceptable. But the text gives no indication of this but rather stresses the fact that the person offering was acceptable or unacceptable, leading us to believe that God was looking on the heart—the attitude of the worshiper—rather than at the specifics of his offering. Even in worship man is capable of deviant behavior and attitudes. Cain shows it and church history confirms it.[2]

## Beam Me Up, Scotty!

*HEBREWS 11:5–6 By faith Enoch was taken away so that he did not see death, "and was not found, because God had taken him"; for before he was taken he had this testimony, that he pleased God. But without faith it is impossible to please Him, for he who comes to God must believe that He is, and that He is a rewarder of those who diligently seek Him. (NKJV)*

The account of Enoch is buried in the Bible's earliest genealogy (Genesis 5). Information there is sparse. We know the name of Enoch's father and the name of his first son, Methuselah. Other than that, all we know is that after this son was born "Enoch walked with God three hundred years" (Genesis 5:22 NKJV). In his three hundredth and sixty-fifth year Enoch "was not, for God took him" (Genesis 5:24 NKJV). Some Jewish sages concluded that this means Enoch died, and speculated that God "took him" to keep him from succumbing to temptation and sinning. Other rabbis and Christian tradition understand the phrase to mean that God took Enoch into heaven without passing through death.

Enoch maintained a close relationship with the Lord. "Walk" is <u>used figuratively</u>. in Scripture of a person's lifestyle. To say, as Genesis 5 does, that "Enoch walked with God" means that for three hundred years Enoch lived in harmony with the Creator's will. What we don't know in Enoch's case is any specific word God may have given him. Abel may have heard God's voice in his parents' instruction about sacrifice. We know that Noah heard God's voice telling him to build an Ark. The fact that the writer of Hebrews can cite no specific instance of Enoch responding to God's voice leads him to

comment, "for before he was taken he had this testimony, that he pleased God" (Hebrews 11:5 NKJV).

For the writer of Hebrews the logic is compelling:

- The Scriptures testify that Enoch "walked with God" (Genesis 5:22 NKJV).

- It is clear from this that Enoch "pleased God" (Hebrews 11:5 NKJV), for as the prophet Amos asks, "Can two walk together, unless they are agreed?" (Amos 3:3 NKJV).

- Thus Enoch must have been a man of faith, for "without faith it is impossible to please Him" (Hebrews 11:6 NKJV).

Then the writer adds what seems obvious: "for he who comes to God must believe that He is, and that He is a rewarder of those who diligently seek Him" (11:6 NKJV). What person who doesn't believe in God would ever approach Him? And what person who wasn't convinced that God is well-disposed toward him would ever "diligently seek Him"? No, to have the Scriptures testify that Enoch "walked with God" is sufficient evidence that Enoch was a man who lived by faith, trusting God and confident of God's love.

## Chartered Cruise to Salvation

> HEBREWS 11:7 *By faith Noah, being divinely warned of things not yet seen, moved with godly fear, prepared an ark for the saving of his household, by which he condemned the world and became heir of the righteousness which is according to faith.* (NKJV)

There's no question about the specific word of God to which Noah responded. Genesis 6 tells us: God told Noah "I will destroy them [all flesh] with the earth" (6:13 NKJV). "Make yourself an ark of gopherwood" (6:14 NKJV). And, "I Myself am bringing floodwaters on the earth, to destroy from under heaven all flesh in which is the breath of life" (6:17 NKJV). Noah's response to this stunning revelation was to spend the next 120 years (Genesis 6:3) building a giant boat over four football fields in length on a dry plain. Motivated by "fear" (respect for and awe) of God, Noah chose to trust the Lord even though no flood of waters had ever threatened humankind before. In fact, in Noah's world before the Great Flood there had not eoven been rain (Genesis 2:5–6). Everything Noah

key point

had seen throughout his life testified against the possibility of flood-waters destroying life on the earth. But Noah believed God, trusting in the unseen rather than in what was visible to the human eye.

The writer to the Hebrews comments that, by responding to God's voice, Noah "condemned the world" (11:7 NKJV). The apostle Peter speaks of the Spirit of Christ testifying to those in Noah's time "while the ark was being prepared" (1 Peter 3:20 NKJV). We can imagine that as the skeleton of the massive ship rose on dry land, people from miles around came to gawk and ridicule. And we can picture Noah passing on the warning he had received from God. But what this word from God provoked in the people of Noah's time was laughter and disbelief. They had no awe of God and no confidence in things which remained unseen. Noah's faith stands in stark contrast to the reaction of those who populated his world. His belief exposed their unbelief, and in this sense "condemned" them.

go to

condemned
John 3:19–20

## Off to See the City

HEBREWS 11:8–16 *By faith Abraham obeyed when he was called to go out to the place which he would receive as an inheritance. And he went out, not knowing where he was going. By faith he dwelt in the land of promise as in a foreign country, dwelling in tents with Isaac and Jacob, the heirs with him of the same promise; for he waited for the city which has foundations, whose builder and maker is God. By faith Sarah herself also received strength to conceive seed, and she bore a child when she was past the age, because she judged Him faithful who had promised. Therefore from one man, and him as good as dead, were born as many as the stars of the sky in multitude—innumerable as the sand which is by the seashore.*

*These all died in faith, not having received the promises, but having seen them afar off were assured of them, embraced them and confessed that they were strangers and pilgrims on the earth. For those who say such things declare plainly that they seek a homeland. And truly if they had called to mind that country from which they had come out, they would have had opportunity to return. But now they desire a better, that is, a heavenly country. Therefore God is not ashamed to be called their God, for He has prepared a city for them.* (NKJV)

Abraham is the Old Testament's prime witness to a life of faith. He was also recognized by the Jewish people as the source of their race,

**go to**

**herds and entourage**
Genesis 13:2, 6;
14:14

key point

and thus as the greatest of Old Testament figures. So the author goes back to two pivotal points in Abraham's life and traces their impact.

Genesis 12 relates the story of God's command to seventy-five-year-old Abraham to leave his home in the city of Ur and go out to an unknown land "that I will show you" (Genesis 12:1 NKJV). At the time Ur was a dominant and prosperous city-state. Excavations there have uncovered evidence of its riches and the skill of its builders, who even designed into homes of the wealthy a kind of air-conditioning. And Abraham was one of the wealthiest in the city, as testified to by the size of his <u>herds and entourage</u>.

Yet despite his age and wealth, Abraham responded to God's voice and abandoned the comforts of Ur to take up the life of a nomad, wandering an under-populated land. The writer makes it clear that Abraham saw beyond God's promise of a homeland for his offspring to something more: to a city "whose builder and maker is God" (Hebrews 11:10 NKJV). Just as the earthly tabernacle was a "copy and shadow" (Hebrews 8:5 NKJV) of a "more perfect tabernacle not made with hands, that is, not of this creation" (Hebrews 9:11 NKJV), so Abraham looked beyond the land to a home in heaven. It was not the visible with which Abraham's faith was concerned, but with the unseen.

Nor did the visible keep Abraham or Sarah from trusting God. His body might be "as good as dead" (Hebrews 11:12 NKJV) as far as his ability to impregnate Sarah, who herself had ceased menstruating (Romans 4:19). But Abraham chose to trust the God who promised despite this evidence. And the result? "Therefore from one man, and him as good as dead, were born, as many as the stars of the sky in multitude—innumerable as the sand which is by the seashore" (Hebrews 11:12 NKJV).

When Abraham was 99 and Sarah was 90, the angel of the Lord told them that they would finally have a child (Genesis 18:10–12). They both thought the idea was hilarious. They couldn't help laughing out loud. Two old people, well past childbearing age, making a baby! They named the promise-child Isaac, meaning *"Laughter."*

Don't try to tell me God doesn't like a good joke!

## Seeing Beyond History

Yet even this evidence that faith "works" is incomplete. For Abraham and the other patriarchs looked beyond history itself and saw "a heavenly country" (Hebrews 11:16 NKJV). They believed with all their hearts that this world was not their home, and that God "has prepared a city for them" (Hebrews 11:16 NKJV).

Perhaps most significant of all is the comment that "therefore God is not ashamed to be called their God" Hebrews (11:16 NKJV). The faith-response of the patriarchs, as those responses were expressed in their commitment to the promises of God, established deeply personal relationships with the Lord—relationships in which He was "their God" and they were "His people."

## The Great Test of Abraham's Faith

**HEBREWS 11:17–19** *By faith Abraham, when he was tested, offered up Isaac, and he who had received the promises offered up his only begotten son, of whom it was said, "In Isaac your seed shall be called," concluding that God was able to raise him up, even from the dead, from which he also received him in a figurative sense. (NKJV)*

This is the third great test of Abraham's faith. Abraham was told to leave Ur and go to an unknown land. And Abraham went. Abraham was told he would have a child with Sarah long after they were capable of having children. Abraham and Sarah believed, and Isaac was born. Now Abraham was told to offer Isaac as a sacrifice.

The story is told in Genesis 22. Several verses deserve special attention. The text tells us that after hearing God's command "Abraham rose early in the morning" (Genesis 22:3 NKJV) to obey God. We would surely understand if Abraham had found reason to delay. Perhaps he needed to lay out work for his staff to do while he was gone. Or perhaps the signs indicated bad weather. Something, anything that might delay the sacrifice of Isaac as a burnt offering.

But Abraham obeyed immediately. As soon as there was enough light to see by he took his son, two servants, wood for the sacrifice, and set out for the place God had told him to offer up Isaac.

The Genesis text also tells us that when Abraham arrived at that place he told the two servants he'd brought along to wait, saying, "The lad and I will go yonder and worship, and we will come back to you" (Genesis 22:5 NKJV). That "we will come back to you" is a striking statement. It was only after the writer of Hebrews gave us the explanation that we fully understood. God had told Abraham that the promises of Genesis 12 would be passed down through his son, Isaac (Genesis 21:12). Abraham was convinced that God would never go back on His word. And so the patriarch reasoned that, if necessary, God would raise Isaac from the dead in order to keep His promise!

Often, trusting God's word and promises seems risky. Abraham had seen God's track record. Even if the worst imaginable thing happened, Abraham would do what God told him to.

## Pardon Me, Pilgrim—Gotta Yield to *This* Temptation!

The writer of Hebrews doesn't yield to the temptation of comparing the sacrifice of Abraham's only son to that of God the Father's sacrifice of His Son on Calvary. Yet the comparison is so obvious that we can hardly avoid pointing it out. God spoke to Abraham and told him, "Take now your son, your only son Isaac, whom you love" (Genesis 22:2 NKJV). Millenniums later God said of Jesus, "This is My beloved Son, in whom I am well pleased" (Matthew 3:17 NKJV).

When Abraham reached Mount Moriah, where God said the sacrifice of Isaac was to take place, he carefully laid out the firewood, bound Isaac, and laid him on the altar. But before Abraham could plunge his knife into his son, God stopped him and pointed to a ram caught in a nearby thicket. That ram was substituted for Abraham's son and died in his place.

key point

But no ram could be offered in place of the Son of God. And so on Calvary's hill, Jesus was crucified, God giving His only begotten Son as a substitute to die in our place. While God spared Abraham the death of his son, God refused to spare Himself, out of love for you and me.

Even so, Abraham's reasoning was correct. The promises given to the first of the patriarchs are to come to complete fulfillment in Jesus. And so, to keep those promises God raised Jesus from the dead, exalting Him as our great High Priest and King.

## Pass It on, Ike!

**HEBREWS 11:20** *By faith Isaac blessed Jacob and Esau concerning things to come. (NKJV)*

The story is a fascinating one. Jacob and Esau were twins. As Isaac neared the end of his life he determined to "bless" his two sons. In the ancient world a parental blessing served both as a powerful prediction of the future and as a parent's last will and testament. What Isaac had to pass on to one of his sons was material possessions, but also a spiritual heritage. One of the boys would inherit the promise God had given first to Abraham and then transmitted to Isaac.

Cultural tradition and protocol demanded that the family birthright, parental blessing, inheritance and clan leadership should be passed to the eldest son.

But here's the sticky wicket. Just before the birth of the twins, God told their mother that the younger, Jacob, would have precedence over the moments-older Esau (Genesis 25:23). Thus Jacob was to receive the promises. In this slightly dysfunctional family, Esau was his father Isaac's favorite. Isaac determined that he would transmit the promises to Esau through his blessing. But Jacob was his mother's favorite, and when she learned of Isaac's plan she plotted with Jacob to pretend he was Esau, and so to steal the blessing.

Rebekah disguised Jacob with animal skins and the smell of the outdoorsman. Because Isaac was nearly blind the plot succeeded, and Isaac blessed the disguised Jacob. When Esau found out, he was distraught and begged his father for a blessing of his own. It was at this point that Isaac surrendered to the will of God. The Genesis text tells us after he realized what had happened, Isaac confirmed what he had given to Jacob, saying, "And indeed he shall be blessed" (Genesis 27:33 NKJV).

## Pass It on, Jake!

**HEBREWS 11:21** *By faith Jacob, when he was dying, blessed each of the sons of Joseph, and worshiped, leaning on the top of his staff. (NKJV)*

Jacob adopted his son Joseph's two sons, and when he blessed them he also favored the younger over the elder (Genesis 48:13–20).

Firmly established tradition guaranteed the right of the elder to inherit the bulk of the family's tangible and intangible assets. But Jacob was, by now, sensitive to God, and by faith favored the younger son.

## Pass It on, Joe!

> HEBREWS 11:22 *By faith Joseph, when he was dying, made mention of the departure of the children of Israel, and gave instructions concerning his bones. (NKJV)*

Joseph had been sold into slavery by his brothers (Genesis 37:28). Taken to Egypt, Joseph rose to become **vizier** of that land. When a famine struck the ancient world, Joseph's action saved Egypt. He was also able to invite his family to come to Egypt, where their descendants would reside for nearly four hundred years. While Joseph did not know how long the Israelites would stay in Egypt, he did know that their future lay in Canaan, the land God had promised to the descendants of Abraham, Isaac, and Jacob. And so when he was dying Joseph made the children of Israel swear to carry his remains with them and bury him in the promised land.

## The Exodus Generation Catches the Vision

> HEBREWS 11:23–31 *By faith Moses, when he was born, was hidden three months by his parents, because they saw he was a beautiful child; and they were not afraid of the king's command. By faith Moses, when he became of age, refused to be called the son of Pharaoh's daughter, choosing rather to suffer affliction with the people of God than to enjoy the passing pleasures of sin, esteeming the reproach of Christ greater riches than the treasures in Egypt; for he looked to the reward. By faith he forsook Egypt, not fearing the wrath of the king; for he endured as seeing Him who is invisible. By faith he kept the Passover and the sprinkling of blood, lest he who destroyed the firstborn should touch them. By faith they passed through the Red Sea as by dry land, whereas the Egyptians, attempting to do so, were drowned.*
>
> *By faith the walls of Jericho fell down after they were encircled for seven days. By faith the harlot Rahab did not perish with those who did not believe, when she had received the spies with peace. (NKJV)*

The Exodus from Egypt initiated another era in sacred history. Now the writer of Hebrews focuses on this critical period and notes that those whom God used to frame it did so "by faith." While we would expect Moses to be held up as an example, some very unexpected people are also singled out.

## Moses's Parents' Daring Faith

HEBREWS 11:23 *By faith Moses, when he was born, was hidden three months by his parents, because they saw he was a beautiful child; and they were not afraid of the king's command.* (NKJV)

The multiplication of the Jewish population (Exodus 1:7–10) in Egypt concerned the royal court. Egypt was under pressure from peoples beyond its borders, and Pharaoh grew afraid that if Egypt was invaded the Israelites might join the enemy. He enslaved the Israelites and put them to hard labor. But the slave population kept growing. Finally, in an act of desperation, Pharaoh decreed that every male child born to his slaves was to be thrown into the Nile River. By faith, Moses's parents refused to obey the king's command and kept Moses hidden.

## Rags to Riches and Back Again

HEBREWS 11:24–26 *By faith Moses, when he became of age, refused to be called the son of Pharaoh's daughter, choosing rather to suffer affliction with the people of God than to enjoy the passing pleasures of sin, esteeming the reproach of Christ greater riches than the treasures in Egypt; for he looked to the reward.* (NKJV)

Even the youngest child hears the story of Moses's adoption by an Egyptian princess in Sunday school. When Moses was three months old, his mother wove a watertight basket-boat and placed her son in it. The child was discovered by the princess, and became an adopted member of the royal family. But Moses spent his earliest years with his own mother, whom the princess employed as a wet-nurse.

Typically children then were nursed until they were three or even four years old. During these formative years young Moses must have heard stories of his ancestors and of the promises God made to Abraham, Isaac, and Jacob. Although later he was given the education reserved for the royal children (Acts 7:22), Moses identified with his own people rather than the people of his adoptive mother. Gradually a dream formed in Moses's mind: he would deliver his people from slavery and lead them to the promised land (Acts 7:23–24)! By age forty he was fully committed.

## The Dream of the Anointed

From a human point of view, this was a costly commitment. As "the son of Pharaoh's daughter" (Hebrews 11:24 NKJV), which was then a title as well as descriptive, Moses had a claim to the throne of Egypt itself! And Egypt was then the most powerful and wealthiest nation in the Eastern world. Yet Moses saw beyond this world's wealth and power. He esteemed "the reproach of Christ greater riches than the treasures in Egypt" (Hebrews 11:26 NKJV). In using the phrase "the reproach of Christ," the writer may be reminding us that like Jesus, Moses chose a course that led to rejection and suffering.

More likely, however, the choice to suffer "the reproach of Christ" (Hebrews 11:26 NKJV) is the faith that holds this entire chapter together. The bruised and battered Hebrew Christians in and around Jerusalem were hanging in the balance between keeping the faith in Jesus Christ and turning back to dead Judaism in order to find peace from persecution that goes with being a follower of Christ. The "reproach of Christ" which Moses chose was the stigma that goes with being Jewish—the "Anointed People" of God—who, by virtue of God's promises, live leaning forward, determined faces fixed on a distant goal, always looking to a brighter future as a nation ultimately ruled by the Messiah.

Their picture of Messiah might not have been very well formed in the Hebrew mind and faith when Moses made his decision to identify himself as one of them. But it was there. If they are not atheists, that mystical hope constantly keeps the Jewish people looking beyond their bitter today to expectations of the coming kingdom of heaven and the promised King.

It started in the Garden of Eden with the promise that a son of the woman would crush the serpent's head (Genesis 3:15). Then Abraham was separated for the purpose of fathering the nation of Messianic hope. You can trace the history of that family, their sufferings, and the progressive development of their dream. Keeping that dream alive required faith because it was based on unseen realities.

## No Mummy for Moses

The Christ-hope was alive in Moses. Moses declined the possibility of power and riches now in favor of doing God's will, and ultimately receiving the far greater reward when Messiah comes. Had Moses chosen to cling to his position as "son of Pharaoh's daughter" (Hebrews 11:24 NKJV), we might even now be looking at his dried-up mummy in some museum. But by rejecting the "passing pleasures of sin" (Hebrews 11:25 NKJV), Moses won a place in Faith's Hall of Fame and is honored even today as Israel's Deliverer and Law Giver, and as the prototype prophet of the Old Testament. On the Mount of the Transfiguration, Moses met the yearned-for Christ, face-to-face.

What a stunning example of rejecting the seen in favor of the unseen! Moses heard God's voice speaking through tales of the patriarchs, and he responded in faith. That choice, more than any other, framed the era that his ministry initiated.

**prototype prophet**
Deuteronomy 18:18

**Mount of the Transfiguration**
Luke 9:28–31

what others say

**Randy Alcorn**

Materialism would dupe us into believing this world is the ultimate world, the destination rather than the route to the Destination. From there it's a short step to racing off to earn, collect, accumulate, take, and consume as if that's all there is to life. Then we wake up one day (if we ever wake up at all) to realize how terribly unhappy we are. Joyless, passionless, we become shriveled caricatures of what we could have been if only we'd lived in light of the person and place we were made for.[3]

## The Fugitive

HEBREWS 11:27 *By faith he forsook Egypt, not fearing the wrath of the king; for he endured as seeing Him who is invisible.* (NKJV)

This is perhaps the most surprising statement in Hebrews 11. Exodus 2 tells us that one day Moses saw an Egyptian overseer abusing a Hebrew slave. Moses killed the Egyptian and hid his body. The next day Moses tried to intervene when he saw one Israelite abusing another. The abuser taunted Moses, asking if he intended to kill him as he had killed the Egyptian the day before.

Exodus 2:14 tells us that when Moses realized that the earlier killing was known, "he feared" (NKJV). Then when Pharaoh heard of the murder "he sought to kill Moses. But Moses fled from the face of Pharaoh" (2:15 NKJV).

In a powerful speech made before the **Sanhedrin**, the martyr Stephen gives us more information about the incident. Moses had "supposed that his brethren would have understood that God would deliver them by his hand, but they did not understand" (Acts 7:25 NKJV). It was after he saw the reaction of the Israelite who rejected his intervention that Moses fled.

## The Fear Factor

It's reasonable to assume from the story, as told in Exodus, that Moses feared Pharaoh's retribution. But Hebrews tells us he didn't fear the king's wrath, "for he endured as seeing Him who is invisible" (Hebrews 11:27 NKJV). Once again Moses was not responding to what was seen—an angry Pharaoh, who might have been delighted to have an excuse to rid himself of a potential rival—for Moses had such a high view of God that he felt safe in the Lord's hands. What, then, did Moses fear?

Two possibilities suggest themselves. The first is that the reaction of the Israelite made him fear that his dream of delivering his people was nothing but a dream: that it originated in his own heart rather than in God's will. That fear, and the doubt it created, may have driven him from Egypt.

The second possibility is that the murder of the Egyptian revealed something about himself that terrified Moses. The sight of the Egyptian beating a fellow Israelite aroused such anger in Moses that he felt compelled to clobber the Egyptian. Somehow the same penchant for violence that moved the Egyptian existed within Moses! And this might well have terrified the idealistic forty-year-old.

Whatever caused Moses's fear, the writer of Hebrews wants us to understand that it was not fear of Pharaoh. Unlike <u>even Abraham</u>, Moses realized that God is in control and that, despite all his earthly power, Pharaoh could not harm him apart from God's permission.

even Abraham
Genesis 12:10–19;
20:1–12

complaining
Exodus 15:24; 16:2;
17:3;
Numbers 11:1; 14:2

## Protected by the Blood

**HEBREWS 11:28** *By faith he kept the Passover and the sprinkling of blood, lest he who destroyed the firstborn should touch them. (NKJV)*

Here the writer touches on the final miracle God used to break Pharaoh's will and win freedom for his people. When devastating miracle after miracle failed to sway the obstinate Pharaoh (Exodus 5–11), the Lord told Moses that the firstborn child in every Egyptian household would die on a single night. However, the Israelites would be spared, provided they sacrificed a lamb and sprinkled its blood on the doorposts to their homes.

Again there was no evidence to suggest either that the deaths would take place or that lamb's blood would provide protection. But Moses, and the people of Israel, responded to the warning with faith, and the firstborn of the Israelites were spared.

## The Case of the Unbelieving Believers

**HEBREWS 11:29** *By faith they passed through the Red sea as by dry land, whereas the Egyptians, attempting to do so, were drowned. (NKJV)*

It's surprising to see this first Exodus generation credited with faith. The behavior of the freed Hebrew slaves usually displayed anything but trust in God. Their murmuring and <u>complaining</u>, their idolatry at the base of Mount Sinai (Exodus 32), culminating in their rejection of God's command to invade Canaan (Numbers 14), mark this generation as one of sacred history's most *unspiritual*. Yet here the author of Hebrews points out that this generation did at least enter the path God cleared for them through the sea. And theirs was a "by faith" response.

How gracious of God to credit even these stubborn people with the little faith they did display. And how gracious of Him to credit us when we too display even a little faith in Him.

key point

# The Second Exodus Generation

**HEBREWS 11:30** *By faith the walls of Jericho fell down after they were encircled for seven days.* (NKJV)

We're not surprised to see faith displayed by the children of the slaves who were led to freedom by Moses. Unlike their parents, the men and women of this generation consistently responded to God's voice. There is no better example than that cited by the writer.

The walled city of Jericho controlled the route that the Israelites would have to take into Canaan's central highlands. The Israelites had neither the time to undertake a siege, nor the equipment needed to make a frontal assault. God, acting as commander of the Israelite army, told Joshua to have the people maintain silence and simply walk around Jericho once a day for six days (Joshua 6). They were then to circle it seven times the seventh day. These instructions made no military sense, but the people acted on the orders of their unseen commander. When the seventh circuit was completed the people shouted—and Jericho's walls fell down.

This incident set the tone for the conquest of Canaan, and powerfully demonstrated that when the people responded to God's voice, victory was theirs.

# Saint of Ill Repute

**HEBREWS 11:31** *By faith the harlot Rahab did not perish with those who did not believe, when she had received the spies with peace.* (NKJV)

All those previously listed in this chapter have been of God's people, the offspring of Abraham, Isaac, and Jacob. Rahab is different. During my Sunday school days, teachers and preachers tried to sugarcoat Rahab. But the Greek and Hebrew words leave no doubt. She was a pagan, a citizen of Jericho. And she was a **harlot**, a lady of the night. One would hardly expect to find her here on this list of heroes of the faith. Yet she too responded to God's voice in her "today." That's faith!

Just before attacking Jericho, Joshua sent spies to check the city defenses. Rahab hid the spies and helped them escape. In return she asked that she and her family would be spared when the city was taken. Her words to the spies give us unique insight into the difference between fear, and faith. Hers was not "blind faith"—she was well-informed about Israel's exploits, and she believed.

JOSHUA 2:9–11 *I know that the LORD has given you the land, that the terror of you has fallen on us, and that all the inhabitants of the land are fainthearted because of you. For we have heard how the LORD dried up the water of the Red Sea for you when you came out of Egypt, and what you did to the two kings of the Amorites who were on the other side of the Jordan, Sihon and Og, whom you utterly destroyed. And as soon as we heard these things, our hearts melted; neither did there remain any more courage in anyone because of you, for the LORD your God, He is God in heaven above and on earth beneath. (NKJV)*

All the inhabitants of Canaan had the same information about the Lord that Rahab possessed. All were awed by the miracles He had performed, and convinced that God had given Canaan to the Israelites. And all were terrified. Yet despite what they knew and feared they fought against God's people and resisted His known will. They heard God's voice yet refused to surrender.

key point

All but Rahab. Rahab acknowledged the Lord as God of heaven and earth. She too heard God's voice in the reports of what He had done for His people. And rather than resist, Rahab came to God to seek refuge.

Knowing truth about God still provokes one of two responses. Human beings either reject Him and resist His will, like the citizens of Jericho, or they surrender and seek refuge in Him, as Rahab did.

It's noteworthy that this onetime pagan prostitute's response of faith not only won mention in the Hebrews Hall of Fame, but Matthew 1:5 places Rahab in the family line of Jesus Himself.

Whatever a person's origins or former way of life, faith brings him or her into the family of God as a full and significant member.

## The Gathering Cloud of Witnesses

HEBREWS 11:32–35b *And what more shall I say? For the time would fail me to tell of Gideon and Barak and Samson and Jephthah, also of David and Samuel and the prophets: who through faith subdued kingdoms, worked righteousness, obtained promises, stopped the mouths of lions, quenched the vio-*

*lence of fire, escaped the edge of the sword, out of weakness were made strong, became valiant in battle, turned to flight the armies of the aliens. Women received their dead raised to life again.* (NKJV)

For some, counting on the unseen produced victories. The Scriptures are filled with stories of victories won by faith, and of how God has used faith's response to His voice to frame the ages. While the phrases above evoke familiar stories, neither the writer nor we have time to examine them all.

For some, counting on the unseen produced suffering and even death.

HEBREWS 11:35b–38 *Others were tortured, not accepting deliverance, that they might obtain a better resurrection. Still others had trial of mockings and scourgings, yes, and of chains and imprisonment. They were stoned, they were sawn in two, were tempted, were slain with the sword. They wandered about in sheepskins and goatskins, being destitute, afflicted, tormented—of whom the world was not worthy. They wandered in deserts and mountains, in dens and caves of the earth.* (NKJV)

ISRAEL, 1500 BC–AD 70—Hebrews 11:35–38 reports a history of harassment, poverty, persecution, torture, and death—pain and suffering that many who responded to God's voice with faith have suffered in this world.

EARTH, AD 1900–1999—In the twentieth century more Christians were killed for believing in Jesus than in all the previous centuries of church history combined.

The "by faith" life has been fully validated as a biblical alternative to a life lived by constantly referring to law's rules and interpretations of those rules. But the writer doesn't want the Jewish Christians of Jerusalem, or any other believer, to suppose that living by faith guarantees an easy or prosperous life. And so he adds a paragraph to remind his readers that living by faith truly is commitment to the unseen.

God has something far better in mind for His people than a few pleasant decades in this world. God has eternity in view, a theme that the writer of Hebrews will develop for his weary and discouraged readers in Hebrews 12. For now, it's enough to know that "success" isn't necessarily a way to identify those who live by faith, nor is suffering evidence of failure to be responsive to God. It fact, the reverse might well be true, and trials and difficulties might be <u>better indications</u> that a person is living a life of faith.

## Cross Over the Bridge

Hebrews 11:35–38 serves as a bridge to bring the original Hebrews readers into the "by-faith kingdom." None of them is an Abraham or Moses or Noah or one of the other historic faith heroes. But in these verses they are likely to find a connection. They know what it is to be persecuted for believing Jesus. They are familiar with "mockings and scourgings" (11:36 NKJV). Some know the inside of the local jail by personal experience.

The people described here are people going through what Hebrew believers are going through. These are faith-heroes with whom they can identify. The connection has been made!

## Previews of Coming Attractions

**HEBREWS 11:39–40** *And all these, having obtained a good testimony through faith, did not receive the promise, God having provided something better for us, that they should not be made perfect apart from us.* (NKJV)

The vision these people were following was a vision of Christ based on the promise of God and their history with Him. It was a vision of *home* (a better country). And it was a vision of *spiritual perfection*.

In contrast, none of the "faith heroes" listed in Hebrews 11 saw fulfillment of the dream in their own lifetimes. They had glimpses, visitations, patterns, blurry pictures, and shadows. Previews of coming attractions—just enough to keep their faith alive. According to what we see of the heroes of Hebrews 10:32–11:40, trouble, loss, struggle, persecution, affliction, and martyrdom are normal consequences of following Jesus.

It's a strange recruiting poster for signing up new visionaries. Yet even with all the challenges, believers have hope of "something out there"—something better. Something worth giving one's life for.

**better indications**
2 Timothy 3:12;
Romans 5:3–4

key point

Sometimes it is the only thing that keeps us going. Since God's Son entered the human scene, we have been able to see the shape of our hopes better than ever. We haven't experienced the fullness of the hoped-for yet. But by faith we see it from here—the day believers through the centuries have been waiting and dying for.

A missionary returned to New York on an ocean liner. When the ship docked bands played and happy crowds swarmed to welcome travelers home. The missionary made his way through all the hustle and bustle, alone. No bands played for him; no happy crowd celebrated his return. That night he sat in a tiny hotel room, feeling discouraged and despondent. And then he realized it—he wasn't home yet!

That's what the writer of Hebrews wants us to realize. As the ages have passed, men and women of faith have lived and died without having "received the promises" (Hebrews 11:13 NKJV). But when the last age that God has framed comes to an end; when history is succeeded by eternity; men and women of faith will all come home, "made perfect" (Hebrews 11:40 NKJV) together.

And then the celebration will never end.

## Chapter Wrap-Up

- "Faith" is expressed in an obedient response to God's voice speaking in our "today." We are to live by faith, not by law.

- The experience of Old Testament "elders" makes it clear that faith has priority in the believer's experience.

- God uses believers' response to His "today" voice to frame the ages.

- Hebrews 11 identifies specific faith responses to illustrate how faith is to be expressed in Christians' lives.

- Every faith-response is significant, but living by faith does not guarantee anyone an easy life.

- The ultimate reward for living life by faith will be experienced only in eternity.

## Study Questions

1. What is the significance of the "seen vs. unseen" theme in the book of Hebrews?

2. What does "the worlds were framed by the word of God" (Hebrews 11:3 NKJV) indicate?

3. What was the specific faith-response of each of these individuals that won him or her a place in Hebrews 11: (a) Abel, (b) Noah, (c) Joseph, (d) Rahab?

4. Why does the writer explain that "without faith it is impossible to please Him" (Hebrews 11:6 NKJV) in his comment on Enoch?

5. What is the critical difference between living "by law" and living "by faith"?

6. What verses in Hebrews 11 might you refer to question a person who insists that God wants His children to be rich?

Chapter Highlights:
- On the Run
- Woodshed Theology
- Score One for God
- It Hurts So Good
- Stop Shouting!

# Hebrews 12:1–13
# It's a Great Day for the Race

## Let's Get Started

The writer has just offered his readers a list of "elders" (Hebrews 11:2 NKJV) who "obtained a good testimony through faith" (11:39 NKJV). He concluded with a litany of the sufferings of many of these men and women of faith. Now he says, "Therefore we also" (12:1 NKJV)!

Modern advertisers work hard to sell the public on the benefits of their product. But why in the world would the writer of Hebrews, speaking to an already discouraged community of Christian Jews, picture them in the company of those whose faith brought suffering? Wouldn't he be wiser to highlight eternal benefits and stay away from any pain they might experience here and now? Or to paint an even more rosy picture of what might lie just around life's corner?

The problem is, of course, that a life of faith is no guarantee of Disneyland. Those who promote a Gospel of Prosperity ignore the fact that Christians are heirs to the same troubles that plague all humankind. They also ignore Scripture's warning that "all who desire to live godly in Christ Jesus will suffer persecution" (2 Timothy 3:12 NKJV). Sooner or later the illusion of a life on earth— of riches, good health, and ease—is shattered by troubles and hardships. In fact, the Christians who read this letter first were already suffering hardships! What they needed wasn't hype, but help. What they needed—and what we still need today, as hard to understand as this might seem—is the ability to put pain in perspective and recognize tribulations as gifts of a loving God.

key point

## On the Run

**HEBREWS 12:1–2** *Therefore we also, since we are surrounded by so great a cloud of witnesses, let us lay aside every weight, and the sin which so easily ensnares us, and let us run with endurance the race that is set before us, looking unto Jesus, the author and finisher of our faith, who for the joy that was set*

**image of a race**
Psalm 19:5;
Ecclesiastes 9:11;
Acts 20:24,
1 Corinthians
9:24–27

**lights in the world**
Matthew 5:14, 16;
Philippians 2:15

*before Him endured the cross, despising the shame, and has sat down at the right hand of the throne of God. (NKJV)*

Scripture writers are fond of the <u>image of a race</u>. The apostle Paul incorporates images of athletic competitions in his second letter to Timothy when he writes, "I have fought the good fight, I have finished the race" (2 Timothy 4:7 NKJV). There are several reasons why the image is so appropriate. Athletes in the ancient world competed not for money but for glory. The prize was a simple wreath fashioned from a branch. But that wreath symbolized excellence. Athletes in any sport had a single and simple goal—to win the prize. This goal brought focus to their lives, and led them to train rigorously.

Paul reminds us that those who compete must be "temperate in all things" (1 Corinthians 9:25 NKJV). They watch their diet and "discipline [their] body and bring it into subjection" (1 Corinthians 9:27 NKJV). They willingly accept the pain of strained muscles, ready to pay any price to win. They look to those who've won before as their examples and determine to emulate them in everything.

It's not surprising, then, that the writer of Hebrews also casts the Christian life as a race, and carefully develops the analogy.

## Standing Room Only

HEBREWS 12:1 . . . *since we are surrounded by so great a cloud of witnesses . . . (NKJV)*

There's been much speculation as to who this "cloud of witnesses" is. To some, the word "cloud" has suggested a great gathering of angels peering down to see how God's people run their race. To others the "cloud" suggests saints who have died, cheering on the living. But each of those interpretations reads too much into the image of the cloud. Ancient literature frequently uses the image of clouds to represent large crowds. The writer is simply reminding his readers that everyone who knows them is watching closely.

This too is a frequent New Testament theme. Jesus spoke of His followers as <u>lights in a dark world,</u> and as a city set on a hill that can't be hidden (Matthew 5:14). Peter urges his readers to live godly lives, "having your conduct honorable among the Gentiles, that when they speak against you as evildoers, they may, by your good works which they observe, glorify God in the day of visitation" (1 Peter 2:12 NKJV).

In Matthew 5:14, Christ was emphasizing that the Christian is watched closely by those who do not yet know the Lord, and the life we lead brings glory or shame to Jesus's name. Universal as the image He used might have been, His context might have been His own boyhood. He grew up in Nazareth, a city that literally "sat on a hill" that rose up from the surrounding terrain.

## The Real Bible Diet

HEBREWS 12:1 . . . *let us lay aside every weight* . . . (NKJV)

No, the writer isn't thinking pounds as he urges his readers to "lay aside every weight." The weights here are encumbrances, whatever keeps a person from going all out in his Christian life.

For some, the "weight" we need to lay aside might be too many hours in front of the TV. For others it might be so great a focus on work that there's not enough time for family and for God. For some the "weight" is seeing money as an end itself, rather than a resource God has entrusted us with so that we might bless others. There are also many other "weights" or hang-ups that hinder the running of a good race—things like oversensitivity (touchiness), narcissism, paranoia, selfishness, prejudice, pride, fear, self-denigration. The list of weights that can trip us up is long and personal.

The "weight" that the writer is concerned with will differ with every individual. Each of us has to evaluate his own attitudes and actions. But the writer has given us criteria we can use to assess our lives. We're in a race to win the prize of a "good testimony through faith" (Hebrews 11:39 NKJV). Anything that hinders us from full commitment to a life of faith is an encumbrance we would do well to shed.

(And yes, He didn't say it would be easy! But read what Arthur Pink has to say on this very page.)

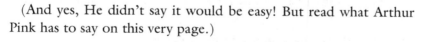

what others say

**Arthur Pink**

The more we love Jesus the easier will it be to lay aside every weight. If our hearts be occupied with the sacrificial love of Christ for us, we shall be constrained thereby to drop all that which displeases Him; and the more we dwell on the joy set before us, the more strength shall we have to run "with patience the race that is set before us."[1]

# Sneaky Snares That Snag Sprinters

HEBREWS 12:1 . . . *and the sin which so easily ensnares us . . .* (NKJV)

Most Christians aren't tripped up by the "big" sins. Murder? Robbery? Rape? These seldom trip up your average, committed follower of Jesus. No, it's usually the so-called "little" sins that "so easily ensnare us."

Note, however, that I said "so-called." To be more biblically accurate, the Bible does not grade sins. Sin is sin. James, Jesus's brother, in his own New Testament Letter, writes:

"For whoever shall keep the whole law, and yet stumble in one point, he is guilty of all." (James 2:10 NKJV; see the entire section, verses 1–13)

He puts **partiality** in the same category as murder—gasp! It's a tough passage. The particular sin that triggers James's statement is the sin of favoring rich people over poor in the church. We sinners have invented the practice of grading some sins "big" and others "little." "White lies and black lies." We do it to hide the bald-faced wickedness of our own sin, to feel better when we compare ourselves with those "really bad sinners."

In the chart below, we can gain insight into the "sin which so easily ensnares us" (Hebrews 12:1 NKJV) Christians by looking at several qualifications for spiritual leadership provided by the apostle Paul in his letter to Titus (1:6–8). The first column is to guide the church in choosing its elders. Actually, most of these qualities are the marks of spiritual maturity expected of all real Jesus believers. Each "godly quality" in the left column has its opposite in the far right column, and it's these ensnaring qualities that Christians fall victim to so easily.

## Qualifications for Spiritual Leadership

| The Godly Quality | Explanation | The Ensnaring Sin |
| --- | --- | --- |
| Blameless | Having unimpeachable integrity | Stretches or shades the truth |
| Not self-willed | Not arrogant or self-willed | Willful, discounts the views of others |
| Not quick-tempered | Not given to anger, not irascible | Touchiness, petulance, grumpiness |

## Qualifications for Spiritual Leadership (cont'd)

| The Godly Quality | Explanation | The Ensnaring Sin |
|---|---|---|
| Not given to wine | Not overly fond of wine; not a drunkard | Dependence on alcohol or drugs, self-medicating |
| Not violent | Not pugnacious | Quarrelsome, quick to take offense |
| Not greedy for money | Not a money-lover | Materialistic, taking pride in possessions |
| Hospitable | Welcoming, open, approachable | Unfriendly, distant |
| Lover of what is good | Focuses on the true, the noble, the pure | Focuses on gossip, on what is wrong or evil |
| Sober-minded | Temperate, sane, balanced | Extreme, hot-headed, unstable |
| Just | Upright, aligned with light | Unfair, biased |
| Holy | Devout, fulfills obligations to God and others | Impious, slack in fulfilling obligations |
| Self-controlled | Restrained, under control | Over-emotional, impetuous, impulsive, driven by appetites |

**keep going**
1 Timothy 2:3; 3:10

**Christian virtues**
2 Corinthians 1:6;
1 Timothy 6:11;
Titus 2:2

A quick look at the third column in the chart helps us understand the nature of the "little" sins that ensnare believers and hinder them in running the race God has set before us. We're all too likely to think of these things as character flaws, or to dismiss them as "just the way we are." We fail to identify them as sins that we're to recognize and "lay aside" (Hebrews 12:1 NKJV). Yet only when we acknowledge that the "traits" we tend to excuse in ourselves truly are "sins" will we confess them and seek the Holy Spirit's aid in purging them from our character.

## It's a Marathon, Not a Hundred-Yard Dash!

HEBREWS 12:1 . . . *and let us run with endurance the race that is set before us,* (NKJV)

The concept of endurance is expressed in several different Greek and Hebrew words. While endurance is closely linked to waiting, endurance isn't passive. Here we're encouraged to "run" with endurance, to keep on going at a steady pace, unwilling to slow down or stop. It's our endurance that enables us to <u>keep going despite hardships</u>. Endurance is frequently included among other <u>vital Christian virtues</u>.

The writer of Hebrews wants us to remember that the race we're to run is one that "is set before us" (Hebrews 12:1 NKJV). God has laid out the track on which each of us is to run. He's planned ahead each bend. He's laid out every hill, and He has carefully prepared for each obstacle we'll be asked to overcome.

Recognizing God's hand in everything that happens is one of the keys to running with endurance.

## Keep Your Eyes on the Champion

**HEBREWS 12:2** . . . *looking unto Jesus, the author and finisher of our faith* . . . *(NKJV)*

Jesus is our example. He's come this way before. He has run His own race on this track. The writer tells us two important things about Jesus. He is the "author" of our faith. And He is the "finisher."

The word "author" is *archegos*. In the first century this word was often used of founders of philosophic schools and, more significantly, of the traditional founders of cities. These founders determined the location of the city, gave it its name, and were viewed as its guardians. The word also may indicate a "trailblazer" or "champion." The writer of Hebrews uses *archegos* twice, once to identify Jesus as the one who laid the foundation of our salvation (Hebrews 2:10), and here to present Jesus as the "trailblazer" who opened up the path along which we're to run, and the "champion" who has already won the race.

The word "finisher" is *teleioten*, built on that familiar root that means to bring something to completion. Other English versions translate it "perfecter." The thought is that Jesus not only laid the foundation for our faith in His death on the cross, but He also reveals the end of our faith in His exaltation to God's right hand. When we look at Jesus we see faith's beginning in suffering and its end in glory!

It's so easy, as we live our lives, to lose the big picture. We focus on what's happening to us today, and agonize over what might happen tomorrow. But when we "[look] unto Jesus" (Hebrews 12:2 NKJV), we realize how petty the problems we face in this world actually are. Looking back we see the salvation won for us on Calvary.

Looking ahead we see the future, secured for us by Jesus's death. With our eyes fixed on Jesus, the author and perfecter of our faith, we gain perspective on our present troubles. And we're encouraged to run the "race that is set before us" with "endurance" (Hebrews 12:1 NKJV). Because the victory party is just ahead!

## Run for the Joy

HEBREWS 12:2 . . . *who for the joy that was set before Him endured the cross, despising the shame, and has sat down at the right hand of the throne of God. (NKJV)*

The derisive phrase "pie in the sky bye and bye" is often used to disparage the Christian's emphasis on eternity. Yet it captures an important truth. We do look ahead to eternity. And we do believe that treasures in heaven are of far greater value than any treasures we might lay up here on earth. At the same time, looking ahead to heaven has a powerful impact on the way we live our lives here and now.

what others say

**Randy Alcorn**

Your life on earth is a dot. From that dot extends a line that goes on for all eternity. Right now you're living *in* the dot. But what are you living *for*? Are you living for the dot or for the line? Are you living for earth or for heaven? Are you living for the short today or the long tomorrow?[2]

The writer reminds us that here on earth Jesus "endured the cross, despising the shame" (Hebrews 12:2 NKJV) associated with a form of execution reserved for the dregs of society. Crucifixion is an ugly, humiliating way to die. Jesus hung naked on a Roman cross, between two of the lowest possible criminals. The shame, disgrace, and indignity He utterly "despised."

However, this word does not mean He was bitter or hateful. It means He realized that it *didn't really matter.* He thought of the shame of the cross as of little consequence compared to what lay ahead—what His death on the cross would accomplish, the exaltation at the end of the ordeal. He "endured" because He chose to live for "the joy that was set before Him" (Hebrews 12:2 NKJV) rather than for any passing pleasures or pain this world might offer.

**sons**

generic term indicating all God's human children, male and female (see chapter 4 of this book)

Jesus is experiencing that joy now, from His seat at the right hand of God's throne. Right now you and I are called to pick up our own cross and follow Jesus (Matthew 16:24). Carrying our cross in the footsteps of Jesus may also lead to shame, ridicule by others, and even death, but not necessarily so. The cross is not only a symbol of Jesus's death; it also stands for God's will for the Savior.

The cross we are called to carry is the risk and reality of the pain which may be (and frequently is) experienced in the course of doing God's will. We cannot know where taking up our cross—accepting and living by God's will for our lives—will lead us. God has a different path for each of us to walk. But what we can know is that when we come to the end of that path there is *joy*!

Jesus lived for that joy. We also live for the "joy that was set before [us]" (Hebrews 12:2 NKJV). No matter how dark our night, we know that joy comes in the morning (Psalm 30:5).

## Woodshed Theology

HEBREWS 12:3–6 *For consider Him who endured such hostility from sinners against Himself, lest you become weary and discouraged in your souls. You have not yet resisted to bloodshed, striving against sin. And you have forgotten the exhortation which speaks to you as to **sons**:*
> *"My son, do not despise the chastening of the LORD,*
> *Nor be discouraged when you are rebuked by Him;*
> *For whom the LORD loves He chastens,*
> *And scourges every son whom He receives." (NKJV)*

The writer has portrayed Jesus as the "author and finisher" (Hebrews 12:2 NKJV) of our faith. His sacrifice launched the new covenant era, and His exaltation to the right hand of God marks out its completion. Now we're asked to "consider" the life Jesus lived here on earth.

The word translated "consider" is *analogistasthe*. Other Greek words are also translated in the same way. Each of these synonyms calls for us to examine something carefully and reach a conclusion. When Jesus told His followers to "consider the ravens" (Luke 12:24 NKJV), He was encouraging His listeners to note how God provided for ravens, and to reach the conclusion that God would surely provide for His children, who are more important to Him than a flock of birds.

Now the writer of Hebrews asks the Jerusalem Christians to take careful account of Jesus's experiences here on earth. Christ "endured hostility" (12:3 NKJV), just as they are enduring hostility. But Christ went even farther. He "resisted to bloodshed, striving against sin" (12:4 NKJV). Even though His bold stand for truth aroused such hatred that His enemies killed Him, Christ stayed the course.

What conclusion should the troubled Jewish Christians reach? They should expect to be treated with hostility, as was the Savior. After all, Jesus had warned His disciples, "If the world hates you, you know that it hated Me before it hated you" (John 15:18 NKJV). He also told them, "'A servant is not greater than his master.' If they persecuted Me, they will also persecute you" (John 15:20 NKJV).

Keeping your focus on Jesus is the writer's prescription against becoming "weary and discouraged" (Hebrews 12:3 NKJV). This phrase, "weary and discouraged," is found in Greek literary works to describe persons who slow down or collapse on a journey. When we "consider [Jesus]" we realize that hardships are no reason to give up or to drop out. After all, He suffered far more than we're called to endure.

## Watch Out for Biblical Amnesia!

It was also clear that the troubled community of Jewish Christians had forgotten a principle stated clearly in the Old Testament. There God's people are exhorted, "Do not despise the chastening of the LORD" (Proverbs 3:11–12 NKJV).

We noted earlier that the concepts of "remember" and "forget" normally refer to behavior rather than to mental acts. A person who "remembers" acts on what is remembered. A person who "forgets" fails to act on some revealed truth. These early Hebrew Christians have failed to take to heart and act on the revealed truth that "whom the LORD loves He chastens" (Hebrews 12:6 NKJV). As a result they've totally misunderstood their troubles and have begun to doubt God's love for them.

You see it in some Christians today. They have been taught that becoming a follower of Christ will bring them health, happiness, success, and wealth. And there is no doubt that being at peace with God makes you a better worker, business person, executive, etc. The tendency is that the believer will be better off. But not always.

**Christ's principles**
Matthew 5–7;
Luke 6 (Sermons on
the Mount and on
the Plain)

Being a Christian may mean turning down (or losing) a job which requires violating <u>Christ's principles</u> of morality, honesty, personal priorities, and treatment of other people. Anything less brings shame to the community of believers and to God. And then, there's the high probability that His followers will be treated as He was for no other reason than their association with Him.

## Don't Forget the Chastening of the Lord

If we look in a dictionary we find a number of synonyms for the word "chasten." Among them are punish, reprimand, chastise, castigate, and discipline. Typically "punish" is listed first, and "punishment" is probably the first image that comes to mind when people read this verse. But neither in the Old Testament nor in the New is it true that whom the Lord loves He "punishes."

At this point in his letter the writer to Hebrews is about to explain just what the verse he quoted does mean, so he can then demonstrate that the challenges and troubles Christians experience are both evidence of an intimate relationship with God as Father, and evidence of His parental love. In order to see this more clearly we need to go back to the Hebrew and Greek words that our translators have rendered "chasten" in the NKJV.

## "Chasten" in the Old Testament

The Hebrew word here is *yasar*, and a derivative, *musar*. The New International Version (NIV) and the New American Standard Bible (NASB) frequently join the NKJV in translating *yasar* as "chasten." But more often the Hebrew word is translated as "discipline" or "instruction." The underlying concept is one of correction and direction, which contribute to a person's training in righteousness.

Proverbs 1:2–3 clearly states the goal of education in Old Testament times. Solomon, the writer of Proverbs, has a clear purpose in mind in recording his sayings.

PROVERBS 1:2–3
*To know wisdom and instruction,*
*To perceive the words of understanding,*
*To receive the instruction of wisdom,*
*Justice, judgment, and equity;* (NKJV)

**go to**

**responsibility of parents**
Deuteronomy 6:6–9

**of the father**
Deuteronomy 8:5

**primarily verbal**
Deuteronomy 8:3;
Proverbs 1:8; 19:27

**not respond**
Isaiah 8:11;
Hosea 5:2;
Proverbs 22:15;
29:17

**expression of love**
Deuteronomy 8:1–5;
Proverbs 3:11–12

**sense of instruct**
Acts 7:22; 22:3

The goal of instruction, of discipline, is to guide the learner into a life of righteousness.

There are several elements of Old Testament discipline/instruction that are particularly important.

- Discipline/instruction is the primary <u>responsibility of parents</u>, and <u>especially of the father</u>.

- Discipline/instruction is <u>primarily verbal</u>.

- There is an element of punishment in discipline/instruction, but this is introduced only when the learner <u>will not respond</u> to parental discipline or to God's guidance.

- Discipline/instruction is an <u>expression of love</u>, not of anger.

Each of these key truths is expressed in the Proverbs passage paraphrased by the writer of Hebrews:

> **PROVERBS 3:11–12**
> *My son, do not despise the chastening of the LORD,*
> *Nor detest His correction;*
> *For whom the LORD loves He corrects,*
> *Just as a father the son in whom he delights.* (NKJV)

## "Chasten" in the New Testament

**Septuagint**
the Greek translation of the Old Testament used in the first century

The Greek words used most often in the **Septuagint** to translate *yasar* and *musar* are *paideuo* (verb) and *paideia* (noun). The Greek words mean "to bring up" or "to train." Twice these Greek words are used in the New Testament with the <u>sense of instruct</u>. Only two times do they mean "to beat" (Luke 23:16, 23) or punish.

The rest of the time these words are clearly used in the Old Testament sense of providing correction or guidance, with a view to training or educating. In the New Testament too, instruction is primarily verbal, for it is God's word that is "profitable for doctrine, for reproof, for correction, for instruction in righteousness" (2 Timothy

3:16 NKJV). Taking the role of a parent to his converts in Philippi, the apostle Paul urges, "The things which you learned and received and heard and saw in me, these do, and the God of peace will be with you" (Philippians 4:9 NKJV). He gives an even clearer picture of discipline/instruction in 1 Thessalonians 2:11–12, as he recalls "how we exhorted, and comforted, and charged every one of you, as a father does his own children, that you would walk worthy of God" (NKJV).

Thus, both the primary method of discipline and its goal remain the same in the Old and New Testament eras. With this background, we can look more closely at the rest of Hebrews 12 and, with the first readers, put our own tribulations in better perspective.

## Me Too

HEBREWS 12:7–8 *If you endure chastening, God deals with you as sons; for what son is there whom a father does not chasten? But if you are without chastening, of which all have become partakers, then you are illegitimate and not sons. (NKJV)*

Just to underscore what we've learned, let's rephrase these verses:

"If you guys accept your difficulties as rebuke and correction, you'll realize that God is dealing with you as sons. After all, good dads correct their children. If you had no troubles then you'd really be in trouble! Then you'd not be sons at all. You'd be illegitimate!"

what others say

### John Philips

It was common enough in the ancient world for a man to father both legitimate and illegitimate children. To prepare the legitimate child of his carefully chosen lawful wife to be his heir he disciplined him by means of a series of tutors and a rigorous program of study and exercise for the mind, while relegating the illegitimate child to a life of careless ease. Discipline was therefore a sign at once of legitimacy and of selection for inheritance.[4]

## "If I Were a Rich Man!"

There's a fascinating illustration of this comment in Psalm 73. The writer, Asaph, tells of a time when he almost stumbled in his journey of faith. He saw the "prosperity of the wicked" (verse 3 NKJV) and was overtaken by envy. How come they had it so good, and he didn't?

He says:

PSALM 73:5–9
*They are not in trouble as other men,*
*Nor are they plagued like other men.*
*Therefore pride serves as their necklace;*
*Violence covers them like a garment.*
*Their **eyes bulge** with abundance;*
*They have more than heart could wish.*
*They scoff and speak wickedly concerning oppression;*
*They speak **loftily**.*
*They set their mouth against the heavens . . .* (NKJV)

**eyes bulge**
their faces are fat

**loftily**
proudly, arrogantly

Comparing his troubles with the trouble-free life of wicked and arrogant men, Asaph was overcome with doubt and self-pity. It just wasn't fair! Here he was trying to live a godly life. How come God was treating him worse than those who totally ignored God and His ways?

Asaph didn't express his doubts because this would have been "untrue to the generation of Your children" (Psalm 73:15 NKJV). But his inner struggle to deal with what he saw as God's unfairness was "too painful for me" (73:16 NKJV). Then one day he went into the sanctuary, and suddenly he saw the answer. Asaph tells us, "Then I understood their end" (73:17 NKJV).

## Punished with Prosperity?

PSALM 73:18–20
*Surely You set them in slippery places;*
*You cast them down to destruction.*
*Oh, how they are brought to desolation, as in a moment!*
*They are utterly consumed with terrors.*
*As a dream when one awakes,*
*So, Lord, when You awake,*
*You shall despise their image.* (NKJV)

God had not *blessed* the wicked with prosperity. He had *punished* them with prosperity! In their prosperity they had never felt a need for God; had never needed to depend on Him. Asaph, in his troubles, felt his need for God's help continually, and so had placed his trust in God rather than in good health or in riches.

key point

Asaph tells us that when this insight came he felt utterly foolish. It was so obvious! Troubles had drawn him closer to God. And prosperity had driven the wicked farther from the Lord! Asaph's troubles had been an unrecognized blessing, while the prosperity of the wicked was a slippery slope down which they would slide to eternal judgment.

With this new perspective Asaph's doubts were transformed to praise, and he exulted.

PSALM 73:23–24
*I am continually with You;*
*You hold me by my right hand.*
*You will guide me with Your counsel,*
*And afterward receive me to glory.* (NKJV)

The truth that a believer's troubles may be evidence of God's love is something that has escaped the troubled community in Jerusalem. And so the writer of Hebrews puts it bluntly. It would be worse *not* to have troubles. Then you'd have to question your relationship with God.

God treats believers as sons, and that means He provides painful experiences to correct and guide us!

## Score One for God

HEBREWS 12:9–10 *Furthermore, we have had human fathers who corrected us, and we paid them respect. Shall we not much more readily be in subjection to the Father of spirits and live? For they indeed for a few days chastened us as seemed best to them, but He for our profit, that we may be partakers of His holiness.* (NKJV)

How are we to react to our trials and our troubles? The same way a child is to respond to his human father. Children need to accept a parent's guidance and discipline and learn from it. That's what paying respect means.

We constantly see examples of disrespect. A harried mom in a grocery story tells her child not to touch the products. The child pays no attention and grabs boxes of sugary cereals or picks up candy bars he wants Mom to buy.

A teenager is asked to do a chore. He mutters, "Later," or simply leaves the room without answering at all. When she's tired of waiting, mom does the chore herself. Another teen is told to finish homework before going to a friend's house. On the way out of the house the teen lies and says that her untouched schoolwork is done.

**go to**

**Honor your father and your mother**
Ephesians 6:1–4

To show respect for a parent means to follow his or her instructions, even when we want to do the opposite. Showing respect for God means the same thing. We show respect for God by following His instructions as we hear His voice in our today. Even when we want desperately to take a different course.

## Vive la Différence!

There's one really big difference between parental discipline and God's discipline. Sometimes parents do know what's best for their kids. Sometimes they act in our best interests. But sometimes they are wrong about what's best. Sometimes they react out of frustration, or anger, or weariness, or their own pain.

Even so, the fifth of the Ten Commandments still applies: "Honor your father and your mother" (Exodus 20:12 NKJV). Even when the child feels his or her parents are wrong, they are to be responded to with respect. God, on the other hand, always knows what's best for us. And God's discipline is always directed toward a specific goal.

**apply it**

Here is the goal: He disciplines us "for our profit, that we may be partakers of His holiness" (Hebrews 12:10 NKJV).

A loving mother's instruction to the young child in the store may be intended to help him develop self-control. Or it may be she's frustrated by the little rascal's hyperactivity. A concerned parent may want to help his teen develop the discipline of putting work before pleasure. Or he may be expressing irritation at the teen's general irresponsibility.

But God always keeps the goal in mind. God disciplines us for *our* benefit. And the benefit is that, as we show the Lord proper respect and respond to His voice, we will grow in holiness. We will become more and more like our Savior in our values, in our attitudes, and in our behavior.

In the case of a parent who instructs his or her child to commit sin (stealing, dealing drugs, lying, etc.), it's hard to remain respectful and obedient. Ephesians 6:1 includes a clarifying phrase—"Children, obey your parents *in the Lord*, for this is right" (NKJV, italics added). Verse 4 adds, "Fathers, do not provoke your children to wrath, but bring them up in the training and admonition of the Lord" (NKJV).

## It Hurts So Good

HEBREWS 12:11 *Now no chastening seems to be joyful for the present, but painful; nevertheless, afterward it yields the peaceable fruit of righteousness to those who have been trained by it.* (NKJV)

It's so obvious that it hardly needs saying, but it's an important reminder. No one *enjoys* the process of chastening (discipline, correction—even verbal correction).

key point

Earlier we saw that even Jesus "learned obedience by the things which He suffered" (Hebrews 5:8 NKJV). I pointed out there that "obeying" implies doing something you wouldn't normally *want* to do. For that young child in the store, obeying means controlling his impulse to grab and touch products on the shelves. He really wants to do—to grab and to touch. Not grabbing and touching *hurts* when his impulse is denied.

For the teenager, sitting down and doing homework when he wants to go out with friends is painful. If he obeys it will *hurt*. But if he refuses to obey, he shows disrespect for his father and fails to learn an important life lesson. He really wants to ignore his schoolwork and go out. Not going out *hurts*—at the time.

All too often when we hear God's voice of guidance, He's calling us to do something that we don't want to do at the time. We don't want to go over to our always-complaining neighbor's house and try to be a friend. We're too exhausted to call the new Christian down the block and invite her to the Bible study we planned to skip. We're too embarrassed to seek out the friend we think our words might have hurt and apologize. We're too busy to listen to our child's chatter about school. We're too fearful of rejection to talk about Jesus with the person who works beside us in the office.

So, when we hear God's voice prompting us we hesitate, and all too often we choose not to respond. It seems to us that obeying would be *just too painful*.

But if we don't respond we miss more than an opportunity to be God's voice in another's life. We miss the opportunity to reap what the writer of Hebrews calls "the peaceable fruit of righteousness" (Hebrews 12:11 NKJV).

"Righteousness" is not a cool concept in today's world. But that's a crying shame, because righteousness (rightness, goodness, justice) is a wonderful, peaceful, harmonious outcome to the man or woman who pays attention to the Father's instruction. Remember the adage: When trouble or pain hits your world, just ask, "What are You trying to teach me, Lord?"

We may find the process of being trained by God painful. But eventually we'll love the fruit of God's training. And so will He.

## News Flash! God Doesn't Give Up on Us

There's a word in verse 6 of Hebrews 12 that I purposely ignored earlier. Verse 6 says, "For whom the LORD loves He chastens [instructs, disciplines]" (NKJV). Then it adds, "and scourges every son whom He receives." With that word "scourges" we get to the "punishment" element in discipline. In fact, the NIV translates the Greek word here as "punishes."

Sometimes there is no substitute for a good spanking! Proverbs never hesitates to recommend a good spanking when it's needed to correct unresponsive youngsters.

- "**Foolishness** is bound up in the heart of a child; the rod of correction will drive it far from him" (Proverbs 22:15 NKJV).

- "He who spares his rod hates his son, but he who loves him disciplines him promptly" (Proverb 13:24 NKJV).

- "The rod and rebuke give wisdom, but a child left to himself brings shame to his mother" (Proverbs 29:15 NKJV).

- "Correct your son, and he will give you rest; yes, he will give delight to your soul" (Proverbs 29:17 NKJV).

There's no hint here of a permissiveness that says anything my child does is all right with me. What is here is the awareness that we all need to learn to do what's right and reject what's wrong, and that a person who resists correction will at times need to be helped along the way with a good spanking.

That's what the writer of Hebrews wants his first readers to understand. God speaks to them and gives them guidance. The directions He gives may not be "joyful for the present," but if we respect God and respond obediently to His voice, "afterward it yields the peaceable fruit of righteousness" (Hebrews 12:11 NKJV). And if we refuse to respond, God loves us enough not to give up on us. He uses His own rod of correction, until we're willing to abandon our willful ways and submit to His love.

## Straighten Up and Fly Right

HEBREWS 12:12–13 *Therefore strengthen the hands which hang down, and the feeble knees, and make straight paths for your feet, so that what is lame may not be dislocated, but rather be healed.* (NKJV)

Hebrew is a picture language. Greek tends to be a concept language. Concept languages use abstract terms to convey meanings. Picture languages use images, word pictures. We can sense the writer's Hebrew roots in these verses. A person whose first language was Greek would probably say something like, "Stop being discouraged! Take heart and get on with it!" Instead the writer gives us a vivid picture of total discouragement.

The first readers of his letter have given up. Their shoulders are slumped. Their hands hang at their sides. Their knees are so feeble they seem about to collapse. And they wander around aimlessly, looking here and there for a way out. Now it's time for them to abandon their defeatist attitude and behavior. It's time to straighten up, stop wandering, and step out boldly to "run with endurance the race that is set before us" (Hebrews 12:1 NKJV).

It's time for us, too. Time to consider Jesus's life. Time to focus on the joy set before us rather than the difficulties we may encounter along the way.

Time to see the difficulties we're afraid to face as opportunities provided by our loving Father to grow in Jesus's likeness, "that we may be partakers of His holiness" (Hebrews 12:10 NKJV).

# What's in It for Me?

Another concept visible in this Hebrew word picture (Hebrews 12:12–13) has to do with the church family's response and involvement with discouraged brothers and sisters under chastening. The exhortation urges members of Christ's family to come alongside hurting friends and help lift up "the hands which hang down" (12:12 NKJV).

That phrase is a throwback to the experience of Moses when Israel was engaged in a pitched battle (Exodus 17:8–16, escpecially verses 11 and 12) with the Amalekites. The battle went Israel's way when Moses held up his hands, but when he could hold them up no longer and his hands hung down the battle turned in the enemy's favor. To keep Israel's troops winning, two men, Aaron and Hur, held Moses's arms up all day. The result was Israeli victory.

Just so, the family of Christ must step up and help lift the hands of its struggling members no matter how they got into the trouble they're in (James 1:5).

We help each other to keep from quitting by:

- lifting each other's drooping hands (in prayer, praise, or work)
- supporting feeble, wobbly legs about to buckle under the pressure
- guiding strugglers onto straight paths, showing the right way to go
- healing, reversing damage done by the disaster

key point

# Stop Shooting the Wounded!

Insiders sometimes accuse the church of being "the only army that shoots its own wounded." They're talking about the church's practice of rejecting Christians who fail. Considered *persona non grata* by their former brothers and sisters, they are often left to try to find healing and a way back without loving support.

If true, that's a terrible indictment for a body whose business is forgiveness and saving the lost! When someone is weak or fails in the war against sin, the church has too often abandoned that person—especially if it's someone less desirable.

When fellow believers are in trouble—whether as a result of their own stupidity, rebellion, or through no traceable fault of their own—that's no time to desert or attack them. Instead, the body/family identifies with (sees themselves in) the sufferer and comes to his aid. Paul cited the principle in 1 Corinthians 12:26: "If one member suffers, all the members suffer with it" (NKJV).

It's a fact, not a choice. All members, whether they know it or believe it or not, in one way or another, suffer with the suffering of one. Knowing and believing, we are equipped to learn and change when disaster strikes our spiritual kin.

Sometimes the member "under God's discipline" is suffering for not only his or her growth and cleansing, but the growth and cleansing of others of the entire spiritual family. Aid is to be given with full understanding that our member may be going through pain and suffering for us! When others in the body are in trouble the members should be asking, "Lord, what are You trying to say to or accomplish in *the rest of us* through our comrade's distress?"

That said, with open hearts and minds, invited the chastening of the Lord to begin to bring to fullness the fruit of holiness/righteousnes, which is the goal for us in the Father's mind.

## Chapter Wrap-Up

- We're called to "run with endurance" (Hebrews 12:1 NKJV) whatever race God sets before us.

- We need to consider how Jesus dealt with hostility and suffering, and determine to follow His lead.

- We need to remember that difficult experiences are evidence that God loves us and is treating us as sons.

- It's through difficult experiences that God trains us, and that His training is "for our profit, that we may be partakers of His holiness" (Hebrews 12:10 NKJV).

- These disciplinary experiences are painful while we go through the process, but in the end yield "the peaceable fruit of righteousness" (Hebrews 12:11 NKJV).

- We need to stop being discouraged or thinking of giving up, and get back to running the race of faith.

## Study Questions

1. What are the "weights" and the "ensnaring sins" that the writer urges his readers to "lay aside" (see Hebrews 12:1)?

2. In what ways is Jesus the "author and finisher" (Hebrews 12:2 NKJV) of our faith?

3. What evidence is there that the Christian Jews to whom this letter was written have "forgotten" Proverbs 3:11–12?

4. What does the word translated "chasten" in this passage mean?

5. What does the writer say a trouble-free life indicates? How does Psalm 73 illustrate this concept?

6. What is the role of "punishment" in discipline?

7. How does a child show respect for his father? How do we show respect for God?

8. What: (a) is God's attitude in disciplining us? (b) is God's goal in disciplining us? (c) does God's discipline feel like to us? (d) is the end result if we respond appropriately?

# Hebrews 12:14-29
# The Great Heaven-and-Earthquake

## Let's Get Started

Throughout his letter to the Jewish Christians in Jerusalem the writer of Hebrews has emphasized the importance of response. Don't harden your hearts when you hear God's voice (Hebrews 3–4). Don't even think of turning back. Go on to maturity in Christ (Hebrews 5–6). Now that you understand the significance of Christ's High Priesthood (Hebrews 7–10), commit yourself to live by faith rather than by law (Hebrews 12). And also in chapter 12, learn to see your troubles as discipline—instruction, correction, guidance—expressions of God the Father's love.

> **what others say**
>
> **D. A. Carson**
>
> All the correct theology in the world will not make a spanking sting less, or make a brutal round of toughening-up exercises fun. Yet it does help to know that there is light at the end of the tunnel, even if you cannot yet see it; to know that God is in control and is committed to His people's good, even thought it still does not look like that to you.[1]

The writer has already given his readers some advice about how to respond to divine discipline. Show respect for God by obeying Him, even when it's painful to obey (Hebrews 12:9–11). Don't give up, but "strengthen the hands which hang down, and the feeble knees" (Hebrews 12:12 NKJV). But the writer has even more suggestions to offer. Suggestions that, if we follow them, will enable us to experience life as active citizens of God's unshakable kingdom.

## Bitter Root Road

**HEBREWS 12:14–15** *Pursue peace with all people, and holiness, without which no one will see the Lord: looking carefully lest anyone fall short of the grace of God; lest any root of bitterness springing up cause trouble, and by this many become defiled. (NKJV)*

The writer of Hebrews encourages his readers to pursue the things that "make for" peace. What does he mean by "peace," and what are those things that "make for" it?

**only those who trust in Christ**
John 8:42–44;
Ephesians 2:1–3

## Peace, Brother!

In both the Old and New Testaments, "peace" is essentially a relational term. The Old Testament word translated "peace," *shalom*, conveys a sense of wholeness and harmony. A person at peace is in harmony with himself, with God, and with others. While at times the word is used of a state of peace between nations, or of prosperity, the peace God gives is available to His people whatever the external circumstances may be. David, while fleeing from the forces of his rebel son, Absalom, says, "I will both lie down in peace, and sleep; for You alone, O LORD, make me dwell in safety" (Psalm 4:8 NKJV).

The essential meaning of "peace" in Scripture as inner harmony and well-being is established in the Old Testament and carried over into the New. Jesus told His disciples, "Peace I leave with you, My peace I give to you; not as the world gives do I give to you. Let not your heart be troubled, neither let it be afraid" (John 14:27 NKJV). Through their relationship with Jesus, Christians are to know the wonderful blessing that David experienced on one of his most difficult days; a peace that comes from a personal relationship with a God they know well, who loves them and will care for them.

This peace that God gives us as individuals is wonderful indeed. But the writer of Hebrews is urging us to pursue peace "with all" (12:14 NKJV). The fact that "people" is italicized in our NKJV text means that the translators supplied the word. "People" is not in the Greek text. It would be better here to supply "believers," for the writer's teaching on discipline is for believers alone, as <u>only those who trust in Christ</u> have a true Father-child relationship with God.

## In Hot Pursuit

In using the word "pursue," the writer makes it very clear that peace is something we need to work at within our own community of believers. "Pursue" is a strong word. It suggests fixing our eyes on a goal and concentrating every effort to reach it. New Testament writers use "pursue" frequently, and in most contexts they too emphasize pursuing interpersonal harmony. Followers of Jesus are to:

- "pursue the things which make for peace and the things by which one may edify another" (Romans 14:19 NKJV).

- "pursue love" (1 Corinthians 14:1 NKJV).

- "always pursue what is good both for yourselves and for all" (1 Thessalonians 5:15 NKJV).

- "pursue righteousness, godliness, faith, love, patience, gentleness" (1 Timothy 6:11 NKJV).

- "pursue righteousness, faith, love, peace with those who call on the Lord out of a pure heart" (2 Timothy 2:22 NKJV).

- "seek peace and pursue it" (1 Peter 3:11 NKJV).

**tender mercies**
compassion

**bearing with**
putting up with

**bond of perfection**
the bond that ties these virtues together perfectly

What, then, are some things we're to pursue in our fellowships that make for peace? In Romans 14 Paul urges the Roman Christians to stop judging one another in matters of conscience. We are to step back in matters not specifically forbidden in Scripture and let each other be responsible to Jesus, as Lord, concerning what we do or don't do. At the same time we need to be sensitive to each other's convictions, and act in love.

apply it

In 1 Corinthians Paul has just concluded his great exposition on the nature of love (1 Corinthians 13). The Corinthians had been measuring one another's spirituality by their visible spiritual gifts. Paul decisively rejects this approach and reminds them that the truly spiritual person is marked by love. Therefore, he writes, "pursue love" (1 Corinthians 14:1 NKJV).

In each of the "pursue" passages the emphasis is on caring for others and living with them in a godly, loving way. Perhaps Colossians 3:12–15 gives us the single best description of how we can "pursue peace" on a community-wide basis.

COLOSSIANS 3:12–15 *Therefore, as the elect of God, holy and beloved, put on **tender mercies**, kindness, humility, meekness, long suffering; **bearing with** one another, and forgiving one another, if anyone has a complaint against another; even as Christ forgave you, so you also must do. But above all these things put on love, which is the **bond of perfection**. And let the peace of God rule in your hearts, to which also you were called in one body; and be thankful. (NKJV)*

**go to**

**seeing the Lord**
2 Corinthians
3:17–18

key point

In a significant sense the way of life described in Colossians 3 *is* the life of holiness. Practical holiness involves the way believers who live in harmony with God's will relate to one another, expressing His character and His life daily in our world.

## I Want to See You, Lord

The writer reminds us that if we fail to pursue a life of peace within the believing community, and holiness before God, "no one will see the Lord" (Hebrews 12:14 NKJV). Don't jump to the conclusion that the writer is talking about not getting to heaven. He isn't. He's talking about seeing the Lord in and through what He is doing in our own lives, and in the lives of our believing brothers and sisters.

God is absolutely holy (Isaiah 6:1–3; Revelation 4:8). His holiness is both an awesome "otherness" (separateness from every created thing and evil in any form) and moral perfection. Anyone who associates with God must be holy—cleansed of sin (1 John 1:7–9), and living a good and self-giving life daily in this present world—a life of righteousness, justice, and love.

New Testament believers in Jesus are set apart as God's holy ones, "saints" (Ephesians 1:1 NKJV), because of their relationship with Jesus. The Holy Spirit comes to live in the person who trusts Jesus, to express the positive dynamic of God's essential holiness through Christians.[2]

As was already noted in Hebrews 12:10, we become "partakers of His holiness" (NKJV) through God's "chastening." (To *"partake"* of God's holiness or likeness is to actually have a share in the holy nature of God!)

what others say

**Maxie D. Dunnam**

The essence of holiness as we find it in the Scriptures is conforming to the character of God. This is the essence of the covenant and a central theme running throughout Scripture.[3]

Holiness comes as God works to reshape us into the likeness of Jesus, using all the painful and difficult circumstances of our lives (Romans 8:28–29). Holiness involves presenting one's whole being to God in living, active, sensible, rubber-meets-the-road worship

(Romans 12:1–18) and indwelling/filling by the Holy Spirit (Acts 1:8; Ephesians 5:17–21). Forgiveness of past sins and cleansing by the Spirit from inner unrighteousness—unjust, unloving attitudes and actions (1 John 1:7–9). This also is holiness.

It's a process. But growth in holiness and personal change is the privilege and charge of every Christian.

## Short on Grace

HEBREWS 12:15 . . . *looking carefully lest anyone fall short of the grace of God.* (NKJV)

The phrase "fall short" means "to lose sight of, to miss." It was all too easy for members of the early Jerusalem church to lose sight of God's grace under the constant pressure of troubles and persecution. It's all too easy for us to do the same today.

The emphasis of chapter 12 is on the grace of God as shown in how He disciplines and instructs His people. It's all too easy to miss God's loving hand in painful experiences, and so to lose sight of His grace. But there are other ways in which we lose sight of God's wonderful grace. In persistent pain we may not see God's grace in the kindness of our family. In overwhelming financial difficulties we may not stop to appreciate the beauty of a sunny day. Driven by a desire for more, we may never realize how graciously God has provided the plenty that we already have. A failure to appreciate evidences of God's grace in a Christian community or in an individual's life can mean disaster for both.

## The Anguish of Bitterness

HEBREWS 12:15 . . . *lest any root of bitterness springing up cause trouble, and by this many become defiled.* (NKJV)

When we keep God's grace in view our hearts are filled with peace, even when our days are filled with troubles. On the other hand, all too often the consequence of missing God's grace is bitterness. And bitterness is infectious, like the rotten apple that spoils the whole barrel.

Old Testament words for bitterness describe an emotion that's close to despair. The bitter person is in anguish, crushed by circumstances. Among the bitter in the Old Testament are Naomi, who moved to a foreign land and there lost her husband and her two sons (Ruth 1:20); a woman who lost her only child (2 Kings 4:27); and Job, whose tragedies made him "bitter of soul" (Job 3:20 NKJV). The emotion associated with bitterness is powerfully expressed by Jeremiah 4:18b–19: "It is bitter, because it reaches to your heart. O my soul, my soul! I am pained in my very heart! My heart makes a noise in me; I cannot hold my peace" (NKJV).

The New Testament emphasizes another aspect of bitterness. Here bitterness is not so much the emotions as the attitudes that grow out of despair. We see these attitudes in several verses that place bitterness in company with similar traits:

- Romans 3:14 (NKJV) quotes a psalm which uses "cursing and bitterness" as synonyms.
- Ephesians 4:31 (NKJV) puts bitterness with "wrath, anger, clamor, and evil speaking."
- James 3:14 associates bitterness with envy and selfishness.

The developed picture is one of a person whose sufferings have turned him into a hostile, antagonistic person dominated by resentment. It's no wonder that the writer of Hebrews warns against the "root of bitterness" that can "cause trouble, and by this many become defiled" (Hebrews 12:15 NKJV).

Nothing can be more disruptive of harmony between Christians than a bitter, hostile individual.

In urging his readers to accept God's discipline as a gift of love, and to be always alert for evidences of God's grace, the writer confronts us with a choice. We can respond to God's discipline appropriately, knowing that this will yield *"the peaceable fruit of righteousness"* (Hebrews 12:11). Or we can continue to wallow in despair, closing our eyes to God's grace, and becoming bitter, resentful persons.

The choice we make will dramatically affect our lives. And the lives of others.

## The Material Man

HEBREWS 12:16–17 . . . *lest there be any fornicator or **profane** person like Esau, who for one morsel of food sold his birthright. For you know that afterward, when he wanted to inherit the* *blessing, he was rejected, for he found no place for* **repentance** *though he sought it diligently with tears.* (NKJV)

**repentance**
here, refers to a change of mind by his father

Esau was the twin brother of Jacob, sons of Isaac and Rebekah. Their story, as told in Genesis 25:21–28:6, underlines how different these fraternal twins were. For one thing, they looked very different. Jacob, in the imagination of this author, was rather pale, not at all athletic, and seemed to feel most at home sitting around chatting with the womenfolk. Esau was a rugged outdoorsman, who loved hunting and other manly activities. It's not surprising that Mom favored Jacob, and Dad favored Esau. After all, Esau was, in his father's cataract-disrupted view, a "man's man."

But the differences between the two went far beyond appearances. Esau was a thoroughgoing materialist with no interest in anything spiritual. One day he came home after hunting, famished. When his brother Jacob offered to trade Esau a bowl of red stew for Esau's birthright, Esau didn't think twice. He was hungry. How could some ephemeral birthright compare to food on the table now!

## Too Little, Too Late, Too Bad

It's important to understand what the birthright entailed. Esau had been born a few seconds before Jacob. That made him the elder brother. And, as the oldest, it meant that under the legal principles of the time Esau was entitled to a larger portion of their father's material wealth, and to his intangible possessions as well. The one great intangible possession of Isaac was the covenant promise that God had given Abraham to pass down to his descendants. That promise guaranteed that the Lord would be the inheritors' God, and that one day their descendants would inherit Canaan.

key point

"God" meant little or nothing to Esau, so he didn't skip a beat in giving away the right to have the Lord as his God. And as far as Canaan was concerned he couldn't have cared less about what happened to its hills and meadows after he died. These and other blessings promised to Abraham simply weren't real to Esau. But that bowl of red stew, well, *that was* real! Esau could almost taste it, and he knew it would fill his empty belly. So this classic example of the material man quickly agreed. "You take the birthright, Jacob. I'll take the stew."

Many years later, when Isaac feared he was about to die, he determined to bless his son Esau. In those days the blessing of a dying man was equivalent to our modern "last will and testament." It was also viewed as a prophetic utterance that to some extent shaped the future. So Isaac sent Esau out to hunt game, intending to bless him after eating a meal that his son provided.

When Rebekah overheard the conversation between Isaac and Esau, she helped Jacob disguise himself as Esau. And blind Isaac gave the blessing he'd intended for Esau to Jacob, including the passing on of the promises given to Abraham to this, his younger son.

prophecy

No one comes off very well in this story. Jacob is a sneak and a cheat. Rebekah practices deceit. Isaac, assuming his wife had shared the prophecy with him, knew that God intended Jacob to have the blessing (Genesis 25:23) but is set on giving it to his own favorite son instead. Isaac appears to have the same weakness for savory food that his son Esau had (compare Genesis 25:28–34 with 27:1–3). Esau shows contempt for God throughout. But at least Jacob valued the blessing and thought that relationship with God was important.

Later, after Isaac surrendered to God's will and confirmed his gift of the blessing to Jacob, Esau became upset. He decided then that he wanted the blessing after all—although it's likely that he was more interested in the material inheritance than any spiritual one. Although Esau cried and wailed, it was too little, too late.

## what others say

### Ronald Youngblood

Esau continued to beg his father for at least one blessing, and he broke down and wept bitterly. It was too late for him to receive the main blessing, however. The best he could hope for was a pitiful shadow or reflection of what Jacob had already received.[4]

### W. Griffith Thomas

Esau had despised his birthright. However it came about, he was evidently conscious of the value of the blessing; and when the New Testament tells us that "he found no place for repentance," it means, of course, that there was no possibility of undoing what had been accomplished. He found no way to change his father's mind, though he sought earnestly to bring this about. There is a sense in which the past is utterly irretrievable.[5]

Esau's experience is now applied by the writer of Hebrews to his readers. Keep on as you have been, living as material men and women who are blind to the grace of God, and one of these days it will be too late for you, too.

And that really is too bad!

## Climb Every Mountain—but Not This One

**HEBREWS 12:18–21** *For you have not come to the mountain that may be touched and that burned with fire, and to blackness and darkness and tempest, and the sound of a trumpet and the voice of words, so that those who heard it begged that the word should not be spoken to them anymore. (For they could not endure what was commanded: "And if so much as a beast touches the mountain, it shall be stoned or shot with an arrow." And so terrible was the sight that Moses said, "I am exceedingly afraid and trembling.") (NKJV)*

**contrasting the era**
Galatians 4:21–31

We now come to what's been called the final warning passage in Hebrews. Like the other so-called warning passages, this one has struck fear in many. The "much more shall we not escape if we turn away" of Hebrews 12:25 (NKJV) (which we'll look at in a moment) seems at first glance a terrifying threat of eternal condemnation. But before we reach that conclusion, let's follow the writer's argument more closely.

## Old Covenant—The Scary Summit of Sinai

**HEBREWS 12:18** *For you have not come to the mountain that may be touched . . . (NKJV)*

Once again we see recurring patterns. The writer is setting out to contrast the seen (Sinai, "the mountain that may be touched") with the unseen ("you have come to Mount Zion the heavenly Jerusalem" Hebrews 12:22 NKJV). At the same time the writer is contrasting the era of Law, symbolized by Sinai, with the era of faith, symbolized by Mount Zion.

Going back into the Old Testament the writer picks up its terrifying description of Sinai at the time God gave the Law.

loves Me
John 14:23–24

EXODUS 19:16–18 *Then it came to pass on the third day, in the morning, that there were thunderings and lightnings, and a thick cloud on the mountain; and the sound of the trumpet was very loud, so that all the people who were in the camp trembled. And Moses brought the people out of the camp to meet with God, and they stood at the foot of the mountain. Now Mount Sinai was completely in smoke because the LORD descended upon it in fire. Its smoke ascended like the smoke of a furnace, and the whole mountain quaked greatly. (NKJV)*

These, and the other details that the writer of Hebrews picks up, were familiar to all his early Jewish Christian readers. And together they underlined the fact that everything about God's appearance to the Exodus generation created terror. Even Moses was "afraid and trembling" (Hebrews 12:20 NKJV).

But "you have not come to the mountain that may be touched" (Hebrews 12:18 NKJV). You haven't come to a terrifying deity, of whom you need to be afraid.

**what others say**

**George H. Guthrie**

You Christians have not come to a Mount Sinai, material, sensible, horrible, where and when the Old Testament dispensation was founded amid scenes of a terrifying character. You are come to the heavenly Zion, spiritual, supersensible, eternal. The writer evinces the awfulness attending the revelation of the old covenant in order to stress the more dire peril of forfeiting far greater Christian gifts and privileges of the new covenant, which are the things themselves and not merely types and symbols.[6]

key point

And this is important. For fear will no more evoke obedience in Christians today than fear did in God's Old Testament people. Once again, remember Jesus's words. "If you love Me, keep My commandments" (John 14:15 NKJV). And, "He who has My commandments and keeps them, it is he who <u>loves Me</u>" (John 14:21 NKJV).

## Not Your Father's Mountain

HEBREWS 12:22–24 *But you have come to Mount Zion and to the city of the living God, the heavenly Jerusalem, to an innumerable company of angels, to the general assembly and church of the firstborn who are registered in heaven, to God the Judge of all, to the spirits of just men made perfect, to Jesus the Mediator of the new covenant, and to the blood of sprinkling that speaks better things than that of Abel.* (NKJV)

What's so special about Mount Zion?

"Mount Zion" is the name given to the ridge on which Solomon's Temple was constructed. It's thus associated with God's forgiveness and with access to the Lord. As Solomon prayed on the day the temple was dedicated,

KINGS 8:27–30 *But will God indeed dwell on the earth? Behold, heaven and the heaven of heavens cannot contain You. How much less this temple which I have built! Yet regard the prayer of Your servant and his supplication, O LORD my God, and listen to the cry and the prayer which Your servant is praying before You today: that Your eyes may be open toward this temple night and day, toward the place of which You said, "My name shall be there," that You may hear the prayer which Your servant makes toward this place. And may You hear the supplication of Your servant and of Your people Israel, when they pray toward this place. Hear in heaven Your dwelling place; and when You hear, forgive.* (NKJV)

## Drama on Mount Moriah

Mount Zion has even more stunning links to God's grace. Tradition tells that another name for Zion was Mount Moriah, and it was to Mount Moriah that God directed Abraham to bring his son—and sacrifice him (Hebrews 11:17–18). Yet when the two came to the mount, and Abraham had laid out the wood on a roughly constructed altar, God stayed Abraham's hand. The knife that had been poised over young Isaac was withdrawn, and God pointed Abraham to a ram caught in a nearby thicket. That day the ram died in the place of Abraham's dearly loved son. But the God who spared Isaac would not spare His own Son. Centuries later, outside the walls of Jerusalem but within sight of the temple constructed on Mount Zion, the Son of God paid the price of humankind's sins.

# New Covenant—The Approachable Pinnacle of Zion

In saying "You have come to Mount Zion" (Hebrews 12:22 NKJV), the writer is underlining the vast difference between Law and grace. The one thunders the terrifying message of human sin and divine punishment. The other joyfully shouts out the Gospel of God's love and forgiveness. Sinai emphasizes God's sheer majesty, God's absolute inapproachability, the terror of God. Zion empha-sizes God's nearness. At Sinai He is the stern lawgiver and judge. At Zion He is our "*Abba* (Daddy) Father."

God has always been both. But Mount Zion shows how His love and mercy overshadow His sterner side. He has not changed. Humans whose minds and hearts are not closed are simply given a chance to know Him as He is.

And to reinforce this message the writer of Hebrews provides a summary of Mount Zion's other attractions.

- *City of God*

  Mount Zion is "the city of the living God" (Hebrews 12:22 NKJV). It is the city that God Himself founded, named, and where He personally dwells. It is a city where there is no dark-ness at all, for the glory of God illuminates it and "the Lamb is its light" (Revelation 21:23 NKJV). It is the land of "no more death, nor sorrow, nor crying. There there shall be no more pain" (Revelation 21:4 NKJV). It is the place where God Himself "will be with them and be their God" (Revelation 21:3 NKJV).

- *Heavenly Jerusalem, City of Angels*

  Mount Zion is "the heavenly Jerusalem" (Hebrews 12:22 NKJV). Mount Zion exists now in the realm of the unseen, where there are "an innumerable company of angels" (12:22 NKJV). Although Mount Zion is unseen it is very real, and that host of angels are "ministering spirits sent forth to minister for those who will inherit salvation" (Hebrews 1:14 NKJV).

- *General Assembly and Church of the Firstborn*

  Mount Zion is the place where "the **general assembly** and church of the firstborn who are registered in heaven" gather (Hebrews 12:23 NKJV). It's the end of life's long journey for the saved; a place of continual celebration and joy.

- *God the Judge of All*

    Mount Zion is where we appear before "God, the Judge of all" (Hebrews 12:23 NKJV), not to be condemned but where "each one's <u>praise will come from God</u>" (1 Corinthians 4:5 NKJV).

- *Spirits of Men Made Perfect*

    Mount Zion is where "the spirits of just men [are] made perfect" (Hebrews 12:23 NKJV). It marks the end of our long struggle with sin, as God completes His new covenant work and finishes our transformation into Jesus's likeness (1 John 3:2).

- *Mediator of the New Covenant*

    Mount Zion is where Jesus sits as "Mediator of the new covenant" (Hebrews 12:24 NKJV). He applies the benefits of His sacrifice to us, providing us with "mercy, and . . . grace to help in time of need" (Hebrews 4:16 NKJV).

- *Sprinkled Blood*

    Mount Zion is that tabernacle in heaven which Jesus entered with His own blood (Hebrews 12:24–28), the sprinkling of which "speaks better things than that of Abel" (12:24 NKJV). <u>Abel's blood</u>, shed by his brother Cain, was conclusive evidence that the curse of sin had passed from Adam and Eve to all humankind. But the blood of Christ stands as an eternal offer of forgiveness of sins and inner transformation, proof positive of the amazing grace and love of God.

**go to**

**praise from God**
1 Corinthians 3:3:10–15;
2 Corinthians 5:10

**Abel's blood**
Genesis 4:1–8

**refused**
rejected, failed to respond to

What a contrast! Mount Sinai thunders God's judgment; Mount Zion reverberates with God's love. Mount Sinai threatens punishment; Mount Zion promises forgiveness. Mount Sinai creates fear; Mount Zion provides peace.

And these are contrasts we need to have clearly in mind as we read the next verses. For the writer of Hebrews clearly states that his readers "have not come to the mountain that may be touched" but that "you have come to Mount Zion" (Hebrews 12:18, 22 NKJV).

We who live in Zion must always take care not to read Mount Sinai into any words New Testament writers address to us.

## <u>Worldwide Shakeup</u>

**HEBREWS 12:25–29** *See that you do not refuse Him who speaks. For if they did not escape who **refused** Him who spoke on earth,* *much more shall we not escape if we turn away from Him who speaks from heaven, whose voice then shook the earth; but now He has promised, saying, "Yet once more I shake not only the earth, but also heaven." Now this, "Yet once more," indicates the removal of those things that are being shaken, as of things that are made, that the things which cannot be shaken may remain. Therefore, since we are receiving a kingdom which cannot be shaken, let us have grace, by which we may serve God acceptably with reverence and godly fear. For our God is a consuming fire. (NKJV)*

The apostle Peter makes the same point as the writer of Hebrews in his second epistle. But Peter, not relying on Old Testament images, says it a little more plainly:

**2 PETER 3:10–11** *But the day of the Lord will come as a thief in the night, in which the heavens will pass away with a great noise, and the elements will melt with fervent heat; both the earth and the works that are in it will be burned up. Therefore, since all these things will be dissolved, what manner of persons ought you to be in holy conduct and godliness, (NKJV)*

The material universe, heaven and earth, are destined for destruction. In view of the future of this world, we need to live as citizens of God's unshakable kingdom.

## All Shook Up

No less than five Hebrew words are translated "shake" or "shaken." All five are synonyms, and any one could replace another with no change in meaning. Any of the words can also be used descriptively, as in "who shakes hands in a pledge" (Proverbs 22:26 NKJV), or figuratively as "make their loins shake" (Psalm 69:23 NKJV).

But the most significant use of these words in the Old Testament is to portray the material universe as something that God can and will completely shatter when He executes judgment on the earth. Thus:

**ISAIAH 2:19** *They shall go into the holes of the rocks, and into the caves of the earth, from the terror of the LORD and the glory of His majesty, when He arises to shake the earth mightily. (NKJV)*

ISAIAH 13:13 *Therefore I will shake the heavens, and the earth will move out of her place, in the wrath of the LORD of hosts and in the day of His fierce anger.* (NKJV)

JOEL 3:16 *The LORD also will roar from Zion, and utter His voice from Jerusalem; the heavens and earth will shake; but the LORD will be a shelter for His people.* (NKJV)

HAGGAI 2:6 *For thus says the LORD of hosts: "Once more (it is a little while) I will shake heaven and earth, the sea and dry land."* (NKJV)

HAGGAI 2:21–22 *I will shake heaven and earth. I will overthrow the throne of kingdoms; I will destroy the strength of the Gentile kingdoms.* (NKJV)

Prophecy

It's no wonder, against this background, that the writer of Hebrews quotes Haggai 2:6 and interprets it to teach "the removal of those things that are being shaken, as of things that are made" (Hebrews 12:27 NKJV). Everything of this creation will be destroyed, and only "the things which cannot be shaken" will remain.

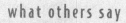
what others say

**Lloyd J. Ogilvie**

God is going to really rock this planet more violently than anything experienced at Sinai, or Mount Saint Helens, or anywhere else. Our Lord is doing this to replace everything changeable. It will be far more terrible than the shaking of the earth at the presence of the Lord in Exodus (Ps.114:11; "When Israel went out of Egypt . . . the sea saw it and trembled . . . Tremble, O earth, at the presence of the Lord, the presence of the God of Jacob) and the presence of the Lord at Sinai (Exodus 19:18: "Now Mount Sinai was completely in smoke, because the Lord descended upon it in fire . . . and the whole mountain quaked greatly") were merely precursors of the appearance of God on the final day. In the last day there would be a shake-up that would engulf the whole world, signaling that the appearance of Christ would take place momentarily. Then Christ would come and reign on earth in all His glory forever and ever.[7]

There's another important contrast in this passage. In Exodus, on the day the Lord descended to Mount Sinai, it's said that "the whole mountain quaked [shook] greatly" (Exodus 19:18 NKJV). It was from that unstable mountain—itself destined to be destroyed when God shakes the earth again—that God announced His law. And

**go to**

**spoken from heaven**
Hebrews 1:2; 2:2–3

although the law was uttered from an unstable platform, "they did not escape who refused Him who spoke on earth" (Hebrews 12:25 NKJV). But now in Jesus God has spoken from heaven. Surely, the writer suggests, no one can escape the consequences of failing to respond to "Him who speaks from heaven" (12:25 NKJV).

Like Peter, the writer of Hebrews points out the practical implications of the contrasts between the shaken and the unshakable. Believers "are receiving a kingdom which cannot be shaken" (Hebrews 12:28 NKJV). We are citizens of the unshakable kingdom. We're not to settle in on this unstable and temporary planet. Surely we must live as citizens of the kingdom that we are receiving from God rather than as citizens of this world.

### Twelve Believeing Responses When Trouble Comes, from Hebrews 12

| Passage | Response |
|---|---|
| verse 3 | Consider Jesus. Look ahead to the joy of completion. |
| verse 5 | Don't regard chastening lightly. |
| verse 7 | Don't faint. Hang in there. |
| verse 10 | Submit to what the Father's trying to do. |
| verses 12–13 | Help one another, steadying, correcting, healing. |
| verse 14 | Pursue peace with everybody. |
| verse 14 | Pursue sanctification. Cooperate with God in change He's bringing. |
| verse 15 | Don't let a brother or sister miss the grace in his/her sufferings. |
| verses 15–17 | Guard against becoming bitter. |
| verse 25 | Listen to what God is saying. |
| verse 27 | Grab hold of the unshakable; let go of what God is shaking. |
| verses 28–29 | Worship. Thank God in the midst of the fire. |

## Got Grace?

HEBREWS 12:28 . . . *let us have grace, by which we may serve God acceptably* (NKJV)

The phrase "have grace" here is used in the sense of "be thankful." We're to appreciate what God has done, and respond out of thankfulness rather than fear. True appreciation for what God has done for us transforms "have to" into "want to," and motivates the only truly acceptable service—that which flows from a grateful, loving heart.

## Fire God

**HEBREWS 12:28** . . . *with reverence and godly fear.* (NKJV)

We of all persons should be fully aware of who God is. We of all persons should revere and respect Him. We of all persons should be in awe of the Creator who stepped into His creation to rescue those who were in active rebellion against Him. We of all persons should know the difference between that which can be shaken and that which is unshakable, between the seen and the unseen, the illusory and the real. And we of all persons should understand the implications of this chapter's final words: "for our God is a consuming fire" (Hebrews 12:29 NKJV).

One day fire will destroy the present heavens and earth. One day those who reject God's grace will be consumed by fire. But that prospect of fire, which terrifies others, warms and comforts us. For when the world ends, we will take the place reserved for us in the kingdom of God's dear Son.

Prophecy

## Chapter Wrap-Up

- It's dangerous to lose sight of God's grace in our troubles. Those who fail to see God's grace in spite of difficult circumstances are likely to become bitter.

- It's also dangerous to be so focused on this world that we lose sight of spiritual realities.

- The reality is that we've come not to Mount Sinai (which represents law) but to Mount Zion (which represents faith and grace). We're to view everything from a Mount Zion perspective.

- From Mount Zion we realize that the material universe is destined to be shaken (destroyed), and so we live to serve God rather than for whatever this world may offer.

- We are moved by thankfulness, for we realize that when this world is destroyed we will fully enter God's kingdom "which cannot be shaken" (Hebrews 12:27 NKJV).

## Study Questions

1. What is the nature of the peace we're to pursue?

2. What is the danger of failing to see the grace of God?

3. What different emphases do the Old and New Testaments place on bitterness?

4. In what way does Esau illustrate the danger that the writer of Hebrews warns against?

5. What is the significance in this passage of Mount Sinai?

6. What is the significance of Mount Zion?

7. Why is it dangerous for Christians to read Scripture from a Mount Sinai perspective?

8. How does the writer apply the contrast between that which can be shaken and that which cannot be shaken?

## Let's Get Started

As this letter to persecuted Hebrew Christians nears its end, the writer can't help providing snippets of practical advice. While the intensive teaching sections of this epistle establish the writer as a master of both the Old and New Testament truth, at heart he's a **pastor**, concerned with the well-being of every individual in the flock. We might almost hear similar words of advice given by a mother to a child heading off to college. As she hugs him good-bye she just can't help saying things like, "Now remember . . . ," "Don't forget . . . ," "I urge you . . . ," and "I appeal to you . . . " We can almost see her child smiling and reassuring her. "Don't worry, Mom. I'll be all right. I'll do just fine."

It's helpful to read chapter 13 with the picture of the mom and her child in mind. The warning sections of Hebrews are long past. The stern demeanor has been dropped, and now nothing but tenderness shines through. These are words of a loving parent who wants nothing less than the best for a child. Surely the writer of Hebrews wants nothing but the best for his first-century readers—and for us.

**pastor**
shepherd

## Keep On Keeping On

HEBREWS 13:1–6 *Let brotherly love continue. Do not forget to entertain strangers, for by so doing some have unwittingly entertained angels. Remember the prisoners as if chained with them—since you yourselves are in the body also. Marriage is honorable among all, and the bed undefiled; but fornicators and adulterers God will judge. Let your conduct be without covetousness; be content with such things as you have. For He Himself has said, "I will never leave you nor forsake you." So we can boldly say:*

> *"The LORD is my helper;*
> *I will not fear.*
> *What can man do to me?" (NKJV)*

**go to**

**exhortations**
Colossians 3:12–17

**hospitality**
Romans 12:13;
1 Timothy 3:2;
Titus 1:8;
1 Peter 4:9

**exhortation**
advice, encouragement, counsel

The chapter begins with a burst of breathless reminders. We know right away that the writer has confidence in his spiritual children. "Let brotherly love continue," he says. The key word here is "continue." There are already many evidences of love in the community to which this letter has been sent. And love is certainly the right place to begin this series of brief exhortations. Earlier we looked at a similar series of **exhortations** in Paul's letter to the Colossians. There he urged, "Above all these things put on love," which he called the virtue that ties all the other virtues to together (Colossians 3:14 NKJV).

It's an appeal today's church seems often to forget in its zealous pursuit to be "right." Being right is good, but it's no substitute for being holy and loving. John reminds us, "God is love" (1 John 4:8 NKJV). We need to have love in our fellowships. Without love, nothing we do will benefit us or anybody else (1 Corinthians 13:3).

## Guess Who's Coming to Dinner?

**HEBREWS 13:2** *Do not forget to entertain strangers, for by so doing some have unwittingly entertained angels. (NKJV)*

One thing that love calls for is "entertaining strangers." In the first century there were no motel chains in every community. Travelers had to depend on the willingness of strangers to take them in. Christians would often seek out fellow believers with whom to stay. It's no wonder that in the first century hospitality was viewed as a virtue (the apostle Peter suggests it's among the gifts of the Holy Spirit, 1 Peter 4:6–10), a significant expression of love.

The writer of Hebrews reminds his readers that entertaining strangers also opens the door to unexpected blessing. After all, both Abraham (Genesis 18) and Lot (Genesis 19) welcomed strangers who turned out to be angels. And those angels saved Lot's life!

**apply it**

Opening up our lives to let others in may seem to be difficult in these days of triple door locks, bars on the windows, 6-foot fences, and warnings to beware of strangers. But we have no idea how God would like to bless us through those we come to know.

## Here's to You and Me, Kid

**HEBREWS 13:3** *Remember the prisoners as if chained with them—those who are mistreated—since you yourselves are in the body also.* (NKJV)

The writer makes it clear that the word "prisoners" here represents all the powerless of society—"those who are mistreated." One thing that "brotherly love" demands is for Christians to identify with the weak and the oppressed (Matthew 5–6; 25:34–36, 41–45). The Old Testament makes it clear that God has special concern for the most vulnerable in society, represented most often in Scripture by the poor.

key point

**DEUTERONOMY 15:7–8** *"If there is among you a poor man of your brethren, within any of the gates in your land which the Lord your God is giving you, you shall not harden your heart nor shut your hand from your poor brother, but you shall open your hand wide to him and willingly lend him sufficient for his need, whatever he needs"* (NKJV).

**PSALM 82:3–4** *"Defend the poor and fatherless; do justice to the afflicted and needy. Deliver the poor and needy; free them from the hand of the wicked"* (NKJV).

**PROVERB 19:17** *"He who has pity on the poor lends to the Lord, and He will pay back what he has given"* (NKJV).

It was all too common even among Christians to dismiss the poor and pander to the well-to-do (James 2:2–6). The writer of Hebrews reminds his readers that the God of love calls us to identify with the oppressed rather than the oppressors, and to care for all "those who are mistreated" (13:3 NKJV).

**fornication**
sex between the unmarried

**adultery**
sex in which at least one of the partners is married to someone else

As long as we are "in the body" we're as vulnerable as anyone to victimization. When it comes to the poor and needy, it's wise to remember we're not speaking of "them," but of "us"!

## Don't Mistake "Love" for "Love"

HEBREWS 13:4 *Marriage is honorable among all, and the bed undefiled; but fornicators and adulterers God will judge.* (NKJV)

The apostle Paul writes extensively on love and marriage in 1 Corinthians 7. The writer of Hebrews simply drops a reminder. There's nothing wrong with marriage or married sex. But God has ruled that sex outside of marriage is out of bounds.

It's appropriate that the writer of Hebrews fits this reminder under his general statement, "Let brotherly love continue" (Hebrews 13:1 NKJV). It's especially appropriate today. While too many young adults are going for "hookups," casual sex without any pretense at relationship, most of our society buys the notion that "love" makes sex right.

"Love" is a very slippery term. At least the Greeks made distinctions when they spoke or wrote of love. *Eros*-love was sexual attraction. *Philos*-love was a friendship-like relationship with benefits for both parties. *Agape*-love, a newcomer on the scene that was filled with meaning by Christianity, was a love whose primary concern was the benefit of the one loved. *Agape*-love was, and still is, defined by the sacrifice of Jesus, who gave Himself totally to rescue people from sin's control.

We don't make those kinds of distinctions in English. Yet it's clear that the "But, we love each other" justification for sex outside of marriage isn't talking about *agape*-love. It may be more than *eros*-love, raw sexual attraction. There may be an element of *philos*-love, which links truly *liking* someone with the benefits we receive from the relationship.

But neither of these so-called loves makes either **fornication** or **adultery** right.

Yet we're not to take the other extreme and view sex within marriage as somehow wrong or dirty. It's not. After all, God created sex when He created human beings male and female (Genesis 1:27). What makes sex right is experiencing it in the context that God intended; the context of a committed, lifelong relationship between one man and one woman. Sure, we need to love each other. But the love we need is *agape*-love, which says I am committed to care for and be with you as long as I'll live on this earth—no matter what.

No wonder the writer of Hebrews wants to make sure that we see sex in the context of love, but in the context of *true* love. That view that justifies sex outside of marriage on the basis of other so-called "loves" stands today, as in the beginning, under the judgment of God.

## More! More! More!

**HEBREWS 13:5–6** *Let your conduct be without covetousness; be content with such things as you have. For He Himself has said, "I will never leave you nor forsake you." So we can boldly say:*
> *The LORD is my helper;*
> *I will not fear.*
> *What can man do to me?"* (NKJV)

The writer of Hebrews tells us, "Be content with such things as you have." The materialist, whose thoughts are consumed by a desire for "the things that are seen," mistakenly assumes that more of what this world has to offer can bring him security and happiness.

Christians look to the unseen. They find security in relationship with their faithful God, and their happiness in serving Him. When our thoughts and hopes are anchored in the Lord, contentment is within our grasp if we will have it.

key point

> **what others say**
>
> **Sue Richards**
>
> My husband of eight years left me at the beginning of my fourth month of pregnancy. I have never felt more rejected, vulnerable, or unloved. No house, no job, no husband, no church. Just an active little boy asking heartbreaking questions, a stomach that gagged at the thought of food, and an empty bed with sheets as cold as the February winds. Yet, somewhere, there was something else too. It was deep inside my heart. It didn't feel overpowering or dramatic, but it gave me courage to get up each morning and make it through the day. How reassuring it was for me in those lonely times to read God's words, "Never will I leave you; never will I forsake you." I held on to those words when I felt totally abandoned, totally alone. In those times, when I was willing to reach out to God and his reassuring words, he faithfully held me up.[2]

# Follow the Leader

HEBREWS 13:7–14 *Remember those who rule over you, who have spoken the word of God to you, whose faith follow, considering the outcome of their conduct. Jesus Christ is the same yesterday, today, and forever. Do not be carried about with various and strange doctrines. For it is good that the heart be established by grace, not with foods which have not profited those who have been occupied with them. We have an altar from which those who serve the tabernacle have no right to eat. For the bodies of those animals, whose blood is brought into the sanctuary by the high priest for sin, are burned outside the camp. Therefore Jesus also, that He might sanctify the people with His own blood, suffered outside the gate. Therefore let us go forth to Him, outside the camp, bearing His reproach. For here we have no continuing city, but we seek the one to come. (NKJV)*

The phrase "rule over you" is unfortunate here. The Greek here simply means "leaders." It's particularly unfortunate as the rest of the verse describes how spiritual leaders are to carry out their function. Leaders:

**key point**

- Speak the word of God
- Provide an example of living by faith
- Demonstrate Christian maturity in their conduct

The writer of Hebrews isn't the only one to put these elements together. Writing to the Philippians the apostle Paul says, "The things which you learned and received and heard and saw in me, these do, and the God of peace will be with you" (Philippians 4:9 NKJV). Of course, they aren't the first to define what today is called "servant leadership." That's something Jesus both taught and demonstrated in Matthew 20:25–28!

**something to ponder**

what others say

### Stacy T. Rinehart

I find it interesting that Jesus never reprimanded his disciples for wanting "to be great." Instead He dramatically redefined the terms of greatness and pointed His disciples in another direction entirely. You can be leaders, He told them, but you must take the route of sacrifice, suffering, and service. "Whoever wants to become great among you must be your servant, and whoever wants to be first must be slave of all" (Mark 10:43–44).[3]

The late pastor-author Ray Stedman, teaching local pastors and students in Bangkok, Thailand, discovered his Chinese-Christian interpreter was misinterpreting something he was saying. Asian churches generally have strong, controlling pastoral leadership. It's deeply engrained in the culture. Ray was trying to get across Jesus's revolutionary idea of servant leadership. Ray said, "The pastor is a servant." In Chinese the interpreter said, "The ruler (pastor) is a ruler!"

Controlling ("ruling") leadership often takes advantage of its followers and inhibits them from developing their own personal ministries. The universal priesthood of believers gets short-circuited. The picture of Jesus as Servant-Leader is distorted. The "ruler" is over his head trying to be and do everything in and for the congregation, while his followers become fat and lazy from doing little or nothing. This old warm fuzzy habit is hard to break because of the leader's overblown ego and the fact that the followers like being, not an army, but a weekly sermon-tasting society.

"Remembering" the servant-leader means not merely to have nice thoughts, but to do something.

## Steady As You Go

HEBREWS 13:8 *Jesus Christ is the same yesterday, today, and forever. (NKJV)*

It's not clear just why the writer interjects this gem here. Except perhaps to remind us that while we are to look to our leaders, those individuals are human and may fall short. Even the best of men and women may disappoint us. But Christ "is the same yesterday, today, and forever." We can always count on Him. He is ready to lead the church and His people if they will tune in to His voice and find practical ways to let Him do what only He is able to do.

## Weird Teachings

HEBREWS 13:9 *Do not be carried about with various and strange doctrines. For it is good that the heart be established by grace, not with foods which have not profited those who have been occupied with them. (NKJV)*

**go to**

**dietary laws**
Leviticus 11

**Judaizers**
Acts 15:1–5;
Galatians 2

**doctrines**
teachings

**Judaizers**
Jewish Christians
who taught that
Gentile believers
must be circumcised
and keep Old
Testament ritual laws

"Various and strange **doctrines**" cropped up often in the first century. The specific reference here is to the belief of some Christian Jews that those who relied on Jesus as Messiah still had to keep the Jewish dietary laws. If you want to know that you're right with God, the teaching went, then eat the right things and never touch the wrong ones.

Many Jewish believers kept insisting that people who believed in Jesus should submit to Old Testament food laws and, in reality, become Jews. We know that many Judean Christians had continuing conflict with the Gentile Christians and among themselves over this issue. This same approach to maintaining a right relationship with God cropped up later in Gentile churches, often brought to them by itinerant "**Judaizers**" from the Hebrew homeland.

The issue proved to be a persistent distraction. Paul confronts those in Colossae who subjected themselves to similar regulations as—"Do not touch, do not taste, do not handle." Such rules "all concern things which perish with the using" and are "according to the commandments and doctrines of men" (Colossians 2:21–22 NKJV). Such practices may look "spiritual," but are "of no value" (Colossians 2:23 NKJV).

Concerning conflict in the church at Rome over what a person should and shouldn't eat, the apostle Paul wrote, "I know and am convinced by the Lord Jesus that there is nothing unclean of itself" (Romans 14:14 NKJV). He adds, "The kingdom of God is not eating and drinking, but righteousness and peace and joy in the Holy Spirit" (Romans 14:17 NKJV).

In his first letter to Timothy, Paul even labels as "doctrines of demons" such various and strange teachings as "forbidding to marry, and commanding to abstain from foods which God created to be received with thanksgiving by those who believe and know the truth" (1 Timothy 4:1–3 NKJV).

It's no wonder the writer of Hebrews confronts those in the Jerusalem church over their emphasis on what they should and shouldn't eat. The Christian's heart is to be "established by grace, not with foods which have not profited those who have been occupied with them" (Hebrews 13:9 NKJV). Concentrate on the grace of God and on responding to that grace, and your heart won't be troubled over your standing with God.

**key point**

# Fast Break

**sanctify**
to make holy

These early Hebrew Christians lived among orthodox Jews and, as we've noted earlier in this book, in many ways were indistinguishable from them. The earliest Christians worshipped at the temple as well as in homes. They lived according to the regulations found in Old Testament law as expanded by generations of rabbis.

But the Jewish community itself had begun to make a distinction between those who trusted Jesus as the Messiah and those who did not. The result had been persecution and increased troubles. The writer of Hebrews has come to the conclusion that it's now time for the Christians to make a clean break. The two divisions within first-century Judaism have different altars, on which different sacrifices have been offered. The traditionalist still brings animals to the Jerusalem temple. The Christian Jews rely on Jesus's blood, offered in heaven, to **sanctify** them. All this confusion about dietary laws makes it clear that remnants of the old faith are confusing adherents of the new. The Hebrews writer's advice?

# Coloring Outside the Lines

**HEBREWS 13:10–14** *We have an altar from which those who serve the tabernacle have no right to eat. For the bodies of those animals, whose blood is brought into the sanctuary by the high priest for sin, are burned outside the camp. Therefore Jesus also, that He might sanctify the people with His own blood, suffered outside the gate. Therefore let us go forth to Him, outside the camp, bearing His reproach. For here we have no continuing city, but we seek the one to come. (NKJV)*

Mount Golgotha (Calvary) was outside the Jerusalem wall, over-looking a marble quarry,[5] on what is known to Christians as the via dolorosa, the road that leads from the Roman praetorium to the quarry.[6]

The continuing debate over what foods a Christian Jew can eat makes it clear that the community is confused about central issues in our relationship with God. The best thing to do in this situation is to quit trying to fit in. It's time to take a stand with Jesus on the uniqueness of faith in Him. As Jesus was taken outside Jerusalem to die, let's follow His example and "go forth to Him, outside the

**way of living**
Hebrews 13:1–9;
Romans 12

camp, bearing His reproach." If this going "outside" means experiencing rejection and reproach, then it's a price Jesus paid before us. And we are called to follow Him.

what others say

**James Thompson**

For the readers to go outside the camp was to take the risk of a total break with the synagogue.[4]

New Covenant worship is different because New Covenant relationship with God is different. Disenfranchised Jewish believers on the verge of losing all their worship centers—the Holy City, the Temple, the priesthood and sacrificial system—needed to grasp the nature of Christian worship, in which the shadows and copies have been shaken and set aside. These are now replaced with spiritual realities in Christ. In Christ, worship moves out of the shrine and into life!

This new worship is not a religious performance. It's a <u>way of living</u>. Worship is servanthood, honoring God by caring for one another, sacrificial living, and giving. It includes hospitality, identification with abused people, marital faithfulness. Contentment—freedom from obsession with material things. Confidence in Christ's faithfulness. Teaching that emphasizes God's love and blessing in Jesus, not Hebrew do's and don'ts.

The "altar" in New Covenant worship is Jesus. Believers gather to Him, where and who He really is. Authentic Christian worship may be "outside the camp" of acceptable, established religion—as is the cross (Hebrews 13:10–13). It does not necessarily fit the approved religious mold, away from things that distract from the worship of God—out there in the world of daily life, where believers "share the abuse of Jesus."[8]

## The New Sacrifices

**HEBREWS 13:15–16** *Therefore by Him let us continually offer the sacrifice of praise to God, that is, the fruit of our lips, giving thanks to His name. But do not forget to do good and to share, for with such sacrifices God is well pleased.* (NKJV)

Martyrdom is big in militant Islam these days. Nothing like blowing yourself up with as many unsuspecting civilians as possible to prove your dedication to Allah. There have been times when similar notions motivated Christians, particularly during the Crusades.

But an obsession to die for one's faith isn't biblical. Yes, there have been times when Christians have been faced with the choice of denying Christ or being tortured and executed. But that's not something Scripture urges us to go out and actively look for. Instead the Bible says, "I beseech you by the mercies of God, that you present your bodies a living sacrifice, holy, acceptable to God" (Romans 12:1 NKJV).

Being a "living sacrifice" is undoubtedly more difficult than being a dying one. The big gesture is spectacular, and may mean you're remembered in your community. The "living sacrifice" isn't likely to attract much attention. Besides, we're confused about just what it means to be a "living sacrifice." What does a person who's a living sacrifice *do*?

key point

If you've ever wondered, the writer of Hebrews spells it out for you:

- *A living sacrifice praises God all the time.* "All the time" is made clear in the phrase "continually offers" (Hebrews 13:15 NKJV). We don't just praise God when we get a raise at work. We praise God when we're fired too. We don't just praise God when the test at the hospital comes back negative. We praise God for positive test results as well.

The NKJV text speaks of "giving thanks to His name" (Hebrews 13:15). The margin has a preferred translation. The original Greek carries on the thought of "continually offering the sacrifice of praise" by adding an explanatory clause: "confessing [not "giving thanks to"] His name."

The Greek word for confess means "to acknowledge." Here the writer of Hebrews reminds us that praising God continually is one way to acknowledge that God's hand is involved in our every experience. We acknowledge that everything God brings into our lives is for our benefit.

- *A living sacrifice doesn't neglect doing good.* "Good works" has a poor reputation in many Christian communities. "Doing good" is thought of as a substitute for salvation by faith. But in Scripture, doing good is an expression of true faith (James 2:14–26) and an expected outcome of salvation by faith (Ephesians 2:8–10).

key point

The word translated "good" here is *eupoias*. It's a compound word constructed of a word that means "to make" or "to do" and the prefix *eu-*, meaning good. The living sacrifice constantly seeks to be a positive force in this world and in the lives of others. The living sacrifice stays alert for ways he can contribute and is ready to do whatever he can for others.

- *A living sacrifice shares.* The word translated "share" means "to have in common." It's the word that New Testament writers use for giving. New Testament giving is focused on meeting people needs. There were no church buildings for the first two and a half centuries of the Christian era, so there was no need to divert funds to their upkeep. Instead, giving was the response of those who had enough to be able to share something to meet the needs of people who had little or nothing. Gifts were primarily directed to those who were "of the household of God" (Ephesians 2:19 NKJV), and to itinerant teachers who depended on gifts for their support. Paul provides a clear description of New Testament giving in 2 Corinthians 8 and 9.

apply it

The attitude that marks living sacrifices in sharing goes beyond unselfishness to selflessness. The committed Christian cares, and that caring is expressed in the use of money as well as in other ways.

As the writer of Hebrews reminds us, "with such sacrifices God is well-pleased" (Hebrews 13:16 NKJV).

what others say

**Watchman Nee**

Do not think that joyful praise is the loudest. Often the loudest praise is from those who have gone through deep distress before God. . . . We must not only raise the note of praise when we stand on the summit and view the land of Canaan, but we must also compose psalms of praise when we walk through the valley of death. This is truly praise.[5]

## Bend a Little

**HEBREWS 13:17–19** *Obey those who rule over you, and be submissive, for they watch out for your souls, as those who must give account. Let them do so with joy and not with grief, for that would be unprofitable for you. Pray for us; for we are confident that we have a good conscience, in all things desiring to live honorably. But I especially urge you to do this, that I may be restored to you the sooner.* (NKJV)

Every year books on leadership sell in the hundreds of thousands. Everyone—in business, and in the church—seems to want to be a great leader. But for some reason there do not seem to be any best sellers on being a great follower. Yet in business and in the church there are far more followers than there are leaders. And for Christians, it's just as important to be great followers as to have great leaders.

Jesus explained to His followers what it took to be great leaders (Matthew 20:25–28). Now the writer of Hebrews has a word to his readers about being great followers.

Unfortunately, most English translations either confuse or actually contradict what the writer is teaching. So let's go through the first two phrases carefully.

## What Does it Mean to "Obey"?

We saw it in verse 7, above. Here the word translated "those who rule" is *hegoumenois*. While it's used in secular Greek of rulers and princes, the original meaning of the word is "to lead" or "to guide." Again the writer is simply referring to leaders, and the phrase "those who rule over you" is deceptive. Especially when Jesus specifically said, "the rulers of the Gentiles lord it over them, and those who are great exercise authority over them," and immediately added, "it shall not be so among you" (Matthew 20:25–26 NKJV).

The word translated "obey" is *peithesthe*. It means to "let yourself be persuaded, or convinced." No believer is to blindly obey even the most gifted of leaders. But every Christian is to maintain an attitude of openness to what leaders have to say.

Finally, the word *hupeikete* is accurately translated "submit to their authority." It was used in this sense in first-century Greek. But originally the word was used to describe soft and yielding substances. The idea isn't so much "do what they tell you" as "be responsive."

Putting this together we come up with an instruction that conveys a very different impression than the one given in the NKJV and other English translations. What the writer of Hebrews is saying is, "When your leaders speak, be sure to maintain a responsive attitude and remain open to their persuasion."

Paul pointed it out in Romans 14. No believer is to play God in another's life. He writes, "For to this end Christ died and rose and lived again, that He might be Lord of both the dead and the living" (verse 9 NKJV). We respect our leaders and are open to what they have to say. But in the end we are personally responsible to hear the living Savior's voice, and to let Jesus be Lord.

Every leader needs great followers; those who are eager to listen and to learn, who remain open to persuasion, but who take responsibility for their own choices. Christian leaders who serve such a flock truly "do so with joy and not with grief" (Hebrews 13:17 NKJV).

## Don't Forget to Pray

The request "Pray for us" (Hebrews 13:18 NKJV) highlights another aspect of being a great follower. That is to support our leaders with our prayers. Our leaders may be truly godly men or women, but this doesn't mean they have no need of our prayers. Most people have only the foggiest idea what their leaders are up against in their day-to-day lives. In addition to everything you deal with in this world, leaders are often singled out for special attacks and temptations. When a particular leader comes to mind, *pray*.

## The Ribbon Around the Package

HEBREWS 13:20–21 *Now may the God of peace who brought up our Lord Jesus from the dead, that great Shepherd of the sheep, through the blood of the everlasting covenant, make you complete in every good work to do His will, working in you what is well pleasing in His sight, through Jesus Christ, to whom be glory forever and ever. Amen.* (NKJV)

This is undoubtedly one of Scripture's most beautiful **benedictions** both as blessing and prayer. It merits a lofty place on the list of Bible passages we'd do well to memorize. It also serves as a pattern we can use when we pray for others.

Every line of this benediction speaks to Hebrew Christians tempted to give up on Christ. The short blessing expresses confidence that they will do what pleases Jesus, because He equips them to do God's will.

## PS

**HEBREWS 13:22–25** *And I appeal to you, brethren, bear with the word of exhortation, for I have written to you in few words. Know that our brother Timothy has been set free, with whom I shall see you if he comes shortly. Greet all those who rule over you, and all the saints. Those from Italy greet you. Grace be with you all. Amen.* (NKJV)

The writer concludes the benediction, above, with an *"Amen"* (Hebrews 13:21 NKJV). He'd finished his letter! But he couldn't resist adding a PS. You can almost see him sitting there, pondering after "finishing" what he thinks of as an all-too-short letter. Then he picks up his pen and scratches a few more words.

"Bear with the word of exhortation" (Hebrews 13:22 NKJV). Then he sets down his pen. Suddenly he has a thought. "I should mention Timothy." So he picks up his pen again, and writes.

"Oh, yes. Timothy has been released [from prison]. If he gets here soon, I'll come with him to visit you." Again he lays down his pen and sits back. He's finished. Well, almost. He picks up his pen one last time.

"Greet your leaders, and all the saints. And, greetings from all of us in Italy."

There! That should do it.

But, as if reluctant to end his letter and so let go of the believers in Jerusalem whom he loves, he adds a final phrase. "**Grace** be with you all" (Hebrews 13:25 NKJV).

And, finally, Amen.

**benedictions**
short blessings or prayers, often used to sum up a teaching

**Amen**
solemn Hebrew word indicating something firm, true, reliable

**Grace**
God's love, forgiveness and mercy to undeserving people—the theme of the book of Hebrews

# Chapter Wrap-Up

- This last chapter of Hebrews contains a variety of brief bits of advice from the writer to his readers.
- The advice begins with an encouragement to keep on showing love within the Christian community.
- The writer includes guidelines on how to be "great followers" of the readers' leaders.
- The writer recommends that this particular community of Christian Jews make a clean break with the Old Testament lifestyle they've been living.
- The writer gives practical guidance on how Christians can be living sacrifices.
- The writer concludes with one of the most beautiful benedictions in Scripture.

# Study Questions

1. What are some of the ways we can express "brotherly love [continually]" (Hebrews 13:1 NKJV)?

2. What is God's prescription for contentment? Are you content? Why or why not?

3. What does the phrase "those who rule over you" (Hebrews 13:7 NKJV) really mean?

4. What convinced the writer of Hebrews to recommend that the early Christian Jews should "go forth . . . outside the camp" (Hebrews 13:13 NKJV)?

5. What are some characteristics of a "great follower"?

6. How does the author recommend you use the benediction in 13:20–21?

# Hebrews in Retrospect

## Let's Get Started

The Letter to the Hebrews is one that few Christians read regularly. Its constant references to unfamiliar portions of the Old Testament make it difficult for the average person to understand. Yet the book of Hebrews explores truths that can enrich and even transform Christian experience.

## What do we gain from a study of Hebrews? Here's a partial list:

1. We gain an appreciation for the unity of Scripture.

2. We gain a better understanding of Jesus.

3. We gain an understanding of Jesus's present ministry as High Priest.

4. We gain an awareness of the importance of listening for God's voice.

5. We gain a better grasp of the difference between living by law and living by faith.

6. We gain perspective on our trials and sufferings.

7. We gain a deeper understanding of the sufficiency of Christ's sacrifice.

8. We gain insight into the difference between the things which are seen and the things which are unseen.

Let's look more closely at each of these benefits.

*We gain an appreciation for the unity of Scripture.* The Bible's collection of 66 individual books, penned over a period of at least 1,500 years by a variety of different authors, truly is one book with a common theme and hundreds of interconnected details. Without divine help there is no way that the writer of Genesis could have understood the significance of what seemed to be a chance encounter between Abraham and Melchizedek. Yet that encounter laid the basis on which Jesus, a member of the tribe of Judah, could be ordained as our High Priest and so supersede the Old Testament's Law system.

We see the intimate link between the Old Testament and New Testament revelations in so many ways. The tabernacle of the Old Testament is a "copy and shadow" (Hebrews 8:5 NKJV) of heavenly realities. The Old Testament sacrificial system offers visual clues to the meaning of Christ's death on Calvary. The symbolism of the veil in the Tabernacle that blocked entrance into the presence of God, and the symbolism of that veil being torn from top to bottom at Christ's death, show how tightly the two Testaments are woven together. The covenant promises of the Old Testament and the unexpected ways in which they are fulfilled by Jesus make the essential unity of Scripture unmistakable.

This truly is God's book, a book whose fundamental harmony is so great that only divine inspiration can explain it. We can trust the Bible. Completely.

*We gain a better understanding of Jesus.* Hebrews is launched with a powerful affirmation of the deity of Jesus. There's no mistaking the fact that Christ is presented to us as the eternal Son of God. At the same time the book of Hebrews emphasizes Jesus's humanity. He lived on our planet as a true human being. He made Himself vulnerable to every trial that humans are heir to. He suffered, and through it all He remained faithful to God and obedient to God's voice.

The writer of Hebrews tells us that because Jesus was tested as we are, He both understands and sympathizes with us in our trials. Even when you fall short, Jesus continues to care and offers both mercy and grace to help in your time of need. Put simply, Jesus is on your side. He doesn't excuse your failings. But He does understand, and He represents you before the throne of God.

*We gain an understanding of Jesus's present ministry as High Priest.* Hebrews emphasizes the fact that Jesus is our living High Priest. He holds the door to the throne of grace wide open for us, guaranteeing that God will hear and respond to our prayers. Jesus is our advocate when we sin, arguing His own shed blood as the basis for our forgiveness. His presence before the throne makes our salvation certain, and assures us of a place in heaven.

Jesus's High Priestly ministry reminds us constantly that the central issue in relationship with God is not what we imagine we can do for God, but acceptance of all that God has already done for us in Christ.

*We gain an awareness of the importance of listening for God's Voice.* One of the most important contributions of Hebrews is to help us realize that God speaks to us in our "today." He thoroughly understands not only our situation but our strengths and weaknesses. And God has worked out, from before the foundation of the world, His solution to our problems. Our challenge in life isn't to find our own way out of our difficulties. Our challenge is to listen actively for God's input: to seek His guidance and to be sensitive to what He has to say to us—and then to obey His voice.

Listening for God's voice stands in contrast to looking to rules or rulers to guide us. Yes, there are some things that Scripture identifies as always wrong. But most of the decisions we make aren't of the "always wrong" or "always right" kind. A teen wonders if she should try out to become a cheerleader. That depends on so many things. The answer to "should she" will differ not only with the circumstances and with the individual, but even with time. Perhaps she shouldn't try out this year, but should next year.

An office worker wonders what to do when he discovers fraud in the company books. Should he talk with a supervisor? Go directly to the business owner? Talk to the police or a regulatory agency? Should he take action now, or look a bit more to find out what's really going on? Or should he just resign, and remove himself from a situation where there's possible criminal activity? It's tempting to invent a rule that tells the potential whistleblower, "You must do X and then Y." But again God's solution takes into account every unique detail of the situation, as well as the strengths, weaknesses, and circumstances of the individual. Only by listening for God's voice and doing what he says can such a person be confident he's making the right decision.

It seems so much easier to simply make up a rule and tell everyone to follow it. But God is eager to give each believer personal guidance that's shaped just for him and for each specific situation. Your freedom to choose is part of God's image in which you were created. God guards your freedom, even when you think you might be better off without it. What a powerful impact learning to listen for God's voice can have on us, and what peace we experience when we turn our problems over to the Lord and commit to do what He tells us.

*We gain a better grasp of the difference between living by law and living by faith.* A law way of life is one that's governed by rules; by stated or unstated lists of do's and don'ts. Too many Christians and too many churches have adopted a law-like system to create conformity, and to give those who follow the rules the illusion of pleasing God. Again, there are some clear do's and don'ts in Scripture. But we're not to expand on Scripture's lists of sins, or let do's and don'ts pattern all our choices.

In contrast, living by faith involves the awareness that God is involved in every aspect of your life. And that He personally will guide you as you rely on Him and listen for His voice. You are to expect His leading and be ready to respond obediently. What the Lord tells you to do may be unexpected. It may even be "unapproved" by many of your friends. But then, very few would have approved of Abraham's choice to leave Ur!

## Time to Dig Out the Old Flak Jacket

After a really awful business meeting which exposed the abysmal immaturity of our church, I was ready to give up hope. Disappointed in myself as pastor, my congregation, and the way we went about doing church, I was ready to throw in the towel, put my tail between my legs, and remove myself to a distant planet. The dream that a church could ever become new and function according to principles discernible in the New Testament was for sale—cheap! We all were inescapably chained to a great weight of historic denominational and cultural traditions that wrapped around our legs and kept us from running in any other direction. Nothing made any difference. Spiritual immaturity clung and chafed like cut hair after a bad haircut.

Flipping through an issue of *NAE Journal,* a series of articles by Wheaton College professor Larry Richards, called "Tomorrow's Church Today" grabbed me by the heart! A group of church leaders had spent a week at Honey Rock Camp in Wisconsin, tearing down the accepted model of the church and, in theory, rebuilding it in a shape which might actually produce disciples.

What they came up with was a church free to reshape itself into a more efficient need-meeting structure, where members could actually learn to be each other's spiritual support system. Church meetings were long enough to include worship and teaching, asking and answering questions, sharing needs and help. Home groups kept people in touch with each other through the week.

I was convinced. At significant risk to my reputation, I dove headlong into the mix of radical ideas from the articles, a book by Watchman Nee, and principles of church life that emerged from a fresh study of the New Testament. The congregation made a few small steps toward change. We made mistakes. But we—two pastors and wives at first but later joined by a group of renewal-minded elders—were honestly determined to try to do what we understood God wanted us to do.

Reactions in and outside the church ranged from interest to disapproval to censure. "You've taken these ideas too far," said an old mentor. As the old structures began to change and going to church began to be an experience in personal interaction and learning to care, expository teaching gradually replaced evangelistic preaching. Some condemned it. Loyal members disappeared, some not leaving without a parting shot or two.

The cost of acting in faith in this instance, trying to do what we understood was God's will for us was costly. When you decide to get serious about what God is telling you to do, it might be well to dig out your old "flak jacket." Not everyone will be thrilled with the change.

Living by faith has its challenges. But it's the only path that leads to rest and to a life actually dedicated to doing God's will.

***We gain perspective on our trials and sufferings.*** One of the greatest contributions of Hebrews is to help us realize that our trials and sufferings aren't divine punishment. Hebrews teaches us that such experiences are expressions of God's love.

Chastening is evidence of our Father's active involvement in our lives.

It's vital that we have and maintain this perspective. Seeing God's grace in our difficulties will keep us from becoming discouraged, and is an antidote to bitterness. Sensing God's love when we're in pain strengthens us to keep on doing God's will, and is vital if we are to become mature in our Christian faith.

***We gain a deeper understanding of the sufficiency of Christ's sacrifice.*** Throughout, Hebrews emphasizes the fact that the death of Christ was sufficient to win our salvation. In contrast to the many sacrifices of the Old Testament era, Christ offered Himself once, and then sat down at the right hand of God the Father.

The writer makes this unmistakably clear, saying, "For by one offering He has perfected forever those who are being sanctified" (Hebrews 10:14 NKJV). There is nothing we can do to add to the effectiveness of what Jesus has done. Our salvation has nothing to do with what we may do for God. It has everything to do with what Jesus has already done for us. We are to rely completely on the blood Jesus shed for us on Calvary, and rejoice in the gift of our salvation.

***We gain insight into the difference between the things which are seen and the things which are unseen.*** This is a theme which is repeated throughout Hebrews. The things that can be seen are temporary. They are copies and shadows of reality. The things men call "treasures" here are destined for destruction. The only true treasures are those that are laid up in heaven.

It's important not simply to see this difference, but to internalize it. When what's truly important to us is eternity, there's a shift in our values, and a consequent change in our behavior. People become more important to us than things, and what we do to serve others is more important than what we might get out of a relationship with them. We're released from a desire for more, and we find contentment in the realization that Jesus will never leave us or forsake us.

Shalom!

# Exhotrations . . .

The final chapter of Hebrews offers a superb list of exhortations, preceded by twelve chapters of solid doctrine and followed by a glorious benediction. Here are some of those exhortations—and the benediction—with verse numbers intact.

- *Verse 1*—Let brotherly love continue.

- *Verse 2*—Do not forget to entertain strangers, for by so doing some have unwittingly entertained angels.

- *Verse 3*—Remember the prisoners as if chained with them—those who are mistreated—since you yourselves are in the body also.

- *Verse 4*—Marriage is honorable among all, and the bed undefiled; but fornicators and adulterers God will judge.

- *Verse 5*—Let your conduct be without covetousness; be content with such things as you have.

- *Verse 7*—Remember those who rule over you, who have spoken the word of God to you, whose faith follow, considering the outcome of their conduct.

- *Verse 8*—Jesus Christ is the same yesterday, today, and forever.

- *Verse 9*—Do not be carried about with various and strange doctrines.

- *Verse 15*—Therefore by Him [Jesus] let us continually offer the sacrifice of praise to God, that is, the fruit of our lips, giving thanks to His name.

- *Verse 16*—But do not forget to do good and to share, for with such sacrifices God is well pleased.

- *Verse 17*—Obey those who rule over you, and be submissive, for they watch out for your souls, as those who must give account. Let them do so with joy and not with grief, for that would be unprofitable for you.

## . . . __Benediction__

*Verse 20–21*—Now may the God of peace who brought up our Lord Jesus from the dead, that great Shepherd of the sheep, through the blood of the everlasting covenant, make you complete in every good work to do His will, working in you what is well pleasing in His sight, through Jesus Christ, to whom be glory forever and ever. Amen.

# Appendix A–The Answers

## Hebrews 1:1–3

1. First, Hebrews was written to an unpopular people about to face severe persecution, which suggests a date prior to Emperor Nero's harassment of Christians in AD 64 or 65.

   Second, when Hebrews was written the traditional institutions of Jewish worship were still functioning. The temple was standing and priests offered sacrifices and carried on with their priestly duties. This suggests a date before AD 70, the year Emperor Titus's Roman legions sacked Jerusalem and burned the temple to the ground.

2. Visions
   Audible Voice
   Angels

3. His Son.

4. The Son (Jesus Christ) is "heir of all things" (Hebrews 1:2).

   The Son is "the brightness of [God's] glory" (Hebrews 1:3).

   The Son is "the express image of [God's] person" (Hebrews 1:3).

   The Son "by Himself purged our sins" (Hebrews 1:3).

   The Son "sat down at the right hand of the Majesty on high" (Hebrews 1:3).

5. This is a personal question, best answered by you in view of your own situation.

6. This is a personal question, best answered by you in view of your own situation.

## Hebrews 1:4–14

1. That angels were to be the mediator between God and humans. God's Laws came to us via angels. Humans could not speak directly to God but to God through angels.

2. At Jesus's birth.
   At Jesus's temptation.
   At Jesus's ascension.

3. (self-reflective answer)

4. God
   Lord

5. Eternal
   Loved righteousness
   Hated lawlessness

6. They are sent forth to minister those who will inherit salvation.

## Hebrews 2:1–4

1. They were tending to "drift away" from the good news they had heard, through not paying close enough attention (Hebrews 2:1 NKJV).

2. The "word spoken through angels" (Hebrews 2:2 NKJV) is the Law and Commandments God revealed to Moses on Mount Sinai. Jews believed the law had been delivered to Moses by a host of heavenly angels (Deuteronomy 33:2; Hebrews 12:18–21).

3. The four judicial terms used in Hebrews 2:2 (NKJV) which show the Mosaic Law was legally valid are: (1) "proved steadfast," which in the original Greek means "proved legally valid." (2) "transgression," which in the original means "infringement, trespass, stepping across a forbidden line"; (3) "disobedience," which means "careless hearing or unwillingness to listen to God's voice"; (4) "just reward," meaning "punishment as earned wages or reward" (Deuteronomy 28:1–68).

4. The four things mentioned in Hebrews 2:3–4 which authenticate the "great salvation" through Jesus Christ are:

   (a) It was first announced by the Lord Himself (Hebrews 2:3).

   (b) It was confirmed by eyewitnesses (Hebrews 2:3).

   (c) God testified to its truthfulness by signs, wonders, and miracles (Hebrews 2:4).

   (d) The Holy Spirit confirmed it by distributing spiritual gifts according to His will (Hebrews 2:4).

5. Some consequences of ignoring the great salvation offered in Christ are: Restlessness (Hebrews 3:18; 4:9); no confidence in approaching God (Hebrews 4:15–16); falling away from Christ (Hebrews 6:4–6); no mediator by which to come to God (Hebrews 7:22–28; John 14:6); settling for religious traditions and symbols rather than experiencing real relationship with God to which the symbols point (Hebrews 8:5–12; 10:1; Mark 7:1–8; 1 Corinthians 10:6); no assurance of forgiveness for sins (Hebrews 9:11–14, 22; 10:1–4, 17).

### Hebrews 2:5–18

1. In Jesus we see an example of the royal glory and honor for which God created human beings.

2. Other meanings of the word for "captain" (Hebrews 2:10): (1) "hero"—Jesus is the rescuer who heroically risked His life to save you. (2) "champion"—Jesus fights believer's spiritual battles and wins the victory for them. (3) "trailblazer"—Everything Jesus won by His life and death—restoration of human glory, honor, and authority at God's right hand—is something we who follow Him will experience with Him.

3. To be "made perfect" is to become able to fulfill the purpose for which a person was created or consecrated. This often involves suffering (Hebrews 2:10–11).

4. Priestly functions Jesus performs in and with His human brothers and sisters in the congregation are: (1) Declaring God's name (Hebrews 2:12). (2) Worshiping God (Hebrews 2:12). (3) Trusting God (Hebrews 2:13). (4) Demonstrating the presence of God (Hebrews 2:13).

### Hebrews 3

1. The ten facts outlined in the first two chapters of Hebrews that builds the case for faith and life focused on Jesus are:

    a. Jesus perfectly represents God; to see Jesus is to see God (Hebrews 1:2–3).

    b. Jesus is God's right hand man (Hebrews 1:3, 8–12).

    c. Jesus is greater than angels (Hebrews 1:4–14).

    d. Jesus reveals God's scheme to rescue spiritual drifters (Hebrews 2:1–4).

    e. Jesus restores damaged humanness (Hebrews 2:9).

    f. Jesus bridges the chasm between God and people (Hebrews 2:10, 17).

    g. Jesus makes bad people holy (Hebrews 2:10–14).

    h. Jesus breaks the devil's power (Hebrews 2:14–16).

    i. Jesus forgives sinners (Hebrews 2:17).

    j. Jesus is able to aid tempted people (Hebrews 2:18).

2. The two roles that Jesus fills in the spiritual family are:

    a. Apostle

    b. High priest

3. According to Hebrews 3, Jesus is the greatest man who ever lived, even greater than Moses.

4. The other four names the Holy Spirit is known as are:

    a. "the Spirit of life in Christ Jesus"

    b. "the Spirit of God"

    c. "the Spirit of Christ"

    d. "the Spirit"

5. The gut issue of Hebrews is not politics, greed, or military strength. The issue is faith, meaning trust in God's promises.

### Hebrews 4:1–13

1. Peace, security, confidence, tranquility.

2. God is its source. It is the same rest God knows; the confidence that He has the right solution to our every problem.

3. Our focus should be on maintaining a close relationship with the Lord so we can hear and respond to His voice.

4. We need to respond with a trust in God that is expressed in obedience. God knows us through and through and so picks the path that is best for each individual.

5. "Today" reminds us that God is present with us and speaks to us in our present situation, always guiding us into His rest.

6. No Bible verse or principle is applicable to every individual in every situation. God considers every factor in difficult situations and He considers our individual strengths and weaknesses in guiding each individual to the best path for him or her to take.

### Hebrews 4:14–5:11

1. Because God's people had sinned. The priests offered sacrifices that enabled them to approach God.

2. Intentional sins, where a person knew what he

should do but failed or refused to do it.

3. Atonement provided covering for sins, so that a person might reestablish fellowship with God.

4. Only the high priest could enter the inner sanctuary, and then only with sacrificial blood, and atone annually for all the sins of God's people.

5. As a true human being Jesus was vulnerable to all the pressures that lead us to sin, but without sinning Himself.

6. It means Jesus was tested by His vulnerability as a true human being. It does not mean that Jesus had a desire to make any sinful choice.

7. A high priest must be human, and must be appointed to his position by God.

8. Melchizedek.

## Hebrews 5:10–6:20

1. The spiritual immaturity of his readers.

2. By responding to God's voice and choosing the good over the bad.

3. The author lists things which only believers can experience.

4. To go back is to shame God by intimating that Christ's sacrifice was not good enough.

5. If they go back they will lose present blessings and live unfruitful lives. If they go on they will be blessed and their lives will be fruitful and significant.

6. God keeps His promises.

7. Jesus is able to provide complete and full access to God's throne.

## Hebrews 7:1–28

1. A priest of the Most High God and King of Salem.

2. His name means King of Righteousness. He ruled the city of Peace. His lack of genealogy or an account of his death symbolizes a permanent priesthood.

3. The blessing establishes his superiority to Abraham, and receiving tithes establishes his superiority to the Aaronic priesthood.

4. That Jesus was fully equipped for His High Priestly ministry.

5. That there is a change in the entire law system of the Old Testament.

6. God remains intent on providing sinful human beings with access into His presence.

7. It means "guarantee," and is significant in that Jesus Himself assures us of permanent access to God.

8. Christ is my advocate, interceding when I sin, and providing grace to enable me to overcome sin.

## Hebrews 8:1–13

1. Every aspect of what happened in Old Testament worship represented heavenly realities, but were not themselves that reality.

2. Everything had to accurately represent the heavenly realities.

3. Nothing was wrong intrinsically. What was wrong was that sinful human beings could not keep it.

4. It provides permanent forgiveness, lasting relationship with God, and both present and future personal transformation. The Old Covenant was unable to accomplish any of these things.

5. It became obsolete and irrelevant.

## Hebrews 9

1. It was the setting in which the priests acted out spiritual salvation realities.

2. Among the lessons are that sin is punishable by death, that God will accept a substitute, and the repeated sacrifices established that the blood of animals could not do the job of bringing a person into a lasting relationship with God.

3. Its presence indicated humans did not have access to God. Its tearing indicated that through Jesus the way to God was now open.

4. By God when He provided skin covering for Adam and Eve after they sinned.

5. The life of an animal or person.

6. Conscience is a witness to our knowledge of right and wrong. Conscience is also a judge that accuses us when we do what we believe to be wrong. Freeing us from the drag of a guilty conscience enables us to serve God with joy.

7. It took a death to inaugurate it.

8. We may be gracious and overlook another's sins. God alone can remove sins, and send the sins away.

9. We accept God's promise of forgiveness, understand what it means, and trust God to enable to experience true freedom from guilt.

## Hebrews 10

1. Because this chapter is a summation, bringing together teachings from earlier chapters.

2. Test yourself, then go back to the text and see how you did.

3. These events and principles underline how

essential it is that his readers make a choice.

4. Excited and enthusiastic about their relationship with Jesus and eager to follow Him.

5. The pressure of persecution and difficulties has made them discouraged and lazy in their faith.

6. They are to endure patiently. They are to focus on doing the will of God now. They are to look forward to Jesus's return. As for most important, which of these three is most important for you to do in your own life?

## Hebrews 11

1. The seen falls short of the reality, even when it symbolizes unseen truths. The unseen is the true and lasting, by which we must learn to live our lives.

2. That God is framing the ages of history, and that as believers respond to his voice we have our part in what God is accomplishing.

3. Abel Offered a blood sacrifice. Noah built an ark. Joseph arranged for his body to be returned to Canaan. Rahab chose to help the Israelite spies.

4. Because Scripture does not record a specific faith response of Enoch.

5. The person living by law assumes that he can keep God's rules and thus please God. The person living by faith relies on what Jesus has done, and focuses on being response to God's voice.

6. Those verses near the end of the chapter that recount the sufferings of believers who are commended for their faith.

## Hebrews 12:1–13

1. They differ for each individual, but in general are 'little" sins or character flaws that hinder our following Jesus closely.

2. He is the founder of our faith, the pioneer who shows us the way to live, the one who preceded us into glory.

3. They have let their troubles discourage them and create doubts about following Jesus.

4. It means to discipline, in the sense of training, to instruct.

5. A trouble-free life indicates that God isn't involved in training you, and that you are not really his child. In Psalm 73 Asaph describes how his troubles kept him close to God, while the trouble-free lives of those he had envied helped them feel they had no need for God.

6. Punishment is limited to correcting those who have refused to respond to discipline.

7. Respect is shown by obeying even when what we are told to do seems painful.

8. (a)Love. (b) Our benefit is that we might be partakers of his holiness. (c) Unpleasant, painful. (d) We become more godly, more like Jesus.

## Hebrews 12:14–29

1. It is interpersonal peace; harmonious relationships with all, and especially believers.

2. Missing God's grace leads to bitterness and disruptions in the Christian community.

3. In the OT the emphasis is on the emotion, in the NT on the effect of bitterness on character and relationships.

4. Esau was concerned only with what he could see and taste and use, and placed no value on unseen realities.

5. It establishes a contrast between the law covenant which, wrongly used, leads to fear of God, and the New Covenant.

6. Mount Zion stands for the New Covenant, and the grace which establishes a father-child relationship with God.

7. Because we have a new covenant relationship with God. Passages read from an Old Covenant perspective will be misunderstood and misapplied.

8. We are to build our lives on the unshakeable, rather than on the things of this world which will all disappear.

## Hebrews 13

1. This is a personal question, best answered by you in view of your own situation.

2. Give thanks in everything. As for the last two sections of this question, again they are personal and you need to give your own answer.

3. It refers to leaders whom God has given to teach and to guide us, and does not imply any person has a right to take the place of Christ or of God's voice.

4. The Christians were beginning to rely on keeping the dietary and other ritual laws to keep them in fellowship with the Lord.

5. A great follower respects leaders and remains open to their teaching and persuasion. But a great follower then looks to Christ as Lord, and takes responsibility for making choices to please Jesus-not human leaders.

6. As a guide for your own prayers.

# Appendix B—The Experts

**Alcorn, Randy**—Founder, Eternal Perspectives Ministry, a former pastor.

**Anders, Max**—Former megachurch pastor, author, editor of Holman New Testament Commentary series.

**Anderson, David R.**—Pastor of Faith Community Church, adjunct professor Dallas Theological Seminary.

**Breedlove, Sally**—Frequent speaker at leadership conferences, Bible study teacher.

**Chambers, Oswald**—Famous preacher and author, died 1917.

**Chrysostom**—One of the fathers of the early church.

**Comfort, Philip Wesley**—Anglican NT scholar, led NT translation team for the Living Bible.

**Dillistone, F. W.**—Christian author, teacher, church man, and biographer. He has served on the faculties of Wycliffe College, Toronto, Virginia Theological Seminary, Episcopal Theological School, Cambridge, and Oriel College, Oxford.

**Ellwell, Walter A.**—Professor at Wheaton College, editor of many standard reference works.

**Froste, Bede**—Well-known Christian author.

**Girard, Audry**—Wife of pastor Robert Girard, author of this work.

**Green, Wilda**—Southern Baptist curriculum writer.

**Heen, Erik**—Professor of New Testament and Greek at The Lutheran Theological Seminary at Philadelphia

**Houtman, Cornelius**—Famous Dutch traveler who opened the route to the East Indies for his country in 1595-1597.

**Hughes, Philip Edgcumbe**—Author of Christian Ethics in Secular Society

**Krey, Philip D. W.**—Dean of The Lutheran Theological Seminary at Philadelphia

**Leo the Great**—Bishop of Rome, AD 440–461

**McArthur, John F.**—Pastor of Grace Community Church, founder of The Masters' Seminary, host of Grace to You radio program.

**McGee, J. Vernon**—A popular radio Bible teacher of 1980s–1990s.

**Miller, Calvin**—Professor at Beeson Theological Seminary, editor of the Jesus Millennium Bible.

**Moo, Douglas J.**—Professor of NT, Wheaton Graduate School, Wheaton, Il.

**Murry, Andrew**—Writer of 19th century devotional commentaries.

**Nouwen, Henri**—Catholic devotional writer, who died recently.

**Packer, J. I.**—Professor at Regent College, Vancouver, frequent contributor to Christianity Today magazine.

**Paythress, Vern S.**—Professor of NT Interpretation, Westminster Theological Seminary.

**Pentecost, J. Dwight**—Retired professor, Dallas Theological Seminary, author of several books.

**Pink, Arthur W.**—British preacher and theologian, died 1952.

**Richards, Sue**—Coauthor of best-selling Zondervan Teen Study Bible.

**Richardson, Don**—Missionary to Sawi people.

**Rinehart, Stacy**—Navigator's staff member, founder of Mentorlink, dedicated to training Christian leaders throughout the world.

**Steadman, Ray**—Founding pastor of Peninsula Bible Church, Palo Alto, CA.

**Thomas, Robert L.**—Author, Professor of New Testament.

**Thompson, James**—Graduate School of Theology, Author of "God's Holy Fire: The Nature and Function of Scripture"

**Vines, Jerry**—Founder, Jerry Vines Ministries, a Baptist minister.

**Woods, Fred M.**—Pastor of Eudora Baptist Church, Memphis, and author of several books.

# Endnotes

## Introduction

1. Henry H. Halley, *Halley's Bible Handbook*, 23rd ed. (Grand Rapids, MI: Zondervan, 1962), 60.

2. F. F. Bruce, *The Epistle to the Hebrews* (Grand Rapids: Eerdmans, 1990), 25.

3. Oswald Chambers, *Still Higher for His Highest* (Grand Rapids, Zondervan, 1973), 7.

5. Bruce, 20.

6. D. A. Hayes, *The New Testament Epistles* (New York: The Methodist Book Concern, nd), 76.

## Hebrews 1:1–3

1. H. T. Andrews, "Hebrews," *The Abingdon Bible Commentary* (New York: Abingdon, 1929), 1295.

2. Larry Richards, *The Bible—God's Word for the Biblically-Inept* (Lancaster: Starburst, 1998), 287.

3. Merrill C. Tenney, *New Testament Survey* (Grand Rapids: Eerdmans, 1961), 358–359.

4. Zane C. Hodges, "Hebrews," *The Bible Knowledge Commentary*, New Testament edition, John F. Walvoord and Roy B. Zuck, editors (Wheaton: Victor, 1983), 780.

5. Ravi Zacharias, "Defending the Faith: The 'Fifth' Gospel," *Decision*, June 2001, 16.

6. Ambrose, Bishop of Milan (AD 340–397) Converted Augustine to Christ; known for kindness and wisdom.

7. Ravi Zacharias, "September 11, 2001: Was God Present or Absent?," *Just Thinking* (Winter 2002), 7.

8. Lane, *Word Bible Commentary*, Vol. 47, Hebrews 1–8 (Dallas: Word, 1991), cxxvii.

9. William Barclay, *The Letter to the Hebrews* (Philadelphia: Wwestminister, 1957), 3

10. Democritus, qtd. in *Roget's International Thesaurus*, revised by Robert L. Chapman (New York: Crowell, 1977) 594.2.

11. Michael Card, *Immanuel: Reflections on the Life of Christ* (Nashville: Nelson 1990).

12. C. S. Lewis, *The Case for Christianity* (New York: Macmillan 1965), 45.

13. John R. W. Stott, *Basic Christianity* (Grand Rapids: Eerdmans 1958), 21.

14. Card, 27.

15. Richards, 554.

16. Ravi Zacharias, "Let My People Think," Radio Broadcast, March 10, 2002.

17. Bruce, 49.

## Hebrews 1:4–14

1. Martin Luther, *Tabletalk*, qtd. Graham, Angels, 8.

2. Billy Graham, *Angels: God's Secret Agents* (New York: Pocket Books, 1975), inside front cover.

3. William Barclay, *Hebrews*, 7–8.

4. Ibid., 8.

5. Ibid., 11–12.

6. Carl F. H. Henry, *God, Revelation and Authority*, vol. 4, 231, qtd. in W. Robert Cook, *The Christian Faith, A Systematic Theology in Outline Form* (Unpublished, copyright 1981 by the author), 223.

7. Graham, Ibid., 37.

8. John Calvin, *Institutes of the Christian Religion*, Vol. 1. Qtd. in Graham, *Angels*, 7.

9. Earl D. Radmacher, *Salvation* (Nashville: Word 2000), 3.

10. Bruce, *Hebrews*, 54

11. Ibid.

12. Lane, *Hebrews*, 26.

13. Johnson Oatman and John Sweeney, "Holy, Holy Is What the Angels Sing," *Singspiration Series* (Grand Rapids: Zondervan, nd).

14. John Milton, *Sonnet on His Blindness*, qtd. in Bruce, *Hebrews*, 64.

15. Barclay, *Hebrews*, 8.
16. Robert Jameison, A. B. Fausset, David Brown, *Commentary, Critical and Explanatory, on the Whole Bible* (Grand Rapids: Zondervan no date) 442 (New Testament).
17. Graham, *Angels*, 111.
18. Alford, *The New Testament for English Readers* (Chicago: Moody, no date), 1448.
19. Bruce, *Hebrews*, 58.
20. Lane, *Hebrews*, 22.
21. Jameison, 442.
22. Madeleine L'Engle, *Walking On Water, Reflections on Faith and Art* (Wheaton: Shaw 1972), 20–21.
23. *Revell Bible Dictionary*, 940
24. James Radford, unpublished sermon, "Which God?", preached at Montezuma Chapel, April 28, 2002.
25. Lane, Ibid., 32.o
26. Graham, qtd. in Eugene Peterson, *The Message*, 405.

**Hebrews 2:1–4**

1. *Revell Bible Dictionary* (Nashville, Fleming H. Revell, 1990), 886.
2. Lane, *Hebrews*, vol.47a, 37.
3. Barclay, *Hebrews*, 13.
4. Richards, *Background Commentary*, 551.
5. Barclay, *Hebrews*, 14.
6. H.T. Andrews, *Abingdon Commentary*, 1295.
7. Paul Johnson, *A History of Christianity* (New York: Athenaeum 1977), 33–34.
8. Lane, 38.
9. Ibid., 38.
10. *Harper Collins Atlas of the Bible*, Ed. James Pritchard (Phoenix: Borders-Harper Collins, 1999), 167.
11. Barclay, 14.
12. Lane, 38.
13. Bruce, 68.
14. Lane, 39.
15. Dean Henry Alford, *New Testament for English Readers* (Chicago: Moody, nd), 1454.
16. Barclay, 15.
17. Ravi Zacharias, "A Conversation with Ravi Zacharias," *Decision* March 2002, Billy Graham Evangelistic Association.
18. Bruce, 66.

**Hebrews 2:5–18**

1. Lane, 46.
2. John Killinger, *For God's Sake Be Human!* (Waco: Word, 1970), 63.
3. Barclay, Ibid., 17.
4. Ronald B. Allen, *The Majesty of Man* (Portland: Multnomah, 1984), 123.
5. Allen, 121.
6. Larry Richards, *The Complete Christian* (Wheaton: Victor, 1975), 23.
7. Irenaeus, 2nd century church leader, qtd. in John Powell, *Fully Human, Fully Alive* (Niles IL: Argus, 1976).
8. Bruce, 79.
9. Lane, 55.
10. Dag Hammarskjold, qtd. in Killinger, 48.
11. Richards, *The Complete Christian*, 22–23.
12. Killinger, 73.
13. Bruce, 80.
14. St. John of the Cross, *The Dark Night of the Soul*, excerpted in Richard Foster and James Bryan Smith, *Devotional Classics* (San Francisco: Harper 1990), 36.
15. Desmond Tutu, *The Wisdom of Desmond Tutu* (Louisville: Westminster John Knox, 1998), 36.
16. Dietrich Bonhoeffer, *Life Together*, excerpted in Foster and Smith, 296.
17. *Crosspoint*, Fall 2002, 57.

**Hebrews 3**

1. John Bunyan, *Pilgrim's Progress*.
2. E. Stanley Jones, *The Christ of the Indian Road* (New York: Abingdon, 1925), 53–54.
3. Ravi Zacharias, *Can Man Live Without God?* (Nashville: W Publishing, 1994), 179.
4. Barclay, *Hebrews*, 23.
5. Ibid., 23.
6. Matt Redman, "The Heart of Worship," Kingsway's Thank You Music, 1999.
7. Ibid., 24.
8. Lawrence O. Richards, *Complete Bible Handbook* (Waco: Word, 1987), 750.
9. Bruce, *Hebrews*, 93.
10. Merrill C. Tenney, *New Testament Survey* (Grand Rapids: Eerdmans, 1953), 355.
11. *Septuagint*, cited by Lane, Hebrews, 76.
12. Bruce, *Hebrews*, 92.

13. Barclay, 22.

14. *New International Version* (NIV) (Grand Rapids: Zondervan) Hebrews 1:3.

15. Rabbi Jose ben Chalafta, qtd. in Barclay, *Hebrews*, 22.

16. Barclay, 22.

17. Lane, *Hebrews*, 80.

18. Richards, *Handbook*, 746–747.

19. Merrill C. Tenney, *New Testament Survey*, 356.

## Hebrews 4:1–13

1. *Encyclopedia of Bible Words* (Grand Rapids: Zondervan, 1991), 524.

2. Sally Breedlove, *Choosing Rest* (Colorado Springs, Navpress, 2002), 24.

3. Ibid., 93.

4. Ray Steadman, *Hebrews* (Downers Grove, Ill, IVP, 1992) 89.

5. Go Figure, *Christianity Today Magazine*, February 2006, 24.

6. Jerry Vines, *God Speaks Today* (Grand Rapid, MI, Zondervan, nd), 56.

7. Wilda Green, *The Disturbing Christ* (Nashville, Broadman Press, 1968), 79.

## Hebrews 4:14–5:11

1. *The Tyndale Bible Dictionary*, Eds. Walter A. Elwell and Philip Wesley Comfort, (Wheaton: Tyndale House Publishers, 2001), 1087.

2. Philip Edgcumbe Hughes, *A Commentary on the Epistle to the Hebrews* (Grand Rapids, MI: Eerdmans, 1977), 180.

3. David R. Anderson, *The King-Priest of Psalm 110 in Hebrews* (New York: Peter Lang Publishing, 2001), 215.

4. Robert H. Smith, *Hebrews* (Minneapolis: Augsburg, 1984), 74.

5. Lawrence O. Richards, *The Bible Reader's Companion* (Colorado Springs: Chariot-Victor, 1991), 859.

## Hebrews 5:12–6:20

1. *The New Testament Milieu*, A. B. Du Toit, Ed. (Halfway House: South Africa, Orion, 1998)

2. John F. MacArthur, *Hebrews* (Chicago, Moody Press, 1983), 172.

3. Philip Edgcumbe Hughes, *A Commentary on the Epistle to the Hebrews* (Grand Rapids, MI: Eerdmans, 1977), 196.

4. James Thompson, *The Letter to the Hebrews* (Austin, TX: R. B. Sweet Co, 1971), 88.

5. Ibid., 173.

6. Oliver Cromwell, source unknown.

7. Robert H. Smith, *Hebrews* (Minneapolis: Augsburg, 1984), 89.

## Hebrews 7:1–28

1. John F. MacArthur, *Hebrews* (Chicago: Moody Press, 1983), 172.

2. Don Richardson, *Eternity in Their Hearts* (Gospel Light Publications, 2006). Richardson uses the incident in Genesis 14 to demonstrate how God is at work in the lives of even pagan people. All have some light, which opens the way for a positive approach to planting churches among them.

3. J. Vernon McGee, *The Epistle to the Hebrews, ch 1–7* (Nashville: Nelson, 1991), 80.

4. Chrysostom in Erik M. Heen & Philip D. W. Krey, eds, *Ancient Christian Commentary on Scripture, Hebrews* (Downers Grove, IL: InterVarsity Press, 2005), 116.

5. Philip Edgcumbe Hughes, *A Commentary on the Epistle to the Hebrews* (Grand Rapids, MI: Eerdmans, 1977), 270.

6. Wilda Green, *The Disturbing Christ* (Nashville: Broadman, 1968), 116.

7. Don Milam, *The Ancient Language of Eden: Rediscovering the Original Language of Jesus—Love, Grace, and Mercy* (Shippensburg. PA, 2003), 118.

## Hebrews 8:1–13

1. Ray Steadman, *Hebrews* (Downers Grove, Il: InterVarsity Press, 1992), 163.

2. J.Veron McGee, *Hebrews 1–7* (Nashville, Nelson, 1991), 188.

3. Fred M. Wood, *The Glory of Galatians* (Nashville: Broadman, 1972), 56.

4. Vern S. Paythress, *The Shadow of Christ in the Law of Moses* (Phillipsburg, NJ: P&R Publishing, 1991), 116.

5. Leo the Great, in Erik M. Heen and Philip D. W. Krey, Eds, *Ancient Christian Commentary on Scripture, Hebrews* (Downers Grove, Il, InterVarsity Press, 2005), 127.

6. F. W. Dillistone, *Jesus Christ and His Cross* (Philadelphia: Westminster Press, nd), 128.

7. Max Anders, *Romans* (Nashville: Holman, 2000), 255.

## Hebrews 9

1. J. Vernon McGee, *The Epistle to the Hebrews, 8–13* (Nashville: Nelson, 1992), 43.

2. Wilda Green, *The Disturbing Christ* (Nashville: Broadman, 1968), 55.

3. Andrew Murray, *The Holiest of All* (Old Tappan, NJ: F. H. Revell, nd.), 431.

4. Tom Fettke and Camp Kirkland, *Known by the Scars* (a Palm Sunday cantata)

5. F. W. Dillistone, *Jesus Christ and His Cross* (Philadelphia: Westminster Press, nd), 69.

6. John F. MacArthur, *Hebrews* (Chicago: Moody Press, 1983), 236.

7. Fettke & Kirkland, *op cit.*

### Hebrews 10

1. Vern S. Paythress, *The Shadow of Christ in the Law of Moses* (Phillipsburg, NJ: P&R Publishing, 1991), 43.

2. J. Dwight Pentecost, *Faith that Endures* (Nashville: Discovery House, 1992), 157.

3. Robert L. Thomas, *New American Standard Hebrew-Aramaic and Greek Dictionaries: Updated Edition*, H8674. (Anaheim: Foundation Publications, 1998, 1981)

4. Audrey I. Girard, *Lord of Cleansing* (Girard, 1999)

5. Oswald Chambers, *Still Higher for His Highest* (Grand Rapids: Zondervan , sixth printing 1973), 51.

6. Earthlink, *Main News*, ©2000. All rights reserved.

7. David R. Anderson, *The King-Priest of Psalm 110 in Hebrews* (Austin, TX: R. B. Sweet Co, 1971), 88.

8. J. I. Packer, *Knowing God* (Downers Grove: InterVarsity, sixth printing, 1973), 29.

9. Andrew Murray, *The Holiest of All* (Old Tappan, NJ: F. H. Revell, nd), 431.

10. Calvin Miller, *Once Upon a Tree* (Grand Rapids, MI: Baker, 1967), 41.

### Hebrews 11

1. Bede Froste, *To the Hebrews* (London: A. R. Mowbray & Co, nd), 58.

2. D. Stuart Briscoe, and Lloyd J. Ogilvie. Vol. 1, *The Preacher's Commentary Series, Volume 1: Genesis*. Formerly *The Communicator's Commentary*. The Preacher's Commentary series (Nashville, Tennessee: Thomas Nelson, 1987), 613.

3. Randy Alcorn, *In Light of Eternity* (Colorado Springs, Co: Waterbrook, 1999), 142.

### Hebrews 12:1–13

1. Arthur Pink, *The Holiest of All* (Old Tappan, NJ: F. H. Revell, nd), 431.

2. Randy Alcorn, *In Light of Eternity* (Colorado Springs, Co: Waterbrook Press, 1999), 143.

3. Ben Sirach, *Ecclesiasticus 30:1* quoted in William Barclay, *Educational Ideals of the Ancient World* (Grand Rapids, MI: Baker Book House, 1959), 31.

4. John Philips, *Exploring Hebrews* (Chicago: Moody Press, 1977), 213.

### Hebrews 12:14–29

1. D. A. Carson, *How Long O Lord* (Grand Rapids, Mi: Baker, 1990), 73.

2. Lawrence O. Richards, General Ed., *Revell Bible Dictionary* (Old Tappen: Fleming H. Revell, 1990), 490.

3. Maxie D. Dunnam, *The Communicator's Commentary: Exodus* (Waco, TX: Word, 1987), 246.

4. Ronald Youngblood, *The Book of Genesis* (Grand Rapids, MI: Baker, 1991), 216.

5. W. H. Griffith Thomas, *Genesis* (Grand Rapids, MI:Baker, 1922), 251.

6. George H. Guthrie, in Herbert C. Alleman, (ed) *New Testament Commentary* (Philadelphia: Muhlenberg Press, 1936), 636.

7. Lloyd J. Ogilvie, *Haggai* in *The Communicators Commentary Series* (Waco, TX: Word, 1992), 266.

### Hebrews 13

1. Henri J. M. Nouwen, *The Wounded Healer*, qtd. in Reuben P. Job, and Norma Shawchuck, (Nashville: Upper Room, 1983), 62.

2. Sue Richards, in *The Women's Devotional Bible* (Grand Rapids, MI: Zondervan, 1990), 1370.

3. Stacy T. Rinehart, *Upside Down* (Colorado Springs: NavPress, 1998), 29.

4. James Thompson, *The Letter to the Hebrews* (Austin, TX: R.B. Sweet Co, 1971), 176.

5. Watchman Nee, *What Shall This Man Do?* (Victory Press, Eastbourne, Sussex, G.B., 1962)

# Index

## A

a little lower than angels,
71, 74
Aaron, 91, 92, 135, 170,
299
Aaron's rod budded, 211,
212–13
forced into idolatry, 193
his family as priests, 136
Aaron's sons 246
Abel, 220–21, 257, 261
Abel's blood, 315
Abel's faith, 259–61
Abigail, 116, 118
Abihu, 246
Abraham, 110, 114, 137,
257, 313, 322, 338
Abraham, his faith
in leaving Ur, 263–64
in offering Isaac, 264–66
saving faith, 254–55
Abrahamic covenant,
178–79
as Hebrew, 7
his legacy, 9
and Melchizedek,
137–44, 171–72
promise of son, 163–64
See also Abraham, his
faith
Absalom, 304
Adam, 69, 110, 220, 315
and blood sacrifice,
259–61
adultery, 321, 324–25
afterlife. See age to come
age to come, 65

Alcorn, Randy
on living for eternity, 287
on materialism, 271
Alexander the Great, iv
Alford, Henry
on angels as wind, fire,
36
Allen, Ronald B.
on Jesus as God and
man, 72
altars, 329–32
Amalekites, 299
Ambrose, Bishop
on God seeking man, 10
Amos, 262
anchor of the soul, 164–65
Anders, Max
on God as Father, 205
Anderson, David R.
on coming boldly to
grace, 242
on Jesus's suffering, 139
Andrews, H. T.
on Hebrews' warning
against relapse, 50
on tests of faith, 4
angel, angels, 37
See also angel, angels,
activities in Bible
angel, angels, activities in
Bible
deliver law at Sinai,
53–54
entertained unawares,
321, 322
figured on Ark of the
Covenant, 211, 212,
213

foretell Jesus's birth, 33
guardians of nations,
65–66
in Hebrews, 25–44
present in Jesus's life, 28
visible on Mount Zion,
312, 314
when they appear, listed,
28–29
in world to come, 65–66
worship Son, 33–35
See also angel, angels,
attributes in Bible
angel, angels, attributes in
Bible, 28–29, 35–37
assist salvation, 43–44
compared with Jesus, 26,
30–31, 41–42
need no priests, 135
not "glorified dead
people," 28
occult beliefs, practices re
angels, 26–27
purpose of angels, 26
some are fallen angels, 29
sons of God, 33
what they can't do, 43
as wind, fire, 35–37
angel worship, 33–34
animal sacrifices, 216–17,
219–24, 229
early Christian view,
239–40
origin, 219–220
See also Abel; sacrifice,
sacrifices
anointed, 39
anxiety, 104

*See also* rest
Apollos, possible Hebrews author, vii
apostasy, 244–45
apostle, apostles, 58–59
  Moses, Jesus, as apostles, 91
Ark of the Covenant
  contents, 212–13
  described, 130, 211
Asaph, 292–94
Ascension, 32
atonement
  explained, 82–83
  High Priest's role, 89
author, as term in Hebrews, 286
  *See also* Book of Hebrews, author
author and finisher, 288–89

# B

backsliding, 157–62
Barak, 258, 275
Barclay, William
  on ancient beliefs about angels, 26–27
  on changed lives as moral miracles, 60
  on drifting from God, 49
  on greatness of Moses, 93
  on Jesus as way to God, 27
  on need to focus on Jesus, 88
  on the prophets, 14
Barnabas, possible Hebrews author, vii, viii
Bathsheba, 117, 118
behind the veil, 164–65
Ben Chalafta, Rabbi Jose
  on Moses as higher than angels, 93
Ben Sirach
  on discipline as benefit,

291
benediction, in Hebrews, 334–35
Berra, Yogi, 52
Bethlehem, 32
Bible
  its divisions, iii–iv
  its languages, iv
  as 66 books, iii
  teachings on Jesus, 31–32
  translations, iv
  understanding the Bible, iii
  as word of God, 119–21
birthright, 308–11
bitterness, 307–8
blood
  blood of Jesus, 218–22
  blood sacrifice, 130
  role in redemption, 214–24
  sprinkled blood, 313, 315
  symbolic meaning, 221
  *See also* sacrifice, sacrifices
boldness, 241–42
Bonhoeffer, Dietrich
  on community in Jesus Christ, 80
book of Acts, 49
book of Hebrews, audience
  consequences of their doubt, 62
  Jewish Christians in 60s AD, 3–9
  softening commitment, 51–52
  tempted to turn back, 47–52
  to whom written, 6–7
  *See also* book of Hebrews, author
book of Hebrews, author
  Barnabas possibly author, viii
  in chains, 248
  characteristics of author,

vi–viii
  from Rome, 5
  *See also* book of Hebrews, characteristics
book of Hebrews, characteristics
  addressed to most alienated group, 8–9
  encourages maturity, 148–55
  frequent warnings, 50
  illuminates Old Testament, v
  introduces concept of rest, 102–21
  Jewish terminology, vi
  key theme, 5
  letter-writing style, v
  meaning of name, 6
  outstanding features, viii
  points to Jesus, v, vi
  quotes God as speaking, 11–12
  sermon style, v
  use of Bible, iii
  use of hymns, 14, 30
  use of word "perfect," 78
  warning passages, 156–62
  when written, 5–6
  why study Hebrews, 337–42
  *See also* book of Hebrews, key structural features
book of Hebrews, key structural features
  addresses how God speaks to us, 3–14
  addresses temptation to turn back, 47–52
  begins with God's past words, 9–10
  depicts salvation under law vs. grace, 53–63
  ending benediction, 334–35
  ends with advice, news, 321–35

eternity, 287
Eve, 110, 220, 315
    and her sons, 259–61
evidence of things not seen,
    253–54
evil, words used in Hebrews,
    154–55
excommunication, 5
Exodus Era, 258
express image of His person,
    18, 19
eyewitnesses, 58–59

# F

faith
    biblical meaning, 107–8
    despite worry, 106–7
    as explained in Hebrews,
        253–54
    God's care through ages,
        256–57
    heroes of faith, 255–56,
        259–78
    as key issue, 98–99
    laying aside distractions,
        283
    life of faith, 253
    living by faith vs. law,
        311–15, 340
    Moses's, Jesus's faith,
93–96
    obedience, 255–56
    responses to trouble, 318
    seeing beyond history,
        264–65
    unseen realities, 254–55
    See also New Covenant;
        Old Covenant
fall of man, 69–70
falling away, 157–59
fear
    fear of God, 319
    meaning in Scripture, 104
Feast of Dedication, 212
Fettke, Tom
    on Jesus's victory on cross,
        219
    on power of Christ, 229
fire, God as consuming fire,

316, 319
firstborn
    firstborn from the dead,
        34
    firstborn in heaven, 312,
        314
    meaning of term, 33–34
food laws, 89, 326, 327–28
footstool, 43, 240
forgiveness
    God's forgiveness,
        199–200
    in New Testament,
        225–27
    of sin, 202
    See also sin
fornication, 321, 324–25
foundation of the world,
    111
free will, 112–13
Frost, Bede
    on faith, 254

# G

Gabriel, 28, 35, 66
Garden of Eden, 69
Gideon, 258, 275
Girard, Audrey Inez
    on the blood of Jesus, 238
Girard, Bob, ix
glory, 72, 75
Gnostics, on Jesus, 30
God, actions
    allows self to be known,
        202–5
    chastens believers, 288–98
    confirms salvation through
        signs, 59–60
    foreknows all, 111–12
    forgets sins, 200–201
    gives free will, 112–13
    guides through his Word,
        119–21
    judges all, 312–13, 315,
        316–17
    makes, keeps promises,
        163–64
    permits intimate
        relationship, 203–5

speaks to his people, 9–10
    writes laws on hearts,
        205–6
    See also God, attributes
God, attributes
    consuming fire, 316, 319
    Father, 204–5
    God of peace, 334
    God's image, 69–70
    God's right hand, 42
    holiness, 306
    his justice, 75–80
    Majesty on high, 22
    resting, 109–10
    revealed in Jesus, 25
    See also God the Father
God, speaking, 12
    to his people, 9–10
    in life's events, 12–13
    by prophets, 13–14
    by revelation, 10–11
    by Son, 14–17
God the Father
    and God the Son, 31–44
    and Jesus as Son, 30–31
    as Jesus's father, 32–33
    See also God, speaking
God's Word. See Bible
godly fear, 319
golden
    censer, 211, 213
    pot of manna, 211, 212,
        213
    table, 212
Goliath, 115
good, words used in
    Hebrews, 154
Good Friday, 32
good works, 55–56
gospel, term used in
    Hebrews, 106
government, 201–2
grace, 335
    claiming grace boldly,
        241–42
    falling short of grace, 307
    at Golgotha, 56–57
    at Sinai, 55–57
    thankfulness and grace,
        318

Graham Billy
  on angels in Bible, 26
  on angels in Christian life,
    29
  on angels watching over
    believers, 44
  on angels as wind, fire,
    35–36
great salvation, 56–63, 85
  *See also* salvation
great Shepherd of the sheep,
  134
great white throne, 230
Greek language, iv
Green, Wilda
  on accepting God's
    promises, 119
  on Christian's three points
    of view, 182
guardian angels, 29
  guardians of nations, 65–66
guilt, and death, 76
Guthrie, George H.
  on Mount Sinai vs. Mount
    Zion, 312

# H

Haggai
  on God's judgment, 317
Hammarskjold, Dag
  on ceasing to believe, 75
Hanukah, 212
hearts, writing laws on
  hearts, 205–6
heaven, 287
  *See also* world to come
heavenly calling, 86–87
heavenly Jerusalem, 312,
  314
Hebrew
  Hebrew language, iv
  Hebrew people, 126–27
  term of reproach, 6–8
Hebrews. *See* Book of
  Hebrews
heir of all things, 18–19
hell, 42
heretical teachings, 326,
  327–28

Herod Agrippa II, 98, 209
Herod's Temple
  early Christians banned,
    97
heroes of faith
  awaiting fulfilment,
    258–59
  divided by era, 257–58
  in Old Testament, 255–56
  seeing only glimpses,
    277–78
High Priest, 148–49
  intentional sin, 128–30
  qualifications, 135–44
Hodges, Zane C.
  on key message of
    Hebrews, 6–7
holiness, 311–15
  holiness of God, 306–7
Holy of Holies, 129
  described in detail, 211,
    212–14
Holy Spirit, attributes in
  Hebrews
  gift, 56–57
  giver of salvation, 60
  guiding into all truth, vi
  Jesus speaks through him,
    57–58
  points to Jesus, 96–97
  speaks through Bible,
    96–97
holy place, 212
Holy Trinity, 60
  *See also* God; God the
    Father; Holy Spirit; Jesus
honor, 75
hope, in Bible, 162–65
hospitality, 322, 323–24
house church, 6
  as Hebrews' first audience,
    101
house of God, 94–96
Hughes, Philip Edgcumbe
  on alienation from God,
    156
  on Christ as sole mediator,
    182
  on Jesus accepting
    suffering, 136

humanity, 66–68
Hur, 299
hymn, 14

# I

Imago Dei, 72
incarnation, 86
Irenaeus
  on fully alive humans as
    God's glory, 73
Isaac, 110, 257, 263, 264,
  313
  Abraham offers him to
    God, 265–66
  blesses Jacob, Esau, 267
  disputed birthright,
    308–11
  Jesus and Isaac, 266
Isaiah, 118, 129
  and angels, 37
  on God's judgment,
    316–17
  on Messiah, 81–82
  on no rest for wicked,
    103–4
  prophesying Jesus's
    sacrifice, 222
  vineyard parable, 160
Israelites, 7, 106, 258
  their faith under Moses,
    Joshua, 273–74
  *See also* Hebrews
Israel's tabernacle, 194–95

# J

Jacob, 110, 257, 258, 263
  the birthright, 308–11
  blesses sons of Joseph,
    267–68
James Radford
  on God as perfect and
    changeless, 41
Jamieson, Robert
  on angels as wind, fire, 36
Jephthah, 258, 275
Jeremiah, 179, 195
Jericho, 274
Jerusalem, 37

Jesus, prophecies
    his birth, 32
    fall of Temple, 98
    suffering servant, 236–37
Jesus Christ, 18
    *See also* Jesus
Jewish Christians in 60s AD
    Abraham's spiritual
        children, 9
    believed selves to be Jews,
        4
    consequences of falling
        away, 155–63
    especially alienated, 8–9
    forbidden entry to
        Temple, 4
    shunned by fellow Jews,
        3–5
Jewish culture in first
    century
    role of law, 255–56
    Temple's destruction, 5, 6,
        209
Jews
    in 60s AD, 3
    and Christianity, 4
    at fall of Jerusalem, 208–9
    and Greek language, iv
    and Moses, 90–96
    and revelation, 15
    *See also* Jewish Christians
        in 60s AD
Job, 11
Joel, 317
John (evangelist), 20
John of the Cross
    on why God permits
        suffering, 79
Johnson, Paul
    on early church as form of
        Judaism, 51
Jones, E. Stanley
    on agnostic vs. Indian
        Christian, 85–86
Jordan River, 37
Joseph, 28, 74, 258
    prophecies, 268
Joshua, 8, 113, 114, 240,
    274
Judaism
    and Christianity, 9, 155–56

*See also* Jews
Judaizers, 327–328
Judas, 139
Judea, 6
Judges and Monarchy Eras,
    258
judgment
    of God, 315–19
    on sin, 245–48
    vs. salvation, 230
just reward, in Hebrews, 54

## K

Keilah, 116, 117, 118
Killinger, John
    on fully human believers,
        77
    on wonder of persons, 68
kingdom that cannot be
    shaken, 65
koine Greek, iv
Kirkland, Camp
    on Jesus's victory on cross,
        219
    on power of Christ, 229
Korah, 246

## L

L'Engle, Madeleine
    on angels, 36
lake of fire, 230
    *See also* judgment
lampstand, 212
Land of Canaan, 7
Lane, William L.
    on angels assisting
        salvation, 44
    on angels as wind, fire, 36
    on anonymity in Old
        Testament, 67
    on central theme of
        Hebrews, 12
    on God's actions as
        perfect, 73–74
    on Jesus as Son of God,
        33
    on loyalty to Christ, 96
    on term "apostle" in
        Hebrews, 58

last days, 14–15
last judgment, 315–19
law
    changed, 189
    changed by Jesus, 175–78
    living by law vs. faith, 340
    New Covenant, 195–209
    Old Covenant, 206
    rejecting law, 245–46
    as shadow of Christ,
        233–37
    vs. faith, 197–98, 311–15
    vs. listening to God, 253
    written on hearts, 198–99
    *See also* New Covenant;
        Old Covenant
Law Covenant, 127
Law, the (Law of Moses),
    53, 180, 255
    *See also* law
leaders, servant leadership,
    326–27
legalism, 326, 327–28
Leo the Great
    on law and grace, 199
Levi, 136, 170, 172
    and Melchizedek, 172
    tithed by Melchizedek,
        173–74
Levites, 136, 172
Lewis, C. S.
    on Jesus's unique claims,
        17–18
life after death. *See* world to
    come
living sacrifices, 330–32
Lord, iv
    *See also* God; Jesus
Lot, 138, 322
love, differing meanings of
    word, 324–25
Luke, possible Hebrews
    author, vii
Luther, Martin
    on angels, 25

## M

MacArthur, John F.
    on blood's significance for
        salvation, 228

attitude, 261
  on last day (day of
    judgment), 317
oil of gladness, 39
Old Covenant
  flaws, 205–6
  no remission of sin,
    214–17
  obsolete, 207–9
  *See also* New Covenant
Old Testament, iii–iv, 53
  and New Testament, 196
  Old Testament law, 253
omniscience, 111–12
outside the camp, 329–32

# P

Packer, James I.
  on knowledge of God,
    242
pain, 296–97
parents, 294–96
Passover, 273
Patriarchal Era, 257–58
Paul, 49
  knew God, 204–5
  lived as Jew, 207–8
  not Hebrews author, vii
  thorn in flesh, 115
  *See also* Paul, his teachings
Paul, his teachings
  on angels, 33, 66
  on Christians as God's
    building, 161
  on forgiveness, 226
  on Jesus as servant,
    236–37
  on legalism, 328
  on New Covenant,
    195–97
  on obedience, 142–43
Paythress, Vern S.
  on Mosaic covenant, 198
  on Old Covenant as mere
    shadow, 234
peace
  in community, 303–11
  meaning in Scripture, 304
Pella, 209

Pentecost, J. Dwight
  on Jesus as sacrifice, 237
Perea, 209
perfect
  meaning in Greek, 78
  meaning in Hebrews,
    150–52
perfection through
  sufferings, 77–79
persecution of Christians,
    239, 276–77
  Christians today, 79
  early Christians, 49–51,
    104
  as God's chastening,
    288–98
  as outcome of godliness,
    77
  and relapse, 50
Peter, 49, 263
  declares Jesus Son of God,
    61–62
Pharaoh, 7, 269, 273
Pharisees, as believers, 50
Philip, possible Hebrews
  author, viii
Philips, John
  on discipline as privilege,
    292
Pink, Arthur
  on distractions from
    Christian life, 283
poor, 323–24
Potiphar's wife, 7
prayer
  for leaders, 334
  words used in Bible, 182
pre-Flood Era, 257
preincarnation, 171
presence of God, 82
  *See also* God; Holy of
    Holies
priest
  all believers as priests,
    80–81, 91
  Jesus as priest, 91
  Melchizedek as priest,
  Moses as priest, 91,
    137–44
  priestly functions, 81–82

priest's role, 77–79
  *See also* High Priest;
    priesthood
priesthood
  bridge to God, 126
  changed by Jesus, 174–78
  Old Testament origin,
    126–27
  *See also* priesthood, in Old
    Testament
priesthood, in Old
  Testament
  compared with Jesus's
    priesthood, 177, 181
  intentional sins, 128–30
  significance, 126
  unintentional sins, 127–28
priesthood of all believers,
    80–81, 91
prince (angel)
  of Greece, 65–66
  of Persia, 65–66
Priscilla, possible Hebrews
  author, viii
prisoners, 321
  as powerless people,
    323–24
Promise Covenants, 178–80
Promised Land, 8, 114
prophets, 258, 275
  400-year dry spell, 15
  prophesying New
    Covenant, 205
  ways they revealed God,
    13–14
propitiation, 83, 130, 183
prosperity
  as punishment for wicked,
    292–95
Psalms, as hymns, 30
  Psalm 8, 66–68
  Psalm 45 as messianic
    psalm, 38
  Psalm 102, 40–41
  Psalm 110 as messianic,
    42–43
punishment, 54, 297–98
  God's chastening, 288–98
  wicked punished by
    prosperity, 292–95

purged our sins, 21–22

# R

race (footrace), as image,
281, 282, 285–86,
287–88
Radmacher, Earl
on simplicity in prayer, 30
Rahab, 258
her faith, 274–75
Rahman, Abdul, 239
Rebecca, and the birthright,
308–11
Rebekah, 267
Red Sea, and angels, 37
Redman, Matt
on Jesus as heart of
worship, 88
remembering, 200–201
repentance
and sanctification, 239
too late for repentance,
308–11
respect
for God, 294–95
for parents, 295–96
rest
amid difficulties, 115
entering God's rest, 105–9
God as resting, 109–10
God's rest, 103–4
meaning in Hebrews, 102
meaning for today,
114–15
rest and obedience, 115–19
rest in Psalms, 113–14
rest vs. stress, 102–3
resurrection, 32
and sanctification, 238
revelation, 10–12
general, 10–11
special, 11
Revell Bible Dictionary
on salvation, 47
reverence for God, 319
reward, 54
Richards, Larry, ix, 341
on believers as family of
God, 73

on Christ's holding all
things together, 21
on Jesus linking God and
man, 89
on Jesus vs. Moses, 96
on Jesus's suffering, 140
on message of Hebrews,
77
on original audience for
Hebrews, 5
on slipping away from
truth, 49
Richards, Sue, ix
on God's care for us, 325
right and left in Scripture,
191
right hand of God, 191
righteousness, 152–53
and obedience, 296–97
Rinehart, Stacy T.
on greatness in Christian
leadership
rulers, 326–27

# S

sacrifice, sacrifices
Christians as living
sacrifices, 330–32
Christ's sacrifice as
sufficient, 342
in Old Covenant, 223–24
Old vs. New Testament,
240
purpose, 234–35
saints, 306
saints of Old Testament,
223
salvation
angels' role, 43–44
confirmed through signs,
59–60
and consequences of sin, 77
consistent with God's
character, 72, 73–74
defined, 43
and faith, 106–7
and falling away, 157–59
and God's chastening,
288–98

and good works, 55–56
guaranteed by Jesus,
183–84
in Hebrews, 57–63
Jesus's role, 17
and judgment, 230
meaning of word, 42
and New Covenant, 206–7
in Old Testament, 54–55
past, present, and future,
206–7
refusing salvation, 315–16
rejecting salvation, 61–63
as theme of Bible, 47
Samaria, 6
Samson, 258, 275
Samuel, 258, 275
sanctification
its meaning, 237–38
its scope, 238–39
See also sacrifice
Sarah, 163–64, 255, 257
laughing, 264
sat down at right hand, 22
Saul, 116
scourging, 297–98
Scripture, Scriptures
its unity, 337–38
See also Bible
second coming, 241
seen vs. unseen, 342
See also Old Covenant
seraph, seraphim, 35, 66
See also angel, angels
shadow, 233–37
See also Old Covenant
"shaken," 316–18
shalom, 47
sharing, 330–332
Shepherd of the sheep, 334
shooting the wounded,
299–300
showbread, 211, 212
signs and wonders, 59–60
Silas, possible Hebrews
author, viii
sin, 127
conscience, 223–25
death and sin, 75–80
forgiveness of sin,

199–200, 202–3,
225–27
God forgetting sins,
200–201
Jesus purging sin, 21–22
little sins, 284–85
Old Testament system,
55–56
priests and sin, 126–31
punishment for sin,
200–202
renouncing Jesus, 244–48
sacrifice for sin, 234–35
salvation from sin, 183–84
sins that ensnare, 284–85
sin under Old Covenant,
55–57
*See also* sin offering
sin offering, 244–45
burned outside camp, 329–32
Singh, Sadhu Sunder, 85
on Christ as necessity, 86
"sinners," as non-observant
Jews, 79
slave, 236
Smith, Robert H.
on hope of Christians, 165
on Jesus's suffering, 139
social justice, 323–24
Sodom, 110, 138
and angels, 37
Solomon, 313
Son, 14–17
Son of David, 33
Son of God, 31, 71
son of man, Son of Man,
67, 71
*See also* Jesus
sons, believers as sons,
72–73
spanking, 297–98
special revelation
progressive revelation, 13
and prophets, 13–14
Son as revelation, 14–17
spirit, spirits, 35
*See also* angel, angels; Holy
Spirit
Spirit of Christ, 263
spirits of just men made

perfect, 313, 315
spiritual leaders, 326–27
spiritual leadership, 284–85
spiritual maturity, 148–55
sprinkled blood, 313, 315
Stedman, Ray
on clinging to past, 190
on failure to trust God, 105
on translation difficulties,
327
Stephen, 272
stone tablets, 211, 214
Stott, John R. W.
on Christ as center of
Christianity, 18
strange doctrines, 326,
327–28
stress, 102–3
string of pearls, 30–31
substance of things hoped
for, 253–54
suffering
as divine discipline, 303
as God's chastening,
288–98, 341–42
helping suffering
Christians, 299–300
pain, 296–97
and rest in God, 115
and salvation, 288
suffering for faith, 276–77
symbols, 223–24

# T

Tabernacle, 190, 326
detailed description, 211–14
key features, 194
priests' duties, 214–17
*See also* Old Covenant
Tempe, Arizona, 52
Temple
destroyed 70 AD, 97–98
Herod's Temple, 97
Titus as destroyer, 5
Ten Commandments, 8, 53
conveyed by angels, 37
*See also* Mount Sinai
Tenney, Merrill C.
on impact of Temple's fall,

98
on Jews rejecting
Christians, 90
on when Hebrews written,
6
Thomas (apostle), 40
Thomas, W. Griffith
on Esau's too-late
repentance, 310
Thompson, James
on break with Judaism,
330
on Hebrews encouraging
steadfastness, 162
on Jesus' once-for-all
sacrifice, 159
thorn in flesh, 115
through whom also He
made the worlds, 18, 19
Timothy
possible Hebrews author,
viii
reported as set free, 335
tithe, 167–68, 171–72
Titus (emperor), 5
Torah
and Christian Jews, 189
its composition, 9–10
many meanings of torah,
176
Touched by an Angel, 25
transgression, 54
trouble, 318
trust in God, 82, 106
Tutu, Bishop Desmond
on interdependence, 89

# U

unbelief, 255–56
*See also* faith
universal priesthood, 80–81
unseen realities, 254–55
upholding all things, 20
Ur, 264

# V

veil of Temple torn, 217–18
Vines, Jerry
on Holy Spirit furthering

revelation, 118
vineyard image, 160–62

# W

Way, 4
way, way of living, 329–32
wicked, 292–95
Wilderness of Sin, 53
women, as "sons" of God, 72
wonders, 59
Wood, D. R. W.
  on meaning of
    propitiation, 130

Wood, Fred
  on legalism, 198
Word, Word of God, 37–38
  in Hebrews, 119–21
  *See also* Bible
world to come, 65–83
  *See also* salvation
worry, 104–5
  *See also* rest
worship
  of God, 81
  under New Covenant,
    329–32
  under Old Covenant, 176

# Y

Yom Kippur, 129
  rituals, 215–16
Youngblood, Ronald
  on Esau's too-late
    repentance, 310

# Z

Zacharias, Ravi
  on Christ vs. chaos, 86
  on God speaking to us, 10
  on new life in Christ, 60
  on sin as action against
    God, 22
Zealots, 3
Ziklag, 116–17

CPSIA information can be obtained
at www.ICGtesting.com
Printed in the USA
LVOW03s1934150216

475240LV00009B/61/P